The Economic
Emergence of
Women

THE ECONOMIC EMERGENCE OF WOMEN

Barbara R. Bergmann

Basic Books, Inc., Publishers

NEW YORK

Library of Congress Cataloging-in-Publication Data

Bergmann, Barbara R.
   The economic emergence of women.

   Bibliography: p. 353.
   Includes index.
   1. Women—United States—Economic conditions.
2. Women—Employment—United States.   3. Sex discrimina-
tion against women—United States.   4. Housewives—
United States.   I. Title.
HQ1426.B429   1986   305.4'2'0973   85–73876
ISBN   0–465–01796–7

To my mother, Nellie, and my daughter, Sarah

Contents

List of Tables

List of Figures

Acknowledgments

I want to thank those who have read substantial sections of the manuscript and have given me valuable suggestions for improving it. They include Carol Ullman, Harriet Presser, Suzanne W. Helburn, Phyllis Wallace, Paula England, Fred Bergmann, Marianne Ferber, Francine Blau, Steven Fraser, Glen Loury, Heidi Hartmann, Nancy Folbre, Anne Stevens, and Mary Gray. Throughout the years I have benefited from discussions with Charles Brown, Myra Strober, and Harriet Presser. Ruth Weyand, Mary Gray, Donna Lenhoff, Judith Vladeck, and Karen H. Baker provided some of the case material on discrimination. Earl Mellor of the Bureau of Labor Statistics was extremely helpful in providing unpublished data on wages.

Valuable research help was given by Terence Alexander, Suzanne Greenspun, and Lynn Rogers.

In many ways, the University of Maryland has offered an ideal environment for the incubation of this book. Giving a course on sex roles in the economy has allowed me to develop the ideas, and to hear the reactions of students. I have had generous access to computers; the computer time for the special tabulations included in this book was donated by the University's Computer Science Center. Finally, the University is not so free of sex discrimination as to cast doubt on the ideas about the labor market I present here.

The Economic
Emergence of
Women

CHAPTER 1

The Breakup of the Sex-Role Caste System

WE ARE WITNESSING the breakup of the ancient system of sex roles under which men were assigned a monopoly of access to money-making and mature women were restricted to the home. The forces behind the release of women from obligatory domesticity are not of recent origin; the move of women into paid work started modestly more than a century ago, and its origins go back at least two centuries. The social and economic forces promoting the emergence of women are far from spent; they continue to reinforce each other and to grow stronger. An economic cataclysm or a wave of religious fanaticism (like that which has overtaken Iran) could bring a regression. But barring such upheavals, women are unlikely to retreat back into domesticity. On the contrary, the emergence of women into fuller participation in the economy and in society will probably accelerate.

Not everyone welcomes the change in women's roles. Some despair at what they see as the ruination of a system that provided a warm and comfortable home life. They mourn the passing of the sheltered existence that most women and children had. But many women and young girls relish their new freedoms and opportunities. Many mothers and fathers are delighted that their daughters will have a chance to express their talents and will be able, if they wish, to avoid complete dependence on the good will of a "breadwinner."

As women's behavior and positions change, men's are changing too. Some men are starting to take a more active part in the daily care of their children. But men's contribution to the financial support of their children is decreasing. Every year, more men abdicate their traditional role of provider for the children they have sired. About 30 percent of children in the United States live apart from their fathers, and in a majority of cases the father contributes little or nothing toward the child's support.

Men still retain a commanding position in the job market, but that position, too, is coming into question. Women are striving for a greater share of the better jobs, trying to break out of the ghetto of traditional women's occupations. At the same time, the comparable worth movement agitates for higher pay for women. If that campaign succeeds to a significant degree, as it has in a number of countries, the balance of economic power, now overwhelmingly in men's favor, will shift further in the direction of equality.

A majority of women have by now emerged from the home, but many habits, policies, and institutions survive from the era when all mature women were expected to be lifelong housewives. Discrimination in employment by sex, still virulent today, is a remnant of the time when it was considered good policy to reserve as many jobs as possible for men, for only they were thought to have a real and legitimate need for wages. The welfare system, another remnant from the past, was devised in an era when mothers were assumed to be needed at home full time, and in any case had a poor chance of landing a job with a wage that would sustain them and their children. Males grew up expecting to be waited on in the home, and to be exempted from any share in cooking and cleaning. Most husbands still expect that, even though their wives now spend time and energy at paid work. Employers continue to set up work schedules, transfers, and leave-of-absence provisions much as they used to in the days when most workers were men who maintained a full-time housewife.

The new conditions require new habits, policies, and institutions.

Our most urgent priority is to complete the task of driving sex discrimination and race discrimination from the workplace. This will enable women to earn enough, not just to keep out of poverty, but to stay in the mainstream, even if they lack a man's support. A second necessity is to find and implement a way of helping single parents to live decently. The welfare system traps single mothers into remaining poverty-stricken pseudo-housewives and sentences their children to deprivation. It underwrites sexual and reproductive irresponsibility by relieving both women and men of providing out of their earnings for the children they create. It should be replaced with a system under which single parents would be earners, but would have government guarantees of child support payments out of the earnings of the other parent, health care, and high quality child care. A third priority is the promotion of new and more flexible work schedules and new facilities for child care that will help employed people, with no full-time homemaker to depend on, to carry on their home lives and raise their children with less strain.

THE LONG TRANSITION FROM DOMESTICITY

In 1870 only 14 percent of women of working age in the United States were employed. In subsequent decades, the percentage of women in the job market rose slowly but quite steadily. It doubled between 1870 and 1940, and then doubled again between 1940 and 1986. By 1986, 56 percent of women were in the job market, and the percentage was still growing. Of women under age sixty-five, about two thirds are now in the labor force.

The labor force participation rate of American women of working age passed 50 percent in the late 1970s. The decade of the 1970s thus marked the beginning of an era in which an employed woman could see herself as part of a majority, and within the mainstream. By the same token, the 1970s marked the start of minority status for the woman devoted exclusively to domestic service at home for husband and children. After that, it was no longer possible to sustain the image

of the typical woman as a housewife who had no access to money of
her own, and no interests beyond the home.

The changes in women's economic role have been unfolding gradually, as a result of long-standing tendencies in the economy and society.
In each of the last ten decades, the proportion of adult women working
for pay has risen. A development that has gone on steadily for a century
has not occurred by chance or the whim of fashion, nor is it easily
reversible.

The growth of women's labor force participation has an origin
deep within the economic system, arising from the process of technological change. Advances in labor productivity have raised the wages
employers were willing to pay workers of both sexes. The real value
of a week's pay check has quadrupled since the beginning of the century.
Although women's wages continue to be far lower than men's, they
are a lot higher than they used to be. And it is higher wages that have
made women's time too valuable to be devoted entirely to homemaking.

The fall in the birth rate has been another powerful cause of change
in women's economic participation. In the United States, women are
averaging half as many babies as in 1900, one quarter as many as in
1800. The birth rate is not independent of economic factors—it is
affected by them and affects them in turn. Having a job cuts the number
of babies a woman wants to have—and having fewer children leaves
space in a woman's life for a job.

These same forces are at work in all technologically advanced
countries, whether they have private enterprise economies or state socialism. Developments of the same nature in so many countries cannot
arise from minor or local or temporary causes, but result from factors
close to the mainspring of economic functioning.

The economic forces that have furthered women's emergence are
far from exhausted. Women's participation in the money economy
will most likely grow until it equals men's. In terms of numbers in
paid employment, American women are already almost three quarters
of the way there. Less-developed countries will follow as their economies mature.

SEX ROLES IN ECONOMIC FUNCTIONING

In the past, women's place in the economy was an assignment to sole responsibility for the care of children, and to housework and other work that could efficiently be combined in the home with child care. Men were given sole responsibility for earning money, and exempted from taking a share in "women's work." Most people accepted these automatic assignments by sex as biologically right and inevitable, and as a necessary provision for the nurture of children. Until recently, only a tiny minority of men and women thought that assigning people economic functions based entirely on their sex might be unjust or inefficient or unnecessarily constricting.

Women's economic specialization has been a source of limitation, boredom, deprivation for many of them and of powerlessness for virtually all of them. Of course many men have been denied opportunities, for reasons of class or race or religion or origin. But the denial of opportunities to women has always been more severe, more pervasive, and harder to evade. Different economic assignments for men and women gave them different lives. One's sex determined the likelihood of having paid work that an intelligent person could find interesting and enjoyable. A talented person's sex determined the likelihood that the talent could be developed and expressed. It has determined whether one exercised power over others, or was narrowly, perhaps tyrannically, constrained by others' power. One's sex has largely determined how and with whom one spent time, the likelihood that one would suffer economic deprivation, boredom, isolation, physical abuse. Men's and women's different place in the economy has given them different chances for respect, and honor.

Heidi Hartmann has argued that women have been subordinated to men in all aspects of life because they have lacked direct access to economic resources on the same basis as men.[1] Women have had to seek indirect access to economic resources through their personal relations with men, and the resulting dependence has put them at a crucial disadvantage.

Through the nineteenth century, women were prohibited or discouraged from learning or practicing most trades or professions, from borrowing, or making contracts. In the beginning of that century they could work as domestic servants or low-paid factory hands, but not much else. Later, teaching jobs at low wages opened up.[2] A woman's only way to have a respectable status and a well-provided home in which she could comfortably raise children was to be a housewife. That meant sharing a man's income, and in return devoting herself entirely to running his home. She had to have sex with him on demand, bear and raise as many children as he engendered, keep him in good humor, and obey him on pain of violent punishment, if he chose. Many marriages were partnerships based on love and respect between the woman and the man.[3] Most women probably wanted children, and many enjoyed the sex, were reconciled to the housekeeping, and felt affection for the men they married. But that is a daunting job description. And it was the only way a nineteenth-century woman could earn a decent living.

The difference in status and opportunities between today's women and those of the 1800s appears enormous. With freedom of contraception and abortion, women don't have to have babies they don't want. Higher education is now as available to them as to men. Women's confidence and self-esteem are far higher than in the past. More kinds of jobs are open to them. Women don't have to stay at home after they marry, isolated from business, the professions, the chance to earn money.

Nevertheless, today's women still are at a considerable economic disadvantage relative to men. Marriage still is the only route to parenthood that promises a comfortable life. And women still have poorer access to good jobs than do men.

WOMAN'S PLACE IN THE LABOR MARKET

In a modern economy, access to economic resources for most people is through jobs. The labor market is the place where the degree of equality between the sexes is contested and decided. In the American labor market, today as in the past, the vast majority of the "good" jobs—those with interesting work, promotional possibilities, and good pay—are held by men. Full-time women workers are paid less than two thirds what full-time men are paid. A woman with a college degree can expect to receive a lower scale of pay than a male high-school graduate, and far less than a male college graduate with the same length of experience.

In the past decade, there has been rapid change in a few fields, principally those where schools control entry. The proportion of women among new lawyers and physicians has grown rapidly. Some advances have been made in the proportion of women in managerial jobs. On the other hand, few women have penetrated the blue-collar skilled craft jobs or the higher reaches of business and governmental management. Overall, the gap between men's pay and women's is diminishing very slowly.

There is a great deal of evidence that women's poor labor-market position is in large part due to discrimination in placement and pay, and that, despite some progress, discrimination continues to play a significant role. Statistical studies of women's and men's pay and qualifications suggest that only about a third of the gap between men's and women's pay can be accounted for by differences between the sexes in experience or education. This evidence is backed up by court testimony about conditions in many workplaces.

The result of discriminatory actions by a high proportion of individual employers is that women, rejected for the better jobs, have to throw themselves on the market cheaply; a woman college graduate, after a fruitless search for a job worthy of her education, eventually may succumb and take a job as a secretary. Many employers specify a few occupations as female, push all of their women applicants into them, and assign to them the low wage the market specifies for labor services considered second-rate. Some of the jobs marked out as appropriate for women pay little more to a full-time worker than the benefits given to a welfare client who stays home all day.

The idea that our economy is shot through with unfairness is not accepted in all quarters. Many economists deny even the possibility that qualified women could be dealt with unfairly by employers. Seeing nothing amiss, they deny that government intervention is needed to improve women's place in the labor market. They convince themselves through purely theoretical exercises, based on made-up and untested assumptions, that systematic and long-lasting discrimination is simply impossible.[4] Having proved to their own satisfaction that employers' lapses from impartiality are unimportant or nonexistent, they are led to believe that women's low position must derive from the free choice of the women themselves.[5] Women, they say, occupy the lowest rungs of the ladder at the lowest pay voluntarily. Any woman who doesn't want to doesn't have to, these economists imply.

More women are coming to believe that they are unjustly treated, despite the continued insistence of some academic economists that the job market is perfectly fair. Women's groups, along with some unions, are demanding pay equity—that pay scales be revamped to raise the wages paid in the traditionally female occupations. And increasingly women are trying to overcome the barriers to jobs that have been off-limits to them.

THE FUTURE OF THE TWO-PARENT FAMILY

The traditional husband-wife family had a woman full time in and around the home, on permanent assignment to clean it up, care for the children, prepare the meals, see to everyone's comfort. The marriage ceremony was supposed to obligate her and her husband to stay together until one of them died. There was a strong taboo against having children out of wedlock. These arrangements made life comfortable and secure for many people, at least for those who had a white man with a good job as part of their family. But the comfort and security were based on constraints on women and men both. Women who wanted children were all but forced into such an arrangement by the denial of any alternative means of getting money. Men and women were denied the right to exit easily from an unsatisfying marriage, although the double standard allowed men a wide-ranging sexual freedom both before and during marriage.

The emergence of women into the paid labor force on a large scale has contributed to weakening or destroying these arrangements. Home comforts are reduced and disrupted because the wife is absent much of the day. High-quality child care no longer is built into each family. The wife herself is buffeted by competing demands on her time. Half of the marriages now end in divorce, as wives' jobs allow both wives and husbands to terminate marriages they are unhappy in. The custom of being married before having a child is eroding, especially among blacks, but among whites as well. By 1984, 28 percent of births to women eighteen to twenty-four years old were out of wedlock. The comforts and the stability of the husband-wife family have been impaired. Its very existence as the basic social unit in our society has been brought into question.

People holding to religious traditions of female subservience preach against the emergence of women into the marketplace and the weakening of the husband-wife family it has caused. They sympathize not at all with the constricted life of the obligatory housewife. They think the comfort and security of the traditional family, and the God-given authority of the husband, has been traded away for a mess of pottage— the house, the appliances, gadgets, cars, vacations financed with the help of the wife's paycheck.

One does not have to be a devotee of Old Testament attitudes to recognize that valuable things have been lost in women's transition to a place in the market economy. Children no longer spend their first years in a quiet and protected environment, basking in the attention of a person lovingly and entirely devoted to their well-being. The assumption that a marriage was for life created feelings of security that now have been lost. Anxiety and rush have become more commonplace. But the old system had heavy costs for women—it sacrificed their freedom to the convenience of men and to children's secure nurture.

The old-fashioned family at its best provided stability, warmth, company, adequate financing, a sustaining flow of caring and help. All of those are excellent things that we should not have to do without. It should not require a caste-like sex-role system, and the subordination of women, to provide them. But we can recapture some of the comfort and security of the traditional family only by reforms that take account of the new realities. The sacrifices required to raise children and maintain a comfortable home have to be redistributed between the husband and wife. New schedules of working hours, new purchases of services, and new habits of sharing domestic chores would reduce conflict, and make marriage more equitable.

CHANGES IN MEN'S LIVES

Women have taken on tasks and duties previously typical only of men, but men have been much slower to take on activities and responsibilities typical of women. This is hardly surprising, since men's superior status has required them to hold themselves aloof from "women's work." So far, men's slowness to take on more housework—cooking, cleaning, laundry—appears to have produced gains for them. Those whose wives have a job enjoy a substantial increase in income with very little increase in effort on their part. Some of the increase in divorces may be due to friction over housework.

Wives' increasing economic independence is another cause of increased divorce. The foundation stone of lifetime monogamous marriage has been the wife's lack of ability to support herself at anything but a very low level. Males have had responsibility for providing the money their wives and children lived on. Men have prided themselves on this role and taken their central identity from it; it has been the counterpart for men of the child-care role for women. In the past when some men deserted their wives and children, their families were left destitute. Now that wives have jobs, husbands can leave with less of a wrench to their consciences. Many men have gone on to found second families, and some have abandoned them in their turn.

It is hard to believe that the happiness of men would best be served by the conversion of a high proportion of adult males to rogue elephant status, living only fitfully with females and the young, of use to them only at mating time. But unless the husband-wife family based on long-run trust can be revitalized to accommodate to the new roles of women, that is the direction in which men may be headed.

In all likelihood, men's financial wings will be somewhat clipped in future. Divorced fathers, and fathers of out-of-wedlock children have not been rigorously forced to share their income with their children. Currently fewer than a quarter of absent fathers make substantial, steady contributions. Men's ability to escape supporting the children they sire is being reduced as public anger over the burden of welfare grows and as computerization allows closer financial monitoring of individuals.

Men's preeminence in the labor market will weaken as women compete with men on previously male turf. And the flow of women to the traditional women's occupations puts downward pressure on wage levels in all parts of the labor market—including the parts where men predominate.

LOOKING TO THE FUTURE: THE ROLE OF POLICY

Generally, feminists look to a future in which women and men are equal in opportunity, in respect, and in the burdens they carry. They advocate the use of government policies to further these goals. However, some feminists have grander ambitions. They say that a mere equalization among men and women in the chance for high status and reward is not what they are after. Some insist that the abolition of capitalism is necessary for true equality. Others emphasize the goal of diminishing differences in status and rewards, in making competition less fierce, and management and supervision more collegial. They want our economy and our society to adopt what they claim is a female style of cooperation. They advocate an abandonment of the male style of competition and hierarchy. It is by no means clear that these "styles" are really associated with gender. Nor is it clear that one style or the other produces better results and happier lives, or that a less competitive style is attainable. Nor is it a foregone conclusion that socialism is preferable to capitalism for women or for men.

That women and men should have equal opportunity in whatever system emerges seems a more realistic, if more limited, goal. The achievement of that goal is not yet in sight, however. At this point it is difficult to know whether we are witnessing a trend toward similarity in the roles of men and women, or are instead moving toward new forms of separate roles. Nor will the new roles necessarily be more comfortable, more just. Our main task, through public policy, through private debate, through discussion in the communications media, is to get rid of old habits and institutions that are sources of injustice or are out of line with the new realities. New modes of behavior, more appropriate to the new situation, have to be found and made habitual.

The still-common habit of reserving jobs with a "family wage" for men was rationalized on the ground that men were the sole support of their families. That rationalization served male superiority, but even as an excuse it has become outdated. A majority of husbands have been joined in the labor market by their wives and are no longer their families' sole earners. Millions of single mothers struggle to support their children with their earnings and need jobs with wages that will enable them and their children to live decently. Yet the mindsets and behavior patterns that have always kept women out of the better jobs survive largely intact. Many men still disdain to have women as superiors on the job, or even as coworkers. Many women, sensing that unconventional behavior brings trouble, still restrict their ambitions to traditional jobs. Sex discrimination in employment has been against the law in the United States since 1964 and has diminished, but it is far from dead. Unless we can create a fair labor market, the era of independence for women will be one of poverty for many of them and subordination for most.

The current system for helping the rapidly growing numbers of single parents badly needs reform. The welfare system is almost universally acknowledged to be a failure. The outlines of the present welfare system were laid down in the 1930s, when no one expected that a mother would or could take a job. But if single mothers are to live at a decent standard, they must have substantial earnings of their own—there is simply no other way. Absent fathers will have to make child-support payments, whether the children were born in wedlock or not. Child-support payments will have to be administered like tax collections. When they are, sexual relations with women will be less of a lark for men than they are now. Intercourse will carry risk of long-term consequences for men, as it always has for women.

Marriage can become a loving alliance of two economically and socially equal people. For this to happen, attitudes toward housework will have to be reformed. Husbands will have to change more diapers, sweep more floors, wash more clothes. Of all needed changes in habits and attitudes, this may be the hardest to accomplish. The adoption of flexible, shorter work hours by employers would facilitate sharing of housework between husbands and wives. The current standard workweek dates from a time when most full-time workers had full-time housewives to wait on them.

To some degree, free enterprise is rescuing the overbusy two-earner family. Establishments for out-of-home child care and "fast food" proliferate. These developments enable families to buy some of the services formerly performed by the wife and allow wives to reduce their hours of housework. New public and private ventures should be started to further this trend. Innovative housing and neighborhoods could allow two-earner couples with children to live and work in a safe environment, close to their jobs, where their need for child care and other services can be met efficiently.

It is by no means certain that habits and institutions can be changed to bring about an equitable society. The alternative is a sad one. A failure to reform the labor market would mean a continuation of low pay for women. But the increasing divorce rate and the lower marriage rate mean that progressively fewer men would be sharing their paychecks with women and children. More women and children would slide into poverty or near-poverty as men spent their "family wage" on themselves. Within the husband-wife family, the overload of duties on the wife would continue.

The Soviet Union, which has been and still is ahead of the United States and Western Europe in having women in paid employment, presents a dismal example of where we will be headed without such reforms. The official Soviet ideology touts equality between women and men. Yet there is a hangover of old and inappropriate attitudes and habits governing the relations between the sexes. Women are rare in the top jobs and hold no high political positions. Men openly express attitudes of superiority over women and leave all of the heavy burden of housework to their fully employed wives. The result is a high divorce rate, the disillusionment of women with marriage, a high rate of alcoholism among the men.[6]

Japan presents another grim example.[7] There, as in the West, women have been coming into the labor market. But Japanese women are almost invariably shunted into marginal positions. The jobs open to them are defined as part-time and temporary. Many Japanese companies have a policy of hiring no women college graduates. Women in Japan remain frankly inferior, their condition an ugly blot on Japan's brilliant economic success.

The United States and Western Europe are hardly condemned to follow the bad examples of the Soviet Union or Japan in the relations of men and women. Our flexibility and pragmatism give us a huge advantage. But we need work, study, and experimentation to find the right mix of policies, and political means to carry them out. Both men and women must take part in the work of refashioning our habits and institutions so they are just, comfortable, and safe for women, men, and children.

It may be possible to move toward a world in which both men and women can develop and contribute, free of restrictions based on gender, and free also of prejudice on account of race, origin, sexual orientation, or age. It may be possible for adults to join in stable family unions for economic and social sustenance in which the loving and generous care and support of children are assured. If we can imagine such a world, then it may be in our power to devise the means to move toward it.

CHAPTER 2

The Economic Impetus
Behind Women's Emergence

THE LIBERATION of women from exclusive domesticity did not originate in feminist books, or a war, or a big inflation, although they contributed to its progress. The rising enrollment of women in the paid labor force is a straightforward consequence of the industrial revolution of two hundred years ago. That revolution has produced a long and continuing rise in the productivity of labor. Economic progress has steadily raised the wage of an hour's labor—the price of a human being's time. Women have always had to sell their time cheaper than men. But the price employers have paid for women's time has risen along with the price paid for men's. The key to women's economic emergence is that women's time has risen in price until it has become, in the eyes of family members, too valuable to be spent entirely in the home.

The rise in women's employment has made changes that are visible not only in the workplace but also in the schools, the divorce courts, the kitchens, the child-care centers. Behavior has changed and so have attitudes about what kinds of lives are possible, decent, and desirable for women. The cash wages that more and more women earn motivate and finance the new modes of behavior. The prospect of good jobs motivates college education for more women, and women's earnings pay for some of the tuition. Women's earnings finance the paid-for child care and finance the independent lives women lead after divorce. The idea that women should have the same rights as men gains acceptance as more women can and do pay for the bread on their own tables.

The tide of women into paid employment has been rising quite steadily for more than a century. But until recently very little attention was paid; possibly the liberation of women from exclusive domesticity was news that people did not want to hear. The progressively greater numbers of employed women started drawing public attention only toward the end of the 1970s; by then, people could not help noticing, because employed women had become the majority.

If we look back beyond the nineteenth century—the heyday of the housewife—to our preindustrial past, we see an era in which most wives did more than just housekeeping work. They did farm chores, or helped out in small-scale crafts enterprises run out of the home. As industrialization progressed, however, people moved to cities, and the work of urban men was moved to sites away from the home. Most married women became isolated from all work but housekeeping and child-rearing. An urban husband in modest circumstances could take pride that he was now like a rich man in one respect at least: His wife had nothing to do with earning money, only with spending it.[1]

We can sight the modest beginnings of wives' emergence from that isolation from earning in the latter half of the nineteenth century. The labor market then was uninviting to women—the largest single paid occupation open to them was domestic service. Many of the women who worked for pay then did so because they lacked a father, husband, brother, or a son to keep them at home in comfort. Black and immigrant women from poverty-stricken families made up a considerable part of the female work force, and their status and condition were such that no one would want to emulate them. To society at large, and particularly to women enjoying the economic protection of a man, the condition of those women who worked for pay as servants or in factories appeared pitiful.

Gradually, however, conditions changed. Some of those women who had men who might pay for their keep started to join the work force. Among them were women with ambition to practice a profession or run a business, and a few with literary ambitions—the "thousand scribbling women" of whose competition Hawthorne had so bitterly complained. But women of more common gifts made up the bulk of the new entrants.[2] Some of them enjoyed the work they were allowed to take up, and all of them enjoyed the money that went with it. The economic and social forces favoring the emergence of women from full-time unpaid domesticity grew increasingly more important. As more and more women joined the parade from the home into paid work, attitudes toward employed women changed. What had been a mixture of pity and opprobrium became acceptance and even, in some quarters at least, admiration.

THE STEADY MARCH TO EMPLOYMENT

In 1986, there were 67 million men and 52 million women in the United States labor force, either employed or looking for work* (see table 2–1). In 1870 women were about 16 percent of the labor force. By 1986, their share had grown to 44 percent. What is notable about the numbers in table 2–1 is the evidence they give of the steadiness in the advance in women's participation. Every decade after 1880 shows an increase in the percentage of the labor force that is female. The movement of women into the labor force is not, of course, just an American phenomenon. It has been going on in every industrialized country in the world.†

---

* According to the definition in current use by the statistical agencies of the United States, a person is counted as being "in the labor force" if he or she is employed, or is actively searching for a job. To qualify as "employed," a person does not have to be working full time; any part-time job suffices. Those working on an unpaid basis in a family moneymaking enterprise are also, in theory at least, included in the U.S. labor force. In practice, few farm wives are counted, despite the fact that most of them are involved in some aspects of the work of farming.

† Differing statistical treatment of farm women in different countries makes international comparisons of historical trends in women's labor force statistics difficult. In France and Japan, for example, the inclusion of farm women in the economically active population and the exclusion of housewives causes a measured decline in women's labor force participation over long periods. However, in these countries, as in the United States, urban women's participation in nonagricultural occupations has grown steadily in the twentieth century. For material on England (which does not count farm wives as participants) and France (which does), see Louise A. Tilly and Joan W. Scott, *Women, Work and Family* (New York: Holt, Rinehart, and Winston, 1978), chap. 4.

TABLE 2–1
Labor Force Participants by Sex, 1870–1986

Year	Labor Force (Millions)		Women as a Percent of Total
	Men	Women	
1870	11	2	16
1880	15	3	16
1890	18	4	17
1900	23	5	18
1920	32	8	20
1930	37	10	22
1940	42	14	25
1950	44	18	29
1960	46	23	33
1970	51	32	38
1980	61	45	43
March, 1986	65	52	44

NOTE: Labor force figures are published only back to 1890. The series has been extended back to 1870 by using the "gainful workers" series. Post-World War II figures exclude the armed forces.
SOURCE: U.S. Bureau of the Census, *Historical Statistics of the United States* (Washington, D.C.: 1960), U.S. Government Printing Office, and U.S. Bureau of Labor Statistics. Labor Force Statistics derived from the *Current Population Survey: A Data Book,* vol. 1, BLS Bulletin 2096, Sept. 1982; and *Employment and Earnings,* April 1986.

Women's labor force participation rate—the ratio of females in the labor force to the female population of working age*—has grown almost continually since 1870 (see table 2–2). It fell back for a few years after World War II, when Rosie the Riveter was displaced, and in an occasional year of recession. Since 1948, women's labor force participation rate has risen in every year but three. By contrast, men's participation rate, which was fairly constant between 1890 and 1950, has been dropping at a moderate rate since 1950. The drop in men's participation rate is mostly due to a decline in participation of men age sixty-five or over.† The participation of women sixty-five or over has

* The data from 1950 on refer to a population age sixteen or over; from 1890 to 1940, age fourteen or over; from 1870 to 1880, age ten or over.
† In 1890 it is estimated that 68 percent of men over sixty-five were in the labor force; 45 percent of such men participated in 1950; currently only about 17 percent of them do. Another source of drop in men's participation rates is the reduction in black men's participation.

TABLE 2–2
Labor Force Participation Rates by Sex and Age,
1870–1986
(percent)

Year	All Persons		Persons Under 65	
	Men	Women	Men	Women
1870	82	14	—	—
1880	84	15	—	—
1890	84	18	85	19
1900	86	20	87	21
1920	85	23	87	24
1930	82	24	84	25
1940	83	28	86	30
1950	83	33	88	36
1960	83	38	90	42
1970	80	43	87	50
1980	77	52	86	60
March, 1986	76	55	85	64

SOURCE: See table 2–1.

remained quite steady; currently 7 percent of them are in the labor market, about the same percentage as in 1890.

If we look just at people under sixty-five, the convergence of women's and men's participation rates is even more striking. Back in 1890, the participation rate for women under sixty-five was about one fifth that of men under sixty-five. By 1940, the women's rate had moved up to about one third that of men's. In 1986, the participation rate for women under sixty-five was just over three quarters that of men.

Between 1970 and 1980, the number of women in the labor force grew by 41 percent. But that rapid rate of growth was nothing really new—there had been a 39 percent growth in the 1960s and a healthy 29 percent growth in each of the two previous decades. However, by the 1970s these large rates of growth meant large absolute increases. An additional 13 million women were recruited to the United States labor force in the 1970s. And by the end of the decade a majority of women were in the labor force.

CHANGES IN LIFE PATTERNS

In each succeeding decade over the past hundred years, more and more women participated in the labor market. But numbers of workers do not tell the whole story. As time went by, the pattern of women's lives changed. Successive generations of women spent more years in the labor market than their mothers and grandmothers had done, and worked in phases of their lives their mothers would have considered sacred to domesticity.

A significant proportion of women born in the latter half of the nineteenth century never spent a day of their lives in a paid job. However, by 1890 considerable numbers of young, unmarried women were holding jobs, as women of their age had done over the centuries. In 1890 most young women left the labor force very promptly when they married. Some of them were dismissed by their employers upon their marriage, but most of them probably gave up their jobs before the wedding voluntarily, as a matter of custom. This retirement from paid work must surely have accorded with the desires of their husbands, for whom the possession of a stay-at-home wife was a matter of pride.

As time passed, newly married women started staying in their jobs until they became pregnant with their first child, at which time they retired. Some of them retired for good. But as the years went on, it became more common for women to come back to paid jobs when their youngest child finished high school. At the same time, the number of children women were having decreased, reducing the number of years between the birth of the first child and the departure from home of the last. And as time went on, more women returned to take a job while still having a child of school age.

Today, a considerable proportion of mothers of newborns, probably a majority, take some time out of the labor force, but many of these women go back to a job after a few months at home with the baby. Some new mothers stay home from work after the birth of a child only long enough to recover physically from the delivery. A recent study found that as many as one fifth of employed mothers-to-be stayed on the job until the final month of pregnancy and resumed working

FIGURE 2-1

Labor Force Participation by Age of U.S. Women Born 1886–1965

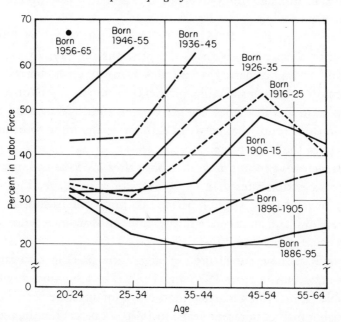

SOURCE: Linda J. Waite, "U.S. Women at Work," *Population Bulletin*, vol. 36, no. 2 (Washington, D.C.: Population Reference Bureau Inc., May 1981).

shortly after childbirth. Most of this group did not reduce their hours on the job after the birth.[3]

Just as every parade has a vanguard, it also has a rear guard—women whose lives have a pattern more typical of the nineteenth than of the twentieth century. There are today young women who have never been employed and who possibly never will be. Many of these women became pregnant while going to high school and, married or on welfare, have been devoting their lives ever since to child care and keeping house full time. In the nineteenth century, women from the most prosperous families stayed out of the labor force. Their counterparts today are in the most prestigious professions. The women who now go directly from school to domesticity are likely to be from less-privileged backgrounds.

Figure 2–1 illustrates how life patterns have changed. Of women born from 1886 to 1895, about 30 percent were in the labor force in their early twenties. The rest were at home, most with children. As more of this cohort of women married, their labor force participation dropped still further. A very slight increase in participation is visible for this group after age thirty-five, but only a small proportion of them ever returned to a job.

Women born from 1926 to 1935 had a pattern quite different from that of the women born in the previous century. At each age they have had higher participation rates than the group born earlier. In their midthirties, considerable numbers of them took jobs once their youngest child was in school. By the time of the 1970 Census, when women in this group were between thirty-five and forty-four, half of them were in the labor force.

Each successive cohort of women born after 1935 has had strikingly higher participation rates than its predecessor at each age. This is the result of fewer babies, shorter periods of nonparticipation after the birth of a child, and an increase in the number of women who do not drop out at all.

Table 2–3 shows the change in labor force participation rates by mothers between the years 1970 and 1985. The table documents the remarkable rate at which married mothers of infants have been coming into the labor market in recent years. In 1970, 24 percent of the married women who had children one year old or younger were in the labor force. By 1985, almost half the married women with children one year or younger were in the labor force. In all, 62 percent of mothers with children under eighteen at home were labor force participants in 1985.

A majority of mothers who have jobs are now working full time, 71 percent in 1985. Of women with children under three who are employed, 67 percent work full time.

THE RISE IN THE PRICE OF TIME

We want now to seek reasons for the century-long movement of women from the home, an emergence that is by no means completed. In the course of those hundred years, there were periods of war and periods of peace. There were prosperous periods when the number of

TABLE 2–3
Labor Force Participation Rates of Mothers, by Age of
Youngest Child, 1970 and 1985
(percent)

	1970	1985
All mothers, with:		
Children under 18 years old	42.1	62.1
Children 6 to 17 years old, none younger	51.5	69.9
Children under 6 years old	32.3	53.5
Children under 3 years old	27.3	49.5
Never married, with:		
Children under 18 years old	N.A.	51.6
Children 6 to 17 years old, none younger	N.A.	64.1
Children under 6 years old	N.A.	46.5
Children under 3 years old	N.A.	42.2
Married, husband present, with:		
Children under 18 years old	39.9	60.8
Children 6 to 17 years old, none younger	49.2	67.8
Children under 6 years old	30.5	53.4
Children under 3 years old	25.9	50.5
youngest child 2 years old	30.5	54.0
youngest child 1 year old or younger	24.0	49.4
Divorced, with:		
Children under 18 years old	75.6	79.1
Children 6 to 17 years old, none younger	82.4	83.4
Children under 6 years old	63.3	67.5
Children under 3 years old	52.1	52.2

NOTE: Data for never-married women are not available for 1970, and the totals for that year do not include them.
SOURCES: U.S. Bureau of Labor Statistics, USDL 85–381, table 1 (September 19, 1985), USDL 84–321 (July 26, 1984), table 1; and Howard Hayghe, "Rise in Mothers' Labor Force Activity Includes Those with Infants," *Monthly Labor Review*, vol. 109, no. 2 (February 1986):43–45.

jobs grew rapidly, and periods of depression when the number of jobs shrank and unemployment was high. There were years of inflation and years of price stability or decline. There were, during that century, times when the agitation in favor of equality for women was at a high level, and times when little was heard on that vexing subject.

Throughout the entire period, however, the rise in women's participation in paid work went on with no important reversals from one decade to another. This suggests that it was not singular events such

FIGURE 2-2

Estimated Weekly Earnings of Women Workers, 1890–1984
(in dollars of 1984 purchasing power)

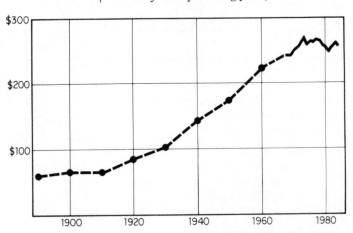

SOURCE: Information for years prior to 1967 adapted by the author from wage and price data in *Historical Statistics of the United States: Colonial Times to 1957* (Washington, D.C.: Government Printing Office, 1960). Later data from unpublished tabulations of the U.S. Bureau of Labor Statistics.

as wars or bursts of inflation or shifts in ideological fashion that were at the root of this development. We must look for causes that exerted a steadily increasing push throughout that period.

An important part of the explanation of women's exodus from exclusive domesticity is the substantial increase over the decades in the wage rate—the price paid for the time they might spend on a job. While the benefit from working at a paid job was rising, the benefit of staying home was declining, as women had fewer children. The benefits of going out to work were bound to catch up with and surpass the benefits of staying home for more and more women.

The hourly wage earned by the average employed women has been rising fairly steadily since the industrial revolution. Some of that wage rise has been canceled by inflation in the prices of goods workers buy. However, when we look at "real wages"—wages that have been corrected for inflation—the trend is unmistakably and substantially upward. The data indicate that women's real wages have more than quadrupled since 1890 (see figure 2-2). The quantity of commodities a woman could buy with the earnings from an hour's work at a job has grown by 1.64 percent per year, on average, between 1890 and 1985.

In contrast to the increased reward for the time on the job, the reward to the time of housewives probably decreased on average. An hour of care for a new baby in the 1980s produces the same benefit as an hour of baby care a half century previously. An hour of home baking produces the same pie. However, the mother of the 1980s has fewer babies. If she is devoted to full-time domesticity on a long-term basis she does less baby care than her counterparts of a half century earlier and spends more time at lower-priority tasks such as pie-baking.

A women considering leaving full-time domesticity and going to work compares her life in the two situations. She considers the financial reward of outside work and considers how much she values the leisure and housework she would have to forgo. (She knows that if she makes the move, she will be relieved of doing few if any of the basic house-keeping services. She will have to cut corners in doing them and cut into her own time for rest and recreation.) Even if the value of the activities of a housewife at home had stayed the same throughout that period, the rise in the real wage rate would have made the trade-off of the home activities for job activities more than twice as sweet in 1983 as it had been in 1939, and more than four times sweeter than in 1890.

Economic dislocations connected to the food and fuel inflation of the 1970s caused the rise in the real wage to falter, after an unbroken run-up of thirty years after World War II. In the period between 1973 and 1984, real wages fell in seven years and rose in five. However, the momentum derived from decades of rising real wages, and the continuing momentum of social changes, have ensured a continuation of the rise in women's employment.

WHY THE REAL WAGE GREW

If the rise in the real hourly wage available to women workers is the main cause of the outpouring of women from the home, it behooves us to ask why that rise has occurred and what the prospects are for its continuance. Progressively higher wages over the long term can be attributed to progressively higher worker productivity. As time has gone on, the average worker has produced a greater volume of output of improved quality in an hour of work.

The most important source of increase in worker productivity in our economy is technological change. New and better processes of production, new products, more efficient machines, and better management are introduced year by year. The improvement in the technology of the productive process has been going on in Western capitalist countries since the start of the industrial revolution in the latter part of the eighteenth century.

In any country, a bad recession or a disruptive turn in economic policy or in the political setup may interrupt progress. The rapid rise in fuel prices in the 1970s caused economic disruptions that hurt productivity. Nevertheless, the basic progressiveness of Western capitalist economies seems to be deeply embedded, and the process of fairly continual improvement shows no sign of ending. On the contrary, we appear to be on the threshold of a period of very rapid technological change as the computerization of the productive process spreads.

A second, related factor leading to greater worker productivity has been the continual growth in our stock of capital goods—the productive equipment of the workplace. This growth in capital allows us to implement the advances in scientific and technological knowledge by creating improved and more plentiful machinery and equipment. An economy's workers become more productive as the capital stock with which they work improves in quality and quantity.*

The workers in any particular plant usually have very little to do with the increase in the quantity and quality of the equipment with which they work. Rather, these improvements in equipment are due to the ingenuity of scientists and engineers, the planning of management, and the financial investment of the company's stockholders and creditors.

If the improvement in capital structure were narrowly confined to just a few companies, the workers in those companies would be unlikely to have gotten much of a share in the increase of per-worker production. Most if not all of it would have gone to the stockholders

---

* There is a third major factor leading to higher worker productivity: Workers have had more education on average as time has passed. This issue, as it pertains to women workers, is discussed in the next chapter.

and the management. However, this process of improvement in the quantity and quality of capitalization has permeated large parts of the economy, and as profits have increased, the competition for good workers has encouraged an increase in the level of real wages throughout the economy. Karl Marx had predicted that the competition of capitalists would "immiserate" the workers, but the opposite has turned out to be the case.

When the size of the national income increases relative to the size of the labor force, workers tend to get a share of the increase in the form of increased real wages. Female workers' wages have remained well below those of men, but as men's wages have moved up, women's have also. Had this not happened, female workers would have fallen farther and farther behind the male workers. There has been little or no tendency for this to happen, despite the fact that the supply of female workers has been increasing faster than the supply of male workers.

MEN'S WAGES AND WOMEN'S EMPLOYMENT

The same process of technological change and capital accumulation that has increased women's wage levels has increased men's wage levels as well. A rise in the husband's wage makes the family less needy, better provided with goods. Each successive addition to family income is devoted to buying goods that, while desirable, are perhaps increasingly less vital to health and comfort.* Further additions to family income become less urgent, so the rise in men's wages works against the entry into employment of wives.

The rise in men's wage levels reduces the utility the family would derive from a second paycheck of a *given size.* At the same time, the rise in women's pay *increases the size* of that potential second paycheck. These two effects work in opposite directions, and which predominates depends on how close the family is to satiation with purchased goods.

---

* Economists summarize this by saying that the marginal utility of income falls as income rises.

Today's families still appear to be far away from satiation; the continual development of new products bolsters the desire for additional income. So the rise in the family's standard of living deriving from the husband's higher wage has done little to dampen the desire to cash in on the wife's improved earning opportunities. The utility the family sees as coming from the wife's paycheck has on balance grown, until it has overshadowed the benefit derived from her full-time presence in the home.*

In households where the husband is a physician, dentist, independent businessman, or corporate executive and has an income that is considerably above average, a high proportion of the wives are still at home. The benefit of additional dollars to such a family is relatively low. Moreover, if the wife does not have the training or inclination for professional work, it is relatively difficult for her to find work befitting the social status she derives from her husband. Such families constitute the last bastion of the full-time housewife.

THE "NEED" OF COUPLES FOR THE MONEY

Over the long term, the economy has grown progressively richer and more rewarding to work in. Families in which only the husband holds a job have grown better off, and wives have better opportunities for earnings as well. However, the explanation that most people give of why more women are holding jobs has nothing to do with richness and increased reward. On the contrary, they speak of an increasingly dire "need." What they seem to be saying is that without women's employment, families are deprived, and that women "need" to go out to work to remedy that deprivation.

Of course, the "need" explanation and the higher-wage explanation both point to the centrality of the monetary reward. An in-

---

* If the introduction of new products flags, a continued rise in wage levels would eventually bring about a situation in which the benefit of family members' extra hours in the labor force would be dropping rather than rising. Family members (not necessarily only the wife) would eventually want to increase their home time and curtail their time at paid work, particularly if work schedules were to become less standardized and more flexible.

creasing number of women, many with children, do not have a husband on whose paycheck they can rely, and for them the "need" argument holds water. However, the argument is somewhat misleading, possibly deliberately so when applied to the general case of married women with employed husbands.

People commonly talk of the wife's salary as though it were a "requirement" or "necessity" for many or most couples. For example, the historian Alice Kessler-Harris says, "[A]s the requirements of keeping a home have changed, so too has the framework of women's lives. Whereas once only poor and working-class families required two incomes to operate a household, in contemporary America the need for two incomes cuts across class lines."[4] There is a problem, however, in interpreting middle-class wives' "need" to work as a financial "requirement." As we have noted, a husband in the 1980s commands a salary that is (after accounting for inflation) perhaps four times as large as his counterpart at the turn of the century, whose wife did not "need" to work. If today's family is so well provided for by the salary of the husband alone, in what sense does the family "need" the wife's paycheck?

Before going farther, it will be worth our while to demystify "need," an ambiguous word that implies different degrees of urgency in different contexts. When we speak of the "needs" of extremely poor people, we are talking of what they must have to avoid severe deprivation or possibly even death. However, when people in more ordinary circumstances say they "need" some product, usually they do not mean that without it they would die or even be in grave difficulty.

On the contrary, the most common usage of the term "need" implies no real urgency whatever: Frequently we say we "need" a product we customarily use but have run out of or used up. When we use the word in that context, the term "need" merely means that our attention is focused on the product because we are in the process of going out and buying it. This is what we mean when we say that we "need" a jar of mayonnaise.

Sometimes we say we "need" a product that, given our income, is just outside of our grasp and that would be one of the first items purchased if more income came our way. Thus we might say, "Our family needs a second car, but we can't afford one." But the "need" for a product we don't currently buy cannot be particularly acute, since that product demonstrably has lower priority than all the products we do buy with our current income. We are really saying that the product is in the focus of our attention. The same psychological process is at work when we say we "need" more money. Here the expression of "need" represents a mental focus on the hoped-for and much-desired next upward step in our standard of living.

When a married woman whose husband is employed says she is taking a paid job because of her "need" for the money, she is doing two things simultaneously. She is using the term in its ordinary economic context, to signify that her mind is focused on the goods she will buy with the new income. However, she is probably also doing a bit of punning by evoking the term "need" as it is used in the context of extreme deprivation, to plead an urgency of "need" somewhat beyond the usual. The reason for the extra burden the word "need" carries when a woman takes a job is that she is committing a stigmatized act.

The married woman who takes a job, even in current circumstances, still is somewhat afraid of being seen to be neglecting her children, a very serious accusation to be faced by any mother. By the same act she can also be seen as injuring her husband, who loses some of her services and loses his previous status as sole breadwinner. To top it off, all of these allegedly bad things are done so she may earn "pin money"—money that will be spent on unimportant things. A woman's allusion to her family's "need" for the money neatly fends off such accusations (and self-accusations) of callousness and triviality and invites inferences of self-sacrifice on her part.[5]

For some women, the invocation of the "need" for the money also serves to draw attention away from other benefits that working outside the home might bring, benefits that some consider illicit when enjoyed by women. On the job, she may enjoy the company of other adults (demonstrating, to some eyes, that she lacks complete devotion to her children). She may be accorded some prestige on account of her accomplishments (demonstrating selfishness and false pride). She may relish a sense of independence (demonstrating incomplete loyalty to her family role). She may find an outlet for talents and aggressiveness that are not allowed expression in the housewife role (thereby demonstrating a lack of true femininity). In sum, focusing on "need" serves to squelch accusations that she is not a true woman.

While the rhetoric of "needs" has been pressed into service to smother criticism of women's move to paid work, it has not been used without some damage to the cause of equality between women and men. The propaganda that has trumpeted the financial "need" that has caused many women to take jobs has by implication downgraded their other reasons for wanting jobs. The false dichotomy between women who "have to work" and women who "don't have to" undercuts the right of the woman whose husband has a well-paying job to pursue a career.[6]

The invocation of the "need" for women to work reached a crescendo during the inflationary period from 1969 to 1981. Those were years in which women's labor force participation was growing rapidly. That was also, as we have seen, the period in which the participation rate of women in jobs passed the 50 percent mark and in which the continuing entry of women into the labor force became salient to the general public. People were starting to cast around for explanations for women's greater participation in the labor market, and the most common reason cited both by individual women themselves and by the media in that period was that inflation was forcing women into the labor market.

It is a common observation that people feel aggrieved and victimized during inflationary periods, even if their paychecks are increasing at the same rate that prices are increasing. They take the rise in the prices of the goods they buy as attacks on their standard of living. Whatever gratification they get from the dollar size of their paycheck is more than canceled out by the chagrin over the price increases.

During the inflation of the 1970s, real hourly wages did cease to rise, and for a variety of reasons, after-tax real incomes may have been falling to some degree.* So there may have been some justified feelings of deprivation. However, the most likely reason for the inflation explanation's popularity was that it fitted in so well with a desire to make women's move to the labor market look involuntary and reluctant.

The rhetoric of "needs" has also been employed to argue that women should not take jobs. Her children have been said to "need" her full-time devotion, her husband to "need" her undivided attention to the tending of their home. As in the case of the "need" for her

---

* Social Security taxes rose in terms of percentage of income, and inflation was pushing people with no increase in real income into higher income-tax brackets.

salary, the use of the word has a large element of special pleading, and the alleged "need" tends to appear and to disappear as the nature of the pleadings changes.

While the invocation of "need" is in most cases used to lay down a smoke screen, one-earner couples, even though more affluent than in the past, may feel *relatively* deprived. As time goes on, it becomes increasingly difficult for one-earner couples to "keep up with the Joneses," more and more of whom are two-earner couples. This will be discussed in the next chapter.

THE EFFECT OF LABOR-SAVING DEVICES IN THE HOME

Labor-saving devices in the home probably have encouraged labor force participation by wives. These devices reduced the time required to maintain a given standard of meal preparation and cleanliness and freed time of the wife for use on a job. The invention, production, and diffusion of household devices is an integral part of the process of technological change and capital accumulation that has raised real wage levels. However, the labor-saving effect of home appliances probably is minor compared to the effect of the rise in real wages.

Cooking, washing, cleaning, and shopping have gotten very much easier over the past century thanks to piped-in water, running hot water, electric lighting, the replacement of coal- or wood-burning stoves by gas or electric ones, the flush toilet, and the refrigerator. With the exception of automatic washers and dryers, the important labor-saving household devices were in common use, at least for city dwellers, by 1930. Thus, their effect in freeing the time of women cannot have precipitated women's labor force influx in the 1970s and 1980s.[7]

Moreover, there is one pivotal domestic task whose time requirements no piece of machinery can change: the care of a child in the home. (Of course, the reduction in the number of children per household has reduced time spent in child care, but that is a separate issue dealt with in the next chapter.) Being continually on call for the children and rendering them personalized, loving, and attentive care has been and continues to be the essential *raison d'être* of the housewife occupation. New products have brought minor changes in some of the techniques of home child care—disposable diapers or amusing the child with television come to mind. But home appliances cannot reduce the need for the mother to spend time in the company of the child, watching over its safety, and being on call to comfort the child and keep it in order. Only child care by substitutes for the mother can do that.

A 1965 study of how people spent their time shows that by then housewives had more free time than their employed husbands, on average. And in a survey done in 1975 housewives reported less time spent in housework than had been reported in 1965.[8] This trend probably owes more to the rise of fast food and the increase in the use of nursery schools than to home appliances. Whatever its cause, by the late 1960s the housewife may have appeared to others, and felt herself to be, increasingly underemployed.

NEW PRODUCTS AS A SPUR TO WORK

New mechanized household appliances have made wives' housekeeping easier, but they may have affected wives' work behavior in another way as well. Clair Brown has suggested that the desire to acquire these and other new consumer goods has been a major force propelling women into the paid labor force.[9] In theory this is certainly possible, although it is an effect that seems difficult to measure, and difficult to compare in importance relative to other effects.

One product introduced in the past hundred years stands out as particularly likely to have occasioned a rearrangement of priorities: the automobile. Expenses of households for automobiles and for their fuel, maintenance, and insurance consume 19 percent of the family budget in the United States.[10] If the introduction of automobiles into widespread use is indeed a major factor in drawing housewives out into the labor market, then it is possible that we have underestimated the extent to which husbands' desires have played a part. Husbands were for a number of decades the sole drivers of, and the major enthusiasts for, the automobile. Perhaps the most common image of family decision-making concerning the wife's work—wives pushing to go out to work over the sullen but somewhat soft opposition of their husbands—is not accurate. Perhaps husbands have been more instrumental in the demise of the housewife occupation than has been realized.

In addition to new products, there are new ways of selling them. Television advertisements have increased people's hunger for goods outside their current budgets. The vividness of television advertising, the sight of fictional families luxuriating in newly-minted material comforts may well have caused many real families to reassess their priorities. Large numbers of families certainly ended up trading part of the wife's household services and much of her leisure for cash used to buy things they saw on their home screens.

THE GROWTH OF "SUITABLE" OCCUPATIONS

Valerie K. Oppenheimer has expounded the theory that the growth in jobs considered suitable for women has been an important factor in the growth of women's labor force participation.[11] The occupations that have seemed suitable, according to Oppenheimer, are those that have reminded people of the tasks that women have traditionally performed. Nursing the sick, caring for and teaching small children, and sewing are examples. Clerical work was considered clean and ladylike. The suitable-jobs theory emphasizes the importance of the changes in the nature of the paid work that became available. By contrast, the wage-increase theory I have emphasized points to the increase in the pay for that work as the leading factor in drawing women in.

The two theories are by no means mutually exclusive. Both emphasize the importance of changes in the methods of production. In the wage-change theory, improved productivity increases the demand for labor, leading to higher wages, which attracts women to leave being housewives. In the suitable-jobs theory, changes in technology and also in the kinds of things produced have altered the nature of the jobs that employers want to fill, and this is pointed to as the main force behind women's greater employment. The suitable-jobs theory can have both supply-side and demand-side implications. Employers may have expanded the demand for women's labor because they considered new jobs they were creating to be suitable for them. Or women themselves may have supplied more labor as they found that an increasing number of jobs had duties congenial to them.*

In trying to assess the validity of the suitable-jobs theory, we have to think about what "suitability" means. There are certain societies in Africa where women do all of the heavy agricultural work, all of the business dealings, and all of the work of family care. The men are at leisure full time. In such a society, presumably no tasks are unsuitable for women. The designation of some jobs as unsuitable for women in any particular society is a matter of social convention rather than a reflection of women's inherent disabilities or inborn dislikes for certain kinds of work. People's ideas about suitability can and do change when the economy changes.

It is certainly true that the number of jobs considered suitable for women have grown very rapidly in industrialized countries since the turn of the century. Women have indeed come forward to occupy such jobs in large numbers. However, some of the jobs currently considered suitable that have had high growth rates were originally not thought suitable for women.

Clerks were once exclusively male, and their jobs were considered unsuitable for women by employers.[12] As long as there were few if any women clerks, most women probably considered the work unfeminine and therefore unsuitable for them. For there to be a change, a few employers had to decide that hiring women as clerks was a reasonable and profitable thing to do. They had to find a few women to take the jobs, which probably was not difficult. Once that happened, the growth of the idea among employers and among women workers that such jobs were suitable for women was only a matter of time. The job of bank teller,[13] which once required a male to signal the bank's financial probity and expertise, has also gone from all male to predominantly female.

---

* In terms of supply and demand curves, the wage-change theory suggests a shift upward in the demand curve for women's labor and a move along a fixed supply curve. The suitable-jobs theory posits a shift in both the supply curve and the demand curve.

A change in the sex typing of a job takes effort and innovation by employers. It appears to happen most easily in wartime, when labor shortages develop and when the mobilization of all resources available to the society may be required. The immediate postwar period typically brings an almost complete reversion to the prewar situation, but traces of the wartime experience remain, and the seeds of subsequent change may have been sown.[14] In peacetime, reclassifications happen relatively infrequently.

Since changing the sex typing of occupations is difficult, the incorporation of newly entering women workers into jobs probably goes more smoothly if jobs of a type already considered suitable for them become available in larger numbers. If that happens, few additional occupations need to have their sex identity changed. However, history suggests that attitudes toward suitability can and do change in response to large, fresh supplies of women's labor. Higher-than-average rates of growth in clerical and retail sales jobs already considered suitable for women has facilitated women's labor force entry during the twentieth century. But the idea that the massive move of women into paid work depended on that happening probably is invalid.

MIGHT THE TREND REVERSE ITSELF?

The increase in women's labor force participation over the past century is rooted in the long-term rise in the real wage—the price of women's time, a rise based on technological change and capital accumulation. Even in periods where the growth in the real wage sputters, comes to a halt, and temporarily reverses itself, the momentum built up by decades of growth continues to pull women into the paid work force.

Barring war or political changes severe enough to destroy the competitive dynamic of the capitalist economy, we can anticipate further technological advance and capital accumulation. The computer revolution should raise productivity to new heights. Thus the economic factors that have led to women's emergence from exclusive domesticity should continue to advance.

Changes in social practices and attitudes have reinforced the purely economic factors. As we shall document in the next chapter, birth rates have fallen, more women are getting a college education, and divorce rates are higher. All of these developments have furthered the move of women into the labor force, and the increase in women's participation has in turn furthered these developments. There has been a revival of an ideology of equality between the sexes. Furthermore, the passing of the 50 percent mark in women's labor force participation means that the force of social conformity will work more strongly in the future to push women into the labor force rather than to keep them out of it.

Apart from economic or political catastrophe, two sets of economic developments might conceivably interfere with the continuation of these trends. One is the development of ways of carrying on business through computer terminals in a worker's home. Women might be pressured to remain at home to combine child care with earning. Although women who did this would still be earning money, they would be even more isolated from other adults than housewives are, since they would have less leisure than housewives. They would have even less chance of promotion than women workers now have.

The growing ability of multinational enterprises to utilize low-paid labor profitably in underdeveloped countries may disrupt the trend toward higher real wages in the developed countries. This in effect enlarges many-fold the labor force available to owners of advanced capital equipment. It is putting downward pressure on the real wage of both men and women in the United States as well as in Europe. If the labor forces of the underdeveloped countries are joined with the labor forces of the developed countries into a worldwide labor market, serious problems for currently highly paid workers in the developed countries can be anticipated. In that worldwide labor market, wage levels and the treatment of women workers might be closer to a Korean standard than to the standard current in the United States or Sweden.

But computerization of the economy and the internationalization of the labor market are just beginning, and it is difficult to predict their pace or their effects. They will certainly not come overnight. For the next several decades we can anticipate that the economic forces bringing women out of domesticity will strengthen and that a reversal is highly unlikely.

CHAPTER 3

The Social Factors:

Births, Schools,

Divorces, Ideas

Yesterday's women viewed their marriage as lifelong and expected big families. Many of them knew that their parents had supported their brothers' education and aspirations while scanting theirs. Yesterday's women were used to hearing themselves described as weak and silly, and many of them thought it advantageous to describe themselves in that way.

Today's women understand that their marriages are for as long as they and their husbands both wish. Many give birth to one child and some now choose to have no children at all. There are still fathers and mothers who favor their sons over their daughters, but such parents are far fewer. Besides, today's daughters fight back. When they get to college, today's women are studying business management in large numbers, and many are headed for medicine or law. There are still those who think of women as weak and silly. More and more, though, people who think that way are learning to keep such ideas to themselves.

These social developments, to which we now turn, have furthered and been furthered by the rise in women's employment. They have increased the incentives for women to take employment and made it harder for women to remain housewives. The new social behavior and the new economic behavior reinforce each other.

It is easy to see how the social and economic factors interact. The reduction in the number of children per woman reduces the pull to stay home. Once a woman is out at paid work, the financial sacrifice involved in having another baby becomes obvious, and a deterrent to having it. A divorced woman needs an independent income, and all married women now understand that divorce is a possibility for them. Once a married woman has her own income, she and her husband may have less incentive to preserve their marriage. The spread of higher education for women and changes in attitudes toward women's roles have opened more and better jobs for women. In turn, the prospect of better jobs has affected girls' educational plans and the plans of their parents for them.

CHANGES IN BIRTH RATES

The fall in birth rates has been going on even longer than the rise in women's employment. The number of children per woman fell throughout the nineteenth century (see figure 3–1). While fewer babies have meant more jobs for wives, and vice versa, the drop in fertility is of great economic consequence in many other respects. A family with fewer children will have different expenditure patterns, make different residential choices. For the community, the birth rate affects the demand for schools, the supply of soldiers to the army, the supply of young people's labor. It affects the ratio of working people to retired people, and thus the extent to which the average working person will have to be taxed to support the average retired person.

The decline in fertility has not been as smooth as the rise in em-

FIGURE 3–1
Total Fertility Rate, White Women, 1800–1982

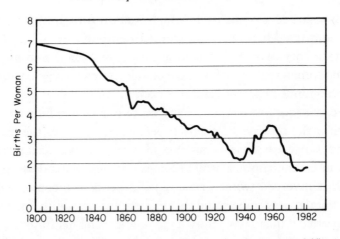

NOTE: A total fertility rate is the sum of the birth rates by year of age for women in childbearing years. For a particular year, this sum yields the number of births average women would have in their lifetime if at each age they acted as women in that age group were acting in that year.
SOURCE: Arland Thornton and Deborah Freedman, "The Changing American Family," *Population Bulletin*, vol. 38, no. 4 (October 1983):17.

ployment and wages for women. The baby boom that erupted after the close of World War II in 1945 sent birth rates climbing back to levels as high as those in the 1920s.* By 1956 the downward trend in birth rate had reasserted itself, and that trend continued into the late 1970s. Since then, birth rates appear to have risen somewhat. As those born during the baby boom pass through their most fertile period, there will be an increase in the absolute number of children.

The average age at marriage is rising, and the number of people who do not marry is also rising. The number of women remaining childless appears to be on the rise. So is the age of the mother at first birth. These developments suggest that larger numbers of women will have a continuous job experience at the start of their careers.

White American women born in the first half of the nineteenth century and who became mothers averaged more than five children. A third had seven or more children, and families with twelve children were not uncommon. White women born in the first fifteen years of the twentieth century averaged 2.9 children per mother. White wives in their twenties in the 1980s say they expect to have an average

* Much of the increase in birth rates during the baby boom proved to be bunching of births rather than an increase in the number of babies born per woman.

of 2.1 children, and only 30 percent expect to have more than two children.[1]

Black women have historically had higher birth rates than white women, despite their higher rate of labor force participation. They participated in the baby boom, and like white women have had generally declining rates before and since. In 1983, black birth rates exceeded white rates by almost 50 percent.[2]

In the developed countries, the proportion of the population making its living in agriculture, where birth rates are high, has fallen steadily and dramatically.[3] In 1870, a total of 53.2 percent of American workers were on the farm, while only 3.5 percent were there in 1984. In the United States in 1910, rural birth rates were two thirds higher than urban birth rates and even in 1950 were 40 percent higher.

WHY BIRTH RATES HAVE FALLEN

One reason for the long-term fall in the birth rate is that having children has been getting progressively less economically rewarding. A second reason is the increasing cost of a child, both in terms of outlay required and wages and opportunities forgone, usually by the mother. A third is the improved means of preventing births.

At a time when most families were on the farm or had a small business based on a craft and centered in the home, the mother could work productively in the family enterprise while caring for the younger children. The older children provided cheap and reliable labor for the enterprise. The economic benefits the family derived from the children might surpass the costs of raising them. At the very least, there would be economic benefits to offset some of those costs.

A farm or a small enterprise represents a set of valuable assets that ordinarily would be passed on to the children. The existence of these assets gave the parents considerable power over the children, who had an incentive to stay close to and remain on good terms with the parents. The children were expected to run the enterprise in the parents' old age, and to help to support them out of the proceeds.

Now family farms and small family crafts enterprises are far fewer. Since the industrial revolution, people have increasingly made their living by working for large-scale enterprises they do not own. To a man with a job in such an enterprise, the purely economic benefits of a child appear to be nil. With greater numbers of young people going to college, and needing support into their twenties, the costs of bringing up a child have on average grown considerably. Government pension systems have reduced the dependence of old people on their children's support.

Under modern conditions, the family has little economic leverage it can bring to bear to influence their children's behavior. There will be little or no inheritance in most cases; whatever the family can give is presented to the children in the form of a college education. Moreover, the children have opportunities to go off and get jobs on their own. They feel no obligation to live with or close to the parents, much less to contribute out of their wages to their parents' income.

Nancy Folbre, one of the economic historians who has elaborated this argument, suggests that in the past the fathers reaped considerable benefits from children. Now, with changed economic conditions, fathers have lost their enthusiasm for large numbers of children and are cooperating with their wives in fertility control. Since all of the burden of bringing the children into the world and almost all of the work of bringing them up has been borne by the mother, mothers have been glad to fall in with this sentiment.[4]

WOMEN'S ABILITY TO CONTROL PREGNANCIES AND BIRTHS

Birth rates have been lowered by improvements in the means of contraception and the increase in their availability. Demographers believe that 40 percent of the women born in the 1840s, 60 percent of those born in the 1870s, and 70 percent of those born in the 1910s practiced some method of birth control.[5] By the 1930s use of contraceptive devices were almost universal among white urban Protestants and Jews.[6]

Catholics were slower to adopt the use of artificial birth control but now do so with the same frequency as other groups despite the continued doctrinal opposition of their church to the practice.

Prior to the 1960s, birth-control methods of relatively low reliability, such as coitus interruptus and douches, were commonly used. To get an abortion, a women had to go outside the law to find a back-alley "butcher." Abortionists were unskillful, dirty, and rushed. Their services, though expensive, were both painful and dangerous; deaths were not uncommon.

A vigorous campaign in the 1920s led by Margaret Sanger[7] popularized mechanical contraceptive devices. A contraceptive pill of high reliability was licensed for sale in 1960, and oral contraceptives have since been adopted by a considerable proportion of women. Sterilization also has increased. By 1982, the man or the woman had been sterilized in 41 percent of couples desiring to prevent births. About 38 percent of the sterilizations had been undergone by husbands.[8]

Margaret Sanger's campaign for contraception had been carried on in the face of laws in most localities forbidding and punishing the sale of contraceptive devices. It was against the law to send contraceptive devices or information concerning them through the U.S. mails. The principal political force behind such laws were religious groups, most notably the Roman Catholic church. Physicians were not active on behalf of freedom to use contraception, and the medical profession had promoted state laws against abortion in the nineteenth century. Prior to the 1960s, many doctors and clinics had a policy of refusing to fit a woman with a diaphragm, then the most reliable contraceptive device, unless she had already had a baby.

Laws restricting the use by married couples of contraceptive devices were declared unconstitutional by the U.S. Supreme Court in 1965; the principle was extended to unmarried people in 1972.[9] Laws limiting in any way women's ability to have an abortion in the first three months of pregnancy were ruled an unconstitutional invasion of privacy by the Court in 1973. Since then, legal abortions have grown to be an important form of fertility control. In 1982 there were 1.6 million abortions in the United States, 426 for every 1,000 live births. Although a majority appears to favor a woman's freedom to choose an abortion, vocal and politically potent opposition to that freedom continues, again led by religious groups.[10]

Mechanical contraceptive methods, some of them crude, progressively reduced the average number of children born per woman over the whole population. But through the 1960s, the prospect of an unwanted pregnancy still was a large and daunting possibility for any woman. Couples could not plan the timing and number of their children with a high degree of confidence, so plans did not count for much. With highly effective contraception, backed up by safe and legal abortion, it has now become possible for a woman to make and carry out firm plans for her life in a way that was never possible before. Now that effective planning of fertility can be counted on, education and career planning can proceed with more confidence. More women are looking ahead, and in doing so, they are planning for fewer children than might have been born without plans. Thus effective contraception, and the freedom to have an abortion in case of contraceptive failure, have lowered the number of desired births and the number of undesired births.

Despite the ample means now available to prevent them, there are still unwanted births. In response to a 1982 survey, mothers characterized 10.5 percent of the 70.2 million children they had given birth to as "unwanted at conception." Another 29.0 percent of the children were characterized as "mistimed."[11] Contraceptive failures are more common among the less educated. Among teenagers, failure to use contraception at all is common. Girls are still imbued with the idea that they are debased by having sex, so they have to pretend to be swept away by passion, a state hardly compatible with contraceptive forethought.[12] Obviously, there remains considerable room for a further reduction in birth rates.

A number of economists speculated that decisions about having children might be thought of in the same way as decisions about buying consumer durables.[13] They reasoned that additional income for the family might mean the inclusion in the expanded budget not only of an additional television set or a second car but also of an additional baby or two. This treatment of the fertility decision, much criticized by most demographers, led to the prediction that as average family income rose, the number of children desired would increase. The difference between children and other consumer durables proved the undoing of this prediction. Children, far more than durables, commit an adult's time for years to come. Children cannot be scrapped or sold.

Those who predicted rising birth rates largely ignored the increased value of the mother's time; the higher divorce rates; and the increasing power of women, on whom the major burden of child-rearing falls, to control their fertility.

EFFECT OF LOWER BIRTH RATES ON LABOR FORCE PARTICIPATION

In Moslem countries, the frank purpose of the seclusion of women in the home is to isolate them from men who are not their husbands. In the West, the rationale given for the wife's seclusion from economic activities outside the home has been her care of the couple's children. Thus fewer children has brought a relaxation of that seclusion.

One hundred years ago, a woman might expect a large number of children and foresee that much of the rest of her life would be spent caring for them. Seeing seven children into adulthood might take thirty years or longer. A fall in the number of children per mother has reduced the number of years of child care and increased the number of years in which the mother has an "empty nest."

Women's life expectancy has increased, thanks in part to reductions in the number of pregnancies and to reduction in the likelihood that a pregnancy will result in death. This also has served to increase the years of life mothers spend without children in their homes.

Even among women who are housewives, those who have decided to have one or two children have different expectations and attitudes than those who are willing to have more. A mother at home with one or two young children, who has no intention of having any more, can at least contemplate the possibility of taking a job in six years or less. She is unlikely to view child care as a lifetime vocation.

By contrast, a mother with many children and who anticipates the possibility of more can see motherhood as an all-absorbing occupation into an indefinite future. She knows that a considerable proportion of the time at least one of her children will have some illness or other and will require continual attention. The larger the number of children,

TABLE 3-1
Labor Force Participation of Married People by Number of Children, March 1984

		Number of Couples* (thousands)				
		Children Under 18				
	All Married Couples	0	1	2	3	4+
In Labor force:						
Husband only	14,076	5,988	2,682	3,225	1,463	717
Both spouses	26,128	11,184	6,334	5,892	2,031	688
Wife only	1,943	1,462	199	178	75	28
Total	42,147	18,634	9,215	9,295	3,569	1,433
		Proportion of Couples				
		Children Under 18				
	All Married Couples	0	1	2	3	4+
In Labor force:						
Husband only	.33	.32	.29	.35	.41	.50
Both spouses	.62	.60	.69	.63	.57	.48
Wife only	.05	.08	.02	.02	.02	.02
Total	1.00	1.00	1.00	1.00	1.00	1.00

* Includes only families with two spouses present in which at least one spouse is in the labor force. "Husband only" signifies husband alone was in the labor force, or husband plus other family members other than the wife. A small proportion of families in which the husband is a nonearner but two or more of the family members (possibly including the wife) are in the labor force were also excluded on grounds of ambiguity. Most such families have no children.
SOURCE: U.S. Bureau of Labor Statistics, "Number of Working Mothers Now at Record Levels," USDL 84-321 (July 26, 1984).

the higher the likelihood of having one with a severe physical or mental problem, requiring a full-time caretaker indefinitely. The more children a mother has, the larger would be the child-care costs and the smaller would be the net financial benefit from her paycheck were she to take a job.

The data show that the fewer young children a mother has the more likely is she to participate in paid work (see table 3-1). However, participation remains substantial regardless of the number of children. Among married couples, 69 percent with one child under eighteen have both spouses participating. The drop in wives' participation for couples with three children is surprisingly modest—only 12 percentage points. Almost half of the couples with four or more children have both spouses holding jobs.

TABLE 3–2
Bachelor's Degrees Awarded by Sex,
1870–1982

	Degrees (thousands)		Women's Degrees as a
	Men	Women	Percent of Men's
1870	8	1	13
1880	10	3	30
1890	13	3	23
1900	22	5	23
1910	29	8	28
1920	32	17	53
1930	—	—	—
1940	—	—	—
1950	330	104	32
1960	256	139	55
1970	487	346	71
1980	526	473	90
1982	526	499	95

SOURCES: *Historical Statistics of the United States, 1960* (Washington, D.C.: U.S. Government Printing Office, 1960), pp. 211–
12; *Statistical Abstract of the United States, 1985* (Washington, D.C.:
U.S. Government Printing Office, 1984), p. 157.

Fewer children have meant that more mothers are in paid jobs,
but the effect has been relatively small.[14] The reduction in the number
of children per family cannot account for the entire increase in women's
employment in recent years, or even much of it.

THE EFFECT OF EDUCATION

Women have always graduated from high school in greater numbers
than men. However, until recently, far more men than women went
on to higher education. In 1870 women received only eighteen degrees
for every hundred that men received, but by 1982 women got almost
ninety-five for every hundred received by men (see table 3–2). Currently the number of women and men among college undergraduates

TABLE 3–3
Degrees Conferred on Women
in Selected Professions, 1960 and 1982

	1960	1982
Medicine (M.D.)		
Degrees to Women	387	3,947
Percent of total	5.5	25.0
Dentistry (D.D.S. or D.M.D.)		
Degrees to Women	26	815
Percent of total	0.8	15.4
Law (LL.B. or J.D.)		
Degrees to Women	230	12,026
Percent of total	2.5	33.4
Engineering		
Degrees to Women	171	10,874
Percent of total	0.4	10.8

SOURCE: *Statistical Abstract of the United States, 1985* (Washington, D.C.: U.S. Government Printing Office, 1984), p. 159.

is about equal, but women have yet to attain numerical equality in postgraduate education.

The number of women earning college degrees took a quantum leap after World War II. Men made an even bigger advance at that time, as a result of government programs subsidizing the education of veterans of the armed services. However, women have been making progress relative to men in the past three decades at a rapid rate.

The extent of the recent increase in professional degrees awarded to women is particularly striking (see table 3–3). The increase testifies to a greater interest on the part of women in practicing these professions, a greater willingness of their parents to support them through expensive years of study, and a decrease in sex discrimination in admissions by professional schools.

Going to college improves the jobs a woman can get: women college graduates working full time year round have earnings 40 percent higher than women who have only a high-school diploma. Not only does a college graduate command higher pay, her job is more likely to have higher status and more interesting work. A college-educated woman who stays home has to give up more in terms of pay, prestige, and engrossing activities. As economists put it, her opportunity cost is higher. This is the reason that women who are college graduates are currently 24 percent more likely to be in the labor force than are those who are only high-school graduates.

In addition to its direct effect in motivating employment, education influences women's employment through its effect on childbearing. Women with more education use contraceptives more and suffer less from contraceptive failure. They desire fewer children and bear fewer children.[15]

While it is clear that more education motivates employment, it is certainly reasonable to suppose that there is some influence in the other direction. The increasing awareness that their daughters will hold a job for a considerable part of their adult lives encourages parents to contribute to daughters' college expenses, where previously many were willing to contribute only to sons'. Increasing affluence resulting from the long-term rise in wage rates also has encouraged this tendency. Finally, increasing attendance of daughters at college has affected the labor-force participation of mothers. More mothers are taking jobs to pay for offsprings' college expenses than would be the case if a smaller proportion of daughters attended college.

THE DEMISE OF MARRIAGE FOR LIFE

The traditional view of marriage in this country and Western Europe has been that the bride would acquire a permanent source of financial support for herself and any children she might have. This view was enshrined in the husband's legal duty to be the family's sole provider of financial support, a legal theory that lives on in somewhat attenuated form. Except under unusual circumstances, it was contemplated that a marriage would be terminated only by the death of one of the spouses.

Women were encouraged by their parents to search for spouses who would be "good earners." Having found and captured the affections of a man willing to marry her, a woman was taught by the prevailing culture that any effort to sell her own labor in a hostile marketplace would be unnecessary and undesirable. A wife was not, of

FIGURE 3–2
Divorce Rates, 1860–1982

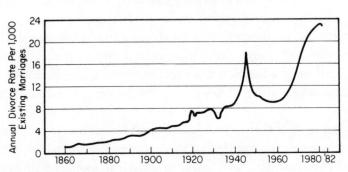

NOTE: Divorces per year per 1,000 existing marriages.
SOURCE: Adapted from Arland Thornton and Deborah Freedman, "The Changing American Family," *Population Bulletin,* vol. 38, no. 4 (October 1983):7.

course, infallibly secure. She might be impoverished by her husband's failure as worker or businessman or farmer. He might sink into alcoholism, go to prison, or die an early death, leaving her with no source of income. But in that case, her parents, her numerous brothers and sisters, or perhaps her children, might come to the rescue.

The one calamity from which she was supposed to be safe was her husband's desire to terminate the marriage, provided she remained faithful to her marriage vows. In reality, we may speculate that even if divorce was unlikely, desertion was an ever-present threat. The huge size of the country and the existence of the frontier allowed men to escape and make a new start somewhere else, possibly with a new wife. Many husbands tired of the brand of domesticity provided by their wives probably escaped in that way.

It is difficult to estimate the incidence of marital breakup due to desertion in the nineteenth century, but formal divorce was uncommon. Divorce rates were, however, on the rise in the latter part of the nineteenth century, and the twentieth century saw continued growth (see figure 3–2). There was one divorce a year per thousand married couples in 1860, and nine a year per thousand married couples a century later. After 1960 a rapid spurt took place, during which divorce rates more than doubled. It is currently estimated that one in two marriages will end in divorce.[16]*

---

* The divorce rate was 22.6 divorces per year per 1,000 married women in 1981. This means that, on average, the likelihood of divorce for any couple in a year was .0226. This modest-seeming per-year probability looks intuitively inconsistent with the statement that 50 percent of

Separations by mutual agreement or by desertion remain common. However, separations more frequently end in formal divorce than was the case in prior years. Marital instability from causes other than death is at an all-time high. However, the fall in the death rate has lowered the proportion of marriages in a given year that end due to a spouse's death.

Women's labor force participation is affected by divorce in a number of ways. First, the divorced wife seldom receives substantial alimony or child-support payments from her former husband (see chapters 9 and 10). If she has children, she has the option of living in poverty on the welfare rolls. Most divorced women choose instead to work at a paying job. Divorced women have relatively high labor force participation; about 80 percent of divorced women with custody of children are in the job market. While remarriage is frequent, unremarried divorcées are a sizable group, currently constituting about 10 percent of all ever-married women.

Young girls see quite plainly that they cannot depend on their own marriages to last for their whole lives. Some see their own mothers thrust out into the cold, and all of them see it happen to the mothers of classmates. They understand that the economic security of a housewife is precarious. As time passes, it is likely that a smaller and smaller proportion of young girls will plan to spend long years in that precarious status.

In matters of divorce and jobs for women, we can again see that causation runs in both directions. Conflicts about the sharing of housework in two-earner couples may make separation and divorce more likely. Women with independent access to money income are more likely to want to end a distasteful marriage. Husbands of women with earnings undoubtedly find it easier on their consciences to terminate their marriages than do husbands of housewives.

While women's earnings motivate or permit some divorces, they probably improve the quality of life in the marriages that persist. Aside from the simple fact that dual-earner couples have more money than

---

marriages end in divorce. To show crudely that the two numbers are not inconsistent, we can calculate the probability that an event with a likelihood of .0226 in each trial will not occur even once in 30 independent trials:

$$(1 - .0226)^{30} = .50$$

they would otherwise have, the husband is relieved from the strain of being the sole provider. His periods of unemployment or illness are less stressful. Moreover, the spouses may interact more as equals, which may make life pleasanter.

A SHORTAGE OF HUSBANDS?

The proportion of the adult female population not currently married has grown, from 29.5 percent in 1965 to 38.6 percent in 1983.[17] About half of this rise comes from an increase in the proportion of women who have never married. The other half results from a rise in the proportion of divorcées who have not remarried. These figures suggest a lesser availability of men for marriage, a greater desire and ability on the part of women to remain husbandless, or a combination of the two. Some observers have suggested that a husband shortage has been an important factor in women's move toward financial independence.

Barbara Ehrenreich contends that much of the change in sex roles and much of the change in thinking about sex roles derives from an increasing desire by men to be free from the financial burden of supporting a wife and children.[18] Men, she says, have been more and more avoiding permanent commitment to one woman. Some have shunned the "ball and chain" of marriage and family altogether. Other men have practiced "serial polygamy" through multiple marriages and divorces. Either way, women have been left without the promise of reliable support.

Ehrenreich makes no mention of the possibility that some of the reduced interest in marriage may come from women, who need it less now. Nor does she venture an explanation of the waning of men's willingness to serve as the reliable lifelong support of one woman. But she says that the lesser availability of male financial support has left women with no alternative but to be prepared to fend for themselves. The result, she says, is increased interest in jobs on the part of women and the rise of the ideology of feminism.

Marcia Guttentag and Paul F. Secord[19] also stress the reduced availability of support from a husband and consider it the leading cause of women's increasing independence. They cite a progressive reduction in the ratio of men to women, which fell from 1.05 early in this century to 0.92 in 1970 because of lower death rates for women, wars that take male lives, and a cessation of male-intensive immigration. The scarcity of men means that some women will have to remain unmarried. Guttentag and Secord cite evidence going back through medieval and ancient times that societies with an excess of women have tended to allow women relatively more independence.

Current attitudes inhibit men from marrying women who are better educated or more successful than themselves and inhibit women from marrying men who are less educated or successful than they are. Women have gained on men in education and in career success, so marriage partners for better educated, more successful women are relatively scarcer.

The tradition that men marry women younger than themselves creates husband shortages for older women. When population increases rapidly, the tradition creates a shortage of husbands for young women as well. Twenty years after the baby boom started, and for years thereafter, the number of women of age twenty was larger than the number of men who were twenty-two because of the rapid rise in births. Thus the women of the baby boom generation will spend longer periods of their lives without husbands than would be the case had they been born in times of more moderate population growth.

The sexual revolution—a reduction in the taboo on sex for women outside of marriage—has made the cohabitation of unmarried couples more common. The tax laws also encourage cohabitation rather than marriage (see chapter 9). In August 1984 there were two million of such households, accounting for just 4 percent of all couples in the United States.[20] Their numbers appear to be growing rapidly. In this less formal alternative to marriage, the female partner is not as likely to consider financial dependence on the man to be a long-term possibility and is more likely to hold on to a job and perhaps a career. In any case, the existence of such relationships reduces the numbers of people available for marriage, in which dependence of the woman on the man still is common.

The hypothesis of spouse unavailability, as expounded by Guttentag and Secord and by Ehrenreich, is not incompatible with the hypothesis that improved economic incentives have brought many additional women onto the job market. The two causes may operate at the same time. It is certainly likely that some part of the increased interest of women in taking jobs is due to their lessened dependence on marriage as a source of financial support. However, the husband shortage cannot possibly account for all of women's increased labor force participation. Much of the increased employment of women in recent years is due to the entry of married mothers of young children. This is the part of the population least likely to be worried about and least immediately affected by a shortage of husbands.

CHANGING NORMS OF BEHAVIOR

Thus far we have largely ignored the fact that people do not make decisions as to work and lifestyle without regard to what others are doing. Economic textbooks tend to portray the individual as considering the pros and cons of various courses of conduct in isolation from other individuals. But this ignores humans' follow-the-herd tendencies. There is more to people's decision-making than comparing the material advantages of available alternatives. Women (and their husbands and children) are highly attentive to what their friends and neighbors are choosing to do. All of us feel powerful pressures to conform our conduct to what is perceived to be the norm.

At the early stages of the move of women into paid work, the norm was clearly the stay-at-home housewife doing her womanly duty by her husband and her children. The happy feeling of approval that comes to those who conform to majority practice was among the benefits of continuing as a housewife. The disapproval visited on the nonconformists reduced the attraction of taking a job. The purely economic incentives were such that an increasing number of women did enter the labor force despite the penalties of unconventionality. Nevertheless, those penalties must surely have slowed down the flow of wives into jobs.

Since the 50 percent mark in women's labor force participation was approached and passed in the 1970s, the shoe has been shifting to the other foot, so to speak. It has begun to be the full-time housewife who is now seen as failing to conform and who has been subjected to the pain of nonconformity. Housewives are starting to be thought of as lazy, as timid, as unenterprising. While in the past, desire for conformity slowed down the movement of women into paid work, we can expect that in the future the desire for conformity to the new norm of the working wife will speed it up.

People want to conform in terms of their work behavior; they also want to "keep up with the Joneses" in patterns of expenditure. As more and more married couples have put two earners into the labor force, the standard of living of a two-earner couple has become increasingly the norm. In 1986, a married couple with both spouses employed had on average 56 percent higher total earnings than a couple in which only the husband had a job.

The "Joneses" most of us want to keep up with are not the very rich people we read about in *People* magazine or the style section of the newspaper. We want to keep up with our peer group: our friends, the people we went to school with, our coworkers on the job who are roughly at our level, the parents of our children's friends. Most American families are now members of a peer group in which more than half of the couples have two paychecks to spend. These couples have used the wife's salary to set a new standard for emulation.

As the two-earner "Joneses" with whom one wants to keep up are growing more numerous in each peer group, the onus of failing to keep up is growing correspondingly greater. The remaining one-earner families find themselves still farther down in the pecking order of their peer group with each succeeding year. This should have the effect of further speeding the demise of the full-time housewife, especially among younger couples.

Some sociologists have suggested that the competition of American families for social status through conspicuous consumption has all along played a crucial part in the rise of women's labor force participation.[21] They argue that as more men work for large corporations with complex structures, the prestige to be assigned to men's job titles has grown more difficult for outsiders to gauge. Thus the assignment of status to a family on the basis of the husband's job title has become less certain, and to relieve the uncertainty, new markers of status were developed. The purchase and display of expensive goods became a substitute method of displaying status, and wives were enlisted in the battle for status through expenditure.

While this theory seems to be in line with much that we are currently observing, it is less convincing as an explanation of a process that has been going on since the nineteenth century. To Thorstein Veblen, the originator of the idea of "conspicuous consumption," the centerpiece of a man's display was his economically useless wife. A man tended to lose status if his wife took a job. The farther back in time we look, the more peculiar her job would have seemed and the more status he would have lost. Until recently, the loss of the man's status as sole breadwinner—as a man whose wife "doesn't have to work"—would have been a severe one. This was widely seen as a problem for the wife who wanted to take a job, and some of those who stayed home said it was because "he wouldn't let me."

In short, striving for relative status may be an increasingly important cause of women's increasing appearance in the job market. But this probably is a recent development, as only recently has wives' work outside the home ceased to cause a loss of status.

THE REVIVAL OF FEMINIST IDEOLOGY

The idea that women should function in the economy and in the community as the equivalents and equals of men goes back at least to Plato's *Republic*. At the start of the fifteenth century, Christine de Pisan, who made a living as a professional writer, argued in her book *Livre de la Cité des Dames* that women's position was unjust. In 1792, Mary Wollstonecraft's *Vindication of the Rights of Women* expressed ideas of equality of the two sexes essentially identical to the ideas of today. In mid-nineteenth-century America, anti-slavery agitation energized a considerable group of able and eloquent women—the Grimké sisters, Susan B. Anthony, and Elizabeth Cady Stanton—who went on to spend the rest of their lives campaigning for women's rights. In England, the philosopher and economist John Stuart Mill was considerably influenced by the feminist ideas of his friend and later wife, Harriet Taylor. His 1869 treatise *On the Subjection of Women* spread those ideas in a wide circle. The economist and poet Charlotte Perkins Gilman published *Women and Economics* in 1899. Toward the end of the nineteenth century, both in England and the United States, the attention of advocates of feminism was concentrated on gaining women the right to vote, finally achieved in 1920 in the United States, and in 1928 in Great Britain.

After women gained suffrage, the movement for women's equality seemed to languish for a time. The "flappers" of the 1920s wore shorter skirts, and they moved about, drank, and danced with greater freedom than their mothers had done. However, the persona the "flappers" presented to the public was that of lighthearted and somewhat empty-headed seekers of pleasure rather than that of women who might want to or be able to compete with men in the world of business and public affairs. During this period and into the 1930s, 1940s, and 1950s, it was not unusual to hear women deride the suffragist leaders who had led the fight for the vote as overly harsh and strident. Perhaps, it was said, that kind of "masculine" woman was needed then, but the need for her had passed, and what was needed and wanted now was a more "feminine" type of woman.

Two books signaled and led the reawakening of feminist sentiment. In 1949, just as the baby-boom period was starting, Simone de Beauvoir published in France *The Second Sex,* which reached the United States in a translation in 1953.[22] The book enumerates for the reader the customs, assumptions, educational practices, laws, literature, modes of speech, and jokes that show to the young girl and the mature woman that she is an inferior and limited being and that convince her to occupy the place in the economy and society marked out for her.

A decade after *The Second Sex* appeared in English, Betty Friedan published *The Feminine Mystique.*[23] That book was an attack on the "working conditions" of the housewife occupation—the boring and mindless nature of many of the duties and the powerlessness and isolation it entailed. It also was an attack on the castelike assignment of all married women to that occupation without regard to their individual talents. Hypocritical exaltation of the housewife occupation, much of it by men who never would consider occupying such a limiting niche, had been going on since the "cult of domesticity" for women had taken hold in the nineteenth century. So lengthy and unchallenged had been the public praise for housewifery as a highly desirable— indeed, the only desirable—career for women, that Friedan's brilliantly articulate attack came as a surprise. Its freshness and directness made it immensely popular.

The 1960s saw the founding of a number of organizations to promote the advancement of women in economic and political roles and to preserve women's right to regulate their own fertility.* These organizations have worked through the information media and the election process with varying effectiveness. The Equal Rights Amendment to the U.S. Constitution passed the Congress in 1972. It fell short of ratification in state legislatures despite public-opinion polls showing support of a majority of both men and women.

Since the 1970s, especially at universities, research and writing by people committed to greater equality between the sexes has flourished. Feminist historians have challenged modes of writing history that make women invisible. Feminist sociologists have investigated societal differentiation between men and women as a form of oppression rather than as a benign adaptation to reproductive necessities. Feminist demographers have looked at how the burden on women of raising children affects birth rates. Feminist psychologists have begun a campaign to dislodge Freudian phallocentrism and to direct women patients away from therapists who advise them to adapt themselves to a male-dominated society. Feminists in education and counseling have begun to devise methods to reduce the conditioning for inferiority that girls receive in schools.

THE WEB OF CAUSES FOR WOMEN'S EMERGENCE

How can we rate the importance of the factors encouraging women's liberation from compulsory and exclusive domesticity? The "social" factors—fewer births per women, less stable marriages, better education for women, the rise of an ideology of equality—must have been important. They have supported and furthered that liberation and indeed have been indispensable to it. However, the most important source of

---

* The National Organization for Women, The Women's Equity Action League, the National Women's Political Caucus, The National Abortion Rights Action League.

that liberation is elsewhere—in advancing technology, which has been the source of the long, upward trend in the real reward the economy pays for human beings' time.

Technological change has done more, of course, than raise wage rates. It has reduced the strain of housekeeping. Technological change also created new consumer goods that families have coveted, encouraging a willingness to trade women's time for access to them. The changes in occupational structure of industry, which have been cited by many authors as influencing women's movement to jobs, are themselves results of technological change. The almost continual flow of new products and new methods of production accustom us to change of all kinds, including change in social habits and patterns.

Most of the "social" factors, with the possible and partial exception of the fall in birth rates, can be accounted for as responses to the changing economic environment. By contrast, the dynamic of continually evolving technology is independent of these "social" factors. Its origin is deep in the structure of advanced economies—in the rewards that are given for innovation and capital accumulation.* The one social factor that may have arisen independent of economic trends—the fall in the birth rate—has been powerfully affected by the changing technology of contraception.

The rise in the real wage has faltered since the 1970s. By the 1970s, however, the trends in the social forces favoring women's independence—in education, ideology, and in consumption norms—had gathered momentum. Whatever their origin in economic forces, these social trends now have a life of their own.

The view that technology and economic factors have been the key elements in women's emergence into the money economy is not as congenial to our egos as the view that attributes change to the spread of liberating ideas. But the importance of economic factors in women's escape from obligatory domesticity does not mean that consciousness-raising is of no use or that policy is irrelevant. There is a great deal of work we can usefully do to make the social and economic structure of our society more fit for human habitation. In succeeding chapters we shall explore some of the possibilities for work of that sort.

---

* This view has a great deal in common with the Marxist "materialist" theory of history, which in broad outline teaches that technology dictates economic structure, which then dictates everything else. Needless to say, adopting such a view of the process of women's emergence does not commit us to prefer socialism to capitalism.

CHAPTER 4

"Women's Place" in
the Labor Market

WHEN IRENE LoRe applied to Chase Manhattan Bank for a job as an executive trainee and didn't get an answer promptly, she assumed her application had been lost. She sent in a second one, and eventually two answers came from the bank. One, addressed to "Mr. LoRe," asked the applicant to come in for an interview. The other, addressed to "Ms. LoRe," advised her that there were no job openings.*

The American labor market must be described as generally hospitable to women—after all, it has absorbed millions of female entrants at rising real wages. But employers' hospitality has been extended most readily to women who have been willing to settle down to work in a "woman's job." Employers have offered women an abundance of jobs, but at a wage far lower than that paid in jobs open to men of comparable

* Irene LoRe was one of a group of women who filed suit against Chase Manhattan Bank in 1976 charging a wide-ranging policy of discrimination aimed at preventing women from achieving managerial, professional, or official positions. The suit was settled, with the bank paying $1.8 million as part of the settlement. As is usual in such settlements, the bank did not admit that it had discriminated. For description of the charges see *LoRe* v. *Chase Manhattan Corp.*, 15 FEP Cases 724 (1977).

education and experience. Women have had promotion opportunities far inferior to those of men, and jobs in many occupations have been closed to them.

To women like Irene LoRe, unwilling to settle for a place in the female job ghetto and looking for the pay, duties, on-the-job-training, and promotion possibilities routinely offered to men, the labor market has been a great deal less hospitable. Many employers have routinely excluded women from jobs in all occupations except the relatively few commonly accepted as appropriate to women. It has not been uncommon for male coworkers or managers to harass the woman who succeeds in being taken on in a "man's job." Thanks to governmental action and to changes in attitudes, there has been some progress against sex discrimination, but outright exclusion and harassment still occur.

The advantage in pay that men have over women in the American labor market is really remarkably large. Women's annual pay in full-time work averaged 68 percent of men's in 1985.[1] Another fact vividly conveys the extent of men's advantage: A woman with a college degree who works full time takes home little more pay on average than a man with comparable years of experience who failed to graduate from high school. The most important reason that women have such poor position in the labor market is that they are not allowed to compete on a fair basis and that employers regularly and habitually act to disadvantage women. Despite a great deal of evidence showing discrimination, not everyone concedes that this is true, however.

A long line of economists over the years have devoted themselves to arguing that women's grossly inferior position in the workplace has very little to do with unfairness or with the sexist prejudices of employers. Nothing bad or unjust is going on, they say; people get their jobs through a process that is with rare exceptions fair and competitive. Women and men are judged as individuals and treated according to their merits. But, say these economists, the vast majority of women don't want to or can't compete effectively for the better jobs and find it in their best interests to stick to the female-type jobs. The woman who could do well in a male-type job and wants one, but who has been excluded, is a very rare bird, these economists are saying. The current situation is in everybody's best interests and does not need reform.

Those who claim that there is no problem of unfairness toward women say that the pay in most jobs, including the predominantly female occupations, is set by supply and demand in a competitive, fair, and free market process. Those who argue in this line say that women choose poorly rewarded jobs because they are consonant with "their" family responsibilities. They say that even if women wanted other jobs, employers would be right to exclude them. Women allegedly engage in behavior that employers allegedly cannot tolerate in anyone considered for promotion to a higher-status, better-paid job. They avoid expensive training; interrupt their careers for childbearing and child-raising; and are unwilling to travel extensively, to take transfers from one city to another, or to work overtime.

According to this line of argument, women's access to good jobs and high pay has been closed off by their own unwillingness or inability to go through what men do to get ahead, rather than by discriminating employers or harassing coworkers. Women are also accused of low native ability for certain kinds of work. All in all, say the adherents of this school of thought, the overwhelming majority of women lack competence and commitment, and that is why they do poorly.[2]

It is possible, as some economists do, to spin simplified theories about a world in which sex (and race) discrimination could have no part whatever, and on that basis to proclaim that discrimination in actuality is nil. But no one with any experience and sense could have much doubt that some employers have excluded and do exclude women from some jobs. Millions of women have experienced at first hand the putdowns, the lack of respect, the sexual harassment, the refusal to take any woman's abilities seriously that are the hallmark of a discriminatory situation. Large numbers of men have committed these acts, and many other men have witnessed them. Thousands of pages of court transcripts attest to them, containing testimony like that given by a group of male employees of Pizza Hut, who said in court that their general manager had complained that it was regrettable that a certain store manager was doing such a good job. She was a woman, he said, and a woman should not be making as much money as she was.[3]

The casebooks are full of sworn testimony of rankly unfair behavior toward women workers. In many establishments, a woman has only had to ask for a promotion or a raise for harassing behavior to begin, leading to her quitting or being fired. The strict segregation of function by sex seen in many workplaces, with no woman with any vestige of authority, suggests not that "*Most* women don't want those jobs" but rather that "*No* woman, whatever her desires, is allowed anywhere near them."

Without doubt some women do plan their working lives to have time to perform the domestic chores loaded onto their shoulders, from which men have kept themselves largely free. Some women do restrict the kind of jobs they look for, and some take part-time jobs to ease their load. Nor could anyone be unaware that young girls feel social pressure to follow certain lines of training and work and to shun others.

But in fixing the causes of women's low place in the labor market we do not have to choose either discrimination or women's accommodation to the largely unshared burden of housework and child care. We do not have to choose one explanation and label the other's influence as absent or trivial. Accommodation and discrimination both go on and are mutually reinforcing. Beliefs concerning women's primary devotion to domesticity may motivate some employers to discriminate against women. Discrimination discourages some women from giving a higher priority to possible careers and turns some of them away from the serious pursuit of career success. It rationalizes a husband's assumption that priority must be given to his career. His larger paycheck gives him the power to resist suggestions that they share more evenly the burden of housework and child care.

The real question is not whether discrimination is entirely absent but whether discrimination is an important factor in the sharp differences in status and pay between the sexes. If discrimination against women is only spotty, and the differences in pay and position largely attributable to women's free and informed choices, then we might be better off without governmental pressure on employers to change their personnel practices. However, the best evidence we have strongly suggests that discrimination, although diminishing, still is an important force in the labor market and still causes substantial injustice and serious deprivation. This being the case, programs designed to further reduce discrimination deserve the serious attention we give them in subsequent chapters.

In this chapter, we shall first of all describe the situation of women in the labor market and compare their jobs and wages with those of men. Then we shall look closely at the ideas of those who believe that

these differences between the sexes in pay and position result almost
entirely from the desires and interests of women themselves and so are
benign and require no remedy. Next, we present a statistical analysis
that suggests that such views are are not supported by the evidence. In
the subsequent two chapters we shall describe the reasons for discrimination against women, the forms that discrimination takes, and its
consequences.

WOMEN'S JOBS, WOMEN'S PAY

Women's organizations have succeeded in publicizing the gross dis-
crepancy between the pay of men and women. When people express
a sense of grievance about women's position in the world of work, it
usually attaches to the pay gap. Less is said about the fact that men and
women hold different kinds of jobs.

One can see from everyday experience that some occupations have
virtually no women and that a high proportion of women work in
predominantly female occupations. Jobs that carry authority and prestige tend to be occupied by men. The skilled blue-collar jobs are also
mostly male. Sex-based differences in job assignments are obvious even
to young children. They very quickly grab hold of the idea that it is
natural, right, and inevitable that there are men's jobs and women's
jobs. Children come to believe that holding a sex-appropriate job is an
important way in which a man demonstrates manhood or a woman
shows femininity. Many adults apparently maintain the beliefs about
occupational roles they formed in childhood. Little popular sense of
grievance or injustice appears to attach to the segregation of occupations
by sex, and the women's movement has not really been successful in
generating much.

People do understand that there is a connection between occupational segregation and women's low wages. "Women have jobs that
are low-paying" is a common explanation of the pay gap. That simple
way of putting it manages delicately to avoid any reference to unfairness. It suggests that the wage each job pays has somehow or other

TABLE 4–1

Annual Earnings of Men and Women by Educational Level, 1984

Educational Level	Annual Earnings		Women's Earnings as a Percent of Men's
	Men	Women	
Elementary school			
Under 8 yrs.	$15,272	$ 9,798	64
8 yrs.	17,392	10,976	63
High school			
1–3 yrs.	18,575	11,808	64
4 yrs.	22,312	14,076	63
College			
1–3 yrs.	24,737	16,241	66
4 yrs.	33,086	19,885	60
5 yrs. or more	39,829	25,370	64
Average	$25,884	$16,036	62

SOURCE: U.S. Bureau of the Census, Current Population Reports, *Money Income of Households, Families, and Persons in the United States: 1984,* Series P–60, no. 151. (Washington, D.C.: U.S. Bureau of the Census, 1986). Data refers to women and men who worked full time year-round.

been set without regard to whether the job is customarily a man's or a woman's. It also suggests that women have somehow had the bad luck to land in or choose just those jobs that happen to pay the worst.

That way of explaining the pay gap pushes under the rug two important problems that women have. First, women's options to go into any jobs other than "women's jobs" have been limited by discrimination. Second, the pay of the jobs they can get is kept low by their limited options. The next two chapters are devoted to spelling out the nature of those problems and the connection between them.

Government statistics give us an idea of the magnitudes involved. Surveys taken by the U.S. Census Bureau show that in 1984, a man who worked at a full-time job for at least fifty weeks had earnings for the year of $25,884 on average. A woman working full time had earnings of $16,036. By this measurement, in that year, a woman made sixty-two cents for each man's dollar on average. The earnings by educational level shown in table 4–1 allow us to see that the percentage difference in men's and women's average salaries does not vary much with educational level. Women college graduates working full time earned $19,885 in 1984; this was 60 percent of what male college graduates earned then. Women high-school graduates earned 63 percent of what their male counterparts did. Women *college* graduates earned $2,427 less than male *high-school* graduates.

The trend in earnings is shown in table 4–2 by sex and race. Progress in the relative earnings of women and minority men has been painfully slow and subject to reverse. White women appear to have made very modest gains relative to white men in the 1980s. Black women made substantial gains relative to white men between 1967 and 1983: 25 percent. Their wages are now about 90 percent of white women's.

We can see some of the differences between the sexes in the kinds of jobs they hold in table 4–3, which gives employment by major occupational group by sex for 1972 and 1985. An estimated 60.4 million men and 47.4 million women were employed in 1985. In the clerical and administrative support occupations, women were 81 percent of the total in 1985. By contrast, women were grossly underrepresented in the precision and craft occupations, where they had only 9 percent of the jobs.

Of employed men in 1985, a total of 20 percent were in the precision and craft occupations. Of employed women, only 3 percent were. These craft jobs are relatively high-paying, and they do not require a college education. The male craft worker's $408 weekly paycheck, as compared with the female clerical worker's $270, or the female service worker's $185, shows the crucial advantage of men over women in the part of the population that has not been to college. The inability of noncollege women to get craft jobs virtually condemns such a woman to a low standard of living if she finds herself with a child or two and lacks a man to depend on. This is a theme we shall return to in chapter 10.

Table 4–3 shows that the distribution of women among the major occupational groups did not change dramatically between 1972 and 1985. The most notable change was that women's share of the executive, administrative, and managerial jobs rose from 20 percent in 1972 to 35 percent in 1985. Their share of the crafts jobs rose from 5 percent in 1972 to 9 percent in 1985.

Occupational segregation by sex is in actuality far greater than can be seen from looking just at the major occupational groups of table 4–3. Table A–1 (in the appendix A of this book) presents a much finer

TABLE 4–2
Weekly Earnings of Full-Time Wage and Salary Workers, by Race and Sex, 1967–85

Year	White Males	White Females	Black Males	Black Females
	Weekly Earnings			
1967	$130	$ 79	$ 90	$ 63
1969	146	88	104	73
1970	157	95	113	81
1971	168	102	123	87
1972	172	108	129	99
1973	193	117	149	107
1974	209	125	160	117
1975	225	138	173	130
1976	238	147	187	137
1977	258	157	201	146
1978	278	167	218	157
1979	298	184	227	169
1980	319	202	244	185
1981	349	220	268	205
1982	375	241	278	217
1983	387	254	293	231
1984	400	268	302	241
1985	417	281	304	252

Earnings as a Percent of White Males' Earnings

Year	White Males	White Females	Black Males	Black Females
1967	100	61	69	48
1969	100	60	71	50
1970	100	61	72	52
1971	100	61	73	52
1972	100	63	75	58
1973	100	61	77	55
1974	100	60	77	56
1975	100	61	77	58
1976	100	62	79	58
1977	100	61	78	57
1978	100	60	78	56
1979	100	62	76	57
1980	100	63	76	58
1981	100	63	77	59
1982	100	64	74	58
1983	100	66	76	60
1984	100	67	76	60
1985	100	67	73	60

SOURCE: U.S. Bureau of Labor Statistics, unpublished tabulations. Figures are medians of usual weekly earnings. Data for years prior to 1979 are not strictly comparable with later data.

TABLE 4-3
Workers by Major Occupational Group, by Sex, 1972 and 1985

Occupational Group	1972					1985				
	Thousands of Employed Wkrs.		Percent Women	Percent Distribution Among Occupations		Thousands of Employed Wkrs.		Percent Women	Percent Distribution Among Occupations	
	Men	Women		M	W	Men	Women		M	W
Managerial and professional specialty	10,795	5,314	33%	21%	17%	15,151	11,104	42%	25%	23%
Executive, administrative, managerial	5,846	1,433	20	11	5	7,988	4,353	35	13	9
Professional specialty	4,948	3,881	44	10	12	7,163	6,751	49	12	14
Technical, sales, and administrative support	9,561	14,058	60	19	45	11,715	21,715	65	19	46
Technicians and related support	1,188	740	38	2	2	1,780	1,584	47	3	3
Sales occupations	5,093	3,473	41	10	11	6,554	6,095	48	11	13
Administrative support, including clerical	3,280	9,845	75	6	31	3,381	14,036	81	6	30
Service occupations	4,216	6,614	61	8	21	5,673	8,614	60	9	18
Private household	35	1,405	98	*	4	41	925	96	*	2
Protective service	1,122	78	7	2	*	1,480	233	14	2	0
Service, other	3,059	5,131	63	6	16	4,152	7,456	64	7	16
Precision, production, craft, repair	9,853	493	5	19	2	12,169	1,202	9	20	3
Operators, fabricators, and laborers	13,201	4,183	24	26	13	12,697	4,256	25	21	9
Machine operators, assemblers, inspectors	5,278	3,322	39	10	11	4,697	3,076	40	8	6
Transportation and material moving occs.	3,996	146	4	8	*	4,211	358	8	7	1
Helpers, laborers, others	3,926	715	15	8	2	3,789	822	18	6	2
Farming, forestry, fishing	3,250	593	15	6	2	2,992	579	16	5	1
Total	50,876	31,255	38	100	100	60,397	47,470	44	100	100

* Less than 0.5 percent.

SOURCE: U.S. Bureau of Labor Statistics, *Employment and Earnings* (January 1984 and October 1985). The 1972 figures are annual averages, while the 1985 figures refer to September.

occupational breakdown: It gives full-time employment by sex for the 335 occupations with employment of 25,000 or greater. The occupations in the table are ranked by the percentage of women they employ. Just about half of the women, 49.87 percent, are in the first 54 occupations, all of which are more than 76 percent female and which employ only 3.94 percent of the men. The 131 occupations at the end of the table (occupations 205–335), which employ 49.41 percent of the men, are all more than 83 percent male and employ only 4.76 percent of the women. The relatively well-integrated occupations, which we can take to be those with 30–50 percent women (occupations 101–64), employ about 17 percent of the workers of each sex.

The sales occupational group, which employs almost equal proportions of the men and women, is really a collection of occupations that are quite highly segregated by sex. Sales representatives who sell to business firms (occupation 213 in table A–1) are 85 percent male. Sales workers in retail apparel (occupation 50) and cashiers (occupation 41) are 77 and 82 percent female, respectively. Those selling television and other appliances (occupation 196) are 80 percent male, while those selling cars (occupation 244) are 92 percent male. A stroll through most department stores will verify that within each store the sexes have different functions. Their pay is also different. Women classed as "cashiers" earn close to the minimum wage, while men sell big-ticket items under more lucrative commission arrangements. Even where men and women have identical duties, few of them work as colleagues for the same employer. Some employers (those who pay higher-than-average wages) will hire only men in particular occupational categories; others hire only women in those categories.[4]

Andrea Beller has estimated that in 1981 a total of 63 percent of women would have had to change finely defined occupations for the two sexes to have the same distribution among occupations. This index of segregation has declined about 11 percent over the past two decades.[5]

Information on men's and women's average pay by major occupational group is given in table 4–4. Part of the pay difference between men and women in the same major occupational group is due to the segregation of women into the lower-paying occupations within the group. Another part is due to the fact that employers paying higher-than-average wages for a particular job type tend to hire men for that job. Still another part derives from the habit of employers of paying

TABLE 4–4

Weekly Earnings of Workers by Occupational Group and Sex, 1985

Occupational Group	Men	Women	W/M
Managerial and professional specialty	$583	$399	.68
Executive, administrative, managerial	593	383	.65
Professional specialty	571	408	.71
Technical, sales, and administrative support	420	269	.64
Technicians and related support	472	331	.70
Sales occupations	431	226	.52
Administrative support, including clerical	391	270	.69
Service occupations	272	185	.68
Private household	na	130	na
Protective service	391	278	.71
Service, other	230	188	.82
Precision, production, craft, repair	408	268	.66
Mechanics and repairers	400	392	.98*
Construction trades	394	265	.67
Other	433	253	.58
Operators, fabricators, and laborers	325	216	.66
Machine operators, assemblers, inspectors	341	216	.63
Transportation and material moving occs.	369	252	.68
Helpers, laborers, others	261	209	.80
Farming, forestry, fishing	216	185	.86

* The wage survey for 1984 produced a value of .77 for the ratio of women's to men's wages in the occupational group "Mechanics and repairers." The 1985 value of .98 may derive from sampling error.
SOURCE: U.S. Bureau of Labor Statistics, "Weekly Earnings of Wage and Salary Workers: Fourth Quarter 1985," USDL 86–46 (February 3, 1986). Figures given are medians of usual weekly earnings of full-time workers.

their male and female workers in basically similar jobs very differently. For example, the same employer may pay women selling women's clothes considerably less than men selling men's clothes on the same floor of the same store.

THE "HUMAN CAPITAL" OF WOMEN AND MEN

In the labor market, educational credentials and experience and skill do matter—those with better qualifications have higher average earnings. (Table 4–1 shows how earnings vary with formal education. In 1984, those men who had been to college for four years earned almost $10,000 a year more than those who had ended their education after high-school graduation. For women, the differential for college graduation was almost $6,000.) Some part of the gap in pay between men and women is due to differences between men and women in qualifications. How much of the gap arises from this qualification difference is a crucial question.

Economists started thinking in earnest only recently about how the market sets wage differentials among different workers. Their initial interest was to account for differences in wages among male workers. They took the fact that qualifications pay off, and the additional fact that qualifications may be expensive to acquire; then they constructed from these two facts a rather simple theory of wage differentials.

Just as working with a tool or a machine can make a worker more productive, so the possession of a particular skill or body of knowledge or valuable experience can make a worker more productive. The analogy between skill and capital equipment led to the designation of skill as "human capital." The worker who took education or training and thus acquired "human capital" was described as "investing in himself" (sic). Human capital can be acquired in school, in on-the-job training, or from the experience of working on a job.

Just as a piece of machinery has a cost, so does human capital; tuition may have to be paid and earnings sacrificed during the time spent in school or in training. The difference in wage levels between a skilled and an unskilled worker can then be metaphorically described as the "return" on the investment in the training that created the skill. In theory, each person carefully calculates whether to make a particular investment in his or her human capital. One does this by comparing the cost of acquiring the skill with the expected payoff in terms of enhanced wages over one's working life. The wage of a job tends to reflect the costs of obtaining the amount of human capital the job ires. If those jobs requiring a great deal of training did not pay higher wages than those requiring little, few would invest in the required human capital and few competent persons would show up to apply for the jobs with high training requirements.*

The human capital theory of wages certainly describes well some important aspects of labor-market reality. Beyond that, the neatness of applying the same terms to human beings and machinery appealed strongly to economists. No sooner was the human capital theory of wages formulated and popularized among economists than it came to constitute for many the orthodox and exclusive theory on matters of wages.

Economists have an unfortunate tendency to go overboard on new theories. It was not enough to say that human capital differences accounted for some wage differences; very soon it became the fashion to assert that human capital differences account for *all* wage differences. In particular, race and sex discrimination were declared nonproblems, since the human capital theory sufficed to answer any and all questions about wages. But race and sex discrimination can work to keep people of the wrong race and sex out of the competition for some jobs, thus forcing them to peddle their human capital at cut rates, and this was lost sight of. Questions about the effects of unions and monopolies on wage rates were also for the most part swept under the human capital theory's capacious rug.

For economists who had come to believe that the right answer to any question about wage differences was "human capital," it was easy to jump to the conclusion that women earned lower wages than men solely because they have less human capital than men. It was very short work for these economists to come up with explanations of why women, on average, might decide on rational grounds to "invest in themselves" less than men do.

Women, these theorists observed, worked for pay in the course

* The human capital theory was not a replacement for the theory of supply and demand; rather, it was an elaboration of it. The demand for labor of a particular type—the number of people employers want to hire—depends on the wage they have to pay for such workers and the uses for workers of that type in the production process. The supply of workers of a particular type (for example, those fit to occupy machinists' jobs, those qualified to occupy typists' jobs, accountants, or those who are high-school graduates with no special skills) depends on the cost to the worker of acquiring the human capital that qualifies him or her, the wage that workers of that type can earn, and opportunities to do other kinds of work. Thus the human capital theory of wages tells us about some of the factors that affect the supply and demand for labor of a particular type.

of their lifetimes fewer years than men did. While women were out of the labor force, they would not be accruing a "return" on their "investment" in human capital. Since fewer years worked meant a lower financial payoff for a woman's human capital, her incentive to spend time and money to learn a skill or acquire a credential would be less than a man's, and fewer women might be expected to do so. Further, women's midcareer absences from paid work might cause an erosion or deterioration in their human capital. When women interrupt their careers, the skills they had previously acquired might rust away from lack of use.[6]

The proponents of the theory that women decline to invest in themselves have tended to overlook the fact that women, when they have been able, have spent as much time in school as have men. Female high-school students always have had more discipline and drive than male high-school students, as evidenced by girls' greater propensity to graduate. Women in the past earned fewer college degrees, because parents were more willing to help sons than daughters with the costs of going to college. Blaming women for a failure to "invest in themselves" is a classic case of blaming the victim.

Furthermore, women have themselves chosen (because it was, given the structure of the labor market, their best alternative) to make considerable investments in the human capital necessary to perform as secretaries, nurses, schoolteachers, or social workers. These occupations, despite their human capital requirements, pay considerably less than occupations open to males for which the training occurs on the job, much of it at the expense of the employer. In any case, women's average years of education converged rapidly with those of men in the 1960s and 1970s, with little apparent effect on the wage gap.

Human capital theorists like to speak of on-the-job training as resulting from a decision by a worker to "invest in himself." This manner of speaking neglects the fact that it is employers (and sometimes male-dominated unions) who decide who is to get such training. Women have less on-the-job training than men in part because many employers and unions will not allow women into training programs, or onto career ladders where informal training occurs.

Much of the public discourse about sex differences in behavior, in qualifications, and in pay goes on in generalities, with the numerical measurements left vague. But to say, "Men have more human capital than women" cannot end the argument. We want to know how big women's human capital deficiency is, how much difference a deficiency of a given size makes, and whether that deficiency accounts for all, or part, or none of the wage-gap problem. To find that out, we have to look at concrete evidence of what goes on in the world; theory alone cannot give us the answer.

STATISTICAL EVIDENCE OF DISCRIMINATION

The statistical evidence, to which we now turn, shows that there are human capital differences between the sexes that does account for part of the wage gap. But the evidence also shows that a considerable part of the wage gap cannot be explained away by human capital differences. A great deal of room for explanations involving discrimination still remains. Women who make heavy investments in human capital receive a reward for that investment far inferior to the reward men get.

The information on which such conclusions are based comes from surveys conducted by university researchers in which large samples of men and women were asked about their pay and about their education and work experience. In analyzing such survey data, we can link each person's qualifications with that person's earnings, which allows us to estimate how qualifications affect earnings for men and how qualifications affect earnings for women.

These surveys show the extent to which women have less human capital than men and the extent to which women exhibit behavior that might be interpreted as creating labor market disabilities. They show that women have somewhat fewer years of education than men, somewhat fewer years of experience, and less training. Women also have less continuity on their current jobs, and have more gaps in their work record to stay home and care for children. Some women do tend to look for work convenient to their home, and when they do work, take off days to care for sick children. More women than men work part time.

All of these statements are true, but that does not necessarily imply that discrimination causes none of the wage gap. Until we look at the data we cannot tell whether the effects of these characteristics and behaviors on women's salaries account for the whole wage gap, or amount to no more than the proverbial "hill of beans." In the latter case, we would find considerable warrant for believing that discrimination is the main reason for the wage gap, rather than women's human capital deficiencies and other deficiencies.

But how could a set of such serious-sounding disabilities for women possibly amount to a "hill of beans"? The answer is that we don't know what they amount to until we look at and measure the effect of each allegedly disabling deficit or behavior on wages—men's wages as well as women's.

Some men exhibit the same characteristics and behavior that are supposed to lower the wages of women. How do such men fare? Does such behavior, when it shows up in a man, have a trifling effect or a serious effect on his labor-market success? If certain behavior handicaps men only slightly, then similar behavior should handicap women only slightly, if employers treat both sexes alike. Women and men with similar amounts of human capital and similar behavior should earn on average similar salaries. If they do not, then we can suspect that discrimination is an important problem.

Suppose, for example, we found that men's career interruptions had little effect on their wages—that men with long career interruptions had only a slightly lower salary on average than similar men with no interruptions. If this were the case, then it would not make sense to attribute very much of the wage gap between the sexes to women's career interruptions. If employers had treated women's career interruptions like they treated men's career interruptions—as no big deal— then women's career interruptions should not have been much of a drag on their ability to get good jobs.

Researchers use a form of statistical analysis called multiple regression to measure how each of the alleged disabilities affects wages. If the effect of a particular disability on wages turns out to be substantial, and if women have the disability more frequently than men, then we can say that we have found a legitimate, nondiscriminatory reason for part of the pay gap.

The results of one such statistical analysis are shown in table 4–5. It summarizes the study done in 1979 by Mary Corcoran and Gregory

TABLE 4–5
Accounting for the Wage Gap Between Men and Women

Factor	Average Value in		Percent of Wage Gap Accounted for by the Difference Between Men and Women in Factor
	Men	Women	
Education			
Years of education	12.9	12.7	2
Years of Experience			
Years of experience before present employer	11.3	8.1	3
Years with present employer	8.7	5.7	11
Training			
Years of training on current job	1.7	0.7	11
Indicators of Labor-Force Attachment			
Years out of labor force since school	0.5	5.8	6
Percent of working years part time	10.0	21.0	8
Hours of work per year missed due to:			
own illness	36.5	43.0	0
illness of others	4.0	12.5	0
Placed limits on hours or location of job (percent of persons)	14.5	34.2	2
Plans to stop work (percent of persons)	3.0	8.6	2
Percentage of Gap			
Explained by factors above			45
Not explained			55
Total gap			100

Source: Adapted from Mary Corcoran and Gregory J. Duncan, "Work History, Labor-Force Attachment, and Earnings Differences Between the Races and Sexes," *Journal of Human Resources*, vol. XIV (Winter 1979): 3–20. The analysis in the table refers to whites.

J. Duncan of the University of Michigan on a sample of 5,212 American wage earners. For each worker, the researchers collected information on the person's wage and on the person's education, training, work experience, attitudes toward work, and absenteeism. Thus for each worker, the researchers had information on a great many factors thought to be pertinent to career success. For each such factor, an estimate in percentage terms was made of its effect on the wage gap between the sexes.

For example, the researchers asked about gaps in labor-market participation. It turned out that women in the Corcoran-Duncan sample had on average taken 5.8 years away from paid work since leaving school. Some men also had taken time off, but men's absences averaged only about half a year. Whether a person had taken time away from employment did have an appreciable effect on the wages a person (whether a man or a woman) got when they returned. So the difference between women and men in years out of the labor force did account for part of the wage gap—about 6 percent of it. Another 8 percent of the gap is accounted for by the fact that women had a greater proportion of their working years that were part time.

If we look at years of experience, the women in the Corcoran-Duncan sample had 3.0 fewer years of service with their current employer than men did on average, which accounted for 12 percent of the gap. Another 3 percent was explained by men's lengthier work experience with previous employers. The men in this sample had a little more formal education than the women, but that accounted for only 2 percent of the gap.

The common allegation that women do worse than men because women give low priority to work and high priority to domestic duties was tested by these researchers. Corcoran and Duncan found that only 3 percent of the gap could be attributed to absences on account of workers' illnesses or illness of family members, or to other evidence of a low degree of labor-force attachment. Whatever the differences between men and women in these respects, these factors do not have a big effect on wages for men or women and so cannot explain much of the gap.

Those people in the sample who had been given training by their current employer got higher wages than those who had been given no such training. More men than women had benefited from such training, and this difference amounted to 11 percent of the gap between their salaries.

When we add all this up, the factors listed in table 4–5 account altogether for 45 percent of the gap between men's and women's salaries. While 45 percent could not be dismissed as a "hill of beans," it does leave 55 percent of the gap unaccounted for. Does that mean that the residual 55 percent is a good estimate of the proportion of the gap due to discrimination?

Some economists would argue that 55 percent is an overestimate of the extent to which discrimination is responsible. They would point out, quite correctly, that some of the worker characteristics that might account in a nondiscriminatory way for the wage gap were not included in the analysis. The most obvious omission in this particular study is the failure of the researchers to collect and analyze information concerning the subjects that the workers in the sample had studied in school. If these respondents were typical, more of the men than the women had studied business and engineering. That would account for an additional piece of the gap in a nondiscriminatory way. Moreover, the Corcoran-Duncan study does not give us a measure of attitudes toward work, except indirectly.

Before conceding, however, that 55 percent is an overestimate of the extent of the wage gap due to discrimination, we might consider that there are some disabilities that tend to afflict men more than women that were not studied either. Employed men suffer more from alcoholism than do employed women, yet information on alcohol consumption was not included among the characteristics studied. Men in charge of a vehicle are more likely than women to have a bad accident. Men are far more likely to have criminal records than women. Alcoholism, a criminal record, or an accident-studded driving record are likely to affect one's job performance adversely, or one's ability to get hired for a good job, so people with those problems would tend to have less-than-average earnings. Since the study did not account for any of these factors, it omitted some important and legitimate reasons that ought to boost women's pay relative to men's.

Furthermore, some of the factors making part of the 45 percent of the gap that was "accounted for" may result from discriminatory behavior by employers. The 11 percent of the gap attributed to differences between women and men in "years of training on current job" probably is in large part due to discrimination. In most places of work, the decision as to who gets a training slot is controlled by the employer. Employers' worries that women's training will not pay off because of their supposedly higher turnover provides a rationalization to discriminate against them by excluding them from training.*

Another component of the 45 percent of the gap "accounted for" is the years the worker has spent with his or her present employer.

* See discussion of this issue in chapter 5.

Apparently long service with a single employer pays off, and women get such payoffs less than men do on average. This looks at first glance like a clear-cut case in which women are hurting themselves by failing to stay on the job. However, a different interpretation is plausible. People who are denied promotion or people with no hope of promotion have little incentive to stay with an employer. An employer who puts and keeps women in dead-end jobs on the ground that they are not stable employees finds the prophecy of women's high turnover to be self-fulfilling. Much of women's lower seniority results from discrimination.

When all is said and done, we cannot make a precise estimate of the proportion of the wage gap that is due to discrimination, but we can say with considerable confidence that the statistical evidence points strongly to discrimination as an important force in the labor market. No researcher, whatever his or her preconception of the importance of discrimination, has been able to come forth with credible statistical evidence that the wage gap is substantially accounted for by nondiscriminatory factors.[7] Jacob Mincer and Solomon W. Polachek are leading exponents of the view that the wage gap between the sexes is due to human capital and other deficiencies, and to women's voluntary choices. Yet their own study left 59 percent of the wage gap unaccounted for.[8]*

Those economists who deny the importance of discrimination have apparently been frustrated by their inability to demonstrate statistically that the wage gap is caused by women's measurable lack of devotion to their careers. Some of them are casting around for new explanations. For example, Gary Becker has recently argued:

> ... women with responsibilities for housework would have less energy available for the market than men would. This would reduce the hourly earnings of married women, affect their jobs and occupations, and even lower their investment in market human capital when they worked the same number of hours as married men. Consequently, the housework responsibilities of married women may be the source of much of the difference in earnings and in job segregation between men and women.[9]

* Mincer and Polachek provide in their paper a long list of unmeasured factors that, they conjecture, might have caused the large part of the salary gap they were unable to explain. All of the additional unmeasured factors they list concern possible deficiencies of women. They do not mention discrimination by employers as even a possibility.

Becker (who maintains that it is rational and therefore inevitable for wives to do all the housework) thus is saying that women simply are too tired to put forward the necessary effort to earn good wages. He has no measurements of the energy level of women workers or men (who also have some energy-draining ways of spending time), but that has not inhibited the conjecture. Nor do the ethics of the situation merit his comment.

When a particular employer has been accused of discriminating against women employees, statistical evidence frequently is presented in court on the characteristics of the male and the female workers. The extent to which such characteristics can account for the pay gap is debated by statistical experts retained by both sides. Experts testifying in the defense of employers accused of discrimination have been known to be quite imaginative in suggesting factors other than discrimination that might innocently account for the pay gap.

In one recent case the economist testifying on behalf of the employer noted that many workers of both sexes had not answered the question "job applied for" on the initial application form. He told the judge that the women's lack of answer meant something about their qualifications and intentions. The men's lack of answer meant something, too, but something different from what the women's lack meant. He went on to claim that this (undocumented) difference in the meaning of the blanks on the application form explained and justified a substantial part of the gap in the salaries the company was paying men and women.*

DIRECT EVIDENCE OF DISCRIMINATION

Statistical studies such as the one by Corcoran and Duncan can be said to offer only indirect evidence of discrimination. These studies provide an answer to such contentions as, "The wage gap is due to the fact that women have fewer years of experience than men." They show

---

* The expert giving this testimony was Dr. Finis Welch. The case was *Dalley et al.* v. *Blue Cross/Blue Shield of Michigan.* The judge actually swallowed this explanation.

that such factors leave a great deal of the gap unaccounted for. However, as we have seen, it always is possible to think of other nondiscriminatory causes for the wage gap that have not been measured, and to assert that these factors would, if measured and included in the analysis, explain the rest of the gap. The portion of the gap left unexplained remains large, despite efforts to close it with new data on women's behavior or characteristics.

We do not have to depend solely on indirect statistical evidence. The case of Chase Manhattan Bank cited at the beginning of this chapter is one example of the abundant evidence brought to light by lawsuits accusing employers of discriminating. One well-documented case is that of the Bell System, whose practices were described by the Equal Employment Opportunity Commission in 1972 as part of a complaint it filed against the company.[10] Occupational segregation in the company was very rigid:

> A total sex segregation of jobs is reflected in virtually all . . . Bell System docu-
> ments. Through pictures of males or females, pronoun reference or through
> straight-forward identification, all jobs are strictly classified as male or female.
> This sex denotation of jobs is carried consistently throughout company personnel
> manuals, collective bargaining agreements, job descriptions, company publications,
> general company advertisements, requisitions for employees . . . interviewer's
> aids, training manuals. . . . Crafts jobs, outside sales jobs, and middle and upper
> level management jobs are always identified as male jobs.[11]

The sex-identification of jobs in Bell System literature reflected the reality of the company's practices of assigning workers to jobs. Of the 190,000 craft workers in 1970, 99 percent were male. This company always has trained workers for each job; there can be no presumption that lack of previous training or experience is what kept women down. Women were given some of the lower-level management jobs that involved supervising other women but had almost no chance of penetrating into the higher management levels. Of the 2,650 employees in higher management, only 1.2 percent were female. In the course of interviews, male managers at Bell provided evidence of the pervasiveness of stereotypes of women and of a belief in their lack of competence.*

---

* Although the Bell System signed a consent decree in this case promising to institute affirmative action, there is evidence deriving from a subsequent lawsuit that in at least one of the constituent companies very little progress was made in introducing women into craft jobs through 1983. Michigan Bell Telephone Company, which had 502 women craft workers out of 8,375

Another firm whose discriminatory behavior has been put on the public record is the Western Electric Company.* Thanks to a lawsuit by Cleo Kyriazi, and the research and detective work done by her attorney, Judith Vladeck (who also brought the *LoRe* case), we know a great deal about what went on in the company's Kearny, N.J., plant in the years 1967–76. In his opinion on the case, the judge relates that,†

1. Of Western Electric's 735 employees designated "Officers and Managers," only 1.9 percent were women. No women held a position above that of section chief, the lowest supervisory level.
2. Of the 545 employees designated "Professional," only 6.8 percent were women, and some of those were secretaries and nurses.
3. Of those hired for entry-level blue-collar jobs requiring no skill, education or experience, 97.5 percent of the women were placed into jobs at grade 32, and 2.5 percent were placed into grade 33. Of the men, 47 percent were placed into grade 32, while 53 percent were placed into grade 33.
4. The sex-segregation of jobs was extreme; there were 141 types of jobs for which only men were hired, and 47 jobs into which only women were hired.
5. Female-only jobs were assigned grades and pay scales lower than those assigned to male-only jobs of equivalent skill. For example, the all-male staff chauffeurs, whose only duties were to drive company executives and keep the limousine clean, were rated higher and paid more than the all-female Assistant Telephone Overseers. The latter were required to oversee and coordinate operating activities of the telephone exchange, assign work schedules, instruct telephone personnel, recommend revisions and improvements for service, handle urgent or critical incidents, and make special studies and analyses.
6. The company knowingly permitted male employees to engage in prolonged and cruel sexual harassment in at least one case, and made no move to discipline the perpetrators.

---

in 1970, had 508 out of 5,314 in 1983. Computations made by the author suggest that despite the drop in craft employment over this period, turnover would have given the company opportunities to have had over 2,000 women in craft jobs by the 1980s had men and women been assigned to craft jobs between 1970 and the early 1980s in proportion to their hiring. This estimate is based on the submissions of Michigan Bell of employment data by race by sex by occupational group to the EEOC and produced in connection with the discovery required in the course of a Title VII lawsuit against the company, *Gerlach et al. v. Michigan Bell Telephone Company.*[12]

  * The Bell System and Western Electric were part of American Telephone and Telegraph Company. But the 1973 consent decree signed in the Bell case apparently had no impact on personnel practices at Western Electric.

  † *Kyriazi* v. *Western Elec. Co.,* 461 F. Supp. 894 (1978).

7. While most jobs above entry level were filled through promotion, Western Electric rarely promoted women beyond the lowest grades. (See discussion in chapter 5.)

8. The company provided supervisors with a requisition form to be used when they had a position to fill, which had a place where they could ask for a male, or a female or could express no preference. As the judge in the case dryly remarked, "Not surprisingly, the Requisition for Personnel forms did little to enhance the position of women at Western." (p. 918) On requisition forms for grade 32 openings, supervisors said they wanted a female in 87 out of 96 cases. On requisition forms for higher-level positions, supervisors asked for males for 263 out of 292 openings.

9. Women were disproportionately excluded from training opportunities. Professional women who were sent to training were steered toward courses in nontechnical areas that could not lead to substantial career advancement.

10. The practice during reductions in force was to lay off workers in lower grades while retaining workers in higher grades even if they had lower seniority. As a result of this, women were required to bear a disproportionate share of layoffs.

One has to conclude, on reading the record of Western Electric's practices, that the company presents an unmistakable and classic case of a phenomenon that many economists have concluded does not, and indeed could not, exist. The practices documented for the Bell System, Western Electric, and many other companies are based in part on biased attitudes toward women's abilities. There is considerable independent evidence that women's capabilities are commonly evaluated in a discriminatory way. In one famous series of experiments, a researcher presented an article for evaluation to a group of people. Half of the evaluators were told that the author of the article was "John T. McKay" and half that the author was "Joan T. McKay." The article attributed to the man was evaluated more favorably than the identical article attributed to the woman. Both men and women gave a lower value to the article they were told was written by a woman, but the males showed the greatest tendency in this regard.[13] Women under consideration for employment or promotion are likely to have their qualifications judged more harshly than those of men, even by evaluators who feel themselves to be fair.

A CLOSER LOOK AT THE LABOR MARKET

Analyses of the Corcoran/Duncan variety render the proposition that the "free market" is fair to women highly doubtful. Such statistical analyses strongly suggest that the evidence of specific discriminatory conduct that turns up in court cases is representative of general practices in many establishments and are not isolated incidents. In the next chapter we take a much closer look at occupational segregation, which I shall argue is due in large part to discrimination and is at the root of women's poor position in the labor market. This will lay the stage for the discussion in later chapters of a discrimination-based theory of the wage gap, and of societal and legal remedies for that discrimination.

CHAPTER 5

Sex Segregation on the Job:

The Root of Women's

Disadvantage

Many jobs are considered "men's jobs" or "women's jobs," and that is the key to women's poor position in the labor market. Women are starting to be able to enter into some male preserves, but many jobs remain off-limits. Women continue to have a poor shot at landing good jobs—those that pay best, that allow for some independence of action, that have fewer boring duties, that lead to still better jobs. Not all "men's jobs" are good jobs in that sense, but many of them are. A large proportion of the "women's jobs" are bad jobs—poorly paid, boring, dead-end. What keeps women out of the good jobs? Why would an employer decide to consider only men for a job, especially since male workers cost 60 to 70 percent extra? Why do employers bother to maintain systems of sex segregation in the workplace?

One important reason for the sex segregation of jobs is that workplaces are not "all business." People on the job have to interact and to cooperate with each other. Smooth social interactions make the work go easier. If interactions cause problems, productivity suffers. Some male workers make trouble when they are asked to work along with or take orders from women. Employers don't want the loss in productivity that comes from such trouble, so many employers decide to keep certain jobs off-limits to women.

Employers also have preconceived notions about what women can and can't do well. For example, there appears to be great resistance by employers to letting women into jobs where they drive trucks, or even cars.* They do not want to put women into jobs where they sell or service expensive or advanced equipment. Legal casebooks are full of examples. But it is not necessary to resort to books; the interested observer can easily verify that few women sell cars. In department stores, few women sell refrigerators, vacuum cleaners, or rugs. In the mid-1980s newly opened stores stocking televisions, VCRs, and audio equipment commonly have no women selling. They are there, but serving as cashiers, at low pay. In fast-food restaurants, women are not allowed to be part of the cooking crew. When one asks why, one is told that women are physically incapable of cleaning the hamburger grill.

Conservative economists don't believe discrimination is an important cause of sex segregation on the job. They say that employers fill certain jobs only with men because there are no women applicants for those jobs; or if there are women applicants, none of them is worth what she would be paid. Employers maintain all-male groups of employees because no woman would want those jobs, no woman is or could be trained for them, no women would have the talent for them, no woman would stay on such a job long enough to make it worthwhile for the employer to hire her.

If the conservatives were content to argue that there were "few worthy women applicants" rather than "no worthy women applicants," that would be more plausible. Certainly, jobs that employers have historically filled only with men do not attract many women applicants. Most women take the division of jobs into "men's jobs" and "women's jobs" as a fact of life. They do not waste time or court rejection by trying to breach the boundaries of the female ghetto. But some women

* There is even some resistance to letting women customers try out cars that are for sale.

do want higher-paying jobs, and when coal-mining jobs opened up, there were women who were glad to get them. There is no shortage of women to fill jobs that carry a better chance for promotion than the jobs ordinarily available to them. Some women would give a far better performance in a "man's job" than some of the men in them.

The accounting firm that has several hundred male partners and not a single woman partner did have women working for them who wanted partnership positions. They were women who had accounting degrees, who had successful experience in accounting, who intended to continue their careers without interruption. What the company did not have was a desire to appoint those women to partnership positions. The large construction company that has no woman carpenters, the insurance company that has no females in entry jobs with promotion prospects are not that way because not even one good women candidate could be recruited; nor is the police department that has no females on patrol, the fifty-man economics faculty, the restaurant with seven men in the kitchen and twenty men waiting on tables. It passes belief that there are no women at all in those well-paid jobs because no worthy woman wanted one.

In these days especially, all-male crews are not kept free of women without some vigilance and effort. The women who do aspire to get berths in "men's jobs" are kept off balance by a host of practices and policies that employers and male workers use to exclude and discourage them. Since the passage of the Civil Rights Act, employers are legally enjoined from behavior that excludes women from any job on account of their sex. The law also forbids employers from tolerating harassing behavior toward women by male employees. But much behavior of this type continues unchecked.

While progress is being made in curbing such practices, it is very slow. The failure to make more dramatic progress is responsible for a great deal of poverty, much unused talent, and many lost hopes.

A WOMAN CARPENTER'S STORY

Here are the experiences of a woman who wanted to be a carpenter and who did succeed:

> I started work as a carpenter in the early 1970s. I was able to pressure a local

contractor, a friend, into hiring me as an apprentice. He encouraged me to join the union. I was already on a union job in 1980, but not yet admitted to the union. They were waiting to see if I would "go away." Two other females [were allowed to] join at the same time. Since then none has been allowed to receive apprentice or journeyman books. There were 450 males in the local and the 3 of us. The business agent and I argued about the number of women constantly and he ended by yelling at me that there were "three of you damn women and there will be no more." He's kept it exactly that way.

The first outfit I was employed at, the supervisor was exceptionally good and fair, but the men hired were a rowdy group in general. They were openly hostile and verbally abusive to me and the other females. My carpenter steward treated me with constant verbal sexual abuse in order to be macho and get a laugh on me for the boys to share. I tried to befriend him and toward the end of the season he backed off somewhat but never really stopped.

My next employment was with another bridge contractor. The management was polite but got me off the job as soon as they could. The steward tried to keep me on, arguing that I was as good a worker as any man, but I was laid off anyway. They played strictly by quotas and never kept a female working any longer than necessary even if she was a reliable employee. . . .

A foreman on another job had sworn he'd never have a woman on his crew, and management put me on his crew to spite him. Of course he proceeded to punish me. In the morning he'd boom out a good morning to each man, then made a point of turning his back on me. At lunch break I was excluded from conversations and at times the men wouldn't move over to allow me a space at the table. I was isolated working, too—sent off on a trivial, meaningless job or on a job involving extreme endless repetition. A decent foreman will share with all crew members a repeating job, but it doesn't often work that way. Females usually do the "dirt jobs."

My solution was to find a good company, which I eventually did—that is unlikely for all of us to be able to do. There are too few "good outfits." Since then I have encountered several very good, tolerant, respectful foremen. There is no excuse for the many others who continue mistreatment of females and still get away with it. The union must set a good example, and it will trickle down. So far that has not happened in this area.[1]

This narrative makes it clear what women have to go through if they aspire to cross the line into male job territory and why many simply give up. The story includes sexual harassment, social ostracism by coworkers, lack of encouragement from supervisors, and punitive assignment to the worst part of the work. None of the hostile supervisors of this woman carpenter could have been interested in teaching her any tricks of the trade. The story is silent on how many times she got advice from friends and family members to stop batting her head against the wall and get into a line of work where she would be appreciated.

We see from this story that women have difficulty getting into craft unions, which have also been implicated in the exclusion of blacks from craft jobs.[2] In the construction trades, union membership helps a person to get better-paid jobs.

The woman carpenter's story also makes clear why some managements might shy away from hiring women in male-dominated occupations. Managing construction sites is difficult enough without hiring workers whose presence on the job creates such problems. To some managements, the male supervisors and workers are the mainstay of the business; the woman carpenter is the troublemaker.

The carpenter's account does testify to the fact that there are "good outfits" that are fair to women workers and that exercise discipline against male employees who might harass them. The carpenter's story also testifies to the fact that "quotas" are effective in increasing the number of women working in male-dominated occupations. She is referring to the "goals and timetables" that are part of affirmative-action programs imposed by the Federal Office of Contract Compliance Policy on firms that hold federal contracts.* Some firms obviously conform only grudgingly, and but for the goals would employ no women at all. But as they get experience with women workers these firms may come to conform less grudgingly.

A SURVEY OF SEX SEGREGATION

As yet few employers run "good outfits" that welcome women and men into the same occupations and allow them to interact as equals. The extent to which individual workplaces segregate the sexes by occupation is documented in a landmark study of the records of 393 establishments in California that had been surveyed by the U.S. Employment Service between 1959 and 1979.[3] Sociologists William T. Bielby and James N. Barron looked at those records and scored each

* There is, of course, considerable controversy as to whether goals and timetables are the same things as quotas (see chapter 7).

employer by the extent of sex segregation. An establishment where there was no segregation at all—where men and women shared each occupation in accordance with their share in the establishment's work force—was given a zero score. An establishment in which the segregation was 100 percent perfect—where there was not a single woman in job titles that had men in them and not a single man in job titles that had women in them—was given a score of 100.*

Bielby and Barron use the word "remarkable" to describe their results, and well they might. They found the average sex-segregation score to be 93.4 percent. Of the 393 establishments, 232 had scores of 100 percent; they were perfectly segregated. Only 8.5 percent of the 60,950 workers covered in the survey were employed in establishments whose segregation scores were below 90.

Those establishments that had low segregation scores and did place men and women in the same job categories tended to have them work in different locations, so little on-the-job interaction occurred. One of the few firms in the sample that appeared on paper to have a low degree of sex segregation was a real-estate management firm.[4] It employed 23 men and 126 women as apartment house managers. But on closer examination, it turned out that the men and the women were in actuality completely segregated from each other. The 149 apartment house managers worked and lived in 149 different buildings, providing a classic case of the exception that proves the rule.

Some of the establishments were surveyed twice, about five years apart, so that the extent of change in the degree of segregation could be looked at. Bielby and Barron report, "Two thirds of [those establishments] remained all-male, completely segregated, or almost fully segregated."[5] Of seventy-five organizations, eleven did become substantially less segregated, but seven became substantially more segregated. The rest stayed about the same.

---

* These scores are very sensitive to the classification of occupations. The fewer occupations are distinguished, the lower the segregation score will tend to be. Scores are also affected by the extent to which the firm hires people of both sexes. A firm may get a good score as a nonsegregator by hiring very few women, but mixing the ones it does hire in occupations with men.

OCCUPATIONAL SEGREGATION:
THE OLDEST TRADITION

The division of labor based on sex is and has been common to all societies. A person's other characteristics (such as age, race, class, and family connections) also may determine or influence what that person's productive duties will be. Groups low in the pecking order are found in jobs with less pleasant duties. Such jobs are defined as less prestigious, so that one's place in the social hierarchy is correlated with one's occupation. In primitive economies such assignment systems may have served as an effective tool of economic management.

In a modern economy family connections still are of some value, and being black still is a hindrance to occupational attainment. But we appear to be moving toward a system where males compete for jobs on the basis of merit. Traditions subordinating and segregating women, which go back thousands of years, are dying more slowly. An etiquette of male-female interactions that has the social function of expressing and acknowledging the subordination of women to men still is in place. That etiquette and the traditions behind it remain as powerful inhibitors of the integration of men and women as equals and equivalents on the job.

Occupational segregation, like any other system of dominance and privilege, tends to perpetuate itself through the self-interest of its beneficiaries. Such regimes, whether based on sex, or on racial or religious differences, always produce elaborate rationalizations about why those groups that have drawn the more desirable economic, social, and political assignments deserve to have them (for the good of all, of course) and why those who have drawn the less desirable assignments could perform satisfactorily in no other roles.

JOBS AS BADGES OF GENDER

Working in an occupation that is typed as appropriate to a woman has served, until very recently, to show and confirm a woman's "femininity," just as wearing makeup and high heels does.[6] Belonging to an occupation that is identified as male has been a part of a man's display of "masculinity." People who fail to behave in ways considered appropriate to their sex let themselves in for social penalties, ranging from being stared at, to ridicule and ostracism. As a result, displaying behavior exhibiting "masculinity" or "femininity" amounts to a compulsion in most people. Many of the differences between the sexes in conventional behavior involve hardships for women, with high heels presenting an obvious example. Most women, however, choose to stick to the conventions, disabling as they are, to avoid the greater pain of the label "unfeminine."

Most people appear to conform more or less gladly and contentedly to the behavior typical of their sex with respect to job aspirations, just as they conform willingly in matters of dress, haircut, and general demeanor. After all, few women have much stomach for courting the rejection both on and off the job risked by women who attempt male-typical occupations.

However, men's and women's jobs differ so greatly in advantages that unless there is an explicit and outright prohibition against their doing so, some women do want to breach the walls. There are women who have campaigned ardently for mining jobs, and performed well in them. The major advantage of the men's jobs is higher pay. Some of the men's jobs have relatively entertaining duties and confer high status.* This being the case, at least some women will try to get into those jobs, even if they have to act "unfeminine" to get and hold them.[7]

If more women were allowed to enter all-male jobs, the idea that these jobs are off-limits to women and unfeminine would change. Thus

---

* There is a large literature arguing for and against the contention that women's and men's jobs lead to similar status attainments. See Donald J. Treiman and Kermit Terrell, "Sex and the Process of Status Attainment: A Comparison of Working Women and Men," *American Sociological Review*, vol. 40 (April 1975):174–200.

the preservation of occupational segregation requires that virtually all women be kept out of the men's preserve. Defenses against women interlopers must be constantly in readiness.

Research by Sandra L. Bem and Daryl J. Bem suggests that some few women do have an interest in craft jobs usually reserved for males, even when it is clear that they are "men's jobs."[8] When the Bems showed women advertisements for telephone craft jobs written in such a way as to be obviously angled toward men exclusively, 5 percent of the women said they were interested in the jobs. While this is not a large percentage, it would have provided enough candidates to deseg-regate all job categories. When the Bems changed the language of the ads so that they were sex-neutral, 25 percent of the women to whom the ads were shown expressed an interest. Finally, 45 percent of the women expressed an interest when the ad they were shown was angled toward women. These experiments show the extent to which women do pay attention to clues about which job is for whom, but they also show that it is not women's unalterable disinterest in such jobs that stands in the way of dismantling occupational segregation by sex. What stands in the way is active resistance to sex integration by employers, fellow workers, and labor unions. We turn now to the reasons for this resistance and to the strategies used by those who resist.

MEN'S STAKE IN ALL-MALE WORKING GROUPS

Many men do not want women to join them as coworkers in the same job category. A man may want to exclude women from his occupation because he feels that his image of masculinity, the precious hallmark of a superior status, is enhanced by holding a "man's job." That masculine image might be diluted or compromised by the entry of women colleagues. He may feel that the presence of women in his work group will dissipate the relaxed and clubby all-male atmosphere. He may have doubts about a woman's ability to do the job and may fear extra burdens on him as a result. Conversely, he may fear that a woman will be more competent than he is and thus may undercut his pretensions to superiority. His wife may be unfavorably inclined to the idea of his having a female colleague.*

Male workers may worry, with considerable justification, that the first woman to enter their job category presages the eventual change of identity of that job to a "woman's job." If the boss sees that women can do the job, he may decide to save some money by hiring only women in the future.

The segregation of men and women affects the duties that employers assign to each job. The jobs that are intended for women tend to involve boring, repetitive tasks. Tasks that might train the worker for higher positions or bring the worker into the limelight as a candidate for promotion get assigned to men's jobs. It would certainly be possible, as Rosabeth Kanter[9] has argued, to create fewer or no boring dead-end jobs by spreading the good and the bad duties around in a more even-handed way. However, as things stand, the men are the beneficiaries of the present job structure, and they understand this quite well.

Lester Thurow once remarked[10] that people might discriminate against those of another race but that most men would be unlikely to discriminate against women. After all, women are men's mothers, sisters, daughters, wives, and girlfriends. Thurow forgets that a man might not want his wife or girlfriend to have as good a job as he has. In any case, most men on the job are not dealing with their own female relations but with strangers.

Perhaps a man does have a woman friend or relative or a spouse whom he would like to see placed in a job like his own. He has to worry about the reactions of his male coworkers if he tries to get her taken on. If he has even a single sexist colleague, who may be an otherwise excellent friend and coworker, he may be in for trouble. In situations like that, where each person can blackball the candidate, the most bigoted person's views may be allowed to govern the situation. Since a woman candidate will have a low chance of being taken on, and a low chance of success on the job if she is taken on, the risk of upsetting any one of a man's buddies to advance her cause looms as a big cost for a small expected payoff.

* Wives get upset about the entry of women into husbands' previously all-male work environment, as in the case of police patrols or construction work. Wives of male executives may agitate against the entry of female executives, but not the presence of female secretaries. Wives do have anxieties about their husbands' relations with secretaries, but they know that it would be useless to agitate against their presence.

PRODUCTIVITY AND SOCIAL RELATIONS ON THE JOB

Employers want high productivity from their work force and under-stand that productivity is not just a matter of getting workers capable of doing the job and providing them with good equipment and su-pervision. The productivity of an establishment is crucially affected by the nature of the personal interactions that each employee has with his or her coworkers and supervisor. If these interactions are pleasant and unproblematical, then employees can pay undistracted attention to the details of their work and go at it with a cooperative attitude.

Productivity suffers if there are time-consuming and disruptive fights. It also suffers if male workers on the job refuse to teach the job to new female workers. Disruptive incidents or a flow of offensive remarks may poison the atmosphere of a workplace and cause break-downs in the flow of work. When cooperation is called for, it may be refused, hindering the accomplishment of particular tasks. Workers may sabotage operations to express spite.

When troubles of this sort arise, an employer may have to transfer or fire employees who are causing this kind of trouble, or some whose presence occasions it. The aggressors may be people with considerable experience, special knowledge, and skill, and thus hard to dispense with. For this reason the innocent victims may be sacrificed. In that case, feelings of injustice are generated, which may have troublesome consequences, including lawsuits. Whoever gets the ax, it is disruptive, tedious, and expensive to shake up the staffing of a department or a crew. New people have to be recruited and trained before things are back to normal.

When employers fill jobs they pay attention to the compatibility of the individuals who will occupy them. Of course, the compatibility of two individuals is not unconditional but depends on the roles they will play, in the near term and in the longer-term future. Individuals who might be compatible when A is the boss and B the subordinate might be incompatible if the roles were reversed, or even incompatible as equal colleagues.

Nothing is more obvious than that people bring with them to their work their ideas about status and respect, and their ideas about when it is right and reasonable for one individual to be subordinated to another. Many bring with them the idea that men are and ought to be superior in status to women and that a man ought not to have to treat a woman as an equal, on the job or anywhere else. They may feel that it is wrong for a man to have to take orders from a woman and that he is shamed if he does.

The managers of an establishment may have liberal attitudes, may have a realistic idea of the capabilities of women workers, may want to avoid sex discrimination. Yet they may feel they have to pay attention to these compatibility issues when hiring, assigning, and promoting workers. If there were rigorous enforcement of antidiscrimination laws, or if there were strong ethical feelings against giving in to these sexist traditions, then workers who rebel against and make trouble for women colleagues would be disciplined. Such behavior would become less common, and so less customary. As it is, in the absence of compulsions requiring change, some managers feel compelled to practice occupational segregation. Others, less liberal, are free to indulge their prejudices.

William Foot Whyte's 1949 study of restaurants, a masterpiece of sociological fieldwork, illustrates the problems that arise when men and women are required by their work to interact in a way counter to the etiquette that expresses women's subordination to men.[11] The women who wait on tables have to transmit the customers' orders to another employee, usually a male, who then proceeds to fill them and passes the food or drink back to the waitress. The women's "origination of action" for men and the men's resistance can disrupt service to the customers. Whyte gives us a description of how one restaurant got around the problem:

> On the main serving floor . . . waitresses wrote out slips which they placed on spindles on top of a warming compartment separating them from the countermen. The men picked off the order slips, filled them, and put the plates in the compartment where the waitresses picked them up. In most cases there was no direct face-to-face interaction between waitresses and countermen, and, indeed, the warming compartment was so high that only the taller waitresses could see over its top. . . . One of the countermen described earlier experiences in other restaurants where there had been no such barrier and let us know that to be left out in the open where all the girls could call their orders in was an ordeal to which no man should be subjected. In such places, he said, there was constant wrangling.

This seems to check with experience in the industry. While we observed frictions arising between waitresses and pantry girls, such a relationship can at least be maintained with relative stability. On the other hand, it is difficult to prevent blowups between countermen and waitresses when the girls call their orders in. Most restaurants consciously or unconsciously interpose certain barriers to cut down waitress origination of action for countermen. It may be a warming compartment as in this case, or, as we observed in another restaurant, there was a man pantry supervisor who collected the order slips from the waitresses as they came in and passed them out to the countermen. There are a variety of ways of meeting the problem, but they all seem to involve this principle of social insulation.*

HOW FIRMS KEEP THEMSELVES SEGREGATED

If a firm is to be and continue to be sex-segregated, the processes under which people are hired, assigned to jobs, and promoted must be geared to maintain the segregation. Presumably few employing organizations still have rules that explicitly exclude or segregate people for reasons of race or sex. However, a business of any size has many people with considerable power over the assignment and pay of other people. It is unlikely to be free of discrimination unless there are ways of motivating all people with such power within the establishment to act in a sex-blind and race-blind way. We have a great deal of evidence that many firms either have not tried to do this, or if they have tried, have not had good success.[12]

Some segregation within a firm derives from the fact that certain groups are excluded in the hiring process. In the past, some firms have excluded blacks entirely. A firm that hires men and women high-school graduates but takes only college graduates who are white males will have all of its upper-level jobs occupied by white men. It is not uncommon for firms who do this to try to justify the lack of women

* An interesting question raised by this narrative and not answered by Whyte is why American restaurants typically open themselves to this kind of trouble by employing women to wait on tables and employ men at serving counters and bars to receive the orders from them. In other parts of the world, the staffs of most restaurants appear to consist entirely of males. In American restaurants that offer fine food and/or a luxurious setting, the size of the check allows for tips big enough to attract male waiters. In cheaper restaurants, the owners put up with the friction rather than supplement the tips to an extent necessary to be able to have male waiters.

or blacks in their upper-level jobs by pointing to the lesser qualifications of the women and blacks they currently employ.

When people are being interviewed for a job, they can easily be steered to apply for a job that the firm considers appropriate for their sex. After all, applicants are trying as hard as they can to please the person interviewing them. They know that if they appear stubborn or pushy they may get no job at all. Women candidates (including some Harvard graduates of my acquaintance) commonly are asked whether they can type. Those who demonstrate good clerical skills are likely to be assigned to a clerical job. From the point of view of the organization, that is where their comparative advantage lies. Sometimes the candidate is given a female-job assignment on a take-it-or-leave-it basis; at other times the candidate may be given a signal which job to choose if she wants any. One young woman was urged by the personnel officer of an insurance company to "choose" to be a secretary rather than a claims agent, a job that was mainly male at that company. He said that the secretarial job was good for her because "it would make use of your training." She understood quite well that the secretarial job paid less than the claims agent job and had no promotion prospects, but needing a job, she did what he was urging.[13]

Even where the official policy of the establishment is neutral toward sex segregation or is opposed to it, certain practices connected to the placement of new employees within the firm may contribute to the perpetuation of separate jobs for men and women. It is common in placing a new employee to have the candidate interviewed by the prospective supervisor and coworkers. This certainly serves to weed out people who appear incompatible with the workers already on the job. However, such a practice amounts to allowing relatively low-level employees to blackball candidates. Women may be rejected for openings in "men's jobs" on the grounds that the people on the job have doubts about them, which indeed they may have. Where a blackball procedure is used, the opinions of the most sexist person in a department may be controlling.

Once women employees are aboard, they have to be kept from transferring to men's jobs if segregation is to be maintained. This may be done by a seniority system that forces those who take transfers from female jobs to male jobs to lose seniority. News of vacancies in male jobs have to be kept away from females. When a "man's job" becomes vacant, applicants are very frequently recruited through word of mouth. Men who have the same or similar jobs pass the news of the vacancy to other men they know who might be interested. Women simply do not get to know of the vacancy, or if they do, are not encouraged to apply. As the Bems' research shows, recruitment material that appears from its contents to be addressed solely to men discourages women from expressing an interest. Any woman who agitates for an inappropriate transfer may be ignored; if she persists, she may be harassed, and pretexts may be used to set her up for firing. Sometimes tricks are used.

An example of some of these practices was revealed in court testimony concerning Siemens-Allis, Inc., a company that had opened a plant for the assembly of small motors in Little Rock, Arkansas, in 1970.[14] The plant's machine shop and assembly departments were mostly male. On the other hand, most employees in the electrical department were female. The few males in the electrical department were in certain jobs always assigned to males but that, testimony showed, women could do without difficulty. The judge found persuasive "evidence of a pattern and practice of discrimination in job assignment and steering." The pay in the electrical department was lower than in the other two departments.

The firm, being a government contractor, had written an affirmative-action plan (see chapter 7) whose official purpose was to plan the firm's move toward more adequate representation of women and blacks in all departments and in supervisory positions. The plan document was itself an expression of snide sexism: It claimed that the concentration of women in the electrical department was not discriminatory because:

> There are some things about the job that appeal to the females such as: clean working conditions, routine work, which once learned, gives the female the opportunity to plan the family budget, menu and other responsibilities directly related to family ties.

Apparently some women were willing to give up the routine but low-paid work in the electrical department but had difficulty being assigned or transferred to the machine department. Linda Parker, who had brought the discrimination suit, testified she had asked to be assigned there when she was hired, because she knew the pay was best there, but had been assigned to the electrical department. Jean Smith, another woman in the electrical department, testified that she made an effort to bid on a promotion in the machine shop. Her supervisor took her to the machine shop and showed her the heaviest machine in the department. He told her she would have to lift it to do the job. She later learned that a hoist was used to lift it.

Linda Parker had been the first woman ever promoted to foreman in the Siemens-Allis plant, and at the time of the lawsuit the only one. Despite Parker's six years of superior performance in the foreman position, the plant's production manager had harassed her continually in front of her subordinates and ended up by demoting her to the position she had occupied ten years previously.

The exclusion of women from a job on the fraudulent ground that the work is heavy is apparently common. A woman who three times applied to the state of New Hampshire for a job on the meter patrol was asked whether she could wield a sledgehammer or had construction experience, neither of which had any relation to the job.[15] Bielby and Barron found it a common practice to classify jobs as "light" or "heavy," with women automatically excluded from the latter regardless of their strength. A job might be defined as "heavy work" if it involved lifting one heavy object (perhaps the weight of a five-year-old child) per day. This assignment system may be a hangover from the era (legally ended by the Civil Rights Act of 1964) when protective legislation closed many jobs to women, ostensibly for their own good. However, whatever its origins, the system of labeling jobs as "light" or "heavy" has the effect in many shops of completely excluding women from jobs they would be capable of doing. Of course, the jobs labeled "heavy" are paid at a substantially higher rate.

Sex bias regarding tools or machinery may create a problem for women. It is not surprising that the space between rungs on ladders should be more comfortable for the average man than the average women. Women are not the only ones affected by the overstandardization of equipment; smaller-than-average men also have difficulty. Even cheap items such as scissors are easily available only in right-handed versions.

WOMEN IN "MEN'S JOBS"

If an occasional woman does manage to land a "man's job," the men who resent her incursion may employ tactics against her designed to dislodge her—to get her fired or get her to quit. Not all men feel or act this way. The strength of the exclusionary sentiment varies from job to job, industry to industry, man to man. But enough men do feel this way to create a serious barrier to integration in many establishments. The lack of serious sanctions against such behavior in most workplaces allows it to continue.

In the cases where a woman is assigned to a "man's job," her treatment by coworkers and possibly by supervisors may be designed to prevent her from doing the job well. Regardless of the job, each new worker requires some help from coworkers to get started. She requires help in learning aspects of the work that are undocumented, in dealing with problems that come up in any new job, and she needs to get hints about peculiarities of the work process and the administrative procedures. Where there are multiperson tasks, she needs to be given a chance to learn to cooperate as a team member. If her fellow workers refuse to give that help and instead surround her with an unrelentingly hostile environment, then her productivity, her morale, and her chance of survival on the job may be low.

Male workers may worry that just as a neighborhood can go from white to black, a job can go from male to female. When the first black family buys a house in a white neighborhood, the householders worry that the neighborhood will "tip over" into being all-black and possibly become a slum as well. The male worker who sees the first woman come onto the work floor may anticipate that his occupation is on the way to becoming part of the low-paying female ghetto.* The first black family in a neighborhood may get stones thrown into its picture window, a fire set under its porch, and its children roughed up. The first woman in a "man's job" may experience hostility, sexual harassment, even life-threatening violence. Men who might be inclined toward a liberal attitude may themselves be treated as outcasts if they

---

* In a large organization the firm will find another place for him, but even so, the process is likely to upset his ego.

display it openly. The result may be that no one will make the new woman on the job welcome, no one will help her to learn the ropes, as would routinely be done for a new male colleague.

SEXUAL HARASSMENT

Sexual harassment of women in the workplace plays an important part in keeping males and females segregated. The definition of sexual harassment given by the Working Women's Institute is ". . . any attention of a sexual nature in the context of the work situation which has the effect of making a woman uncomfortable on the job, impeding her ability to do her work or interfering with her employment opportunities. It can be manifested by looks, touches, jokes, innuendoes, gestures, epithets or direct propositions. . . . [by a] direct demand for sexual compliance coupled with the threat of firing if a woman refuses . . . [by] being forced to work in an environment in which, through various means such as sexual slurs and/or the public display of derogatory images of women . . . a woman is subjected to stress or made to feel humiliated because of her sex."[16]

Surveys reveal that a large proportion of women workers experience sexual harassment. Of women workers for the federal government, 42 percent reported having been sexually harassed on the job in the two years previous to the survey.[17]

Women in traditionally female occupations often suffer sexual harassment by superiors. The male boss pressures the female underling for sexual favors, sometimes as a condition of holding the job. He wants the favors partly for their own sake and partly for their demonstration of his superior status and his ability to get her to do what he wants.[18] Sometimes the sexual harassment of a woman in a typically female job is done to show her and her coworkers that she is always a sex object and so cannot be a serious competitor of men. It has the function of keeping her off balance and cooling out any hopes she might have of moving into a job like the harasser's. Here is the experience of one young woman working in the accounting department of a carpet company:

> When I first came to this company, I was introduced to the rest of the office workers as well as the salesmen. When introduced to the head salesman, for whom I do some work, one of the first things he said was, "Oh, good, she's got big boobs." As this was said in front of many of my coworkers, comments about me regarding this physical characteristic are very common.
>
> Once another salesman came up behind me, unzipped his pants, and poked a blunt object in my thigh. This incident was also witnessed by many of my coworkers, and my audible reaction was the topic of conversation for many months.
>
> I believe actions like that have caused me to be held back from promotions and raises. The reason is that many times when I am trying to make a point to one of the salesmen, he might interject with a comment about my physical attributes that has nothing to do with the work. I feel that these comments are timed to be used whenever I am beginning to take control of a work situation and the male coworker feels threatened. This type of comment takes away from my credibility and "puts me in my place." In particular, at one time I asked to take the place of a part-time salesman who was leaving for another job. The salespeople make a lot more money than the office workers, and all the salespeople are men, while most of the office workers are women. The owner laughed when I asked for this position and said, "We need you girls in the back office."*

Testimony in a sex-discrimination lawsuit against The Hertz Corporation brought out that there had been, in the judge's words, a "history of vulgar and indecent language tolerated by management and directed toward women employees. The proof is clear that the order of the day at Hertz was for supervisory men employees to address questions about sexual activity and preference to women rental representatives." The judge gave as an example of an impermissible remark, "Did you get any over the weekend?" The company's defense was that most of the women employees encourage and invite that kind of language. It further argued that the use of sexual questions and comments by managers is not inappropriate. However, the judge found such behavior to be sex discrimination. The women who complained about these remarks had been trying unsuccessfully to move up to supervisory positions themselves (see following material).[19]

---

* This account appeared in a term paper of a student of mine, Deborah J. Wigler. Many of my women students report that they are laughed at when they ask to be considered for promotions to male-dominated positions, or when they ask to do things not usually done on the job by women, such as driving an automobile. The rationalization that women are "needed" for clerical positions and therefore cannot be considered for other jobs is apparently common.

The sexual harassment of women already in male-dominated occupations appears to take the form of insults, which may include mock
propositions to engage in sexual relations. Such behavior appears to be
motivated by a desire to wound and embarrass the woman, to demonstrate the men's contempt for her unfeminine behavior in invading
their territory, to show her that they will not accept her as "one of
the boys," and out of a hope that she will be made sufficiently uncomfortable to abandon the job.[20] This kind of behavior has occurred on
construction sites and on the premises of coal mines. It has also been
complained of in less *macho* contexts—by federal air-traffic controllers
and by women professionals at Harvard University and the Massachusetts Institute of Technology.

People who run surveys of sexual harassment tend to classify the
kinds of harassment into more severe or less severe varieties. They
classify the sexual teasing, jokes, remarks, and questions endured by
the woman in the carpet company and by the Hertz rental agents in
the "less severe" category.[21] In a physical sense such behavior is less
severe than blackmailing a woman to engage in sexual intercourse or
raping her. However, such "less severe" harassment helps to maintain
occupational segregation and can have seriously negative results for
women's careers.

PROMOTIONAL OPPORTUNITIES ON THE JOB

Economists have dubbed the structure of promotion opportunities and
wages within a workplace the "internal labor market."[22] The internal
labor market has formal and informal rules of operation that establish
who can make a serious bid for each of the jobs above entry level. In
most large work establishments, the possibilities of promotion depend
on the job a worker has. From some jobs, relatively long "promotion
ladders" lead upward, with the possibilities of promotion to the upper
echelon. Still other jobs have either short promotion ladders or are
dead-end. Typically male jobs tend to have longer ladders than typically
female jobs, and at least some of the male jobs lead to the upper eche-

lons, while no female jobs may do so. Even if a woman has a job of the type from which men can be promoted up the ladder, the rules operating in the internal labor market in the place she works may make her ineligible for further advancement.

A classic case of differences in promotion possibilities for men and women came to light as a result of a sex discrimination lawsuit against Liberty Mutual Insurance Company.* The firm had two jobs for which it hired new college graduates; one of the jobs was called "claims adjuster" and the other "claims representative." No particular experience and no particular college major were required for either job. Most male graduates were placed in the adjuster jobs, from which a promotion was possible to a position called "claims supervisor" (see figure 5–1). From there, further promotion might be obtained to a series of managerial jobs, with possibilities of further promotion to still higher management positions.

The insurance company treated the female college graduates very differently. Substantially all of them were placed in the "claims representative" job, which paid several thousand dollars less than the claims adjuster's job. From the claims representative job a series of two promotions was possible, to jobs with supervisory responsibility over the female representatives. There, however, the promotion possibilities for the women came to a dead end.†

This example makes clear the connections among occupational segregation by sex, low promotion possibilities for women, and the absence of women in the upper reaches of the hierarchy. It also suggests that the human-capital theory—the idea that it is only a person's education and training, and not their sex or race, that affect their wage— does a poor job of explaining a case of this sort. The new "representatives" and "adjusters" came on the job with identical human capital yet got different wages. Moreover, the male adjusters were being groomed for possible promotion to middle-level and higher-level management jobs, so that in all likelihood their jobs offered more valu-

* *Wetzel v. Liberty Mutual Insurance Company,* 9 FEP Case 219. The evidence brought forth in the suit refers to the late 1960s, but more recent cases against other companies reveal that discrimination in promotion still is a problem.

† Paradoxically, this kind of setup sometimes may result in more rapid rate of promotions for the women than for the men in the company, although all of the women's promotions will be from one low-level job to another. Turnover among the dead-ended female "claims representative supervisors" may be higher than among the male "claims supervisors."

FIGURE 5-1
Liberty Mutual Insurance Company Claims Department—
Technical Employees' Lines of Supervision and Promotion

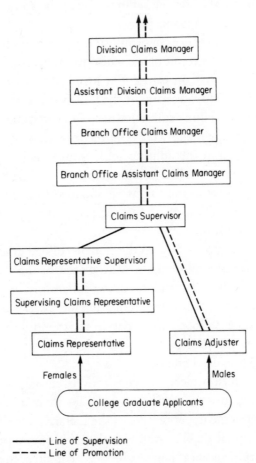

SOURCE: *Wetzel* v. *Liberty Mutual Insurance Company.* Diagram represents situation prior to 1970.

able training, more autonomy, and better contacts with higher-ups than the claims representative's job.*

The female college graduate employee obviously creates something

---

* A died-in-the-wool human-capital theorist would say the adjuster was "investing in himself" more than the representative was "investing in herself," but the facts of the case make such a locution ridiculous because the company made all the decisions as to who got which job. Since the company was allowing the male adjusters to acquire human capital faster than the female representatives, the men should in theory have "paid" for this by receiving lower wages than the women. In fact, they were paid at a higher scale. This example shows that the human capital theory misses essential issues in cases of wage differentials involving women and men.

TABLE 5–1

Promotion of Blue-Collar Workers
at the Western Electric Co. plant in Kearny, N.J.

	Persons Promoted		Percentage Of	
Promoted to Grade	Males	Females	Females in Feeder Grades	Promotions Going to Females
33	235	329	85.5	58.3
34	391	143	55.5	26.8
35	302	19	24.1	5.9
36	201	5	7.5	2.4
37	160	2	1.1	1.2
38	42	0	1.7	0.0
39	9	0	0.4	0.0

SOURCE: Judge Stern's decision in *Kyriazi* v. *Western Electric Co.*, 461 F. Supp. 894 (1978). The table aggregates data from four years shown separately in the judge's opinion. The percentage of females in feeder grades shown in the table is the simple average of such yearly percentages. Data refers to the period January 1973–December 1976.

of a problem for the establishment that wants to keep the upper part of its hierarchy all-male but does not want to appear to be discriminating. The common response, apparently, is to hire very few of them and to put the ones who are hired into positions that have no obvious next step up. A study done in the late 1970s on personnel practices in the New York State government showed the prevalence of sex-segregated promotion ladders, with women's ladders shorter than men's. The very shortest were those that college-educated women were on.[23]

We have detailed statistics on promotions by sex in the Western Electric Company for the period 1973–76, thanks to court records. (See table 5–1, which gives data on blue-collar promotions from one grade to another at the company's Kearny, N.J., plant.) Almost all entry to higher grades was through promotion. More women than men were promoted from grade 32, the lowest grade, to the next higher grade. But in that grade, and at the next three higher grades, men had a much better chance at promotion than women did. For example, women had 24.1 percent of the jobs in grades eligible for promotion to grade 35, but got only 5.9 percent of the promotions to that grade. Thus the likelihood that a woman would be promoted to grade 35 from grade 34 was about one fourth that for a man. A woman's chance to progress from grade 32 to grade 36 was 3 percent of a man's chance. This meant, of course, that women were very rare in grades 36 and above. Promotions to grade 37 and above were "fair" in the sense that women were promoted in approximate proportion to their availability among those considered eligible (almost nil), but this was virtually meaningless in view of the barriers to women's advancement in grades 33–35.

In his opinion on the case, which found that Western Electric had systematically discriminated against women, the judge said of these promotion records:

> This disparity is not explained by seniority, by job qualifications or by occupation . . . [F]emales had substantially greater seniority than males in each grade. The job specifications for the higher-graded positions reveal that the only skills, knowledge or experience required are attainable through experience in Western's lower graded jobs. Moreover, even within the so-called "women's occupations," positions within the higher grades are filled primarily by men. Thus women do not even progress within the occupations into which they have been segregated.[24]

The company's explanation of the lack of promotion for women was that women were simply not interested in being promoted. Supervisors frequently gave that reason to the personnel department for passing over particular women. Thanks to pressure from federal and state antidiscrimination agencies, supervisors were told at one point to start documenting this expressed lack of interest in every instance in which it occurred. But when asked to produce these documents in court, the company replied that not one of the four hundred to five hundred supervisors had provided documentation for a single instance in which a woman had expressed a lack of interest in a promotion. The company's explanation for that was that all of the supervisors had simply forgot.

A more recent case, against the Hertz Corporation,[25] involved the denial of promotions to two women who were car rental agents. They had applied for promotion to station manager on four occasions when vacancies had to be filled. They were turned down four times and the vacancies given to men, some of whom had less experience. The judge started his opinion by saying that the case presented "a disgusting saga in employer-employee relations." He went on to say that Hertz has a long history of discriminating against women and that "a cadre of male management preferred men in management positions at Hertz and disfavored the promotions of women." (p. 125) Although most of the Hertz rental agents are women, and although experience as a rental agent qualified a person to become station manager, very few women had been promoted at Hertz. Those few had been forced to struggle or to file charges to get promotions. Hertz's city manager in Memphis, who was responsible for denying the promotions to the two women who had brought the lawsuit, had been overheard to say that a woman should not be station manager because a woman could not go away for training, because a woman could not follow irate men customers into the men's rest room, and because a woman's place was in the kitchen.

In the Hertz case as in many others, we may speculate whether the "cadre of male management" well and truly represent the firm or are acting as freebooters against basic company policy. In this case, cross-examination of witnesses revealed that high officials of the firm had induced an employee to sign a false statement denying that the city manager had made sexist statements. They also induced one of the previously promoted women managers to sign a statement condemning the women plaintiffs' abilities, when in fact she thought they were both able and qualified for promotion. These false statements were recanted under oath. All this suggests that the resources of the firm were mobilized to back up managers it knew to be discriminatory rather than to treat women employees fairly.

The rental-agent job at Hertz was not perceived as a dead end, at least by some of the women who occupied it, because the next job up involved similar duties plus additional management duties. However, many clerical jobs are currently thought of as a dead end, perhaps because their male bosses do not share any of their duties. Nevertheless, a secretary's job can be a strategic place to learn a considerable amount concerning the business of the establishment. In the nineteenth century, men in clerical jobs were offered possibilities of promotion, but the practice of promoting clerks ended when women entered the field. A secretary may know more about her boss's job than the male hired from the outside to occupy that position. Not infrequently she will have to help to train him, covering for his mistakes as he learns.

ALLOCATING JOBS TO THE MALE
AND FEMALE TERRITORIES

Given that we have occupational segregation, what determines the sex identity of each job? How and why does the assignment get perpetuated? One favorite idea of stand-pat economists led by Solomon W. Polachek, who see no harm in the present situation and oppose government intervention, is that women themselves have chosen certain occupations as particularly advantageous to them.[26] The typical women's occupations are low paying, but a person can enter and exit and then reenter without having to take a deep cut in pay. The falsity of the argument that women have chosen the lowest paying jobs for their own economic advantage was exposed by sociologist Paula England.[27] Working with data on wages, she proved that a person who drops into and out of the work force would get no advantage from choosing the typical women's occupations for the simple reason that the pay in such jobs is so low. Granted, the pay in typically female occupations drops relatively little when a person leaves the labor force and reenters. But there would be greater advantage to taking a typically male job, with a male-level salary, even if it carries penalties for intermittent participation.

Sociologist Valerie K. Oppenheimer, writing in 1969, suggested that women are assigned to jobs and assign themselves to jobs that are reminiscent of the tasks they do as housewives.[28] There is certainly a large element of truth to this hypothesis. The idea that women were suited to care for young children surely facilitated their entry into elementary-teaching assignments. Nursing was something that women had done on an amateur basis in the home. The detachment of the clerical occupation from the realm of male jobs, which occurred in the late nineteenth century, may have been facilitated by the evident ease of refashioning it from a management trainee job into a dead-end helpmeet job.

On the other hand, the shift of clerical jobs from the men's side to the women's seems to have been triggered by the introduction of a mechanical device—the typewriter. The housewife analogy does not do a very good job explaining the shift of the bank-teller occupation;

it was previously thought that tellers had to be male because males knew more about financial matters and were more businesslike.[29] Nor does the assignment of most restaurant cooking jobs to men seem consistent with it.

Another set of explanations listed by Oppenheimer are probably closer to the heart of the matter. Employers avoid having women in jobs where they are supervising men, in mixed groups, or in jobs that might be expected to lead to supervisory positions over men. The key to this set of explanations is the unequal social relations between the sexes in society at large, which carries over to inequality in the workplace.*

A major reason for occupational segregation by sex is that employers tend to keep women out of jobs with on-the-job training opportunities. They save for men those jobs in which the workers learn things that would give them competence for more advanced jobs.[30] The common rationalization is that women have greater turnover, and that an employer's investment in a woman's training is more likely to be lost, as she is more likely to quit. However, the perceptions of differences in turnover behavior between men and women appear to be false. Studies of turnover rates have shown that if women and men in similar jobs are compared, women have turnover rates little different from those of men.[31]

When employers pay attention to group averages, their behavior is sometimes called "statistical discrimination." The employer may know that there are individual women who if given the chance would perform and persist as well or better than the average man. But the employer rules out all women because of a belief that the *average* male candidate is a better bet than the *average* female candidate. Thus membership in what is thought to be a low-performing group destroys opportunities for individuals whose behavior may be very different from the average. Whether the perception of difference in averages is,

* Another of Oppenheimer's suggestions is that women lack motivation (p. 111). Still another of her suggestions is that women's occupations are those in which the employer has a "need for cheap but educated labor" but cannot attract qualified men who will work for low wages (p. 99). The latter is an entirely specious argument based on the mistaken idea that wages are fixed in each occupation by some unspecified process, after which employers sit back and wait to see whether men turn up for the job. As we shall see in following material, it is the assignment of a sex identity to each job that determines each job's wage, not the other way around. If an employer decides to let women into certain jobs that have been occupied by males, the wage will be reduced.

as in the turnover case, false, or whether it is correct, statistical discrimination hurts individuals because of their sex, and is illegal under U.S. law (see chapter 7).

A SEGREGATION CODE IN PERSONNEL ADMINISTRATION

If an employer is set on avoiding situations where women and men are required to act in ways that disregard the subordination of women, then the kinds of jobs that women can have in an establishment are limited. These limitations derive from the taboo on women supervising men, or even acting as equals. Moreover, for each "man's job" that is not on the entry level but requires prior experience within the establishment, training slots at lower levels must be kept for men. This involves further limitations on the jobs women can have.[32]

These limitations form a kind of "segregation code" for personnel administration: (1) avoidance of mixing of men and women where they must interact as equals, (2) avoidance of female supervisors for men, and (3) the reservation of training slots for male candidates for upper-level men's jobs. The code restricts the use of female labor more severely than might be thought. The operation of these limitations and their effect on assignment of jobs by sex can be illustrated by the example of an "internal labor market" shown in figure 5–2. (Unlike the real case shown in figure 5–1 the establishment in figure 5–2 is hypothetical, although not unrealistic.) The firm is shown as having two kinds of operatives, each group having a supervisor, who reports in turn to a low-level executive with "line" functions (IA). The latter reports to a higher-level executive. There is another low-level executive with "staff" functions (IB), who also reports to the higher-level executive. Each of the executives has a secretary. In addition, there are craft workers who fix the machines on which the operatives work and who must interact on an equal basis with the supervisors of the operatives. The craft workers pass through a period as apprentices. Figure 5–2

FIGURE 5-2
Which Jobs Can Women Have in This Organization?

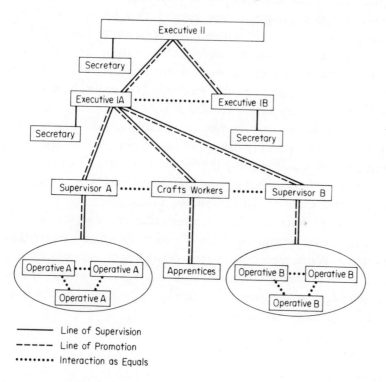

shows lines of supervision, lines of promotion, and lines between jobs in which the workers must interact as equals.

Consider the problem posed for the management of this establishment. It may have an incentive to set up an occupational pattern that will yield a low labor cost, but it also wants to avoid male-female interaction problems. The consideration of low cost suggests that women be used in as many jobs as possible. However, the constraints posed by the interaction problems suggest little use of women. Limitation 1 means that if any occupation is opened to a particular sex, then all members of that occupation must be of that group. Limitation 2 suggests that the most likely slots for women are entry-level positions, which include the operatives, the secretaries, and the apprentices. Limitation 3 suggests that jobs at all levels must be reserved for the sex that is to be given the top-echelon jobs, to provide adequate training opportunities for successors to the present incumbents.

We can start off by assuming that the top executive is likely to be a male, given current ideas about leadership, and the set of persons available with the requisite experience. It then follows from Limitation 3 that Executive IA or Executive IB or both must be male. If Executive IA is male, then one of the supervisors and all of the operatives under that supervisor must also be male. If the crafts are unionized, they are also likely to be male, and this establishes the male character of Executive IA with some certainty, and of the craft apprentices.

This leaves for the women remarkably few jobs—one set of the operatives' jobs, possibly the job of supervisor of those operatives, the secretarial jobs, and possibly the "staff" executive's job. However, the necessity for interactions as equals between Executives IA and IB may suggest that the latter also should be a male job.

This outcome does have features that are observed in reality. If women are in management, they tend to be in staff rather than line positions. Women professionals do tend to be on very short promotion ladders. Moreover, the number of occupations identified as female is considerably smaller than the number identified as male (see table A–1 in appendix A).

TRAINING PREREQUISITES

Some jobs require formal education or training in school prior to starting on the job. If women do not take such training, they cannot present themselves as credible candidates for these jobs. In some cases, discrimination in admissions by schools excluded many women better qualified than men actually admitted. Elite medical and law schools have until recent years behaved in this way. Quotas for women students have in recent years been relaxed and outright exclusions repealed, but it is likely that some discriminatory exclusions continue.

On most college campuses, women still tend to distribute themselves differently among majors than men do, although the differences are lessening. However, the importance of specialized training can be exaggerated. Most male-dominated jobs that recruit college graduates do not require a specific college major. Accounting and engineering constitute the bulk of the male-dominated jobs that do have such a specific schooling prerequisite. Currently women are getting more than one third of undergraduate accounting degrees.

Only engineering, which accounts for 7 percent of college graduates and 2 percent of the full-time labor force, remains overwhelmingly male. Women have increased their participation in engineering, from almost nil in 1960 to 11 percent in 1982. However, women's participation is far lower in engineering than it is in undergraduate mathematics, or in medicine, dentistry, or law (see table 3–3). Perhaps part of the problem is that engineering is the only college major set up so that a student cannot try out an introductory course and then shift in as a sophomore or a junior. One must make a total commitment in high school, at a time when many female students have no information about the field and in any case are under intense social pressure to act in a feminine way.

Jobs that require apprenticeships or other lengthy on-the-job training appear to all intents and purposes to be closed to women.[33] Where employers designate which workers are to be given training, they exclude women disproportionately if not entirely. Where unions are involved in apprenticeship programs, they appear to be particularly resistant to women. Upper limits on the age of apprentice candidates serve to exclude women, many of whom do not awaken to their need for a job with a "family wage" until their late twenties or early thirties. While the law schools, medical schools, and business schools of the United States have enrolled considerable numbers of women students in the past decade, high-school industrial-arts teachers and administrators have managed to keep their student bodies preparing for the male-dominated craft jobs remarkably free of women. These teachers sometimes are called on to propose candidates for apprenticeships, and women cannot get referred through such channels.

CONSEQUENCES OF OCCUPATIONAL SEX SEGREGATION

Occupational segregation affects the demand and supply of labor to each occupation and therefore affects wage levels in the "women's jobs." However, the consequences of occupational segregation go beyond money, important though that is. Having a majority of the job titles effectively off-limits to half the population has costs in terms of human expression and human dignity. Some of the means used to enforce occupational segregation also rob women of their dignity.

Occupational sex segregation means that certain talents and aptitudes do not get expressed; that some people have to spend their lives doing things they hate, when a chance to compete for jobs they would have liked better should and could have been open to them. It reinforces the very system of female subordination that motivates it. Women's situation apart from the workplace is made more difficult because of the reduced options that occupational sex segregation entails.

Productivity considerations have an important part in the generation and maintenance of occupational sex segregation. If and when a significant proportion of the nation's establishments are induced to make an effort to break the tradition of "men's jobs" and "women's jobs," there may be short-run losses in productivity. However, in the longer run productivity should improve. The wastage of women's talent will diminish, and fewer jobs requiring discretion will be in the hands of relatively less able men.

The remedy for occupational segregation by sex and race is affirmative action—a conscious program by employers to end the reservation of certain jobs for white men. After looking at the effects of occupational sex segregation on wages, we shall turn to a discussion of the problems and promises of affirmative action.

CHAPTER 6

Why Are Women's
Wages Low?

THE WAGE a person is paid depends to a considerable extent on the job he or she lands. Women with secretarial jobs averaged $279 a week in 1985. Men who held jobs as dispatchers averaged quite a lot more—$388.* The market, one might say, decided that male dispatchers should get 39 percent more than female secretaries. In that same year, the market decided that women with jobs as dispatchers should get $280, just about the same pay as female secretaries. Wage rates determined in the marketplace by supply and demand are commonly thought of as reasonable, right, and fair in an economic sense. Supply and demand don't sound as though they have anything to do with gender. But the example of the dispatchers suggests that they do. The demand for labor is, after all, in the hands of the people responsible for hiring, placing, and promoting. And many of those people discriminate by sex.

Qualifications are an important part of the supply-and-demand story. You cannot be part of the supply for a particular job unless you

---

* See table 6–1 for source.

have the education, knowledge, talent, and devotion a worker must bring to that job. If a job requires lots of human capital—expensively acquired training and experience—then many people will be excluded from consideration as serious candidates for that job. Another part of the supply-and-demand story is people's opinions about jobs. You may decline to become part of the supply of labor to an occupation if, given the pay, you consider that the duties are too difficult or highly uncongenial.

But there is more to the supply-and-demand story than human capital or preferences for one job over another. Your sex determines whether you are in demand for certain jobs. To put it another way, your sex (your race and your age) may determine whether an employer, looking to fill a particular vacancy, sees you as part of the supply of candidates worthy of consideration. The data suggest, for example, that employers with vacancies for dispatchers who are offering $388 are looking only for male candidates.

JOB CHARACTERISTICS AND PAY LEVELS

To make a good guess about the wage a job pays, you would have to know the amount of education one had to have before getting that job, and the degree of specialized knowledge, talent, and intelligence needed to perform it effectively. If you knew all of those obviously important things about the job, but only them, you would still be likely to make a big mistake in guessing the wage. To be sure of making a really good guess, you would have to know in addition whether the job in question was occupied by a man or a woman.

The human capital the job requires—the value of the qualifications—does affect the pay for a job. But it is not the sole determinant. An examination of weekly wage rates by occupation by sex reported in table 6–1 bears this out. The table lists 24 occupations that pay women less on average than women who are secretaries get, arranged in descending order of women's pay. We can infer that the occupations toward the bottom of the list require less human capital than the oc-

TABLE 6–1

Average Weekly Wages for Women and Men in
Twenty-Five Narrowly Defined Occupations, 1985

Occupation	Women	Men
Secretaries	$278	$365
Stock and Inventory Clerks	$265	$326
Bookkeepers, Accounting, and Auditing Clerks	263	341
Expediters	257	413
Machinists	257	408
Bus Drivers	257	404
General Office Clerks	255	323
Cost and Rate Clerks	254	483
Sales Workers, Furniture, and Home Furnishings	252	307
Grinding, Abrading, Buffing Machine Operators	251	330
Production Inspectors, Checkers, Examiners	249	406
Traffic, Shipping, and Receiving Clerks	247	305
Electrical and Electronic Equipment Assemblers	243	284
Packaging and Filling Machine Operators	234	286
Printing Machine Operators	225	363
Molding and Casting Machine Operators	222	347
Painting and Paint Spraying Machine Operators	218	313
Solderers and Braziers	216	287
Photographic Process Machine Operators	208	297
Butchers and Meat Cutters	204	326
Bakers	202	301
Truck Drivers, Light	200	281
Slicing and Cutting Machine Operators	192	303
Hotel Clerks	191	279
Sales Workers, Apparel	168	281

NOTE: These figures are estimates of medians of usual weekly earnings of employed wage and salary workers who usually work full time. They are based on data collected by the Bureau of the Census for the Bureau of Labor Statistics, but the medians have been computed on a basis that differs slightly from the method used to produce the official BLS estimates. Moreover, BLS does not officially issue figures on wages for groups of less than 50,000, while some of the wages quoted in the table are for groups of size 19,000–50,000. Wage estimates included in the table have a standard error of estimate of less than 10 percent.

cupations at the top of the list. An examination of the titles certainly suggests that. For example, a clothing sales worker does not need the typing skills or literacy of a secretary, her organizing ability, her tact, her ability to learn some aspects of the job of her boss. In fact, people who sell clothing perform duties that require about an hour or so to learn. So the 40 percent pay gap between the woman selling clothing and the woman secretary can easily be understood as a payment for the human capital of the latter.

The occupations listed in table 6–1 are quite narrowly defined. For this reason we can be fairly sure that the male workers in them have jobs that have similar duties to the jobs the female workers have. Thus the men's jobs probably require about the same human capital as the women's jobs under the same job title.

The men in all the occupations listed in table 6–1 average more pay than the women secretaries. Even when we look at jobs toward the bottom of the table, which have human-capital requirements considerably lower than those of the secretarial job, the men in such jobs get more pay than women secretaries. Why is that?

The pay scales reported in table 6–1 certainly would make some people suspect sex discrimination. But those who resist that explanation can certainly bring forth others. Perhaps the men have more experience than the women. They probably do, on average. But most analyses have shown that differences in length of experience account for very little of the pay gap between men and women.[1] Moreover, with a few exceptions, we would not expect workers in the occupations listed in table 6–1 to become more productive with prolonged experience. After five or ten years on the job, a hotel clerk is not going to be any more productive than a hotel clerk who has been on the job a week or so. Thus we would not expect workers in those occupations to differ much in pay as a result of differences in experience. (Those workers who progress in pay with experience are those who progress to higher-level jobs than the ones listed here—jobs with supervisory responsibilities, for example.)

Perhaps the men work longer hours, or nights, and that accounts for their higher pay. The table reports wages only for full-time workers. However, more overtime for the men may account for part of the pay gap between men and women in the same occupation. But again, studies show that women's voluntary restrictions on hours account for very little of the pay gap between men and women.[2] Perhaps the men are working in higher-paying businesses, or are union members. But then why aren't the women there right along with them, unless discrimination is keeping women out of the higher-paying businesses and out of the unionized shops?

Solomon Polachek conjectures that the sex gap in wages is due to women's choice of jobs that are easy to leave and reenter.[3] Those jobs, he says, happen to be low-paying. But that conjecture does not help us much in explaining the differences in pay between men and women in the same occupation. A job as driver of a light truck probably is easy to drop out of and return to. Very little human capital is likely to rust during the break in service. But it is hard to believe that women coming back to work after having a baby purposely look for the truck jobs that pay $200 rather than the ones that pay $281. Yet it is the lower-paying ones that the figures in table 6–1 suggest they consistently find.

Gary S. Becker has conjectured that differences in pay between men and women are in considerable part due to housework differences between the sexes. That does not work too well here, either. Women workers, he says, are tired from doing all the family's housework, while men come to their jobs fresh from their rest and recreation.[4] It is hard to believe, though, that female operators of slicing and cutting machines make $192 and male operators of slicing and cutting machines make $303 because the males, being less tired, do a better job of slicing and cutting.

A far better explanation of why men with less valuable qualifications than female secretaries—less human capital—get more pay than female secretaries is that men and women are not competing in the same market. Men and women are selling themselves and their human capital in segregated markets, a separate market for each sex. Supply and demand in the men's market decrees one set of wages. Supply and demand in the women's market decrees a whole different set of wages, very much lower.

WAGES AND THE SEGREGATION OF MARKETS

The key to the low wages attached to women's jobs is the occupational segregation within a high proportion of workplaces. Many jobs are open just to men, and many others are open just to women. Some jobs—a slowly increasing number—are open to people of either sex.

Up to 1972, want ads in newspapers were sex-segregated, and very few jobs were advertised as open to both sexes. The research of Bielby and Barron suggests that as of the late 1970s more than 90 percent of jobs still were earmarked for one sex or the other.[5] Because such a high proportion of jobs are open only to people of just one sex, it makes sense to talk of a market for male labor and a substantially separate market for female labor.[6]

We speak of a market (the New York Stock Exchange, or the market for eggs, or the market for men's labor), as the "place" where the commodities that cater to a certain kind of demand are sold. Supply and demand in that market sets the price for those commodities. The market that caters to the demand for male labor fills all the jobs open only to men and dictates the wages for those jobs. Similarly, women workers sell their labor in the market that fills all the jobs open only to women and sets the wages for those jobs. (The relatively few jobs that are genuinely open to people of either sex will be discussed separately later.)

The jobs in the occupations that are all-male are filled, obviously, in the male labor market. These include the vast majority of the jobs in occupations appearing at the end of appendix table A–1 (see pp. 317–328)—mechanics, drivers of heavy trucks, those in the construction trades, supervisors of men in mostly male occupations. But there are jobs in occupations toward the middle of table A–1 that are earmarked for men and filled in the male labor market. The occupation "waiters and waitresses," which is 81 percent female, presents an obvious example. Typically a male waiting on tables does not have colleagues who are 81 percent female. Many of the restaurants that employ the 96,000 male waiters have never hired a waitress.* That pattern of sex-typing each of an occupation's jobs applies to a high proportion of occupations throughout the list. In virtually all occupations, some jobs are earmarked for men, to be filled in the male labor market.

Within the men's market, wages get set that balance the supply of men with the demand for men's labor—in jobs that have been re-

---

* Those restaurants that have hired both men and women usually have assigned them to different parts of the restaurant or different shifts, with the males getting the assignments in which the tips are higher. In 1985, full-time waiters reported they averaged $233 and full-time waitresses reported $185 (see table 6–1 for source). Also, restaurants seldom mix table servers of different races, although people of one race may bring the food and people of another race may take away the dirty dishes. Recently, some restaurants have started using males and females interchangeably.

served for men in each occupation.* Within the women's market, the same process is worked out. Within the men's and the women's labor markets, human-capital requirements affect the supply of labor to jobs in each occupation. Each market is independent of the other, at least in the short run.

The workings of supply and demand in the men's and women's labor markets put very different wages on jobs requiring similar human capital, as the wage rates in table 6–1 show. Those jobs filled in the women's market are assigned markedly lower wages than similar jobs filled in the men's market.

But why does the women's labor market ordain such low wages for the jobs open to women and for the human capital women bring to the market? The answer is that job segregation is not just a neutral and benign division of economic functions between the sexes; we are not dealing here with a case of "separate but equal." Rather, we are dealing with a segregation code in personnel administration (see chapter 5) that dictates the absence of women from most jobs that would make them the equal or the superior of males. The realities that underlie that segregation code puts pressure on employers to keep jobs for males. Obviously, under present conditions, hiring women reduces labor costs, and that is why there are jobs open to women. But if there are doubts as to which sex a particular job belongs to, the code of behavior pushes employers to resolve those doubts by giving it to a male.

Adherence to the code of behavior holds down the number of jobs that women are allowed to have. Women are fenced off from a disproportionate share of what we might call "labor-market turf." As a result, the turf assigned to them tends to be relatively overcrowded, as compared to the male share of the turf. That translates into restricted demand for labor in the women's labor market and lowers the wage levels in the jobs that are filled there. It makes the wages low in the traditionally female occupations. It also lowers the pay of the jobs that women hold in occupations that are mixed-sex and mostly male.

The law of supply and demand does affect men's and women's wages. But the supply and the demand in the markets for men's and

---

* We know from the phenomenon of unemployment that the market does not adjust wages downward to equalize the supply of labor to the demand. Employers, for reasons of morale, dislike lowering established wage rates. However, wages in particular occupations slowly realign themselves as the general wage level rises with the rise in productivity. Those occupations with excess supply tend to get lower-than-average wage increases.

women's labor are powerfully affected by discrimination. Discrimination keeps the men's and women's labor markets separate from each other. The exclusion of women from a big share of all of the jobs in the economy is what creates two labor markets where there should be only one. The discriminatory assignment of jobs, to one sex or the other is what sets the level of demand in each market. So the fact that supply and demand affect wages does not prove that wages are fair, or even economically sensible. (This argument is illustrated with supply-and-demand curves in appendix B. See pp. 329–335.)

The wage differential that discrimination engenders does more than force women to have to sell their labor at a low price; it also cuts down the efficiency of the economy. The overcrowding in the women's jobs reduces the productivity of women's labor. Discrimination reduces the size of the traditionally male occupations because it makes labor artificially expensive to hire for those occupations. By the same process, the traditionally female occupations have been enlarged because labor is artificially cheap in the women's labor market. A single sex-blind labor market would allocate labor more efficiently throughout the economy, and productivity would be higher on average.

THE STORY OF THE RELUCTANT SECRETARY

While many women try only for jobs that are obviously open to women, there are women who would like to sell their labor on the men's labor market and who make active efforts to do so. A few succeed; but many fail to connect with a job there and get shunted back into the women's market.

Through court records, we can see the defeat of the efforts of one such woman. Alice Howland applied to Sears, Roebuck & Co. and would have preferred a job selling on commission at one of their stores. At Sears, most of the commission sales jobs are held by men, and the pay they take home is commensurate with the pay in the men's market. Most of Sears' noncommission sales jobs that pay straight hourly salaries are held by women. Their pay is commensurate with wage scales in the women's labor market.

Sears claimed that the reason it has few women in commission sales is that very few women are interested in such jobs. But Howland, whose application showed considerable experience in commission sales, was not offered an interview by Sears. Here is an excerpt from a statement she wrote about it:

> If Sears had called me in for an interview, I would have told the interviewer that I was available for full-time work. Since I needed a job, I might have taken whatever was offered, but my preference definitely would not have been to sell women's clothing. It is boring and there is little to learn, and I know that there is not much money to be made in those departments. I would have preferred a commission sales job: if I am going to put in the hours, I want to be compensated as much as possible for them.
>
> I also would have preferred a commission compensation arrangement to straight salary because I do not like to have to depend on another person's decision to give me a raise for the work I have performed; I would prefer to control my earnings through my own effort.
>
> I have been informed that at Sears such products as furniture, carpeting, drapes, storm window and door, and other installed home improvements are sold on commission. I would have liked to sell any of those products. I would not have objected to making sales calls at customers' homes at all; I do not believe that working nights and having a rotating schedule would have been a problem. . . . If I am going to work, I might as well earn more money rather than less.
>
> I have been informed that Sears states that women generally do not have the capacity to compete with each other or men for sales. As far as I am concerned, that is ridiculous. I like competition.
>
> The job I ultimately found in 1978 was as a secretary. . . . I took it because that was what was available, not because I love secretarial work. In fact, I found secretarial work to have its own pressures—mostly because it is difficult to always be submissive and catering. Sharpening pencils and making coffee for people was certainly not my preferred career. One does not always have a choice, however.*

Male salesmen in the kind of work Alice Howland was hoping to get average $320 a week, compared with a secretary's $278 a week.

* This statement was given as part of the evidence in an eventually unsuccessful sex-discrimination suit against Sears filed by the Equal Employment Opportunity Commission. Sears' chief expert witness, Dr. Joan Haworth, had picked out Howland's application as an example of a woman applicant to Sears who, despite commission sales experience, was in reality not an applicant for a commission sales job. To rebut Dr. Haworth's testimony, the EEOC tracked down Alice Howland and elicited from her the statement quoted above. The judge who tried *EEOC* v. *Sears, Roebuck & Co.* accepted Sears' defense, and decided that the company had not been proved to have practiced discriminatory exclusion of women from commission sales jobs.

Howland would have liked a chance to join a mostly male sales crew. She was confident that she could do as well as they if she were allowed access to Sears customers on the same basis as they and if she were paid at the same commission rate.

Alice Howland ended up as part of the supply to the women's labor market, but not because she preferred the kinds of jobs there. She was forced there by her lack of success in landing one of the jobs filled on the men's labor market and by her need to avoid a long period of unemployment and get work. (She and her husband were supporting seven children.)

When women like Alice Howland are forced to go into the women's labor market, the wage level in that market is lowered because of the forcible increase in supply. Every woman now on the women's labor market who would be allowed into a job in the men's market would reduce the pay gap between the sexes. Her move would push the wage scales in the two markets toward equality by increasing the supply of labor to the men's market and decreasing the supply to the women's.[7]

CROWDING BASED ON EXCLUSION: A SIMPLIFIED EXAMPLE

At this point in the discussion, we want to explore carefully the connection between wage levels and the segregation of each sex into its own "labor-market turf." The crucial point is this: If a group is segregated and furthermore is crowded into a relatively narrow segment of labor-market turf, its members will as a result be less productive, and their economic rewards will be lower.

The line of argument will be made clearer if we resort to a simplified example. Consider an island inhabited by two tribes of people, the Pinks and the Blues, both of whom make their living gathering berries. We shall assume the gatherers of both tribes to be more or less equal on average in talent and energy. If all gatherers were allowed to range over the whole island, individual gatherers' yields would vary with their talent, energy, and luck. Given our assumption that the two tribes have equal average talents, the average yield per gatherer would be the same in both tribes.

However, suppose the island's territory was partitioned between the tribes, so that gatherers were allowed to pick berries only in the territory assigned to their tribe. Were each tribe assigned a share of the territory about proportional to its size, and of equal average quality per acre, then again the yield per gatherer in the two tribes should be about the same. However, suppose the Blue tribe were to be assigned exclusive possession of a disproportionately large share of territory. In that case, the work of members of the Blue tribe would on average bring in a greater yield than the work of members of the Pink tribe. If the land the Blue tribe got was higher in quality than the Pinks, the Pink tribe's disadvantage would be greater still.

The Pink and Blue workers in our example have, by assumption, identical productive potential because their personal characteristics and behavior patterns are taken to be identical. However, as a consequence of the uneven division of the territory, the Pink workers would have to exploit their territory more intensively. They would have to work on less accessible and sparser berry patches. This extra difficulty reduces their per-person take, so the Pinks would have lower productivity than the Blues.

The way things are arranged on our mythical island, no one says to a Pink worker, "Because you are a Pink, we will see to it that you get less than a Blue." The mechanism that arranges for Pinks to get less is a set of rules about who may work where. As long as everyone follows the rules and all hands keep to their place, the Pinks will average less production per person than the Blues and will take home less "pay" for their efforts.

The restriction of the Pinks to a relatively small territory reduces the efficiency of labor on the island as a whole. The total number of berries picked on the island would rise were the territorial restrictions on the Pinks to be relaxed. If some Pinks were allowed into the Blues' territory, it would relieve the overcrowding in the Pinks' part of the island. Labor would be transferred from less accessible berry patches to more accessible patches.

(In our example, a person's income is the berries they gather, so the low productivity the Pinks suffer because of territorial restrictions translates directly into lower income. In a money economy, people work in "berry patches" owned by others in return for money wages. There, low productivity also results in lower wages. This occurs when workers' low productivity is due to their lack of human capital. But it can also happen when workers are confined to a low-productivity activity, as in the case of our berrying example. In a money economy, the process is somewhat more roundabout than in the case of the simple economy of our example, but the principle at work is the same.)

If a boatload of social scientists were to visit the island portrayed in our example, they might hear from theoreticians belonging to the Blue tribe that its success was a sign of innately superior talent and greater attention to business. They might also hear that all Pinks voluntarily restricted themselves to their own territory. If, however, these social scientists observed the segregation of the two tribes, the relative smallness and low quality of the territory the Pinks worked, and the devices used to keep Pinks from infiltrating Blue territory, they might very well conclude that the inequality of rewards was connected to the exclusion of Pinks from the Blues' territory.

(Some rebellious readers may be thinking, "How about hunting? Surely the reason for the Blues' higher income is that they have a talent for hunting while the Pinks can only gather. Perhaps, also, the Pinks have time-consuming hobbies that have not been mentioned but that distract them from effective berrying." The rebellious reader wants, in short, to construct a different example about two *other* tribes and to dispense with the assumption of equal abilities and energies. Obviously, everyone is free to make up examples, and the making up proves nothing. The example of the Pinks and the Blues certainly does not prove anything about women and men and provides no evidence about them. Its function is to clarify the notion that unequal partition of the opportunities leads to unequal reward for work. The evidence about actual women and men is found in the court testimony taken in discrimination cases and in the statistical studies discussed in chapter 4.)

PRODUCTIVITY IN THE SEX-SEGREGATED
LABOR MARKET

The partitioning of the island between the Pinks and the Blues in our example is intended, of course, as an analogy to the sex segregation of the labor market. Lots of women in the labor market stick to the jobs marked out in everyone's minds as "women's jobs." But there are women like Alice Howland who would prefer the better income and the more interesting work that some jobs in the men's territory provide. Some succeed. But some are turned back to the women's territory by the exclusionary practices of employers, and some are rebuffed by the harassment of male coworkers.

On our partitioned island, the number of berries that are picked in the two territories depends on the number of people in each territory. The more crowded a territory, the more intensively will the less-accessible berry patches, which take more work to exploit, be utilized. Analogously, in the labor market, the number of jobs that actually materialize in each of the two labor markets under each job title is not fixed. The more people available in a market, the more jobs will be created, and the more people who can be accommodated with employment.

In our island, the Blues could restrict their attention to relatively productive berry patches. On the other side of the dividing line, the Pinks were forced to work the less accessible berry patches because so few of the better patches were allotted to their territory. That had the effect of lowering the Pinks' productivity. The extra women penned into the women's labor market must work at relatively low-productivity tasks if they are to be absorbed at all. To induce employers to expand the number of women employees and assign them to such tasks, wages have to be relatively low in the "women's jobs."*

The secretarial occupation provides a good example. The number of woman secretaries is not absolutely fixed by technological necessity. Within limits, every establishment has a choice as to how many sec-

---

* Although women's productivity is kept lower than men's by segregation, the productivity of workers of both sexes has tended to rise over time, thanks to the increase in the nature and quantity of productive equipment (see chapter 2).

retaries to keep on the payroll and as to what duties they are to perform. If women secretaries are cheap as compared to men with the same length of training, then the organization can have secretaries on hand to perform some relatively low-priority duties. Extra secretaries can be hired to increase the prestige of certain male workers. Or they can be kept on tap doing relatively little, just in case they are needed during busy periods.

A secretary in a job with low wages and low-priority duties has low productivity, not because she has low potential but because she has been penned into the secretarial pool by exclusion from other jobs she might have filled. The more intelligent and talented women are not allowed to compete with the more intelligent men for most of the leadership jobs and the other jobs conferring power and paying high wages. These women swell the numbers competing for jobs requiring less talent. Similarly, the women who are excluded from jobs in which one receives craft training swell the ranks of those competing for other blue-collar work. The presence of these extra people competing for the dead-end jobs lowers the wages in these poor jobs from what they would otherwise be. So the crowding hurts the less talented workers who would, even in the absence of discrimination, still be in lower-level jobs.[8]

WOMEN OUTSIDE OF THE TYPICALLY
FEMALE OCCUPATIONS

The "women's labor market" fills the jobs open to women, a high proportion of them in the traditionally female occupations. The women's labor market also fills all the jobs that have been earmarked for women in other occupations. Women also have access to a third and much smaller group of jobs—those open to workers of both sexes.

As a result of the classic labor-market research of Francine Blau,[9] we know that there are jobs outside of the mostly female occupations that are earmarked for women, and some jobs outside of the male-dominated occupations that are earmarked for men. Looking at white-collar office occupations, she found that men and women will work in the same occupation but tend not to work together in the same firms. Most firms that hire men in a particular occupation will not hire any women at all in that occupation, and firms that hire women for a particular job title will hire no men for that title. Most vacancies seem to be earmarked for one sex or the other.

When Blau looked at wage patterns, she found that the firms that hired only women in a particular occupation paid those women workers considerably lower wages than were paid by the other firms, those that hired only men for that occupation. Blau's observations suggest that the wage level for a particular job title in a particular establishment is set *after the employer decides whether those jobs will be filled by women or men.* If the firm fills jobs in an ordinarily male-identified job with men, then the employer must pay something approximating the going wage for men in that job—namely, the wage set by the men's labor market. If the firm decides to fill that group of jobs with women, it can take into consideration that fact that the women's major alternative is to get a low-paying "woman's job." Thus, when women get employed in occupations outside the traditionally female-identified jobs, their wages still are set in the same labor market in which women compete for female-identified jobs.

(The idea that employers decide on the sex of the person to be recruited before they decide on a job's pay is one we will return to when we discuss the pay equity campaign in chapter 8. Here we will simply draw attention to the fact that such a procedure combines sex discrimination in hiring with sex discrimination in pay-setting.)

When men get jobs in female-identified jobs, they have to be paid wages that are commensurate with the relatively high pay set in the male labor market for their human capital. That is why male secretaries earn $87 more a week than female secretaries (see table 6–1). Male secretaries certainly have more training and higher skills than light truck drivers or male clothing sales people, whose human capital sells for $281 on the male labor market. The latter earn just about what female secretaries get for their much greater amounts of human capital.

Those few men who do take jobs in predominantly female fields view themselves and are viewed by their employers as in line for supervisory or administrative positions. A male clerk or librarian or teacher is viewed as promotable, while a woman in such a position is viewed as a perpetual underling, at a dead end.[10] Men higher up in the organization will keep a lookout for opportunities to promote a man out of a typically female job, because his position seems to them to be an anomaly from which he needs to be rescued.[11]

Not infrequently, where men and women have the same functions, the men will be given higher pay. Studies of academic institutions have shown that women faculty have lower salaries than male faculty in the same field with the same number of years of experience.[12] Sometimes some slight difference in the jobs of men and women will be created to justify the higher male rate.

In a peculiar (and almost, but not quite, laughable) inversion of human-capital theory, higher pay for men sometimes is justified on the grounds that women are required to have higher or additional qualifications. The nurse supervisors in Denver's hospitals were paid less than male executives with similarly responsible management duties. The difference in their jobs was, according to the Denver personnel director, that the nurse supervisors had to be nurses.[13] The female jail guards in the county of Washington, Oregon, were paid less than the male jail guards. One of the reasons given was that the women guards had to do some typing. Most of the male guards probably were incapable of doing that.[14]

The rare job not earmarked for one sex or the other presents a problem for employers, and that probably is one reason why there are so few of them. The wage in the employer's mind probably is the male-level wage. If this were not the case, the employer could not expect qualified men to be interested in it. When and if a very well-qualified woman candidate shows up, the employer may want to offer her the job but is tempted to do so at a lower wage. If that happens, that woman has in effect been shunted back to the women's labor market, and the job itself has been shifted from the male to the female labor market.

However, there are dangers to the employer in such an approach. The employer is open to a lawsuit charging discrimination if the woman employee finds out that she has male colleagues in the same type of job who are being paid at a higher scale. Lawsuits on such grounds are far more common than suits filed by women not hired or not promoted, and such suits fare better in the courts.

The record of the discrimination suit that Patricia Scott brought against a firm called Océ Industries illustrates the situations that arise when men and women work at the same functions at different salaries.[15] In 1975, Scott was a secretary at Océ Industries. She was promoted to assistant credit manager (ACM). Her predecessor in the job, a man named Ron Norton, had been given a starting salary of $12,000, with a promise of an increase after four to six months if he performed well. However, Ron Norton had not performed well and had been let go. Scott was given his job, but at a salary of $9,460. Scott's work was rated "excellent" and "outstanding." By 1976, her salary had been increased to $11,544. In that year John Gonzales was hired as an assistant credit manager at $15,500 and the following year received a raise to $17,000.

Scott asked for a raise and brought up the disparity between her salary and that of Gonzales. Her supervisor told her she was at a dead end at Océ and didn't need to worry about her salary because she was just going to get married and have children. (The judge in this case remarked that the women ACMs' situations "reflect a viewpoint on the part of Océ's relevant supervisory personnel that a male ACM was an ACM, while a female ACM was little more than a glorified secretary.")

When Patricia Scott compared her pay to a man's and indicated she wanted similar treatment, her supervisor, who had been friendly, turned on her. After her salary request, the treatment of Scott underwent a sharp change. She was stripped of duties, other workers were told to shun her, and a memorandum was drafted to build a case that she was incompetent and uncooperative. Her boss said to her he had been "told I can't fire you, but I can certainly make it tough so you quit." He succeeded.

Patricia Scott's case provides an insight into the problems that women workers face when they stand up for their rights to equitable treatment, and why so few do so. It also provides an insight into the problems firms have when they ease segregation. Scott's bosses could not bring themselves to regard or pay her as they would a man. The result was months of bad feeling, the loss of an employee who might have remained an excellent secretary, and a lawsuit.*

* One of my students reported a situation in some respects the reverse of the Scott case. In the newly established retail stores selling and renting video tapes, there is a sideline of selling video hardware, something traditionally restricted to males. In one large-city chain, the managers sell the hardware on a commission basis. The chain has both male and female managers, but only the male managers are allowed to sell hardware. However, the commissions are put into a common fund and shared by all of the managers, male and female. Clearly, the firm feels obligated to have female managers and is anxious to avoid discontent and a lawsuit.

ARE WOMEN'S OCCUPATIONS CROWDED?

Occupational segregation, which is a commonplace in our society, does not by itself *logically* imply that the job territory earmarked for women is disproportionately crowded. It would be theoretically possible to have the jobs split between the two sexes in such a way that each labor-market segment contained equivalent (although not identical) opportunities, with the result that equally qualified people in each segment would make equal wages. However, the same factors that enforce segregation also lead to relative crowding in the women's sector. (In India the occupations assigned to those castes lowest in social status yield below-average incomes. If the economic situation changed and those occupations started yielding above-average incomes, we might expect to see members of the more powerful upper castes contriving to change the assignment of economic roles to castes so as to occupy those economic niches.)

The split of jobs between the sexes is not the result of a process of equitable sharing but of exclusion and relegation. That is by no means a process that takes due and fair account of the relative numbers of men and women in the labor market. Many male workers are interested in keeping as many of their coworkers as possible males, and in keeping women restricted to clearly separated and subordinate positions. While not all men feel that way or act on such feelings, it is in the interest of males as a group to keep as much labor market turf as possible for themselves. It not only raises their wages above what they otherwise would be, but reserves the more interesting duties for male-identified jobs.[16] Male activities to maximize their own labor market territory puts pressure on the boundaries of the women's turf, and keep it relatively small.

If more jobs were opened up to workers of both sexes and were paid at the male wage rate, we would certainly see women workers moving into such jobs. Women like Alice Howland (who was turned down for a Sears job) are there ready to respond to opportunities like that. We would certainly not see males taking many of the vacated clerical jobs unless the wages employers offered for them rose considerably. So the supply of workers to jobs currently earmarked for men would increase, and the supply of workers to jobs currently earmarked for women would decrease. Wage rates would change, and the wage gap between men and women would be reduced. There are surely enough Alice Howlands willing to move to jobs currently earmarked for men to decrease considerably the crowding in jobs now in the female work ghetto.

Some economists believe that occupational segregation accounts for little of the pay gap, because whatever their occupation, women's pay is lower than that of men in the same occupations. In the narrowly-defined occupations in table 6–1, women's pay ranges between 53 and 86 percent of that of men in corresponding jobs. If women from a female-dominated occupation (say, secretary) moved to a job in a male-dominated occupation (say, printing machine operator) and in their new jobs were paid, not the wages men get there, but the low wages that women currently working in those occupations now earn, they would have failed to improve their earnings. In fact, if women are going to continue to be stuck with low earnings relative to men in every occupation, then no conceivable change in their occupations will make their average earnings rise to the level of men's.

Some observers of the labor market have been led by this undoubted mathematical truth to the mistaken belief that occupational segregation is of little harm to women and that ending it is of little concern.[17] Such a view is incorrect because it ignores the causal connection between occupational segregation and the assignment of wage rates to jobs by the market. Segregation creates the market conditions leading to low pay in female-dominated occupations, in which most women hold jobs. The pay that women get in jobs in the male-dominated occupations is low because employers know that women's alternative job possibilities are the poorly paid, traditionally female jobs. Segregation ends up affecting the pay in all of the jobs women hold, whether they stay in the traditionally female jobs or get the jobs earmarked for women in other occupations. If the sex segregation and sexual earmarking of jobs were to end and women and men were to compete in the same market, women's wages would rise in most occupations.

Some writers have argued against the idea that the women's turf is relatively crowded by pointing out that although women are excluded from many men's jobs, so men are excluded from or exclude themselves from women's jobs.[18] The unstated implication of such arguments is that the exclusions on both sides should balance out. To argue this way, however, is as fallacious as arguing that the tourist-class passengers on a plane have accommodations as roomy as those of the first-class passengers because very few first-class passengers try to sit in the tourist section of the plane. The idea that there ought to be higher- and lower-class passengers on the plane results in the separation of the classes. It also results in the devotion of a disproportionate amount of the plane's space to the first-class passengers. In the labor market, men's lack of interest in taking low-paying jobs in the women's turf does not balance out the exclusion of women from relatively higher-paying jobs.

Some economists have used deductive reasoning to deny that occupational segregation could be discriminatory. They point to competitive pressures on employers that, they say, compel them to minimize costs. After all, an employer can hire a woman for 65 percent of what it costs to hire a man. Any employer who discriminates against women by refusing to hire them for any job they are competent to do and uses high-priced male labor instead will have costs higher than necessary. A nondiscriminating rival would be able to come into the market and hire women for all the jobs they can perform. The nondiscriminator would have lower labor costs than the discriminating employer and could offer the same product for a lower price. In time, competition should put any discriminating employer out of business.[19]

According to this line of reasoning, when we observe that women are poorly represented or not represented at all in a certain job, we should not rush to assume discrimination. But even if incontrovertible evidence were presented that competent women were being turned away by an employer, then governmental intervention still would not really be necessary. The employer in question would, after all, be in the process of committing economic suicide and would not be marring an otherwise discrimination-free labor market for very much longer.

This line of argument has been quite powerful among economists, many of whom refuse to acknowledge that sex (and race) discrimination could be anything but a rare and temporary phenomenon. The argument is just the kind of pure theory that appeals to many economists, based on deductive logic rather than on observation of any actual events.

We see thousands of business failures every year in the United States, so firms do make fatal mistakes; but no one has ever reported seeing a firm that discriminated reduced to ruin by a less bigoted competitor. On the other hand, we do know of firms that have discriminated yet have remained successful. A judge who heard extensive testimony on the personnel practices of the Hertz Corporation declared it to have "a long history of discriminating against women."[20] Yet Hertz manages to remain number one in its industry. Unfortunately for the science of economics, the acceptance and circulation of a theory by economists has never depended on the existence of actual observations that support it. Nor have counterexamples impeded its circulation.

The argument that firms that discriminate are at a fatal competitive disadvantage is based on the picture of economic life painted by economic theorists: atomistic competition, dog eat dog, an unrelenting search for economic advantage in which social relations have no part. To economists, only money counts to a business firm in making decisions. Sociologists, on the other hand, always have understood the force of custom and the durability of caste systems. They have stressed the importance in the workplace of social relations reflecting dominance and subordination based on characteristics such as race, age, and social stratum as well as sex.[21]

The sociological perspective suggests that the iron law of competition has not been sufficient to eliminate discrimination practiced by firms:

1. Competition is not as severe as economic theorists have claimed; a firm can stay in business even if its costs are not the lowest achievable.
2. Social custom circumscribes what people will do, even for profit. American men used to go to the expense and trouble of maintaining very short haircuts. Social pressure rather than tastes or cost-effectiveness dictated that. Similarly, employers are under social pressure to have men in "men's jobs." A universal custom among employers not to hire women for certain jobs would eliminate competitive pressures.
3. Employers consider it unprofitable to hire women for certain jobs, even though in a technical sense they could do the work. Reasons include the greater rate of turnover expected of women, and the social relations of the workplace (see chapter 5).

Gary Becker has argued that if there is discrimination, it takes the form of a desire on the part of employers to exclude women for social and psychological reasons.[22] However, Becker argued, employers will hire them if they are available at a sufficiently big percentage discount. The size of the discount demanded depends on the strength of the prejudice of the particular employer.* This theory seems to imply that as more women enter the labor market, the ruling rate of discount on their labor would rise, as women have to seek jobs with the more prejudiced part of the employer population, whom they had previously been able to avoid. Therefore, the wage gap between the sexes would be expected to have increased over time in the United States. This does not appear to have happened.

A DESIRE TO MAINTAIN PAY DIFFERENCES PROMOTES OCCUPATIONAL SEGREGATION

So far we have been assuming that occupational segregation is responsible for pay differences between men and women. Sometimes the causation goes the other way: A desire to maintain pay differences between the sexes gives employers an incentive to segregate them into different jobs.

In reading the evidence in discrimination cases, it is hard to avoid the conclusion that pay differences between men and women workers sometimes arise because some men simply resent seeing women get salaries as large as those of men. Claudette Bourque, applying for a promotion from a secretary's job to a buyer's position, was told by her supervisor, "I will not pay a woman, any damned woman, the same money that I will pay a man for that position. That's how I feel. I

---

* Becker called the discount a "discrimination coefficient." His theory of sex discrimination is really little more than a footnote to his theory of race discrimination, where such a scenario may have greater plausibility. However, I believe that in the case of race it also is unrealistic and that wages are lowered on account of exclusion.[23]

don't care if it leaves me open for a suit or not. Now you can have the position, but you will have it at the pay that you are presently making."[24]

The theme that marriage or potential marriage is a reason for not paying women higher salaries, mentioned in the case of Patricia Scott at Océ Industries, appears in numbers of cases that have been brought to court. As an example, the director of a state agency in Grand Forks, North Dakota, told one woman who complained about salary inequities that her husband made a good living so she should not worry about additional income. The same man told a woman supervisor in the agency that he would not want to pay her more money than her husband made.[25]

Whatever the causes of the sharp difference in wages for men and women workers, employers who want to have both men and women on their staff, and who want to pay them differently, have an incentive to segregate. Such employers will not allow newly hired women a choice of which entry-level job they are to go into. The women entrants get directed into the female slots by steering and by veiled threats that they will get no job at all if they try to promote a sex-inappropriate assignment for themselves.

Once an employer decides to allow women to fill certain types of jobs, there is a tendency to discontinue hiring or assigning men into that category of job. First of all, the employer has to pay men a great deal more. Second, there are the problems of social interaction when women and men have to interact as peers, as discussed in chapter 5. Third, employers are barred by law from maintaining different pay scales for men and women doing substantially identical work. Even in the absense of such a law, openly paying sex differentials would these days at least be bad for the morale of the women workers, and they might be inclined to stir up trouble. So employers, when they do decide to allow women into a particular job category, tend to rotate the men in those jobs as rapidly as possible to other jobs. (In situations, as in the professions, where men and women are employed in the same job titles, the men frequently are given higher ranks, and higher pay in the same rank. In such situations, wage rates tend to be fixed by a flexible process. Frequently in such situations the pay assigned to individuals is confidential, so people are inhibited from making direct comparisons.)

MOVING JOBS FROM THE MALE TO
THE FEMALE PRESERVE

In our example of the Pink and Blue tribes, the lower income of the
Pinks depended on the location of the boundaries drawn separating
the two tribes' territories. In the labor market, the continued crowding
of the sector of the labor market to which most women are confined
could be relieved in two ways. Employers might simply stop segregating
and earmarking jobs by sex. Alternatively, they could turn over to
women enough job categories in enough firms to relieve the crowding.

The low wages for which women can be hired puts employers
under a continuing temptation to turn over job groups to women
whenever that can be done with ease. Any rise in the wage differential
can be thought of as making employers more attentive to niches within
their organization where women might substitute for men.[26] However,
a number of substantial difficulties face the employer who tries to make
the switch: an awkward period during which males and females have
to be mixed, the problems connected with the training of the new
women by men who are likely to resent their presence, the uncertainty
as to how to recruit suitable women, and the lack of experienced women
in the applicant pool. Employers may also feel uncertainty as to how
relations between the new female employees and males in other job
groups with whom they have to interact in the productive process
will go.

All of these problems and uncertainties are a drag on the transfer
of jobs from the male to the female labor markets. An organization's
health and profitability depend crucially on its personnel decisions.
Employees whose presence causes trouble, even if they are innocent
victims of other employees' bigotry, are bad news to the enterprise,
and the possible cause of heavy losses. Personnel problems can cause a
wide range of serious problems: sabotage of the production process,
damaging the records, alienating customers, the quitting of other valuable employees, the loss of a cheerful and spat-free work environment,
and continuing friction. It is no wonder that managers are conservative
in their employment practices and are not quick to overturn an assignment system that is working passably for one that may cause the

establishment to unravel. Even if substantial savings in payroll might be made, managers like to stick with what works.

The rise in women's labor force participation over the years has meant, of course, that the supply of women's labor has increased relative to the supply of men's labor. Given the degree of segregation in the labor market, we would expect that if no other factors were operating, the crowding of women in their segment of the labor market would have worsened and therefore the differential between women's and men's average wages would have widened. This has not happened, and it is worth our while to ask why.

One way in which the additional supply of women has been accommodated without deterioration in their relative wage has been that, as we have seen, certain large occupations have been turned over to them. The most important set of occupations in which this has occurred has been the clerical jobs. In 1900 about one quarter of the clerical jobs were held by women; in 1981 women had about 80 percent of such jobs. Women also have taken over many of the sales jobs. They had 17 percent of such jobs in 1900 and almost half in 1981. The clerical and sales-job categories in which women have been acceptable also have had rates of growth that far exceed the average growth in overall employment. Total employment grew between three- and fourfold from 1900 to 1981, while clerical employment grew twenty-onefold in the same period for both sexes and seventyfold for women alone. Sales occupations for both sexes grew fivefold, and for women alone thirteenfold. During World War II bank teller jobs were turned over to women. (On the other side of the ledger, domestic servant jobs, which in 1900 employed about 30 percent of all women workers, have sharply declined, and now employ about 2 percent.)[27]

It appears easier to expand the number of traditionally female jobs than to change the sex identity of occupations. The growth in white-collar employment has facilitated the absorption of women under traditionally female job titles and has reduced the pressure to detach additional large occupations from the men's segment.[28] But the increase in the number of women in the labor market does and will create economic pressure to enlarge the borders of the ghetto of jobs open to women. That economic pressure works counter to the social pressure to keep the borders fixed.

Once a certain set of jobs has been opened to women by a substantial number of employers, then many of the inhibitions that kept women out of those jobs fall to the ground. First and probably most important, attitudes of employers, male workers, and women job entrants change, and what might have seemed strange and wrong now seems quite natural. Second, there gets to be in the field a pool of experienced women workers whom employers can rely on.

AS SEGREGATION IS REDUCED

If discrimination were to be significantly reduced, more women would be in jobs now considered to be "men's jobs." The crowding in the "women's jobs" would be relieved, and under new conditions of supply and demand, the market would dictate wages that better approximated the economists' ideal marketplace: Human capital would be rewarded more equally, whether embodied in men or in women.

As more women are welcomed into what has previously been the men's preserve, the crowding in the women's occupations should be relieved by a flow of women into the higher-paying jobs in the men's turf. The wages in the formerly male-identified job titles and the wages in the formerly female-identified job titles would tend to converge, probably through slower growth of the former and more rapid growth of the latter than would otherwise have occurred.

It must be emphasized that for wages to reach substantial equality, it is by no means necessary that all or even a substantial majority of women be willing and able to take jobs in what formerly were male-identified occupations. When people say, "Women wouldn't like those jobs; women couldn't do those jobs," they seem to be implying that unless women had exactly the distribution of same tastes and skills as men, equality could never be achieved. But such a precise equality would not be necessary. Just enough women would have to be willing and able to move to traditionally male occupations to relieve the crowding of the female territory. The traditionally female territory would not, of course, have to be entirely abandoned. Estelle James[29] has estimated that a third of women workers would have to shift to male-identified occupations for equality of wages to be achieved. If that occurred, persons of equivalent talents and education working in the formerly male-identified segment and the formerly female-identified segment would get an equal return on their human capital—their education, their experience, and their skill.

The ratio of women's to men's earnings has appeared to be on the upswing since 1980, although more time is necessary before the trend can be confidently proclaimed. Employers are starting to pay a lower wage to newly hired employees, many of them in male-identified occupations. Employers have justified these moves by an increase in foreign and domestic competition, but they may derive in part from a lowered willingness to pay a large premium for maleness.

Having explored the connection between occupational segregation and wage levels, we are now in a better position to understand the effects of the policy measures—affirmative action and "comparable worth"—that have been proposed to deal with women's low estate in the labor market and to decide whether the advantages of these policies exceed their disadvantages. This is the subject matter of the next chapters.

CHAPTER 7

Fighting Discrimination Through Affirmative Action

D ISCRIMINATION against women in the job market has two major aspects: exclusion and low pay. The two aspects are connected: Women's exclusion from some jobs pushes them into a labor market separate from that of men, a fenced-off market in which supply and demand decree low rates of pay. If more rapid progress is to be made, both aspects of discrimination need to be attacked. The main attack on exclusion is through affirmative action. Under affirmative action, employers draw up and implement plans to recruit women and minority men into jobs in which their presence has been low. The main attack on low wages is through the pay equity campaign. Its goal is to get employers to raise the pay in jobs where women predominate and so to close the wage gap between women and men by direct action.

Title VII of the Civil Rights Act is the basic legal charter of women's rights on the job in the United States. The act was passed by the Congress in 1964 and signed by President Lyndon Johnson. It outlaws virtually all discriminatory employment practices on account of race or sex. Workers who believe they have been injured by sex discrimination of any kind by an employer or a labor union can bring a lawsuit and collect damages if the court decides discrimination has occurred. Class-action suits brought on behalf of groups of employees allow large damage awards in cases where there has been a consistent pattern of discrimination against the group.

Some employers found by a court to have violated the Title VII ban on exclusion by race or sex have been required to implement affirmative-action plans. But the most extensive affirmative-action program has its origin in executive orders issued by successive presidents since Franklin Roosevelt. Originally the orders concerned only race discrimination; sex discrimination was added in 1968. The order currently in force, issued by President Johnson, requires firms that sell products to the federal government to formulate and implement detailed plans for getting women and minority men into jobs from which they have been excluded. Minority and white women and minority men are to be represented in all occupational groups in accordance with their availability in the labor force.

Pay equity started out as the theme of a number of lawsuits complaining that employers' pay scales discriminated against workers in traditionally female occupations and thus violated Title VII. It has blossomed into a political campaign by women's groups and certain unions to persuade or force employers, particularly public-sector employers, to realign their wage scales.

Title VII lawsuits, affirmative action, and pay equity wage realignments have been responsible for some improvements in the position of women and minorities.[1] They have not moved mountains. (See table 4–2, which shows that black and white women and black men have all made some progress, albeit slow and subject to reversal.) But to the extent that these antidiscrimination policies have been applied, they have made gains possible that would otherwise not have occurred. An important task that lies ahead is finding ways to make them work better. Antidiscrimination remedies currently are difficult to administer, are expensive, work very slowly, and frequently produce inadequate results.

Affirmative-action requirements and the pay equity campaign have both raised loud protests. Affirmative action, its critics claim, is unfair to white men. Furthermore, they say, affirmative action harms the intended beneficiaries more than it helps them and forces employers to hire people who are poorly qualified. While the opponents of affirmative action convey anger, the opponents of pay equity convey amused disbelief. They mock the idea that wages that have been fixed by the market should be readjusted. Adjustments in wages to meet pay equity claims, they say, would create unemployment, would be hopelessly arbitrary, and would be atrociously expensive. The critics of affirmative action and pay equity have little to propose in their place, however, except reliance on the free market. In the past that has not been sufficient to keep the workplace free of unfairness.

In this chapter I shall survey the key decisions in which the federal courts have determined what is and what is not discrimination under Title VII, and discuss the strategy of the act's implementation. The last part of the chapter is devoted to a discussion of the pros and cons of affirmative action. The discussion of pay equity is reserved for the next chapter.

THE CIVIL RIGHTS ACT

A broad statute against discrimination in employment has been on the books in the United States for almost a quarter century. Title VII of the Civil Rights Act of 1964 states:

> It shall be an unlawful employment practice for an employer—(1) to fail or refuse to hire or to discharge any individual, or otherwise to discriminate against any individual with respect to his compensation, terms, conditions, or privileges of employment, because of such individual's race, color, religion, sex, or national origin; or (2) to limit, segregate, or classify his employees or applicants for employment in any way which would deprive or tend to deprive any individual of employment opportunities or otherwise adversely affect his status as an employee, because of such individual's race, color, religion, sex, or national origin.[2]

The act, which outlaws discrimination in hiring, placement, promotion, pay, and fringe benefits, was passed as the result of a bitterly contested crusade against racial injustice led by Martin Luther King, Jr., A. Phillip Randolph, and Clarence Mitchell. The civil disobedience campaign that led to the passage of the Civil Rights Act was sparked by the refusal of a black woman, Rosa Parks, to give up her seat in a crowded Montgomery, Alabama, bus to a white man, although she was required by local law to do so.

The inclusion of the word "sex" in the passage of the act quoted was originally proposed by a white-supremacist representative. By this maneuver he had hoped to harm the prospects for passage of Title VII. As a result, the legend has grown up that sex discrimination was outlawed as a result of a trick gone awry. However, historical research[3] has shown that the Congress considered the issue of barring sex discrimination in employment on its merits.* Under the leadership of Representative Martha Griffiths, a Democrat from Michigan, the word "sex" was voted into the bill.†

The Civil Rights Act set up an agency, the Equal Employment Opportunity Commission (EEOC). The commission receives and investigates complaints of discrimination, attempts conciliation, and may bring lawsuits against employers. The commission also issues guidelines concerning the legality under Title VII of a host of personnel practices, guidelines which may, however, be challenged in the courts.

Title VII covers private employers with fifteen or more employees, labor unions, and employment agencies. It allows suits by individuals and suits on behalf of classes of persons. Judges can order employers to hire or promote or reinstate individuals whom they find have been discriminated against, can order salaries changed, and give back-pay awards. The judge may require the losing party to a Title VII suit to pay the attorney's fees of the other side.[4]

---

* The exclusion of a person from restaurants and hotels on the basis of race is forbidden by the public accommodation sections of the Civil Rights Act, but exclusion based on sex is not barred, so that single-sex restaurants, bars, and hotels are permitted. Private clubs are allowed to exclude people on any basis, including race and sex, but what is private and what is public is subject to definition by the judiciary.

† The year before, the Congress had passed the Equal Pay Act, which mandates equal pay regardless of sex to employees who do "equal work." The effect of EPA will be discussed in the next chapter.

WHAT PRACTICES ARE DISCRIMINATORY?

The laws passed by Congress are for the most part broadly drafted, and Title VII is no exception. It has been left to the courts to define what behavior is discriminatory and what is not and to set the nature of the evidence to be required as proof of discriminatory behavior.

SEX AS A PREDICTOR OF PERFORMANCE

Title VII generally prohibits employers from classifying people according to sex, race, religion, or national origin, and treating them differently for those reasons. There is, however, an exception. The framers of the act recognized that sex or religion or national origin (but not race) of employees might in special circumstances be a legitimate concern of an employer. For example, Congress did not want to force a Catholic school preparing young men for the priesthood to hire women or Protestants as teachers. The language of the act refers to "instances where religion, sex, or national origin is a bona fide occupational qualification reasonably necessary to the normal operation of that particular business or enterprise."[5]

The interpretation of the bona fide occupational qualification (BFOQ) by the courts was clearly of crucial importance to the application of the act. It is easy for an employer to come up with reasons why men might be better suited than women for any job that had in the past been limited to men. If an employer was able to declare the male sex to be a BFOQ for most of the typically male jobs, then the act would not be of much help to women.

In a landmark case, Claudine Cheatwood charged that her employer, South Central Bell Telephone, had discriminated against her by refusing to consider her or any women for the post of commercial representative. The main duties involved visiting customers' premises and dealing with financial matters, complaints, and delinquencies. The commercial representative also occasionally had to collect coin boxes (which typically weighed 60 pounds but might weigh up to 90 pounds) from pay telephones.

The company's defense was that being male was a BFOQ for that job. In the course of the commercial representative's work tires on the company car might occasionally have to be changed, and the representative would have to enter bars, poolrooms, and other such locations. Rest rooms might be unaccessible. Much was made of the weight-lifting requirements of the job, and medical testimony was given concerning problems women might have in doing that.

The court rejected the company's BFOQ defense and said that the company had committed discrimination in failing to consider Cheatwood's application:

> A thorough consideration of the evidence makes clear that it is "rational" rather than merely capricious, for the employer to discriminate against women as a class in filling this position, i.e., on the average, men can perform these tasks somewhat more efficiently and perhaps somewhat more safely than women. . . . [But] it appears to this Court that it will not impose a hardship on this Employer to determine on an individual basis whether a person is qualified for the position of commercial representative. On the other hand, it is manifest that the use of this class distinction deprives some women of what they regard as a lucrative and otherwise desirable position.[6]

In the Cheatwood case, the court imposed on the company the requirement that it consider candidates individually, rather than relying on its view, which the court considered correct, that women were *on average* less qualified than men.* As noted in chapter 5, an employer using facts or suppositions about women's average ability in coming to decisions about the hiring, assignment, or promotion of individual women is said to be engaging in statistical discrimination. The employer is penalizing an individual for belonging to a group, rather than judging the individual's characteristics or actual performance. If some group really does have a relatively poor track record in performance, and if testing for candidates is unavailable, unreliable, or expensive, turning away candidates on the basis of their sex or race might reduce costs for an employer.[7] Some economists come quite close to endorsing such behavior.

Under judicial interpretation of Title VII, the exclusion of women based on statistical discrimination is not permitted. It makes no dif-

---

* From the present perspective, it is difficult to take at face value, as the judge seems to have done, the issues raised concerning rest rooms, poolhalls, and tire changes. It would not be surprising if the company simply thought it appropriate that its commercial customers be dealt with by male employees and wanted to continue that practice.

ference if an employer's contention about women's lesser abilities is true on average. People have the right to be considered on their own merits and not be disadvantaged by their sex. (This issue will come up again in our discussion of affirmative action.)

PENSIONS

Some employers were running pension plans that awarded monthly pension checks to retired women that were 20 percent lower than those awarded to men with equivalent service. Employers argued that women on average live longer than men, so the amount of pension money that men and women retirees would collect between retirement and death would on average be equal. Thus, the lower monthly payments to women were not discriminatory, employers claimed.

The U.S. Supreme Court accepted the women's argument that individual women were being disadvantaged by the assumption that they were like the average woman in terms of mortality.[8] Some women die soon after retirement, while some men live into their nineties. Whatever the age at which a retired man dies, there are women dying at the same age who had been forced to live on a lower pension income just because they were women. In fact, 80 percent of retired men and women can be paired up as dying at the same age.[9] Employers now are required to give equal pension checks to women and men with equivalent service.

CUSTOMER PREFERENCES

The courts have ruled consistently that employers do not have the right to exclude women from any job on the grounds that their customers or their other employees would rather have men on the job and that their business would be hurt if they were forced to hire women. An employer may plead "business necessity," but that plea has been rejected unless the business could show that it would not be able to carry on unless women were excluded.

In one case, a hotel claimed that people giving receptions preferred to have male waiters serving them, a defense that was disallowed by the court.[10] Two of the key cases have involved the rights of men to jobs usually performed by women. Hospitals do not have the right to refuse to assign male nurses to female patients.[11] Males cannot be excluded as flight attendants despite surveys showing that passengers prefer women in that role. In the flight attendants' case, the Appeals Court said:

> While we recognize that the public's expectation of finding one sex in a particular role may cause some initial difficulty, it would be totally anomalous if we were to allow the preferences and prejudices of the customers to determine whether the sex discrimination [practiced by an employer] was valid. Indeed, it was, to a large extent, these very prejudices the Act was meant to overcome. Thus, we feel that customer preference may be taken into account only when it is based on the company's inability to perform the primary function or service it offers.[12]

PROTECTIVE LEGISLATION

In the nineteenth and early twentieth centuries, many of the states passed "protective" laws that forbade women from filling a long list of jobs or working long hours or at night. (Nurses, of course, were excluded from the prohibition of night work.*) These laws had had the enthusiastic support of certain women's advocacy groups such as the National Women's Trade Union League (so-called "social feminists") who believed that they were necessary to save women from exploitation by employers. However, laws restricting the use of women's labor had also been supported by male labor unions to exclude women's competition from jobs men wanted.[13]

A key decision came in the case of Leah Rosenfeld, an employee of Southern Pacific Company, who wanted a job assignment that would have required her to lift fifty pounds and work more than ten hours per day at peak periods. California labor laws prohibited giving a job with such requirements to a woman. The court concluded that such laws conflicted with the policy of nondiscrimination mandated by Title VII and declared them invalid.[14]

The demise of protective labor legislation opened up for women job opportunities previously closed to them. Bartending, an occupation that had been barred to women by law in many localities, appears on the way to becoming a stereotypically female occupation.

---

* Regulations of the military services barring women from positions that would bring them close to combat have traditionally been applied less strictly to nurses.

The courts have severely limited the right of employers to exclude workers by race or sex on the basis of tests or conditions of employment. Unless a test is expressly and closely related to the duties of the job in question, it is open to legal attack if it can be shown to exclude a disproportionate number of women or blacks. This is true even if the test is seemingly sex-neutral or race-neutral.

The key decision came in a lawsuit, *Griggs* v. *Duke Power Co.*, brought by a group of black workers. The company had openly practiced occupational segregation by race until the date Title VII became applicable. After that date, the company instituted a requirement that a worker had to have a high-school diploma and take a written test to be eligible to move into a job that it had previously kept for white men. In its decision striking down these requirements as not permissible under Title VII, the U.S. Supreme Court noted that whites who were not high-school graduates performed well, showing that the requirement was not closely related to success on the job. The act, the Court said, did not preclude testing or measuring procedures but required that the tests "must measure the person for the job and not the person in the abstract."[15]

The Griggs case was important for women because it would have been extremely easy for employers to invent tests or requirements that screened them out almost entirely. As the Duke Power Co. record showed, such tests sometimes were devised to take the place of overt discrimination. Even where such motives were absent, employers have injured women candidates by erecting requirements that disproportionately eliminated women without careful validation that such requirements were necessary.

In particular, the Griggs decision cast doubt on height and weight requirements, which had had the effect of excluding many women from male-dominated jobs such as police officer or firefighter. Employers have been forced to validate such requirements as strictly job-related, and if they could not do so have been forced to abandon them.

SENIORITY SYSTEMS

Title VII of the Civil Rights Act contains an explicit permission for employers to treat employees differently if such treatment is based on a "bona fide" seniority system. The operation of seniority systems have caused women workers considerable disadvantage. When seniority is based on service in a particular department of an employer's establishment, people who want to change departments may be required to relinquish all seniority. Where there has in the past been occupational segregation, or where there is still segregation in assignment to entry-level jobs, such seniority systems inhibit transfers by women or black employees to job titles in which white males predominate.

Seniority systems have had adverse effects on black and female employees who had been hired under affirmative action plans. Subsequent layoffs, concentrated on those with the least seniority, have in numerous cases restored the monopoly of white males. In some cases of this sort, blacks and women have filed lawsuits asking the courts to void their dismissals on the grounds that prior discrimination had prevented people like them from accruing seniority. Such suits have had poor success, unless it could be shown that the particular seniority system involved was designed with discriminatory intent. The courts have declined to remedy the low seniority of women and black employees as a group, even if it resulted from the unlawful exclusion of people like them. Only individual employees who applied during the period of exclusion and were unlawfully turned away would be entitled to a boost in their seniority, the courts have said.[16]

SEX ON THE JOB

The courts have generally been unsympathetic to employers (at least those purveying services not overtly or primarily sexual in nature) who have mixed sex and business and in the course of doing so disadvantaged their women employees. They have ruled against employers who have required that women look attractive and available to male customers—be young, unmarried, and good-looking—while making no such demands on males in similar jobs. For example, they invalidated Northwest Airlines' policy of requiring women but not men to wear contact lenses rather than eyeglasses and to be monitored for weight

maintenance.[17] The courts have followed the EEOC in declaring that
an employer who countenances sexual harassment is guilty of sex
discrimination.[18]

PREGNANCY

Historically, the treatment by employers of employees who became
pregnant has been a grave source of disadvantage to women. Some
employers have routinely terminated any employee who became pregnant. Others have required prolonged leaves without pay, with little
or no guarantee of reinstatement to a comparable job. Pregnant employees have been denied the use of paid sick leave during their period
of disablement and of health-insurance coverage for their medical bills
related to the pregnancy. Some employers had health plans that allowed
no benefits for women employees who became pregnant, but included
pregnancy coverage for the wives of male employees. A number with
provisions of this type had been negotiated by unions.

The first legal attacks on employers' pregnancy policies were
brought by public-school teachers who were being required to retire
from the classroom upon discovery of their "delicate condition." The
motive of the school authorities probably was to protect the innocence
of the pregnant teacher's pupils and keep them from having to confront
the indelicate result of their teacher's participation in a sexual act.
However, the school boards chose to defend their policy on the grounds
of the protection of the health and welfare of the pregnant woman
and her baby. In a series of cases, the U.S. Supreme Court struck down
these policies.[19]

Some employers had structured sick-leave, disability, or health-
insurance plans to cover any health problem, with the sole exception
of disabilities deriving from pregnancy and birth. Women sued on the
grounds that omitting pregnancy from coverage discriminated against
women employees, by definition the only ones who could become
pregnant. Employers responded that pregnancy was not illness, that it
was voluntary, that covering it would be expensive, and that their
plans denied to women no coverage available to men.

In *Gilbert* v. *General Electric Company,* the U.S. Supreme Court
allowed employers to treat disability related to the female role in reproduction as in a class by itself and therefore not as something that

had to be treated on a par with other disabilities. This decision dismayed women's-rights advocates because of its immediate effects on the economic condition of pregnant women employees, particularly single mothers. They were also concerned at the possibility that the Court at some future time might choose to allow "people who became pregnant or might in the future get pregnant" to be picked out on that basis for disadvantageous treatment. Responding to the decision in *Gilbert,* Congress passed an act[20] requiring employers to treat disabilities arising from pregnancy and birth as they treat other disabilities. However, the concern about the future use of pregnancy to women's disadvantage remains. An equal-rights amendment to the Constitution might guarantee that women would suffer no disadvantage due to their childbearing functions. However, it might also preclude any especially favorable treatment.

The right of employers to bar from certain work both pregnant women and women who might become pregnant, on the grounds of hazard to themselves or to a fetus, is an issue that still is unsettled. Some firms have required that women be sterilized to be allowed to hold certain jobs. Concerns that work conditions might damage sperm seldom surface, despite evidence that such damage has occurred in some instances.

THE STRATEGY OF ENFORCEMENT

The Equal Employment Opportunity Commission (EEOC) is the official registrar of discrimination complaints. The EEOC itself can bring a lawsuit against an employer. However, its resources have been quite limited, and it can pursue only a small proportion of cases brought to it. Individuals and groups who have registered their complaint with the EEOC can bring a lawsuit privately against an employer or a union. However, this is an extremely expensive and time-consuming process.

Costs of several hundreds of thousands of dollars and time spans of a decade have not been uncommon.* Even when an employer loses one of these suits, the costs to the employer frequently are not large enough to deter future violations or to cause other employers to consider changing their personnel practices.

The enforcement strategy chosen for Title VII might be called a complaint-oriented strategy—responding to complaints that come into the EEOC. The alternative is an investigative strategy, perhaps on the model of tax enforcement. The Internal Revenue Service does not depend on complaints, but makes investigations of its own, concentrating on cases likely to produce large results. The cases it takes to court are the most important and exemplary of the cases its investigations produce.

While a complaint-oriented enforcement strategy might be a good choice against burglary or murder, there are a number of reasons why it turned out to be a poor choice for an agency like the EEOC, charged with mounting a legal fight against discrimination. A relatively small part of the population commits burglary or murder, while a high proportion of those in a position to commit sex discrimination in employment appear to do so. This means that little will be accomplished if the agency pursues a strategy that would suffice for netting a relatively small number of law-breakers. Rather, its job is to change traditions of behavior that countenance discrimination—traditions that are currently pretty much universal and accepted as proper.

Even if the enforcement agencies had far more resources than they do, there are other reasons for not relying on a complaint-oriented strategy. Many—indeed, most—victims of discrimination may be unaware they are being discriminated against. People who apply for a job and are turned down are in no position to judge whether the refusal has been based on their race or their sex, or represents merely a fair judgment on their qualifications. Sometimes the news of job openings does not get to anyone but members of the race-sex group already incumbent. Rejected job applicants are not in a good position to get

---

* However, an employer adjudged to have discriminated may be ordered to pay the legal fees and other expenses of the case for the complaining employee. This has encouraged lawyers to take and pursue promising cases without collecting fees in advance from the complainant. In practice, this has meant that some victims of discrimination have been able to have recourse to the courts.

together to organize a lawsuit.* Yet such cases, were they brought by an enforcement agency, might be among the most useful in setting patterns of fair behavior for employers.

People already employed by a firm and who are excluded from certain assignments and promotions there may have a very poor idea of what constitutes discrimination under the law. Since occupational segregation is so prevalent, and seemingly so universally accepted without complaint, many women are unaware that it is unlawful for their employer to bar them from any job within the establishment on account of their sex. Many aggrieved workers surmise that a complaint of discrimination will end any chance of further advancement, and indeed may result in harassment and termination. In short, an enforcement strategy that relies on complaints will miss some important cases of discrimination.

The EEOC's enforcement actions have been meager in number, primarily because of the low budget of the agency, but also because of its inefficiencies. Nor has it concentrated to the extent it should have on large and important employers showing a pattern and practice of discrimination. Informed opinion does not rate the agency as having been very effective.[21] In fiscal year 1985, the EEOC had 72,000 complaints but brought only 411 lawsuits. It recovered only $54 million for the victims of discrimination from American businesses in that year, a trifling fraction of their losses.[22]

Another federal agency set up to fight discrimination is the office of Federal Contract Compliance Policy (OFCCP), which is charged with enforcing the executive order barring firms from selling goods and services to the federal government if they discriminate. The OFCCP adopted a strategy of enforcement more promising than that of the EEOC, at least on paper. In a set of carefully drawn regulations, the OFCCP has required each federal contractor with more than fifteen employees to formulate an affirmative action plan.

The heart of such a plan, as specified in OFCCP regulations, is a

---

* Black civil rights organizations, particularly the National Association for the Advancement of Colored People Legal Defense Fund, have been able in some cases to bring suits on behalf of blacks excluded from employment at a particular establishment. Women's rights organizations have not played as prominent a role in this regard, probably because the total exclusion of women is a rare phenomenon. The exclusion of women from particular functions within an establishment is more difficult to detect from outside than total exclusion. Even when it is detected, it has historically been more difficult to arouse indignation and to gather plaintiffs on behalf of women than in the case of racial exclusion.

set of numerical goals for the utilization of groups protected from discrimination. The goals are formulated to give each race-sex group (for example, black females) a share in each type of job equal to its share in the pool of persons available for that job in the labor force. "Availability" is broadly construed in the regulations; employers are not allowed to plead that the current paucity of women truck drivers, for example, means that women's availability for that job is very low. To do that would have allowed employers to perpetuate the current level of exclusion. On the contrary, employers are required to reach out to try to recruit women and blacks for jobs that were nontraditional for them. Where reasonable, employers are to set up training programs to remedy the past lack of opportunities for women and blacks. The regulations specified that the goals were to be accompanied by timetables the firm agreed to follow in fulfilling them.[23] This requirement was supposed to keep the attainment of goals from receding indefinitely into the future.

The OFCCP is supposed to oversee the formulation of acceptable affirmative-action plans and to monitor the fulfillment of the ones it has accepted. Firms that fail to fulfill an acceptable plan are supposed to be debarred by the agency from selling to the federal government. In practice, only a handful of firms, those that resisted even the submission of an affirmative-action plan, have been debarred. Despite the low rate of debarment, the activities of the OFCCP do gain the attention of every large firm, because of the need for the formulation of the affirmative-action plan.

Researchers have attempted to assess the effectiveness of the OFCCP in getting federal contractors to reduce the exclusion of blacks and women by comparing the race-sex composition of contractors' employment with the composition of employment of noncontractors. The consensus of these studies is that the agency has been modestly effective in some instances, but needs strengthening.[24]

THE PLACE OF AFFIRMATIVE ACTION

Affirmative action as a remedy for previous exclusion of women and blacks from certain jobs has been used both under Title VII and by OFCCP under the contract compliance program. In a large number of cases where discrimination has been proven or conceded, federal judges have themselves ordered or countenanced setting up numerical goals for hiring and promotion. However, the usefulness of affirmative action would be severely curtailed if it had to be restricted to such cases.

The legality of affirmative-action plans by employers who have not previously been found by a court to have been discriminating was challenged in a key case.[25] Kaiser Shipyards had few black workers in certain craft jobs and set up a training program with a portion of the slots reserved for blacks. The U.S. Supreme Court rejected a white worker's argument that the firm had discriminated against him because it had denied him a place in the training program in favor of a black worker with less seniority. The Court declared that the race-conscious administration of the training program, with a specified number of slots for black workers, was within the spirit and the letter of Title VII.

So numerical goals and timetables of affirmative action are in some circumstances legal. But are they desirable? On one side it has been argued that they create injustice, are a form of "reverse discrimination," and do harm even to those they are designed to benefit.[26] On the other side it has been claimed that they are indispensable if we are to get rid of discriminatory employment practices. Since I believe that a carefully designed and rigorously enforced affirmative-action program will be necessary if we are to end the disadvantages women suffer in the labor market, I have laid out the arguments concerning the rights and wrongs of such programs at considerable length.

The chief argument in favor of the use of numerical goals and timetables for hiring and promoting is that without them women and blacks are likely to be excluded from many of the better jobs for years to come. Occupational segregation and the discrimination that enforces that segregation derive from management's racist and sexist ideas about who should have the better jobs. Occupational segregation is also motivated by a desire to avoid the social discomfort generated when normally dominant white males are asked to act on the job as equal or subordinate to other kinds of people. Hiring and assignment procedures commonly are designed to ensure that the people who will work together are socially compatible and that the roles they are asked to take are comfortable for all concerned.

Discrimination deriving from this source is self-perpetuating unless some new procedure forces change. The lack of women as colleagues reinforces men's feelings that women are inferior outsiders, which in turn makes it difficult for employers to have men and women working side by side in the same job as equal colleagues. Affirmative action enforced by a government agency offers a way to break the vicious circle—the firm's management is forced to institute selection procedures that get around individual managers' and workers' prejudices. Since the employer's hand is forced, the male workers can be told that the firm has no alternative but to integrate. The power of low-level employees to veto candidates on the basis of race or sex is reduced. The hostility generated by the integration is displaced from the employer to the government. The welcome that affirmative action has received from some employers probably derives from this source.*

The imposition of numerical goals and timetables is the only way that has been found to hold firms accountable. In the absence of numerical goals, the enforcing agency can only collect inevitably vague promises from employers "not to discriminate." Such qualitative promises are essentially worthless because evidence as to their fulfillment cannot be efficiently gathered or assessed. The need for quantitative assessment as a management tool is evidenced by the practices of modern business firms themselves. They engage in numerical planning for all essential processes—production, sales, and investment. Numerical planning allows an organization to make a judgment whether success or failure has occurred; in fact, it creates a definition of success and failure.

Another argument sometimes made in favor of affirmative action, particularly by people whose main interest is the achievement of racial

---

* When the Reagan administration threatened to abolish goals and timetables for government contractors, larger employers, represented by the National Association of Manufacturers, protested, and the Administration was forced to back down.[27]

equality, is that those who have suffered discrimination are at a disadvantage because of the injustices they have suffered in the past and do not come to the starting line (of the scramble for the better jobs) with an equal ability to compete. Those who put forth this argument say that equality of opportunity alone (by which they presumably mean scrupulous impartiality and no imposed numerical goals) would not produce equality of results, which, they say, should be the aim of our policy.

This argument amounts to saying that the general run of minority and female candidates are in truth so inferior to white male candidates that a meritocratic hiring procedure, fairly administered, would result in the hiring of very few more than are currently being hired. But, this argument runs, employers should be forced to hire them anyway to fulfill their goals, so that equality of result will be achieved. Needless to say, such an argument has given a great deal of potent ammunition to the opponents of affirmative action, including those who would like to preserve the status quo of white male monopoly of the best jobs.

What is curious is that these "equality of result" partisans seem to have the same attitude toward the factual question of the importance of currently occurring discrimination as the opponents of affirmative action; both appear to believe that current discrimination is not very important and that the allocation of people to jobs is currently approximately in line with a fair assessment of each person's abilities. On such a view, the only possible result of an effective affirmative action program is that it results in the hiring of people who are less competent than those who would have been hired in the absence of the plan.

Such views, however, fly in the face of the evidence that discrimination still is very much a factor in current personnel decisions. If discrimination still is rife, then a rigorously administered affirmative action program should result in the hiring and promoting of competent female and minority candidates who would have been excluded. In this case, affirmative action promotes the hiring of the more competent and prevents the hiring of the less competent. The strong evidence we have that points to current widespread discrimination (see chapters 4–6) supports the view that meritocratic hiring procedures are on balance promoted by affirmative action rather than thwarted by it.

THOSE HARMED BY AFFIRMATIVE ACTION

Of course, even if affirmative action results in an improvement in the quality of those hired and promoted on average, it is certain that there have been individual white males who were denied jobs or promotions that they might have been awarded on grounds of merit. A great deal has been said about the plight of these men under affirmative action— of their alleged innocence of any wrongdoing in connection with past discrimination and of their not having derived any benefit from discrimination.

Affirmative action programs *will* cause some innocent white men to be treated unfairly, and this is nothing to be smug about or to gloss over. However, what is generally lost sight of in discussions of unfairness under affirmative action is that the absence of affirmative action would cause some injustices, too. If discrimination is common, a lack of remedy would allow injustices to continue to occur. So there will be injustices with affirmative action or without it. The identity of the individuals harmed in the two cases differs, of course. Without affirmative action those harmed are the women and minority males who are competent but passed over because of continuing systematic uncorrected discrimination. With affirmative action, there is the possibility that the goals for hiring of women and minority males have been badly estimated and are larger than those that can be filled with competent people. There is also the possibility that any poorly estimated goals will be rigidly adhered to. In such cases, some white males who would have been selected under a fairly administered sex-blind and race-blind system will not be selected.

In reality, we are always choosing among imperfect alternatives, and the verdict we bring in on affirmative action should not be based on the false idea that the alternative to affirmative action is a perfectly fair system in which everyone is dealt with according to merit. On the contrary, we must compare the benefits and injustices under each imperfect alternative and make a choice. One consideration in making that choice is the identity and number of those benefited and those treated less than fairly. Under affirmative action, a substantial share of the best jobs still are allocated to white males, and the proportion of white males harmed due to overestimated or badly administered goals is likely to be small. On the other hand, the continuation of a discriminatory system hurts a very high proportion of women and minority members because of their complete exclusion from the best jobs. Thus if we have to choose between the imperfections of a discriminatory setup and the imperfections of an affirmative action regime, the latter would appear to disadvantage fewer people unfairly.

A further consideration is that affirmative action will inevitably be applied only to the larger establishments, or those with government contracts. This means that the discriminatory preference for white males will be continued in the smaller establishments for some time to come. Until the great majority of establishments have left off discriminating, it cannot be said that the labor-market advantage accruing to being born a white male has been eliminated. The advantage white males have in the establishments not under affirmative action should more than balance out the marginal disadvantages a few of them may suffer due to mistakes in goal-setting in the larger establishments.

Sometimes the affirmative action goals are of the right order of magnitude but there are mistakes or inefficiencies in finding competent people to fulfill them and some incompetents are hired. In this case, the people unjustly excluded are not white males but the competent women and minorities who should have been recruited to fulfill those goals. In the case of such mistakes white males may be excluded who are more competent than those people actually hired, but their exclusion in this case cannot be labeled an injustice due to affirmative action.

DIFFICULT ISSUES

Up to now, the discussion has been carried on in terms of candidates who are judged "competent" or "not competent." In many hiring and promotion decisions, it is customary by formal or informal means to give each candidate a score representing predicted degree of competence and compatibility and to hire or promote those candidates who have been ranked highest. In such cases, the fulfillment of goals under an affirmative action plan gives an appearance of sharp conflict with meritocratic selection in a way that does not arise explicitly when candidates are rated simply as competent or not. In the latter case, all the personnel department has to do to retain the appearance of fairness is to come up with the designated number of competent women and minorities. In the case where candidates are given ranks or scores, picking the highest-scoring candidates will achieve the preset goals only in rare cases.

This is particularly true if a scoring process is used that predates the affirmative action program, and that regularly filled the top of the list with white males. It will surely continue to do so. In such a situation, meeting the affirmative action goal will require that some of the candidates judged to be of highest competence be passed over to permit the hiring or promotion of some female and minority candidates awarded lower scores. It is in such cases that the most bitterness is generated, and the strongest impression is given that affirmative action favors the unworthy over the worthy.

What can be said here in defense of affirmative action in such cases is that precise rankings of candidates are likely to be less reliable than decisions as to whether candidates fall above or below some cutoff point. Where such ranking procedures have failed to procure the hiring of even one woman or one minority candidate, the suspicion must arise that the procedure is discriminatory, whether intentionally so or not.* Where the selection procedure is informal, the candidates judged "best" are likely to be mostly white male, because the people doing the grading are best attuned to get clues as to competence from people like themselves with whom they are most familiar and most sympathetic. Their mental image of an ideal candidate is a white male.

Even where the ranking is done by objective written examination, with candidates' identities concealed from those who grade the examination papers, it cannot be assumed that the ranks or scores are true indicators of the relative competence the candidates will display on the job. There are plenty of instances where the ranking process probably is irrelevant to a realistic attempt to judge whether the candidate

---

* The case of Theda Skocpel, a sociology professor who was initially refused tenure at Harvard, is instructive. Like many Harvard departments, the Sociology Department had never tenured a single woman professor. What is unique about Skocpel's case is that Harvard's administration looked into the matter and came to the conclusion that the Harvard sociology professors who voted against her promotion had not acted in accordance with her degree of merit.

will perform well. The pencil-and-paper tests commonly given to candidates for entry-level positions and promotions in police and fire departments are examples of this. Where advance knowledge about the formal or informal "examination" given the candidates is available to a favored in-group, or where special grooming or preparation is available to some but not others, women and minority candidates will score relatively poorly, despite the fact that their technical abilities to perform on the job may be similar to those of white males'.

Patrick Fenton recalls how men in an ethnic Irish neighborhood in Brooklyn in the 1950s were helped by an informal network to pass the examination for New York City police officer:

> Old timers would hold impromptu tutoring sessions in the doorways of Irish saloons. "You have to know how to find the common denominator in fractions," one veteran of the tests would instruct. "That comes up all the time." There was also talk of numerators and improper fractions and the use of decimals. . . . We would spend weeks quizzing each other on proper grammar. We knew there would be questions on sentence structure, vocabulary and the use of commas. (None of us ever questioned why we needed to know some of these things to become a New York City cop, or if it might help on the job.) On the day of the exam . . . we congregated at the corner for a last-minute review. . . . The old timers would shout encouragement to us as we turned the corner . . . crowded six to a car. . . . With all the yells going up, you would think the men from some ancient whaling village were leaving on an expedition.[28]

From one point of view, this story is just a heartwarming example of community cohesiveness, but there is a less pleasant side to it. The help those young men were given was part of a process that kept women, as well as black men and men of Italian and Polish origin, off the police force. Most likely, the test was designed and perpetuated for that purpose.

The difficulties of reconciling scores and rankings of candidates with affirmative-action goals has led to the suggestion that all evaluation procedures connected to hiring and promotion should be converted to a pass-fail system, and those to be hired or promoted be selected by lot from among those who had passed. While this suggestion has merit in many cases, in others the nature of the job may be such that getting the best candidates is really crucial to the performance of the function. In such cases, the best prescription probably is a concentration on making the rating or scoring process maximally relevant and scrupulously fair, and working to ensure that the preparation of women and minority candidates for the rating process is on a par with that of the white males.

AFFIRMATIVE ACTION IN PROMOTIONS

The application of affirmative action to promotions is far more difficult than its application to hiring. After a promotion the rejected candidates remain with the organization. If they are brought to believe that the process of selection was in any sense unfair, and if they sense that the promoted person is in a weak position because of his or her race or sex, their resentments can create difficulty both for the organization and the person promoted. Yet promotion processes, even when not on their face discriminatory, tend to have features to them that favor in-groups. There may be positions from which promotion is impossible, regardless of the qualifications of the incumbent. There may be an elaborate grooming process for favored people, which virtually assures their recognition as "most competent." Cynthia Epstein, who has studied professional careers, has found that young men considered to be on a fast track to a good position in the hierarchy will be given varied work assignments and good opportunities of demonstrating their competence.[29] There may also be formal or informal requirements for promotion, such as frequent geographic moves and no breaks in service, which are unrelated to performance in the higher job but serve to put barriers in the way of the promotion of women employees.[30]

The process of selecting who to promote almost always involves ranking candidates. Affirmative-action plans for promotion require that these rankings be removed as the sole arbiter, and this is one of the reasons why such plans are particularly likely to arouse a seething resentment in the disappointed candidates. Another is that the person promoted may become the direct supervisor of the rejected candidates. Aggravation of already present sexism and racism, and a determination to withhold cooperation from the new boss may result.

It is interesting in this context to note that in family-owned businesses modestly talented relatives of the owner are frequently the beneficiaries of a well-understood "affirmative-action program" calling for them to be pushed to the top. In such cases, virulent resentment does not surface, as it does in cases of affirmative action for women and blacks. Perhaps the difference is that in a family business the special status that defines the beneficiaries of the affirmative-action plan adds strength to their position rather than indicates weakness and poor bargaining position. Perhaps even more to the point, nonfamily employees know that their gracious acquiescence is a condition of their continuing to work for the company. This certainly suggests that affirmative-action programs succeed best if the top brass take a genuine interest and if measures for punishing resisters are in force and well publicized.

Fair promotion processes are vital to the economic future of women in the workplace. A look at the tiny representation of women in the upper ranks of most organizations shows that a great deal remains to be accomplished. In the federal government, women hold 46 percent of the jobs but only 6 percent of the "supergrade" jobs held by top management.[31] However, the use of numerical goals in internal promotions must be conceded to be highly problematical. In some instances, headway can be made by dismantling practices and requirements that disproportionately impede the promotions of women. But in others, goals and timetables, with all of the difficulties they carry in the context of promotion, appear to be indispensable to any timely progress.

DRAWBACKS TO THE BENEFICIARIES

A genuine drawback of affirmative action from the point of view of women and minority people is that those selected to be hired must face the suspicion of their workmates that they are not competent. This suspicion is particularly galling to those women and blacks who feel (whether correctly or not) that they were hired on the basis of their perceived merit and would have been hired had no such plan existed. Such people, who may themselves have come to believe the argument that affirmative action inevitably means the hiring of incompetent people, feel that the affirmative-action program has ruined their career by causing them to be labeled incompetent.

Even those who know that they owe their job to an affirmative-action program find the prized job somewhat tainted by the attitudes of colleagues toward those people brought in under affirmative action. While these attitudes are regrettable, the beneficiaries of affirmative action are better off than if they had never been hired at all. Some of the expressions of hostility put down to affirmative action may result from the racism or sexism of their colleagues. That may diminish as their colleagues come to know them as individuals, something that might never have occurred in the absence of affirmative action.

The existence of goals and timetables, and the pressure put on employers to meet them, have the regrettable effect of keeping race and sex salient in personnel matters. Affirmative action should be viewed as a temporary expedient that should be phased out as soon as the reduction of discrimination allows. Those who favor affirmative action should themselves define what criteria are to be used in deciding when to phase it out. However, it is unrealistic to think that with discrimination as prevalent as it is, women and minorities can now be helped without race-conscious and sex-conscious remedies.

THE PRINCIPLE OF INDIVIDUAL CONSIDERATION

One source of opposition to affirmative action comes from those who see such programs as opening the way to a revival of some of the oppressive practices of the past, whose purpose was exclusion on grounds of race and religion. For many decades Jewish students were subject to quotas limiting their admission to elite educational institutions to their representation in the population. Jewish students tended to be disproportionately represented among those with the best grades and scores. So the quotas meant that some Jewish students were rejected in favor of non-Jewish (white) students who scored less well.

Affirmative action for blacks and for women is feared as the opening wedge for strictly proportional quotas for all groups. The campaigns of Hispanics and American Indians for goals for themselves certainly leads us further in this direction. It is also mathematically inescapable that numerical goals for inclusion of some groups puts a ceiling on the advancement of members of other groups. Thus mathematically, the goals in favor of women and blacks operate against white males precisely as the old quotas on Jews did.

The unstated essence of the complaint about quotas is that the above-average performance of certain groups (and the below-average performance of other groups) cannot get proper recognition under affirmative action. It could in principle, but in practice, it is admittedly difficult to arrange. The suggested alternative is that group goals never be set and that we revert to a system of judging individual merit, but now (as perhaps not before) with scrupulous and impeccable fairness. The language of Title VII we quoted would certainly suggest that that is what the framers of the Civil Rights Act hoped eventually to achieve.

The response of partisans of affirmative action that "goals" are not "quotas" because they are more flexibly administered is perhaps an attempt to say (without being too explicit) that if a group cannot fill a proportional goal with good candidates, then the regulations allow the goal to be lowered. But in reality it is difficult to do that. (In fact, the lack of enforcement of the goals has made that issue moot so far.)

What must be balanced against the unfortunate aspects of quotas is the reality of currently operating discrimination, the serious harm that discrimination causes, and the lack of a feasible alternative to deal with it. Affirmative-action goals are temporary expedients meant to remedy a highly discriminatory situation that otherwise could not be dismantled. The situation that most justifies affirmative action is where the "quota" for the excluded group has already been set—by the discriminators—at close to zero. Affirmative action then can be seen as upping an already existing quota into a fairer range.

AFFIRMATIVE ACTION IN WOMEN'S ECONOMIC AGENDA

While some writers have declared affirmative action to have failed, or to have done more harm than good, it is more accurate to say that it has never really been seriously tried on a large enough scale and with a severity of enforcement sufficient to make a big dent in the problem of discrimination. One reason is that progress is not easy in this field because of the inherent difficulties of planning and administering changes in deep-seated behavior. Second, there has been up to now very little real political power behind the antidiscrimination initiatives, even under political regimes whose rhetoric appeared to favor them. Under Democratic administrations, ostensibly committed to the achievement of fair employment practices, the agencies charged with fighting employment discrimination have not been models of energy and efficiency. Republican administrations have tended to be openly hostile, if not to the ideal of fair employment practices, then to any instrument that might be used by the government to promote that goal.

Regrettably, activists for women's rights have shown little initiative in pushing for more vigor in the pursuit of affirmative action. Some of them may have assumed that affirmative action should or would be applied principally to get access to jobs for blacks, an assumption entertained by the enforcement agencies themselves for a considerable period. Certainly, they feel that affirmative-action programs, even effective ones, bring relatively little help to the majority of women workers already committed to the traditional female occupations. These considerations have led to a concentration by women's rights activists on a remedy—pay equity—that would offer a direct improvement in the wages paid in predominantly female occupations.

But even though the implementation of pay equity, which is the subject of the next chapter, would bring significant economic improvement for women, affirmative action to include women workers in all occupations in fair numbers is vital. Without affirmative action, the period in which sex segregation is the rule on the job is likely to be prolonged indefinitely. A continued failure to press affirmative action would rob young women of a chance to choose from a full range of occupations the one most congenial to their talents. Continued segregation would make the efforts to close the pay gap between women and men a continual uphill struggle. And only when women have a share in the roles that men occupy will men and women be comfortable interacting as equals.

CHAPTER 8

Achieving Pay Equity

IN ANY FACTORY or office or government bureau, women holding traditionally female jobs get less pay than men holding traditionally male jobs requiring lower levels of skill, knowledge, and mental capacity. In some workplaces, a woman secretary will be paid less than the male operator of a duplicating machine. The idea has been gaining ground among women that pay differentials like that are unfair and discriminatory. The pay equity movement, with the rallying cry "Equal pay for jobs of comparable worth," aims to get employers to equalize the wage rates for women in traditionally female jobs with wage rates for men in traditionally male jobs requiring equivalent abilities.

The pay equity campaign has aroused in millions of women workers a consciousness that their low pay rates derive from discrimination and ought to be remedied. They are coming to believe that unfair acts, not the impartial laws of economics, are responsible. The power of this idea among women has meant that the pay equity campaign can mobilize political pressure. That makes its success a practical possibility. Perhaps for this reason, the pay equity campaign has provoked a great deal of vocal opposition, much of it taking the raucus, mocking tone that often marks the reaction to any proposed improvement in women's status.[1] Some of the opposition has come from those who have brought themselves to believe that nothing is wrong or unfair about the present alignment of wage practices. Some has come from those who believe it is always bad policy to tamper with the verdict rendered by supply and demand. Some opposition has come from those concerned to keep outside interference with business to a minimum. Finally, there is the opposition of those who share the feelings of the manager who said, "I will not pay a woman, any damned woman, the same money that I will pay a man. . . ."[2]

Even for those inclined to think that the present lineup of wage levels results from discrimination, the demands for the realignment of wage rates pose serious questions: How might pay equity be put into effect? How in practice can we compare men's and women's jobs, and do it in a way that makes economic sense? Where is the money to come from for the extra pay for the women? Will the raises in women's pay cut employers' demand for women workers, forcing women into unemployment? Will higher wages in the traditionally women's jobs tempt women to flock to those jobs when they should be seeking to enter traditionally male jobs? Will pay equity cause inflation?

There is a good basis for believing that realignments of wages do a great deal of good and little appreciable harm and that they serve to remedy some of the results of discrimination. There is considerable warrant for believing that pay equity wage adjustments would create little extra unemployment for women. They can be financed out of economic growth in a relatively painless and inflation-free way. Finally, a widespread success for pay equity would reduce the amount of poverty among women and children.

COMPARING WOMEN'S AND MEN'S JOBS

A discussion of pay equity must start with a description of how a pay equity realignment could typically be made in the case of a particular workplace. After looking at that we will be in a position to inquire whether the proposed procedure for establishing pay equity makes sense.

Pay equity realignments of wages are likely to be called for only in workplaces where women and men are segregated by job title. The essence of pay equity is the aligning of the salaries attached to the women's job titles with the salaries of "comparable" men's jobs. Here, "comparable" jobs means jobs requiring similar levels of skills and mental abilities. In the case of a small employer, the wage changes could be decided by negotiation or by some informal procedure. However, in the case of a large employer, where dozens of job titles and millions of dollars would be involved, a formal systematic study would most likely be undertaken. In the course of that study, each job, after due consideration, would be assigned a numerical score. That score would serve as an index of what a reasonable rate of pay for that job should be. Typically, the study would proceed in the following four steps:

1. Personnel experts would be called in to compile a written detailed description of the duties of each job.
2. The personnel experts would establish a group of "compensable factors" to be used in evaluating the job descriptions. Some of the compensable factors would measure the qualities a person would need in order to fulfill a particular job description. Such factors would typically include the amount of knowledge one had to have to perform the job, the ingenuity one needed to perform it, the amount of independent decision-making involved in carrying out the duties. Other compensable factors might include how disagreeable the working conditions were—whether it had to be performed in a dirty, noisy, or otherwise unpleasant environment, and whether there was appreciable danger of injury. Guidelines as to how to assign grades would also have to be spelled out.
3. For each job to be valued, numerical grades for each of the compensable factors would then be assigned by the personnel experts. This would be done by consulting the job description, the description of the compensable factors, and the guidelines for grading.
4. For each job, a total score could now be calculated, based on the grade given that job for each compensable factor.

Based on the study, target wage rates would be set for the women's jobs, to bring them into line with the pay given to men's jobs with comparable scores. A timetable for increasing the pay of the female jobs would have to be set up.

An example of the pay equity process is provided by the state government of Washington. Early in the 1970s, the Washington Federation of State Employees (a union affiliated with the American Federation of State, County and Municipal Employees, AFL-CIO) and the Washington State Women's Council pressed the state government to look at differences in the salaries it assigned its employees in male- and female-dominated jobs.[3] A comparable worth study was done in 1974. Some of its results are shown in table 8-1, which gives evaluations for six important job titles.

The personnel consultants hired by the state government made use of four compensable factors, "knowledge and skills," "mental demands," "accountability," and "work conditions." As can be seen from the table, the consultants brought with them a selection of ready-made descriptive phrases. Rating jobs comes down to choosing the most appropriate phrase for each factor for each job. With each descriptive phrase goes a range of point scores. The consultants rated a secretarial job to be modestly ahead of an auto mechanic's job in terms of knowledge and skill required, and considerably ahead of a delivery truck driver's job on that factor. (The truck driver's job was essentially judged to be devoid of any skill requirements not found in the general population.) With respect to "mental demands," the secretary's job was judged to be about on par with the mechanic's. However, the secretarial job gained points over the mechanic's for having a greater "influence on outcomes." Both the truck driver and the mechanic were awarded points under the heading of "working conditions," because of the moderate lifting requirements and occasional danger of injury on their jobs. In all, the secretarial job was awarded a score considerably higher than the delivery truck driver's and modestly higher than the mechanic's.

A registered nurse's job was evaluated somewhat higher than a civil engineer's but lower than that of a senior computer systems analyst. The consultants rated the knowledge and skills of the nurse above those of the engineer, in part because the nurse, unlike the engineer, has to have an ability required of supervisors—an ability to persuade and motivate. The nurse was judged to have higher mental demands than the engineer, because the analysis required by her job is less routine, less cut-and-dried. While the actions of both the engineer and the nurse "influence results," the nurse makes decisions that may irrevocably help or hurt patients. The nurse gets more points on the work conditions factor than any of the other occupations listed in the table—she deals with excrement, blood, patients who may be violent.

The final two columns of table 8–1 give the total points awarded each job, and the 1985 salaries each earned. Washington state has paid salaries for the four traditionally male jobs shown in the table roughly in line with their total point scores: Men's jobs with higher point scores get higher salaries. The state claims to have paid attention to the market salaries in each occupation when it set the salaries for its employees. The good correlation between market-set salaries for traditionally male occupations and the scores arrived at in the study suggests that, for men at least, the study did a good job of measuring worker characteristics that the market values.

By contrast, the salaries the state has set for the two female jobs in table 8–1 are obviously way out of line with their scores. Secretaries employed by the state are paid less than delivery truck drivers. Nurses are paid less than auto mechanics. Clearly the market—and the state of Washington—values women's knowledge, skill, ingenuity, and sufferance of difficult working conditions at a rate lower than it values the same characteristics in men.

After the study, the advocates of comparable worth for the employees of the state of Washington, led by their union urged that the governor and the state legislature move to raise salary levels in women's jobs in accordance with the results of the comparable worth study. However, by 1983 little had been accomplished. In that year a lawsuit, *AFSCME* v. *State of Washington,* was filed. The trial judge in the case ruled that salaries in women's occupations should be raised immediately and back wages paid. In 1985 an appeals court reversed the trial judge's ruling. In 1986, the state and the union agreed on a compromise settlement of the case. The salaries in jobs that are currently low relative to their point scores will be gradually raised. The settlement calls for the full achievement of comparable worth by the year 1993, a quarter century after the original agitation for comparable worth started.

TABLE 8–1

Evaluations of Six Job Titles from the Comparable Worth Study Done for the Employees of the State of Washington

	Knowledge and Skills	Mental Demands	Accountability	Work Conditions	Total Points	Salary as of 1/85
Delivery Truck Driver	No previous exp. required. Brief on-the-job learning period required. (61)	Standardized work routines. Recall rather than analysis required. (10)	Duties routine, work closely controlled. (13)	Moderate lifting, some danger. Conditions occasionally undesirable. (13)	97	$382
Auto Mechanic	Mechanical skill required. (106)	Similar procedures and methods, analysis of recurring nature. (26)	Methods clearly defined, work frequently reviewed. (30)	Moderate lifting, some danger. Conditions occasionally undesirable. (13)	175	465
Secretary (Grade III)	Activities require vocational competence and/or adeptness. Capability in dealing with others required. (122)	Similar procedures and methods, analysis of recurring nature. (35)	Methods clearly defined, work frequently reviewed. Actions influence results. (40)	Job at a desk. Little lifting, danger minimal. (0)	197	306

TABLE 8-1 (Continued)

	Knowledge and Skills	Mental Demands	Accountability	Work Conditions	Total Points	Salary as of 1/85
Civil Engineer	Comprehension of complex principles and practices. Capability in dealing with others required. (160)	Varying or complex procedures. Routine analysis. (53)	Activities generally defined, review after the fact. Actions influence results. (61)	Moderate lifting, some danger. Conditions occasionally undesirable. (13)	287	513
Registered Nurse	Comprehension of complex principles and practices. Requires capability to persuade and motivate. (184)	Varying or complex procedures. Non-routine analysis. (70)	Activities generally defined, review after the fact. Actions influence results. (70)	Moderate lifting, some danger. Disagreeable conditions much of the time. (17)	341	411
Sr. Computer Systems Analyst	Comprehension of complex principles and practices. Capability in dealing with others required. (212)	Varying or complex procedures. Non-routine analysis. (80)	Activities generally defined, review after the fact. Actions influence results. Moderate fiscal impact. (80)	Job at a desk. Little lifting, danger minimal. (0)	372	553

SOURCE: Characterization of job requirements is taken from "State of Washington, Comparable Worth Study, September 1974," prepared by Norman D. Willis in consultation with Ann O. Worcester (Norman D. Willis & Associates, Management Consultants). Salaries and point scores are from an unpublished tabulation made for the author by Helen Remick, Director, Office of Affirmative Action, University of Washington.

PAY EQUITY AND TRADITIONAL JOB EVALUATION

The critics of pay equity have claimed that the comparisons employers will be required to make between jobs to realign pay scales will inevitably be arbitrary and irrational. However, the methodology used for pay equity is similar in almost all respects to the job evaluation procedures that a considerable proportion of large employers—business firms and government bureaus—actually use to set the pay for many of their jobs. Like pay equity, job evaluation requires job descriptions, gives grades for compensable factors, and adds up a value score for each job.

Pay equity evaluations do have some unavoidable elements of subjectivity, as the Washington state example in table 8–1 makes obvious. Judgments about "knowledge" or "working conditions" cannot be completely objective. Yet the same degree of subjectivity has been found tolerable by employers in the job evaluation studies they have commissioned and utilized.[4]

The use of job evaluation in setting pay scales gained popularity with employers many decades before the idea of pay equity came to the fore, and it continues to be popular with them. Job evaluation serves several important purposes for employers. A large employer will have a great variety of job titles, many of them unique to that establishment. That means it would be difficult or impossible to find out market wage rates for many jobs. So in practice some method of assigning wages other than by reference to the market must be adopted. For such firms, the only alternative to a systematic internal job-evaluation scheme would be a set of wage rates based largely on internal politicking. That would be bound to produce inconsistent results and generate worker unrest and dissatisfaction. Job evaluation schemes have the advantage of making the determination of relative wages appear to the workers to be scientific and therefore less arguable.

Because many employers already use job evaluations, the use of similar procedures to compare women's and men's jobs is a natural and reasonable extension of current practices. The job evaluation procedures are well established and familiar, and many groups of experienced consultants offer such services.

FIGURE 8–1

Use of Male and Female Job Clusters to Avoid Paying Male-Level Wage Scales to Women

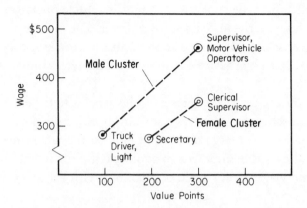

NOTE: The figure illustrates the usual implementation of job evaluation results within a single establishment. Wages are from unpublished BLS tabulations for 1985. Value points are derived from Washington state job evaluations.

There is, however, a crucial difference between pay equity calculations and job evaluation as currently practiced in most establishments. The essence of pay equity is that the women's and men's jobs are rated by the same system. By contrast, in job evaluation systems, employers commonly will use some stratagem or other to avoid comparing the male and the female jobs directly. In one commonly used ploy, the jobs are split into a number of groups or clusters. Some of the clusters will consist mostly of jobs that women hold, and some will be made up mostly of jobs that men hold. By design, clusters will be sex-segregated to a high degree. Each cluster will be evaluated and assigned wages separately. In each cluster, nomenclature, grading methods, and point systems unique to that cluster may be used to give the impression that the evaluations of the jobs in one cluster have no relation at all to the evaluations of jobs in any other cluster.

For each cluster of jobs, the employer will pick a job whose market wage is easily determined because the duties are fairly standard from one employer to another. For such a job, designated as a "key job," the employer will pay market wages. Then the employer will set the pay of any job in relation to the key job in its cluster. The pay of a job will be higher or lower than that of the key job for that cluster, depending on the job's total value score.

In figure 8–1 this use of clusters and key jobs is illustrated. Secretary is the key job for the women, and light truck driver is the key job for the men. A female office supervisor will be in the same cluster as the secretary job, and the male supervisor of motor vehicle operators will be in the same cluster as the male light truck driver. The male supervisor will get a weekly salary $100 or so more than the female supervisor. Yet their jobs, if rated by the same system, would have a similar value score.

The use of the cluster system preserves the benefits to the employer of job evaluation schemes—it offers a seemingly objective process for assigning wage levels to a large number of jobs. At the same time, the cluster system allows the employer to avoid paying for female occupations the same wages as for male occupations with the same value point score.

Sometimes the desired differential between male and female wages is achieved by superimposing a distinguishing label on some of the job titles, such as "management" or "exempt."* This label is then used to justify paying certain workers (invariably mostly men) more than other workers with the same job evaluation point score.

Some job evaluation schemes are "fixed" to produce low pay for women by discounting the factors that distinguish women's jobs and rewarding highly the factors that distinguish men's. Giving high points for physical strength requirements, and few points for requirements of fine attention to detail or boredom, are examples. Occasionally the "fix" is achieved simply by inaccuracy, as in the case of the job evaluation training manual used by one well-known firm of personnel consultants that identified "running a typewriter" as being in the same low-level category as "running a mimeograph machine."

If job evaluation schemes are to be used in pay equity adjustments, these "fixes" have to be removed. The "fixes" mar a potentially useful way of building a fair and economically sound wage structure; properly cleaned-up job evaluation schemes provide a promising methodology for the removal of sex bias from wage scales, one pioneered by business itself.

---

* The provisions of the Fair Labor Standards Act, which allow some workers to be designated as exempt from receiving premium pay for overtime, frequently are used in this way. Male-identified jobs are designated as "exempt," and a premium wage rate is applied to exempt jobs. This works particularly well in firms where very few workers do overtime work.

PAY EQUITY VERSUS THE MARKET

Pay equity carries job evaluation to its logical conclusion. All of an employer's jobs are subject to the same evaluation procedure. In pay equity any two jobs that are awarded the same score are awarded the same pay, regardless of the sex identification of the job. This certainly violates the command of the marketplace. The market allows the employer to segregate jobs by sex and to attach to the women's jobs lower salaries than those attached to comparable men's jobs.

The opponents of pay equity cite the violation of the market's command; they claim that such a violation is pay equity's fatal flaw. Granted, economic efficiency and fairness *are* served if we follow the command of an unbiased market. However, if discrimination is conceded to be serious and widespread in the market, then following the market means validating unfairness. If discrimination has skewed the market outcome, an alternative way of assigning wage rates may be economically more valid. Of course, not every alternative technique that might be proposed is necessarily an improvement over the market. Before we adopt pay equity as a remedy, we need to ask what validity the evaluation techniques of pay equity have. We need to inquire whether using them can be expected to make things better or worse.

The original slogan of "equal pay for jobs of comparable worth" carried with it the suggestion that a job should be evaluated by looking at the benefit the employer gets from the services the worker in the job performs. This would have made little sense. Sometimes a function vital to a business, such as tending the furnace that runs an entire factory, can be performed by an untrained, unskilled employee. While such an employee might be given a modest premium for being extra careful and alert, there would be no valid reason to pay the particular employee singled out to do such a vital job a great deal more than would be paid to any other worker in the shop with the same low skills. In practice, pay equity evaluations have not been tied at all closely to the value the employer derives from the employee's service.* Rather,

---

* Job evaluation schemes do give a minor amount of credit for the importance of the outcome of the worker's actions. In the example given in table 8–1, this is taken care of under the accountability factor.

The Economic Emergence of Women

these evaluations have focused on the duties of the job and on the qualities the worker must bring to the job to perform those duties successfully.

Many of the qualities the worker must bring to the job are built up by investments in human capital, so pay equity or job evaluation techniques, if well conceived and well carried out, do serve to give us a measure of the human capital necessary to perform adequately in each job. They also measure the talent workers must have to do non-routine tasks, an inborn form of human capital the market also pays for. In the Washington state evaluation, the compensable factor "knowledge and skills" is highly correlated with length and intensity of education and training. The compensable factor "mental demands" measures the problem-solving abilities required on the job, abilities that are created and enhanced by education. Jobs with high "account-ability" scores require that workers have the experience and education that fit them to make well-considered independent judgments. So three of the four compensable factors relate to the human capital requirements of the job.

The compensable factor "work conditions" does not relate to human capital, but to the likes and dislikes of workers for certain kinds of conditions faced on the job. Work that takes place in a factory or out-of-doors, is physically heavy, and carries some chance for injury is less favored by workers than clean, light work in an office. Giving points for unfavored work conditions is a way of acknowledging that the market awards extra pay for a job that workers would otherwise shun.

Thus each compensable factor measures aspects of jobs that affect the wage assigned to jobs in the market, and would continue to affect wages were the market to be purged of discriminatory behavior. Those who design job evaluations attempt to include all such aspects, and to give each aspect its proper importance in the outcome.[5] Compensable factors with relatively minor effect on market wages are given little weight in calculating the total job evaluation score.*

* This is sometimes done by taking jobs for which market salaries are available, and evaluating them using the same scoring system (say, from zero to 100) for each compensable factor. Then regression methods are used to estimate how many wage dollars per point the market awards in the case of each factor. After this has been done, the scoring system can be revised, so that a point for any factor counts the same in terms of market dollars. In the Washington state example given in table 8–1, about ten times more points can be awarded for "mental demands" as for "work conditions," because market wages vary little with work conditions. The low premium

There are some aspects of pay determination that the compensable factors do not account for. Short-run changes in supply or demand may temporarily push a job's pay above or below the level consonant with the job's human capital requirements and working conditions. The compensable factors measure the aspects of a job that affect its relative position in the salary scale only in the longer run.

Pay equity wage realignment pushes an employer's wage scales closer to the pattern they would have in a nondiscriminatory market that was in long-run equilibrium. In such a market, the wage a job paid would depend on the qualifications the job required and on the working conditions, not on the sex of the incumbents. Such a market would be more economically efficient and certainly more fair than the present market, in which discrimination plays such a big role. In such a market, the human capital of men and women would be paid for at the same rate.

The methods that have been proposed for making pay equity adjustments are based on the economically orthodox idea that people who have the same potential productivity—who embody the same level of "human capital"—should be paid similarly, perhaps after due allowance for the job's unpleasantness. However, now that the human capital theory may be turned to the benefit of women workers, some economists are starting to say that wages ought not reflect human capital requirements after all. The compensable factors, which reflect human capital requirements of jobs, may not account for the habitual flocking of women into occupations that have been traditional for them. Perhaps women are willing to endure low wages in these occupations and just want to do the traditional thing. Perhaps the work and conditions in these jobs appeal to some aspect of women's minds. If that were the case, then the pay in such occupations could be legitimately depressed below the level that would be expected on the basis of the occupations' human capital requirements.[6]

It is theoretically possible that women's choice rather than discrimination causes the crowding in the women's labor market. However, this theoretical possibility is refuted by the evidence on occupational wages by sex, which points to the existence of significant

---

the labor market gives to people who suffer difficult work conditions is documented in Charles E. Brown, "Equalizing Differences in the Labor Market," *Quarterly Journal of Economics* (February 1980):113–34.

discrimination, as do the mountains of trial evidence. Men in the women's traditional occupations do get male-level pay, consonant with their human capital (see table 6–1). The large number of women available for these jobs does not depress the pay of the men in them.

THE PRACTICAL POLITICS OF PAY EQUITY

The pay equity campaign in the United States originated with Winn Newman and Ruth Weyand, who were lawyers on the staff of the International Union of Electrical Workers. Newman and Weyand got the idea of suing employers under the antidiscrimination laws for practicing "sex-based wage discrimination." They reasoned that if suits on this basis were successful, back pay awards to women employees might cost large employers billions of dollars. The example of large awards might convince other employers to realign their wage scales voluntarily.

Two laws in the United States forbid sex-based differences in pay: the Equal Pay Act and the Civil Rights Act. Congress passed the Equal Pay Act in 1963, the year before the Civil Rights Act. Its provisions require an employer to give men and women employees "equal pay for equal work." The courts have interpreted this legislation to mean that pay need be equalized only among those men and women doing virtually identical work for the same employer. If the work is merely similar, equality of pay is not required under the Equal Pay Act. Even on this narrow interpretation, millions of dollars' worth of claims have been paid under the act. However, most employers practice strict occupational segregation by sex. So most of them have few or no women doing work identical to any man's. For this reason, the Equal Pay Act can contribute only modestly to closing the salary gap.

Title VII of the Civil Rights Act prohibits sex-based differences in pay and does not require proof of "equal work." Lawyers for women employees have hoped that its provisions could serve as a basis for courts to order realignments of wage scales in establishments practicing occupational segregation. They have reasoned that the pay scales in certain jobs are relatively low just because the workers are women. If the employer had chosen to reserve those same jobs for men, the wage rate the employer would have assigned to those jobs would be much higher, as table 6–1 shows. Thus the low wages assigned to the women's jobs are a form of "sex-based wage discrimination." A realignment of pay scales to raise the wages for the female jobs would provide the appropriate remedy.

In one of the first lawsuits brought under this theory, nurses employed by the city of Denver argued that their pay was lower than that set for males with lower levels of qualification.[7] For example, the city paid nurses, who had a professional education and had responsibility for human lives, less than tree trimmers, who did not need a high-school diploma. Supervisors of nursing, with management functions affecting the life and death of patients, had lower pay than low-level administration jobs filled by males in other parts of the city government. The nurse supervisors' jobs were in the same low-pay job cluster as the nurses, while the male administrators were in higher-paying clusters with other males.

The city of Denver responded that it made periodic surveys of nursing salaries in the Denver area. It paid the nurses in its own hospitals at the market rate indicated by the survey. With respect to the nurse supervisors, the city personnel officer admitted in court that their duties were comparable to those of male administrators paid considerably more. When asked what accounted for the difference in pay, he answered that the nurse supervisors were nurses. The extra qualification required for the nurse supervisor job thus became in effect a justification for paying those women less.

The judge who heard the case accepted the argument that paying market wages was not discrimination under Title VII. He extolled the free market as a way of setting wages, and he made reference to the welter of difficulty he would be in if he were required to take charge of wage-setting for the employees of the city of Denver. The judge threw out the charges of discrimination the nurses had brought, and his decision was upheld on appeal. As we have seen, a court of appeals on similar grounds rejected the comparable worth claims of the women employees of the state of Washington.

Fortunately, wage adjustments can be made apart from lawsuits, if there is enough pressure behind them. Despite judicial hostility to the pay equity concept, other state and local governments have come under political or union pressure to make pay equity wage realignments. Legislative bodies have commissioned job evaluation studies, and appropriated funds to raise the pay for the female job titles. Political pressure to do this probably will continue even if lawsuits continue to fail. Legislation has been introduced to study the wage levels of federal employees, with the purpose of justifying a realignment.

If wages are realigned for a significant proportion of employees in the public sector, there will be an effect, through the labor market, on private employers, even if they are legally immune from forced realignment. If private employers fail to raise wages in the women's occupations they will lose the best women workers to the public sector, which is sizable enough to absorb a considerable proportion of them. In all likelihood there would be some upward readjustment of wages in female occupations by private employers to avoid this.

The equity campaign is just starting to affect private employers. A few employers are starting to feel pressure to make wage realignments from unions.* In the past, unions have not generally been interested in using their bargaining leverage to advance women workers relative to male workers.[8] Even in unions where women workers have been a majority of the members, the union hierarchy has almost invariably been in male hands, and the reservation of jobs for male workers at high relative wages has been carefully preserved. The pay equity campaign of AFSCME represents a break in union traditions of acquiescence to inferior pay for women. Other unions may follow the lead of AFSCME, but in some situations, the formation of women-led workplace organizations to push for pay equity adjustments may be necessary.

Another way to push pay equity realignments would be to have the federal government issue a set of pay guidelines. Opponents of pay equity adjustments enjoy frightening the business community with the nightmare of a large and stupidly run federal agency that would fix by administrative fiat the wage rate for every job in every business in the

---

* The best-publicized cases have been those of universities. Yale, Columbia, and New York University have had pay equity negotiations, with some improvements for women resulting.

country.* Such an inclusive approach would be expensive, unwieldy, and unnecessarily intrusive. However, an agency might set up minimum wage recommendations for the largest of the typically female occupations—typist, secretary, retail sales clerk, child-care worker, teacher, social worker, librarian, nurse. This is the approach taken by Australia, and it has worked effectively to raise women's wages, apparently without adverse economic consequences to the women or to the society generally.[9] Another approach would be for EEOC or the Labor Department to recommend wage ratios for a group of common male and female occupations. For example, the recommendation might be that an employer pay secretaries a certain percent more than that employer pays truck drivers. Such pay patterns could be required of government contractors, along with affirmative action.

DISPLACEMENT EFFECTS

Opponents of pay equity have argued that raising the price of women's labor in the stereotypically female occupations can be expected to shrink the amount of labor that employers will wish to employ in such occupations. Some employers might want to replace their women workers with men if they are forced to pay wages high enough to attract men. Because affirmative action has so far not been vigorously pushed, the absorption into typically male occupations of those women workers who might be displaced can by no means be guaranteed.

The interesting question is not whether there will be displacement effects, but how large they will be. In thinking about this issue, we can look at the experience of countries that have made large relative adjustments in women's pay relative to men's. The experiment has been tried in Australia on quite a significant scale. There, the custom has been for administrative boards to set minimum wages for a wide range of occupations, and the minimums they set apparently do influ-

---

* Such controls would not, however, be unprecedented. Wage boards with broad jurisdiction operated during World War II and during the Korean War.

ence the wages employers actually pay. In the late 1970s, the minimum-pay boards decided to get rid of a big part of the gap between men's and women's pay on average, and women's pay rose by 30 percent.[10] Two economists, Robert Gregory and Ronald Duncan, studied the effects on women's employment of these substantial upward pay adjustments. They concluded that the disemployment of women must have been quite small.[11] Pay adjustments for women in Great Britain seem to have had the same result: little or no extra unemployment for women workers.[12]

Gregory and Duncan's explanation of the low rate of displacement is that men's and women's occupations complement each other in the productive process. At least in the short and medium run, employers find it difficult to reorganize the productive process to allow them to cut down on the employment of some occupational groups but not others. Nor does there appear to be much replacement of women by men in the traditional women's jobs. Ironically, the pervasiveness of sex segregation, the fixed ideas of employers about who should do which job, and the reluctance of men in most circumstances to enter occupations perceived as being appropriate to women appear to have protected women's jobs, even as their wage rates rose substantially. Whether this low disemployment effect will hold up in the longer run remains to be seen.

A strong affirmative-action program would reduce the disemployment effects of pay equity. The drop in demand for women's labor could be fully or partially counterbalanced by increased hiring of women in previously male-typical occupations. Whatever the net disemployment effects of the pay equity adjustments do turn out to be, they must be considered as a trade-off for the higher wages women would get while employed. Higher unemployment rates for women would translate into longer spells of unemployment for those women who become unemployed. It is important to realize, however, that those employed at higher wages thanks to pay equity adjustments, and those banished to the unemployment office for longer stays, are not two distinct groups, one gaining and the other losing. There is considerable circulation of individuals into and out of jobs. The woman who becomes unemployed and has to spend an extra week out of a job because of pay equity reforms might well find that at the end of her spell of unemployment her new job has higher pay. The research done so far implies that the gains to women from higher pay while employed would swamp the losses due to higher unemployment rates.* It suggests, in fact, that the latter would hardly be noticeable.

PAY EQUITY AND AFFIRMATIVE ACTION

Some opponents of pay equity argue that women could be helped without any need for the dislocations that would arise from the implementation of pay equity. They recommend instead stronger efforts to get women to enter previously male fields, and a revitalized campaign to win for women access to the better jobs.

A successful affirmative action program could raise wage scales in the currently female occupations. The crowding of women into the female-stereotyped occupations would be diminished as more jobs reserved for men became open to people of both sexes. Male workers would not replace the women in the jobs they had left as long as the wages in them remained subpar for men. This reduction in the supply of labor to the traditionally female occupations would tend to raise the wages paid in them. In fact, a vigorous affirmative-action program should have the same effect on wages as a well-planned and well-implemented pay equity program. Moreover, affirmative action has added benefits that pay equity reforms lack. Affirmative action allows women workers to have access to jobs they may enjoy and be good at, and it promotes the equality of men and women by casting them as equals on the job. It causes the adjustment of wages through the market mechanism and avoids any disemployment effects.

In fact, if affirmative action were proceeding rapidly, a pay equity campaign might be redundant. The argument for pay equity boils down to saying that whatever progress there has been through affirmative action, little or none of the benefit has accrued to the women in tra-

---

* The average length of time a woman who suffered unemployment in 1984 spent unemployed was 11.5 weeks.[13] A rise in the unemployment rate by 10 percent might increase that by about a week. One week additional in unemployment is a reduction of yearly income by 2 percent, without allowing for unemployment insurance. That 2 percent reduction has to be balanced against the 30 percent rise in pay that pay equity adjustments might bring.

ditional jobs. Pay equity would help those women in a timely way. The effect of affirmative action on wages in traditionally female occupations is at best indirect and tardy.

The pay equity campaign reflects the view of many activists who have felt that it would not make sense to concentrate exclusively or even primarily on getting women switched into traditionally male jobs. They argue for direct action to improve the wages paid in currently female occupations. They see little evidence so far that affirmative action has had a positive impact on the wages in the traditionally female occupations. Most of the women gaining entry to the previously male-dominated higher-paying occupations are young, recent labor force entrants. The majority of the women who entered the labor force in years past and are currently working have, through choice or lack of a better alternative, already committed themselves to jobs that are stereotypically female. A high proportion of the women currently holding jobs as secretaries, nurses, librarians, nursery-school teachers, social workers, and cleaners probably will continue in such jobs for the rest of their work lives. Many women would not be able or do not want to change to typically male occupations. Some have invested in lengthy, difficult, and expensive training for the jobs they hold. They have adjusted their lives to the rhythm and locations of these jobs and would be comfortable in them if only they were paid a male-level wage for the work they are doing. The only way such women can be helped is by a rise in the rate of pay for women in their current occupations. If this is not done, then all the effort to improve women's economic status will benefit only the younger women; for the majority, little will have been achieved.

The suggestion has been made that equitable wages in traditionally female jobs would hurt women by inducing them to hang on to such jobs, and would inhibit them from responding to the opening of traditionally male jobs.[14] The argument may have some merit, but it comes with poor grace from those who maintain that pay equity would force women out of the traditional women's jobs by drastically reducing the number of such jobs. It is also remarkable that those who stoutly defend the status quo, and the "choice" of women to go into currently low-paying jobs, and who have long claimed that such jobs are uniquely advantageous to women, should be the very ones to bemoan the putative choice of women to stay in those jobs once their pay has been raised. A classic case of crocodile tears, it would appear.

EFFECTS ON EMPLOYERS

An establishment that has realigned its wages will have a wage structure very different from that of most other establishments—at least while the pay equity movement is in its infancy. It may simply have raised the wages in its female jobs and kept its wages for male jobs in line with those in other establishments. In this case, it will have a considerably larger wage bill than they, which might well handicap a private employer in a competitive industry. A more likely way of accomplishing a realignment is by giving the female job titles larger increases than the male job titles. If at the same time, other establishments were giving males and females equal percentage increases, then the establishment making the pay equity adjustment is going to find itself with wages in traditionally male jobs that are lower than those in other firms.

Establishments that realign their wage structures by letting male wages lag behind wages in other establishments may experience a loss of labor in traditionally male jobs and an inability to recruit able men to fill them. While some may see this as a drawback to pay equity, properly regarded it is an advantage. In fact, this is a case of pay equity strengthening the motive for employers to practice affirmative action. Such a situation should push the firm to recruit women as trainees for its traditionally male jobs.

PAYING FOR PAY EQUITY

If pay equity adjustments become widespread, they might add $2 billion to $3 billion a week to women's pay checks, or $100 billion to $150 billion a year. These figures are rough approximations, calculated at 1982 levels.* As time goes on, and the level of money wages grows higher, the amounts involved grow.

---

* See following material for the basis of this estimate. The purpose of going back to 1982 is to show how these sums of money might have been mobilized in the period 1982–84.

To put these numbers in perspective and to facilitate the discussion of where such sums of money might come from, figure 8-2 shows the division of the entire national income of the United States for 1982.[15] Of the total national income of $2,450 billion, the compensation of employees—wages and fringe benefits—accounted for the largest share, $1,866 billion, or 76 percent. Corporate profits and income of non-corporate businesses and farms amounted together to $274 billion, or 11 percent. Other payments—rent and net interest—took $301 billion, or 13 percent.

Of the $1,866 billion paid in wages and worker benefits, about $1,325 billion went to men and $541 billion to women.[16] Thus male workers, who were 56 percent of those receiving wage income, received about 70 percent of the wage dollars, and women only 30 percent. Men's large share of the wage dollars is mainly a result of their higher average wage rates. However, a higher proportion of men than women worked full time year-round, and that accounts for part of the size of their share of the wage dollars. Pay equity adjustments would affect directly only the wage rates and any fringe benefits tied to the rate of wages.

If adjustments to wages were made so that jobs with equal scores on job evaluations were to get equal wage rates, only part of the gap between men's and women's wage rates would be closed. The remainder of the gap is due to the fact that women have fewer of the more responsible jobs, so that men would have higher scores on average in the job evaluations. This in turn is due partly to women's fewer years of experience and partly to discriminatory exclusions. The experience deficiency would lessen with the passage of time, while the exclusions would have to be attacked through affirmative action. Roughly one third of the gap would be closed by pay equity readjustments.

To close one third of the pay gap in the whole economy in a single year, on the assumption that the dollar amount of men's paychecks would remain unchanged while women's pay advanced, would have required in 1982 that about $117 billion be added to women's paychecks.[17] This would have increased women's pay by 22 percent. Such a sum would have amounted to 6 percent of the entire wage bill and 5 percent of total national income that year.

Certainly, changes of that magnitude in a single year would be

TABLE 8–2
How to Pay for Pay Equity

Across-the-Board Distribution of Increases (no progress in closing the gap)			
	Men	Women	Both Sexes
Original Wage Bill (in 1982)	$1325	$541	$1866
18 percent Increase (1982–4)	238	97	335
Final Wage Bill	1563	638	2201

Concentrating Part of the Increase on Women (closing about a third of the gap)			
	Men	Women	Both Sexes
Original Wage Bill	$1325	$541	$1866
Pay Equity Increase of 22 percent for Women	0	117	117
Amended Wage Bill	(1325)	(658)	(1983)
11 percent Increase on Amended Wage Bill	146	72	218
Total Wage Increase	146	189	335
Final Wage Bill	1471	730	2201

NOTE: Original wage bill based on national income and Current Population Reports data for 1982; wages by sex based on Bureau of Labor Statistics data for 1982–4, as reported in the *Economic Report of the President, Transmitted to the Congress, February 1985,* table B–41, p. 279.

FIGURE 8–2

Pay Equity Adjustments, Compared to Total Wages and Profits

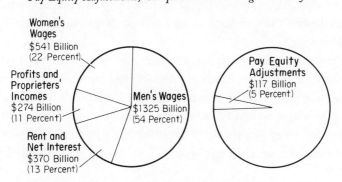

Women's Wages $541 Billion (22 Percent)

Profits and Proprieters' Incomes $274 Billion (11 Percent)

Men's Wages $1325 Billion (54 Percent)

Rent and Net Interest $370 Billion (13 Percent)

Pay Equity Adjustments $117 Billion (5 Percent)

SOURCE: Income shares from the *Economic Report of the President, February 1985.*

difficult for the economy to swallow and digest. However, if the changes were (as surely they will be) phased in over time, the difficulty would ease considerably. In that case, the funds to make the pay equity adjustments might come out of the regular increases in the money compensation rates for workers that normally occur each year. Worker compensation rates per hour increased by 8.1 percent in 1982, by 4.3 percent in 1983, and by 4.7 percent in 1984.[18] This adds up, with compounding, to 18 percent over three years. These increases, as has been usual, were spread fairly evenly between male and female workers. Both male workers and female workers got their pay increased by about 18 percent, meaning that the percentage gap between the sexes changed very little.

Suppose instead that for that limited period of three years, 6 percent (out of the 18 percent) had been concentrated on raising the wage scales of women workers (see table 8–2). That probably would have been about sufficient to finance pay equity adjustments for women throughout the economy. The remainder of the pay increase money would have been available to spread evenly between male salaries and the newly beefed-up women's salaries.* What it adds up to is that an 18 percent across-the-board increase in money wage rates *that actually occurred* could have been converted into a 35 percent increase for women and an 11 percent increase for men.

Of the 18 percent increase in wages that actually occurred over that three-year period, about 12 percent made up for inflation and did not result in an advance in workers' real income. Looked at in another way, price inflation produced the funds to finance two thirds of the wage increase. The rest was financed out of productivity improvements, which allowed the production and sale of extra goods with the same labor force.

If pay equity increases for women over the three-year period had been financed out of the funds usually devoted to money wage increases, leaving room only for increases totaling 11 percent for male workers, men's real wages would have been at a virtual standstill for that period (to be exact, they would have experienced a decline of one third of one percent per year). That would have meant a standstill in living

---

* Only 11 percent (rather than 12 percent) is left over after the catch-up increase in women's pay financed by the 6 percent of total pay, because the base pay to which the increase must be applied has risen.

standards for single males and one-earner couples over the three-year period. Single or divorced women (many of them with children), who are the largest group in poverty, would have experienced a substantial rise in real income. Two-earner couples, who are now in the majority in the economically active age groups, would end up about even with what their situation would have been in the absence of pay equity, about 6 percent ahead in real terms over the three years.

But does the money for pay equity have to come from funds that would otherwise go to increase the salaries of men? Might not some or all of it come out of profits? A look at the way national income is shared out (see figure 8–2) shows that it would be unrealistic to expect to get all or even a large part of the pay equity adjustment money out of the share of national incomes going to profits. Corporate profits and proprietors' incomes are 11 percent of income, while the pay equity adjustment is in the neighborhood of 5 percent. A pay equity process that cut profit shares in half is unlikely, even if it were considered wise.

While profits might absorb some fraction of the costs, one would expect that firms that had to make big adjustments and felt unable to keep increases to the men low enough to make up for them would avoid infringements on their profits by raising prices. The resulting increase in the rate of inflation above what it would otherwise be would not be large—perhaps an addition of 1 or 2 percent, or even less if the adjustments went on over a five- to ten-year period. In terms of shares of labor and profit in the gross national product, the net real result probably would be about the same however the dollar amounts for the women's increases were raised.

THE SOCIAL RESULTS OF PAY EQUITY ADJUSTMENTS

Is it wrong that men's salaries should have to stand still in real terms or even drop off slightly for a few years while women's salaries partially catch up? That judgment is possible only if one believes things are best as they are. Such a judgment would have to overlook all the evidence that a large part of the differences in salary scales derives from discrimination against women. It would also have to overlook the emerging social reality that women are increasingly living independently of men and that men are no longer sharing their high wages with women and children to the extent that they used to.

In the next chapters, we turn to the changes in economic relations within the family, to the economic effects of the increase in divorce and single parenthood, and to the decline of housewifery as our largest occupation. We will also discuss the reforms that will be necessary to accommodate these changes. As we review the issues involved, it will become obvious that higher wages for women workers will be a necessary part of such reforms if we are to turn the corner in the fight on poverty and the dependence of women on welfare.

CHAPTER 9

The Job of Housewife

To BE A HOUSEWIFE is to be a member of a very peculiar occupation, one with characteristics like no other. The nature of the duties to be performed, the method of payment, the form of supervision, the tenure system, the "market" in which the "workers" find "jobs," and the physical hazards are all very different from the way things are in other occupations. The differences are so great that one tends not to think of a housewife as belonging to an occupation in the usual sense. It is sometimes said that a housewife "doesn't work." The truth is, of course, that a housewife does work, does get a reward for her work, and not infrequently gets fired or quits. One dictionary defines an occupation as "an activity that serves as one's regular source of livelihood." Being a housewife is an activity that gets one food, clothing, and a place to live. It certainly meets the dictionary's definition of having an occupation.

By tradition and by law, the housewife is not counted as working for an "employer." The reward she gets for her work is not legally defined as a "wage." That reward may be access to goods and services rather than cash. This arrangement has implications for her status, her sense of independence, and her participation in planning the family budget. Because she has been considered to be merely an economic and social appendage of her husband, she was never taxed as other workers. Her old-age support was not arranged on the same basis as that of other workers.

In the era when all women were expected to spend their mature years as housewives, when almost all men maintained housewives, and when divorce was uncommon, none of this was thought to merit comment or was considered a problem. Now, however, we are in a transition period in which about half of the married men maintain housewives while the other half have employed spouses. The housewife's pay, taxes, postdivorce support, and provision for old age raise policy questions that paradoxically get more insistent as the housewife occupation dwindles. In some respects, housewives are gravely disadvantaged. In other respects, families with housewives are given extra advantages that families with two earners are denied. The way the tax and Social Security laws treat the housewife need examination and reform. The postdivorce situation of women who have been long-term housewives needs to be improved.

The proportion of adult women who report themselves as engaged exclusively in keeping house has been dwindling throughout this century. But even in its dwindled state, the housewife occupation is very large. In fact, it is still the largest single occupation in the United States economy. In January 1986, a total of 29.9 million women in the United States (or 32 percent of the women aged 16 years or over) described themselves to the census taker as "keeping house."* By comparison, workers of both sexes in professional and managerial occupations— physicians, nurses, lawyers, teachers, engineers, social workers, business executives, government officials—amounted altogether to only 26.4 million. Workers of both sexes in clerical and allied jobs amounted to 17.5 million.[1]

A housewife is a married woman who holds no paid job and who works within the home performing services for her own family. She may also contribute some unpaid volunteer work. But her principal attention is to child care, food preparation, housecleaning, laundry, grocery shopping, and a host of other chores and errands. Many if not all of these services will be performed whether the family maintains a housewife or not. However, a family that maintains a competent person devoted full time to performing these services generally benefits from

* In January 1986, 468,000 men reported that they were not in the labor force because they were keeping house.

having them performed well and carefully and in a timely manner. A one-earner family has a higher standard of living than a two-earner family with the same money income because of the family's greater enjoyment of high-quality services.

While the advantages of having a housewife in the family are considerable, so are the disadvantages. Most obviously, the family loses the money income that the person serving as housewife might contribute to the collective budget. There are other disadvantages, concentrated on the shoulders of the person playing the housewife role. A housewife works alone, or with only the company of small children, and many housewives are, as a result, extremely lonely. The husband of a housewife, with his monopoly of direct access to money, has the opportunity to be tyrannical. Sometimes, he acts violently toward her. He may desert, leaving her unprepared to earn a good living. For all these reasons, the housewife occupation is one of the most problem-ridden in the economy.

Being a housewife is no longer a lifetime vocation for most women. Many of the women who tell the census taker they are not in the labor force because they are "keeping house" are taking a temporary spell in the housewife occupation. The shorter the time a person spends as a housewife, the less severe the problems are likely to be. When looked at objectively, the long-term housewife's occupation turns out to be one of the riskiest, both physically and financially. But even short spells as a housewife can produce severe disadvantages.

The housewife usually is thought of as outside the economy. Housewives' services are not included as part of the gross national product, and housewives lack cash payments designated as wages. But there certainly is an economic side to the housewife role. The nature and value of the productive services delivered by the housewife, the nature and value of the pay, and how these get set raise issues worthy of examination.

While there has been some agitation to include housewives' services in the gross national product and to pay them cash wages, the important issues of public policy with respect to housewives lie elsewhere. The treatment of the "displaced homemaker"—a person who has been a housewife for a long time but whose "job" has ended through separation or divorce—is a national scandal. Another set of important policy questions, debated in the Congress every few years, is the treatment of the housewife and the employed wife in matters of taxation and Social Security. Present laws favor the housewife-maintaining family in important ways and penalize the family with an employed wife. Another issue concerns the wisdom of encouraging women to assume the housewife role after the birth of a baby, by instituting generous maternity-leave policies.

THE DUTIES OF THE HOUSEWIFE

"The hand that rocks the cradle rules the world," goes one attempt to persuade women that they should rest content with being housewives. At the other extreme, John Kenneth Galbraith has called the housewife a "cryptoservant."[2] Both of these are irritating ideas, probably intentionally so.

Many of the housewife's duties are those of the servant, and the servant job is the one closest to the housewife's in the money economy. Unlike the servant, the housewife is a family member and therefore partakes to some degree in whatever deference is due to the bank account, class position, and occupation of the husband. She also partakes, as a servant does not, of whatever luxury the husband's salary affords in living space, food, clothing, and entertainment. She does have more discretion than a servant ordinarily has, and she may have the management of the family's finances in her hands. In some respects the housewife's working conditions are more onerous than the servant's: The housewife works seven days a week and is on call twenty-four hours a day for the service of the whole family.

Personal relations are important in a regular job, but they are a much more important part of the housewife's job. The children she takes care of are her own. The housewife's relation to the husband, including their sexual relation, is a factor in her ability to keep her position as wife. Of course, the feelings of love that the housewife and her husband may share enhance the marriage and may make the performance of her work "a labor of love." Yet sexual relations are notoriously changeable in their tenor. If they go sour, the housewife may lose her position. The connection between the economic and the sexual means that the housewife's economic security is hostage to personal whims.

To continue the servant analogy, female servants in the nineteenth century, and probably throughout the course of history, had sexual duties to the father of the house and possibly to the grown sons as well. This was certainly true if they were slaves or indentured servants. These days, good servants are rare, and if unwelcome attentions are forced on them, they can quit and go elsewhere. Only the prostitute and the housewife now have jobs in which a requirement to engage in sex relations is part of the duties. In any other job, the imposition of such a requirement is considered sexual harassment and is outlawed under the Civil Rights Act.

The sexual part of the housewife's job has become more crucial with the advent of easy and frequent divorce. When marriage was understood to go on until death, falling out of love, or meeting someone you liked better was considered no excuse to end it. In the present era, even an excuse is unnecessary. There are some other jobs besides the housewife's where a person performing competently in the technical aspects of the work will be displaced because the boss develops a sexual desire for another person. But surely, the best ones do not have that characteristic.

A great deal of what we are saying about the housewife also applies, to some degree, to many of the wives who have paid jobs. Most do housework seven days a week, in addition to their paid job. The majority of them have wages that are considerably lower than their husbands'. For a woman in that situation, the continuation of the marriage allows her to have a far higher standard of living than she could achieve independently. In this sense, she, like the housewife, gets part of her livelihood by being her husband's wife and doing whatever is necessary to maintain that status.

THE HOUSEWIFE'S MOBILITY PROBLEMS

The housewife has problems in moving from one job to another that exceed those in other jobs. For most people it is easier to move from one job to another within the same occupation than to change occupations. But the housewife, unlike nurses or carpenters or secretaries or economists, cannot search overtly for other vacancies of a similar type while occupying her present "job." For that matter, even after it has ended, she cannot search overtly for another "meal ticket"—her search must be presented to herself and to others as a search for love. If anything, her experience as a housewife is a hindrance in finding a new spot in the same profession. She now counts as secondhand merchandise, with some expensive appendages—her children by her previous husband—trailing after her. She is no longer as young as she was.

In short, gaining another housewife berth with a new husband is not easy. A survey by the Census Bureau in 1985 found that 35 percent of women who had ever been divorced had not remarried. Of those who did find new partners, the median interval between divorce and remarriage was 4.6 years.[3]

If the housewife wants to move into another occupation—namely, a paying job—the similarity of the duties of the housewife and the duties of the servant create difficulties. Apparently most employers do not consider the experience of the housewife to be valuable in performing paid jobs. Of course, this attitude may grow out of sexism. An equivalent set of duties attached to a man's job might well be thought of as valuable experience, possibly for some managerial jobs.

The nature of the financial arrangements of housewife-maintaining families creates difficulties for the housewife if she wants to "quit her job" by quitting the marriage. It may be difficult or impossible for her to accumulate a cash reserve that would carry her through until she finds some other source of livelihood, usually a job in another occupation. If she can make such an accumulation, it may have to be done by stealth. The "live-in" feature of the housewife's job increases the difficulty of quitting by increasing the size of the cash accumulation needed to change jobs. In most other occupations a person who quits a particular job does not have to move out of his or her living quarters at the time of the quit. Such a person usually can live for a while on the goodwill built up with the landlord and on the stocks of staples in the kitchen.

To the financial difficulties of quitting a marriage must be added the formidable logistical difficulties—finding new residential quarters and arranging to move there. A housewife's lack of credit in her own name may also create problems at such a time. We are speaking here of the difficulties of a transition for the housewife from her present job to some other way of getting a living. The longer-term prospects are not good, either, principally because most of the high-paying jobs are marked off for men.

PHYSICAL HAZARDS

It is estimated that about 14 million women are injured in the home each year.[4] Accidents are not the only source of injury. Large numbers of women are the victims of intentional violence from their husbands. A survey found that 4 percent of women living with a husband or male partner at the time of the survey had in the previous twelve months been kicked, bitten, hit with a fist, hit with an object, been beaten up, threatened with a knife or a gun, or had a knife or gun used against them. Nine percent of the women said that at some time in the past they had been victims of those kinds of abuse from the man they lived with. If we include what the survey characterized as less severe forms of violence—having something thrown at them, or being pushed, grabbed, shoved, or slapped—then 10 percent of the women reported violent abuse in the previous twelve months and 21 percent had at some time experienced it.[5]

Police officers have not considered a husband's violent behavior against his wife to be a crime. If called to a home on a complaint of violence, apparently most police officers consider that the appropriate course of action is to conciliate the matter rather than to arrest the husband and charge him with a criminal offense. Many men, including many police officers, believe that men have the right to beat their wives. A housewife will lose her economic support if her husband has to spend time in jail, and this makes judges reluctant to jail battering husbands. Beaten-up wives themselves worry about this. A housewife often refuses to press charges, or withdraws them if they have been pressed. This kind of behavior reinforces police officers' attitude in refusing to make arrests.

There has been considerable speculation about why wives continue to live with violent spouses. Some have argued that such wives derive a masochistic enjoyment from being hurt, or feel that they have deserved punishment. Whether this is true or not, there is very likely an economic aspect to the wife's behavior. Such a woman will have no immediate way to make money, and is likely to have young children whom she feels she must keep with her and whom she would have to feed and shelter. She may not have relatives in the same city with extra space and money they would be willing to put at her disposal. To such a woman, the difficulties of leaving a violent husband may appear insurmountable. There is literally no place for her to go.

Feminists have opened up an offensive against wife-battering by bringing lawsuits against municipal authorities in cases where the police have failed to protect women from their batterers. Where permanent injury has been sustained, multimillion-dollar judgments have been obtained, and these will certainly motivate authorities to indoctrinate police officers to behave more aggressively against batterers than they have been wont to do in the past.

Feminists also have begun organizing shelters for battered women in many cities throughout the United States. These serve as a place of resort for a woman and her children with nowhere else to go. From the shelter, she can apply for welfare and look for a job and a place to live. The shelter movement has received some financial help from the federal government. Recently there has been an attack on the shelter movement from the religious right wing on the grounds that shelters are "antifamily" and "rest and recreation centers for tired housewives." Those who attack shelters want to shore up the husband's authority in the family and apparently believe that the right to administer physical punishment to his wife is necessary or.helpful to the maintenance of that authority.

MEASURING THE ECONOMIC VALUE OF THE HOUSEWIFE

The housewife's activities result in the production of a great many excellent things: meals on the table, clean rooms, clean clothes, and children cared for. We can arrive at measures of the value of the housewife's services by drawing on the obvious parallels between her activities and similar productive activities in the market economy. However, as will become apparent, there is more than one way to arrive at a measurement, and determining which method is the best is no simple matter.

There is no housework task that does not have analogies in the commercial economy. For food preparation and cooking, there are restaurant meals. For housecleaning, there are paid cleaners. For transportation of family members, there are taxis and chauffeurs. There are commercial laundries. The people who perform these tasks for pay are, of course, covered in the U.S. government's tally of production and income, the gross national product accounts. Yet the productive value of the unpaid housework by family members is not covered. Why is that?

The accounts, which were set up for the United States in the 1930s and 1940s, were envisaged primarily as a device for measuring levels of production and income generation in the money economy. Certain items not traded for money did get included, but housework services were not among them. Originally housework may have been excluded from the national income accounts because the changes in the amount performed were thought to be small and to lack relevance to policy. Sexism may also have played a part, considering some of the nontraded items that room was found for, such as the food grown by farmers that is eaten on farms.

These days, however, when catering to the self-image of housewives is considered good politics both on the right and the left, it probably is the valuation problem that has kept housework from being part of the gross national product. No less than three alternative methodologies suggest themselves for valuing housework. However, any of them if adopted might prove embarrassing to the statistical agency.

One way to estimate the value of the housework performed by a housewife would be to equate it to the salary of a full-time servant. This method of estimation probably would be considered to be in bad taste and certainly would not endear the statistical agency to housewives and their partisans. A major purpose of putting housework in the gross national product is to add dignity to the status of housewives, so such a methodology is worse than useless.

A second method of valuing the housewife's productive contribution goes to the opposite extreme. It involves listing the activities of a housewife and finding the specialized occupation in the money economy that is closest to each one. The list that proponents of this kind of measure get together usually includes cook, dishwasher, chauffeur, cleaner, interior designer, nursemaid, dietician, laundress, and so on. The housewife's time at each activity is then valued at the appropriate specialist's pay scale. Many of the occupations cited are mostly male, and many of them are high-paying, in part because women frequently are excluded from them. Housewives work long hours, so this method can easily produce an estimate higher than the average male salary and two to three times as high as the average pay of a woman working at a full-time job. The Chase Manhattan Bank published an estimate based on this method for 1972 that came to a value of $257.53 for a 100-hour work week. In that year white males employed full time averaged $172 and white females $108.*

A third methodology would equate the value of housework to the wage the housewife herself could earn on a full-time job. This method gives a different value to the housework of the college graduate and that of the high-school graduate, despite the fact that they may be doing identical housework.

Given the problem of measuring the housewife's contribution to the national economy, it certainly is no wonder that the economists and statisticians who compile the national economic accounts have been slow to include those contributions. However, those who are pressing for their inclusion might ask themselves how much real benefit would result.

Up to this point, I have emphasized the similarities between housework and services available for purchase in the money economy. However, a word ought to be said about the differences. Oscar Wilde rightly spoke against those who know the price of everything and the value of nothing. What is it worth to have one's own mother devoted to one's care twenty-four hours a day? On the other hand, what is the true cost of living for and through others, of giving up for a lifetime the possibility of achievements outside the home? Accounting for such benefits and costs by putting price tags on them would not do them

* The 100-hour work week is questionable. (See table 11–2, p. 263.) This "assemblage" method is popular with those giving expert testimony concerning the value of a housewife. Such testimony commonly is offered on behalf of a widower suing someone responsible for his wife's accidental death. The Chase Manhattan Bank's calculation is given in A. C. Scott, "The Value of Housework For Love or Money?" *Ms. Magazine* (June, 1972):56–58.

justice. However, they need to be in our consciousness as we think about the housewife, contemplate the decline and eventual disappearance of the housewife occupation, and consider what might be done to replace some of the good things that are being lost in the course of that decline.

PAY FOR HOUSEWIVES

The housewife, despite the productive work she does, receives no sum of money she can call her wage. This lack of a wage has struck many people as an important injustice, which they say ought to be remedied.[6] Perhaps what is most galling is that while the housewife's duties resemble those of a servant, the financial arrangements she has with her husband somewhat resemble those of someone even lower down on the status ladder—namely, the slave. Slaves get no sum of money designated as a wage but do get room, board, and clothing. The legal impunity with which the husband has been able to chastise the wife physically has reinforced the slave analogy. The slave who ran away might be captured and brought back by law. The housewife was constrained to stay by the poverty of the economic and social alternatives open to her. In some cultures, the bridegroom buys the bride for a considerable sum from her father.

The truth of the matter is that both the housewife and the slave do receive a recompense for their work. The slave is at the mercy of the master for the amount of the recompense and for his or her very life. By contrast, custom constrains the husband to allow the wife a standard of living similar to his own. Unless the husband has expensive vices (gambling, drink, and resort to other women are the classic ones), the wife generally cannot complain that the share he accords her is unfair. It is not the lack of recompense but the form it takes that creates practical and psychological problems, especially if the two spouses do not have an amicable relationship.

The housewife's contributions to the family and the return she gets for making them are both obscured by legal and popular ideas that each spouse is unilaterally rendering duties to the other rather than making an exchange of economically valuable services. A husband is seen as having a duty to support the wife, with no conditions specified. The wife is seen as having a duty to keep the house, again unconditionally. The connection between the husband's monetary support and the wife's housework is further obscured by the fact that the standard of living of the wife seems to be inversely related to the amount of housework she does. Those wives who do no housework whatever often enjoy the highest standard of living. Many of those who do the most housework have the lowest standard of living.

The wives of the richest husbands get a pure grant of their living expenses from their husband. Their situation certainly is not typical but seems to have set the pattern for thinking about the economic relations of all husbands and wives. All husbands are thought of as contributing support as a pure grant. Where, as is the usual case, servants cannot be afforded, the wife "has to do the housework." The fraction of wives exempted from housework has always been small; nowadays it is minuscule. The monetary contributions of the husband are in most situations connected to the performance of the housework by the wife. After all, if she stops doing the housework, the marriage will probably end. So there is in reality an exchange of the wife's housework for the husband's continuance in the marriage, and for his continuing to supply her with room, board, and other benefits.

When the husband works, he helps his employer to produce an output and is paid by that employer in money. His income is embodied in his paycheck. Presumably, all of that paycheck becomes the family's income and goes into the family budget. It is consumed when the dollars are used for family members' expenses. The husband's recompense from his employer gets converted into consumer goods for him, consumer goods for other members of the family, and some that are enjoyed jointly, such as the family living quarters.

The housewife's productive activities also contribute to the family's ability to consume, and it is not farfetched to call that contribution an addition on her part to the family income. That contribution is as real as the monetary contribution out of the husband's paycheck. As we have seen, there is more than one way of valuing the housewife's services, but they are real and substantial nonetheless. The income contributed by the wife is consumed almost as it is being produced.

By contrast, the income contributed by the husband may ling
in the bank before melting away in consumption.

Is the housewife paid? By analogy with the husband, the value of
her housework services constitutes an income she has earned. Granted,
she immediately and automatically contributes her "income" to the
family. But many husbands contribute all of their income to the family,
too.

Husband and wife share both the money income and get a benefit
from the housework, which we might call the "service income." In
the last analysis, the recompense of each for their exertions is their
share in both kinds of incomes. The recompense of the housewife
includes a share in the goods and services purchased out of the family's
cash budget—clothing, a roof over her head, participation in family
vacations, travel, medical care, trips to the movies, and so on. She also
benefits from her own services, as when she partakes of a family meal
she has cooked, or gets satisfaction from the development of a child
she has nurtured. She ends up with a certain total level of consumption—and whether we call that her share or her pay should not much
matter.

What, then, do the "pay for housework" advocates complain of?
It is attitudes they are complaining of more than material deprivation.
The husband's money contribution seems more real or important than
the wife's service contribution. His contribution is more visible and
seems more concrete. Psychologically, a sum of money perhaps is more
easily comprehended than a multitude of actions that constitute housework. The nature of the husband's contribution renders him more
powerful in the family and creates the impression that he supports her
with no return and that she is parasitical. If she had money to contribute
to their joint budget, all of those ideas might disappear or at least be
softened.

If the housewife had a wage, she might have more say over the
way the family's money income gets spent. Of course, there are families
in which the husband's pay is all delivered entirely to the wife's control
and all spending is controlled by the wife. However, if the husband
wants, he can keep control of all the money and dole it out to the wife
at his pleasure. She may have no fixed sum that is given to her for her
own needs or even for household expenses. She may be in the humil-
iating position of continually having to ask for small sums. Informal

surveys among my students whose mothers are housewives suggest that about 20 percent of them are in that situation. The opportunities for petty tyranny in such an arrangement are endless.

Suppose it became common practice for the husband of a housewife to render up to her some fraction of his cash wage and acknowledge that he was paying her a wage for housework. Each spouse could not go off and spend the money under their control independently. On the contrary, both the husband and the wife would have to put up almost all of that money for food purchases, the rent or the mortgage, car expenses, and so on. Perhaps the wife would feel freer to buy things for herself, but this is far from clear.

Another possible source of a cash wage for housework would be the government. But where would the government get the funds? One possibility would be to put a large special tax on the husbands of housewives. The money collected, with a suitable subtraction for administrative expenses, might be sent by the Internal Revenue Service to the housewives. The housewives' self-esteem might be enhanced by the receipt of the government checks, but the benefits would be entirely in terms of status.

Another scheme, which would have important substantive results, would be to send government paychecks to housewives out of the ordinary revenue of the government. Presumably there would have to be a tax increase to finance it. The additional taxes would be paid by housewife-maintaining families as well as by single people and two-earner couples. However, the latter two groups would receive no benefit from the extra taxes. The net effect would be a transfer of purchasing power from the pockets of single people and two-earner families into the pockets of families that maintained housewives. But single-earner families are already better off in terms of living standards than two-earner couples of identical cash income. Sending the former a check for the wife's housework financed in part by taxes of the latter would be asking the less well off to contribute to the more well off. Such a scheme also would encourage women to become and remain housewives.

To sum up this discussion, those who have sought to put pay for housewives on the feminist agenda appear to have made a mistake.

MATERNITY AND CHILDREARING LEAVE

Most women who enter the housewife occupation do so when they have a baby. Not all new mothers leave their jobs. About a quarter of women currently giving birth to a baby do not leave the labor force at all, and another quarter return before the child's first birthday.*

There always has been some sentiment for the allowance of long and generously paid maternity leaves for employed women. Lengths of three months, six months, a year, or even several years have been proposed. Such leaves would allow women with jobs to be housewives for considerable periods, and with pay to boot. Since they would be keeping one foot in the labor market at all times, the appearance of dependency would be avoided. Women in dead-end, boring, arduous jobs would no doubt welcome such leaves, and others might also. The leaves might be considered society's or the employer's contribution to the raising of children. They would make the life of the mother easier, allow her to devote herself to the child entirely, and would keep some very young babies out of day-care centers.

Long paid maternity and child-raising leaves are really another version of pay for housewives. The rhetoric on leaves emphasizes the welfare of the child rather than the worth of the mother's services. But in economic terms the two are very similar. However, the stipend for maternity leave is usually proportional to the wife's wage.

A policy requiring employers to give such paid leaves has important disadvantages for women. If the employer must pay a woman's salary for a long maternity leave, employers will have a further incentive to keep women out of the high-paying fields. Even more than now, women will be confined to jobs in which the duties follow an easily learned routine and in which one person can easily be replaced by another. In such jobs, the pay would be lowered to make up for the cost of the maternity leave. More women would take long maternity leaves, and every woman who has a baby would be under social pressure to take the maternity leave, at possible damage to her career. Another disadvantage of long paid maternity leaves for child-rearing is that

* See discussion in chapter 2.

they reinforce the idea that child care, and the other family service chores that women do when they stay home, are women's work.

An alternative to long leaves for mothers would be work-reduction arrangements for both spouses that allowed couples to share child care and housework. Both the mother and the father might reduce the intensity of their paid work for a considerable period after the birth of their baby. Perhaps both could go on half-time for two years or so, or perhaps the father and mother might take alternate weeks or months or quarters of a year off. Under such a system, neither mothers nor fathers would sacrifice career opportunities disproportionately. However, both parents would be at a disadvantage relative to one-earner couples and childless people in highly competitive fields, unless special rules were instituted to take care of that too. Such a system would restore to young children a period of nurturance passed in the quiet and (relatively germ-free) isolation of their own homes, at all times under the attention and care of a parent.*

We might call such a system "two-parent nurturance leave." From many points of view, including probably that of the child, it would be superior both to the housewife-breadwinner setup, and to the two-earners-with-baby setup, with its overextended "supermom." The Swedes have taken modest steps to work toward such a system. In Sweden, the health insurance system provides for paid leave when a baby is born, which mothers and fathers may share. To encourage fathers to participate in child care, the father is entitled to ten days of leave, which does not count against the couple's allotment and which is lost if not taken.[7] However, in Sweden only a small percentage of new fathers currently take advantage of the leave.

The Swedish example shows that instituting such a system would by no means be easy. Men have an interest in continuing to be exempt from household chores, and from career interruption. And as long as wages of women are far inferior to those of men, any scheme that involves men taking unpaid or partly-paid leave is relatively expensive for the family.

---

* Currently some parents achieve this by working alternative shifts. (See discussion in chapter 11.) However, such arrangements are not available to everyone, and furthermore drastically reduce the time the parents can spend in each other's company.

THE DISPLACED HOMEMAKER

The major problem for the long-term housewife, apart from the possibility that she may not enjoy the duties (including the personal part of the duties) of the housewife job or may have aspirations beyond homemaking, is the possibility that the financial flows she gets through the marriage will be terminated or substantially reduced. This might happen through separation or divorce. It also might happen if the husband becomes mentally or physically disabled; becomes an alcoholic, drug addict, or compulsive gambler; is a failure in his job or profession; becomes permanently unemployed; is sent to prison; or dies before retirement, leaving little provision for her. None of these events reducing or ending her income can be ruled out. In fact, such events do occur in the lives of a substantial number of women. As a result, the housewife's position is very risky.

Divorce and separation now are quite common. Half the marriages currently starting will end in divorce.[8] Many of the women involved in divorces remarry, but for the homemakers among them a longer or shorter period of financial stress is usual. Of women between 35 and 65 in 1983, there were about 150 divorced (and not remarried) women for every 1,000 women who were currently married. The ratio of the divorced to the married in that age group was about 50 per 1,000 in 1960, so the proportion of such women living as divorcées more than tripled in 23 years.[9]

If a divorce occurs at the start of a marriage and before any children have been born, the economic consequences for the wife are likely to be minor. In all probability, she will not have retired from the labor market. If, however, there are young children, or if the marriage has gone on for a considerable time and the wife has not held a full-time job recently, her economic and social situation can be very difficult indeed. Her standard of living inevitably takes a precipitous drop. Those first marriages that end in divorce or separation last nine years on average. Of such marriages, 31 percent had lasted more than ten years, and 18 percent had lasted fifteen years or more.[10] About 57 percent of divorces are granted to couples with children under eighteen.[11]

The difference in the economic roles of the wife and the husband in the housewife-maintaining family may be considered by the parties to be optimal while the marriage remains intact. When the marriage breaks apart, that difference becomes a source of deprivation to the wife. The husband leaves and takes with him his male-sized income-earning capacity, expanded, as we have seen, by sex discrimination operating in his favor. She may in the past have supported him through law school or medical school or business school. His income-earning capacity also may have been enhanced by the housewife's support services and entertaining. With all family care duties devolved on the housewife, the husband was freed to devote to his job as much of his time as he chose, and he could move around geographically whenever that would increase his earning power.

The man who divorces a housewife will ordinarily be able, if he wishes, to promptly replace the wife's homemaking services, either by purchasing substitutes or by remarrying. The former housewife, on the other hand, will have to move into the labor market, where she will find that her lack of recent experience, together with the limited nature of the jobs open to women, condemn her to low-status, dead-end work at poor pay.

A wife will take on the housewife role and allow herself to become unfit for well-paid (women's) work under an implicit promise that she will never need to be financially independent. A divorce against the wishes of the wife constitutes a violation of that promise, and she ought to receive a sizable indemnity for her foregone opportunities. Even if she is unhappy and wishes on her own to leave the marriage, she will suffer severely unless indemnified for her loss of earning power over the course of the marriage.

The housewife's situation has been considerably worsened by the advent of no-fault divorce in most states. Under the previous system, a husband could not divorce his wife unless he could prove that she had committed adultery. In the absence of such evidence, his only way of gaining his freedom was by having her sue him for divorce. To get her agreement to do that, he had to offer her a generous financial settlement. That somewhat redressed the imbalance of financial power between them.[12]

Under no-fault divorce, either party can ask for and get a divorce merely by expressing an unwillingness to continue in the marriage. This has robbed the housewife of any bargaining power to get the husband to agree to any sizable indemnity. Judges in divorce cases commonly make small child-support awards and deny to former housewives any long-term continuing support for themselves from their former husbands. The rationale these judges have adopted is that we have entered an era where women have chosen independence. A judge applying such an idea to a housewife, who has specifically given up financial independence to benefit her husband and children, is punishing her for what the judge sees as the ideological sins of feminists. Only 14 percent of divorced women report being awarded alimony, most for a limited duration. The average payment in 1983 was $3,976 per year, and many did not receive all the payments to which they were entitled.[13]

The most difficult situation is faced by women who have played the housewife role most or all of their adult lives, only to be divorced in their late forties or their fifties by their husbands.[14] At the time these women were married, all of the social pressures operated in the direction of encouraging women to assume the housewife role. Most did so without serious thought of the alternatives. Looking ahead to the possibility of divorce would have been considered disloyal, and needlessly destructive to the marriage. When the divorce comes late in life, usually it is very late for the woman to start on a serious career of her own, even if she has the resources, will, and self-confidence. She finds that many of the married people she considered good friends are not willing to continue as friends. Lonely, neglected, robbed of their previous status and of almost everything that made life worth living, many divorced housewives eke out a miserable existence in a marginal job.

Isabel Sawhill has described the betrayal of older divorced housewives:

> One view is that marriage is a partnership with a lifelong commitment to another individual and a complete sharing of economic costs and rewards. Implicit in the lifelong-partnership view is the idea that the risk of divorce is small and that alimony provides a kind of insurance against this risk. . . . A second view of marriage is that it is a limited partnership in which husbands share their incomes with their wives, but only for as long as their marriage is intact. . . . The real problem arises when women agree to marry and be homemakers under the terms of the lifelong-partnership model and later discover that the limited-partnership model is in effect.[15]

Sawhill has suggested that where there are children, divorced housewives and those children who live with them should continue to share the ex-husband's income. The income of the ex-couple should be divided so that the standard of living in the two households would be about equal.[16] Where there are no children, or where they have grown up, Sawhill believes that ex-housewives should receive from their ex-husbands a monthly alimony payment that would recompense the wives for the loss of their earning power during the marriage. The alimony payment would be the difference between the ex-wife's current earnings and an estimate of the earnings she would have currently had she never left the labor force.

The problems faced by the displaced homemaker affect the life of the homemaker whose marriage is intact. She and her husband both know that if he were to decide on a divorce, her economic and social situation would seriously deteriorate. This realization gives the husband power to get his way when there is a disagreement between them. If he wants to use that power in a harsh and dictatorial way, the house-wife's situation can be made very difficult.

TAX POLICY AND THE HOUSEWIFE

We turn now to the treatment of housewives and employed wives in matters of taxation.

The United States has consistently followed a system of income taxation based on two principles. One is the principle of progressive taxation—that people with higher incomes should pay higher shares of their incomes to the tax collector. The second is that a married couple should be taxed on the sum of their incomes, and the spouses not be allowed to calculate their taxes as though they were single people. In recent decades, U.S. tax laws have been revised numerous times. However all revisions, including the revisions of 1986, have kept these principles intact.

A low-income person who marries a high-income person is not allowed by the U.S. tax code to pay the low taxes that would be levied on a low-income person living alone. Rather, such a person is made

TABLE 9-1
*How Income Taxes in the United States
Vary with Marital Status*

The Two-Earner Marriage Penalty	
Man with income of $30,000	
Woman with income of $20,000	
Their taxes as single people ($4,638 + 2,250)	$6,888
Their tax as a married couple	7,554
The Housewife Bonus	
Man with income of $30,000	
His tax as a single person	$4,638
His tax if married to a housewife, no children	3,150
The Single Parent Penalty	
Tax of single mother earning $40,000, two-person family	$5,712
Tax of married couple earning $40,000, two-person family	4,854

NOTE: Based on proposals for taxes to take affect in 1988 as detailed in *Tax Reform Act of 1986: Report of the Committee on Finance, United States Senate,* Report 99–313, May 21, 1986. The use of the standard deduction is assumed in all cases.

to pay the higher taxes thought appropriate to a member of an affluent family. While that has a measure of justice to it, it creates a *two-earner marriage penalty*—when two people marry. and both continue to earn income, the taxes they owe as a couple may be greater than the sum of the taxes the two of them owed as single people.

In order to keep the marriage penalty from becoming more than a few thousand dollars per couple, the tax rules have been written so that a married couple with a given income pays less tax than one single person with the same income. That creates a second anomaly—the *housewife bonus*. A man married to a woman with no income pays considerably less than he would as a single person.

There is still a third anomaly in the U.S. tax code—the *single-parent penalty*. A mother who is not currently married, and is the only earner in her family, is not permitted the same generous treatment accorded to the single-earner married couple. She is treated as an intermediate case between singles and marrieds.

These tax anomalies are illustrated in table 9–1. The numbers in the table are based on current plans for taxes in 1988. A two-earner couple who as single people would have paid a total of $6,888 in taxes would owe $7,554 after their marriage, thus suffering a rise in taxes of $666 or almost 10 percent. By contrast, the man who is married to a nonemployed wife would pay $1,488 less than he would as a single person, a tax reduction of almost a third. The single mother supporting a nonearning child in our example is forced to pay $858 more than a man supporting a nonearning wife, an 18 percent tax penalty.

The marriage penalty encourages people who are living together without benefit of formal marriage to stay that way. For those who do get married, the tax system encourages wives to remain housewives or to become housewives. In our example, a couple's taxes increase from $3,150 to $7,554, a sum of $4,404, if the wife takes a job that pays $20,000.

Most couples view the husband's employment as beyond question but view the wife's employment as something on which a decision might be made either way. Thus they would tend to view the $4,404 addition to their tax bill not as an extra burden on both of their salaries but as the tax on the $20,000 that the wife might earn. By that way of thinking, her salary carries a higher tax rate than the rate on husband's salary, and a rate almost double the rate she paid as a single woman.

The idea behind a progressive tax structure is that better-off people should carry a more-than-proportional share of supporting public expenditure, while the burden on lower-income people should be relatively light. The principle is straightforward when comparing individuals. When comparing individuals with married couples or comparing one- and two-earner families, however, what is fair and what is unfair becomes more problematical.

Should two-earner couples be allowed to pay taxes as though they were single? One argument against the idea is that when people marry, their expenses diminish because they share a dwelling unit, so they can afford higher taxes. These days, however, many couples live together before their marriage. It seems unreasonable to force such couples to pay extra taxes for the act of getting married.

On balance, there is a lot to be said for requiring people to file on the basis of their own incomes without regard to the income of other family members, and for abolishing special tax rates for married people.

This is the way taxes are structured in Sweden.[17] If such a system was adopted in the United States, married single earners would have to pay considerably more tax than they currently do.

A more radical proposal, by Rolande Cuvillier,[18] would go farther than getting rid of the tax break currently enjoyed by the one-earner couple. Cuvillier would make the one-earner couple pay extra taxes. They would be required to pay tax on the value of the services performed by the housewife. Cuvillier reasons that having a housewife increases the family's real income. She simply carries the idea of taxation to its logical conclusion and argues that the family should be taxed on that part of its real income consisting of housewife-performed services. After all, says Cuvillier, the housewife is part of the community, and public services are delivered to her at public expense. She, or her husband on her behalf, should pay her share of this public expense.

Presumably only the extra services delivered by the housewife beyond those performed by two-earner couples would be taxed. In computing taxable income, an amount equal to some fraction of a servant's wage would be added to the cash income of couples maintaining a housewife.

SOCIAL SECURITY AND THE HOUSEWIFE

The Social Security system, on which Americans depend to give them income in old age, was established in the 1930s. Each person who has ever held a job covered under Social Security has an individual account in which that person's earnings are recorded. The rhetoric used to convince a basically conservative population that the system was a reasonable one portrayed the benefits as being drawn from a fund that had been built up out of the worker's own contributions as well as contributions by the employer on the worker's behalf. In reality, benefit formulas were constructed to replace a greater portion of the wage income of the lower-earning workers than of high-earning workers, and extra benefits were paid to the retired male workers who were married.*

At the time Social Security was set up and the principles of the benefit formula were established, most women spent their married years out of the labor force. If they were to receive Social Security benefits, they would have to do so in their capacity as wives or widows of male workers. The solution adopted was to award to each retired couple a "spouse benefit" equal to 50 percent of the husband's benefit. Wives who had earnings in their own right might elect to take benefits based on those earnings, or might elect the spouse benefit, but not both.

The net effect of such arrangements is that the benefits a person gets are not proportional to that person's contributions. People who have had low earnings get more Social Security benefits per dollar of contribution than high wage earners. A married man gets more than a single man who has made the same contributions. Many woman who have made contributions to Social Security end up by accepting the spouse benefit, which they could have received with no contributions at all. In a sense, these women receive nothing for their contributions.

Table 9–2 shows examples of the results of this kind of arrangement, which have been chosen to highlight the features of the system. In the first case shown (Dennis and Deborah), the man's salary had averaged $11,000 in terms of 1985 wage levels, and the wife's salary had been the same. They have a choice of taking the benefits the two of them were entitled to on the basis of their own earnings, or taking the husband's benefit plus the 50 percent spouse benefit. Obviously they would choose the former, giving them a benefit of $10,936. By contrast, the one-earner couple (Edgar and Elsie) can retire on an annual benefit of $13,047, which includes the $8,698 the husband would have been entitled to as a retired single man, plus the 50 percent spouse benefit.

The combined earnings of the first couple are equal to those of the second couple, and the two couples would have paid identical Social Security taxes. Moreover, the first couple would have put out more work effort, and led a less comfortable life than the second couple, who would have had the services of a housewife. Nevertheless, the

* See note to table 9–2.

TABLE 9–2
Benefits to Couples Under the Social Security
System for People Retiring in 1985

	Average Indexed Earnings	Benefits for Couples Based on	
		Own Earnings	Spouse Benefit
Dennis	$11,000	$5,468	$5,468
Deborah	11,000	5,468	2,734
Total	$22,000	$10,936	$8,202
Edgar	$22,000	$8,698	$8,698
Elsie	—	—	4,349
Total	$22,000	$8,698	$13,047

NOTE: Benefits are based on 1985 formulas for people retiring at 65, which give 90 percent of the first $280 per month of average indexed earnings, 32 percent of earnings between $280 and $1,691, and 15 percent of earnings between $1,691 and $3,291. Average indexed earnings are computed by taking earnings for each of the previous 25 years, adjusting them to account for changes in average salary levels between the year in question and the retirement year, and then taking the average of such adjusted earnings. The lowest 5 years are excluded from the average. Detailed information on benefit structures are contained in U.S. Department of Health and Human Services, *Social Security Handbook*, 8th ed. (1984).

one-earner couple would be awarded a benefit that was 19 percent higher than that awarded the two-earner couple.

If the two wives in our example become widowed, they would get very different benefits. Elsie, who had never contributed to the Social Security system, would get a widow's benefit of $8,698. Deborah would get much less, only $5,468, despite a lifetime of contributions.

These examples suggest that the Social Security system, like the income-tax system, is more generous to families with housewives than to families of employed women. This is certainly the case if we restrict our attention to benefits going to retired married couples and to widows. The system is generous to those housewives who manage to stay married to their husbands. But it is extremely harsh to those housewives who become divorced.

Until 1978, a divorced women who had been married to a man less than twenty years was entitled to no Social Security benefit whatsoever on the basis of her former marriage. Spouse benefits would have been payable only for the retired ex-husband's new wife, if any. If the divorced wife had been a housewife, or had a poor or spotty earnings record under her own name, her financial situation in old age would be very poor. Currently, divorced women whose marriage lasted for at least ten years qualify for benefits based on the ex-husband's earnings. However, while the ex-husband is alive, a divorced wife receives no benefits until he retires, and then is entitled only to a payment equal to the spouse benefit. Thus if Edgar divorced Elsie, he and a new wife would retire with a benefit of $13,047, but Elsie would be reduced to living on $4,349. However, if Edgar died, Elsie's benefit would rise to $8,698, the same amount the second wife would receive.

The problem of old-age support for divorced housewives has stirred suggestions that the Social Security system should give housewives direct credit for their service at home by putting "earnings" credits into their records. When wives received benefits under such a system, the benefits would be based on the woman's own credits—any earnings the woman had plus her housewife credits.

On what basis would the housewife's credits be computed? Some have suggested that credit for all the earnings of a couple be shared between spouses. Under earnings-sharing, the separate Social Security accounts of the husband and wife each would be credited with one half of their total earnings. Men married to housewives would get credit in their own accounts for only 50 percent of their earnings. This certainly would have the virtue of making explicit the economic partnership implicit in the marriage and of vesting in the wife the right to future benefits based on economic activity during the marriage. But men have been highly vocal against "giving away credits that belong to them." Other schemes that have been suggested to extend explicit coverage to housewives would allow couples to pay for extra credits to the wife's account (as is permitted in some other countries), or alternatively require them to make such payments. Still another would give the husband full credit for his earnings but would award an extra 50 percent to the wife's account. Under the latter scheme, the rest of the community would continue the current subsidies to housewife-maintaining couples.[19]

All of these schemes involve basing pension checks on each person's "own" account. This might have the effect of giving housewives more dignity; their work would be recognized as worthy of social credit, and they would appear to be less dependent.

A still more fundamental reform of Social Security would reduce the effect of a person's earnings on the size of that person's retirement benefit check. Under a so-called two-tiered or double-decker setup, every old person would get a stipend unrelated to the person's earning history. To that stipend would be added a relatively small amount based on the earnings record. This would make the system more "like welfare" rather than the purely contributory system it appears (falsely) to most people to be. The two-tier system would help the displaced housewife more than any other. It would also reduce the unfair advantage the current system gives to the one-earner over two-earner couples with the same income. For those reasons it is the most desirable of the reforms that have been proposed.

FEMINIST THINKING ABOUT THE FULL-TIME HOMEMAKER

The role of the housewife has a major place in feminist thought. Betty Friedan's book *The Feminine Mystique,* which was influential in initiating the current wave of feminism in the United States, had as its central theme the disadvantages to women from assuming the housewife role. All feminists believe that women should not be forced into assuming that role and that alternative choices should be available.

There is a second strand of feminist thinking concerning housewives that derives from the solidarity feminists feel with all women, housewives included. This solidarity expresses itself in a concern to alleviate injuries (physical, psychological, financial) that housewives have suffered. It also leads feminists to join in efforts to shore up the dignity of the housewife.

There is still a third strand of thought about homemakers. Some people who consider themselves feminists think it would be desirable for even larger numbers of people to assume the stay-at-home housekeeper role than now do so. They see it as indispensable for the proper raising of children. They would prefer it if members of both sexes were candidates for the role, or if mothers and fathers could alternate. However, whether that were possible or not, they favor public policies making it financially easier for families to support a full-time homemaker. They tend to favor multi-year parental leaves with pay for childrearing.

Much of the attention of feminists has gone toward trying to help the housewife. Rolande Cuvillier, quoted earlier in connection with taxation, argues that the net effect of many pro-housewife measures is not to help women at all. Rather, such measures help men to retain someone dedicated to serving them in the home, at the expense of the rest of society. Thus policy measures that encourage women to become or remain housewives, such as tax breaks for housewife-maintaining families, help perpetuate the inequality of the sexes. When the scarce resources of the feminist movement are devoted to pushing measures that have that effect, support and attention are diverted away from reforms that would help the employed woman, the single mother, or the battered housewife.

The disadvantages to playing the role of full-time homemaker are so great that it is unlikely that significant numbers of men would want to serve in it. If the occupation continues to exist, it will continue to be part of the female domain and hence inherently disadvantaged. Since this is the case, equality of the sexes and women's welfare would be better served if younger women were to avoid entering the role even temporarily and if the socially sanctioned "option" to assume the role were to disappear. Policies that reward families for having housewives, or encourage women to assume the housewife role, do harm to women and should be avoided.

After we have passed through a phase where unpaid family care services have been largely replaced by purchased substitutes, and after equality of opportunity has been established in the workplace, it will be time to consider reviving the occupation of full-time homemaker. Then we can see if it can become an honorable, safe, and secure occupation for both mothers and fathers.

CHAPTER 10

Poverty and Single Parents

IN MOST of the human societies we know about, both past and present, the male parent has been an important person in the life of his children. Typically he has lived with them and made substantial contributions toward the expense of raising them. Today we are seeing a loosening of the economic and social bonds between men and their children, as out-of-wedlock births and divorces increase. Millions of mothers—a rapidly increasing proportion of all mothers—are bringing up children by themselves, supporting them out of their wages or with a welfare check from the government, with little or no help from the fathers. Recapturing for children the financial help of their absent fathers is one of the major tasks of public policy facing us.

The increase in the number of women raising children without the help of a man has more than one cause. Women's opportunities for earnings have gradually improved, allowing more of them a choice about whether to be independent of a man. Men have less compunction than they used to about leaving their wives and children. The taboos against sex for women outside of marriage have eased.

Most of the children living apart from their father in the United States get little or no economic contribution from him. The estrangement of so many men from so many of their children signals a breakdown in the social arrangements that have served to funnel economic resources from male adults to children. The result of this breakdown is inadequate provision for an increasingly large proportion of children. Many "economically fatherless" children, together with their mothers, live in a state of extreme deprivation. Today in the United States, more than one third of the poverty population consists of single mothers and their children. Fatherless families constitute an increasing share of all poor families.

Women who rear children without the financial help of a man face a difficult task in an unfriendly economic environment. For some, the best they can do is get along on a poverty-level welfare grant, living in a decrepit apartment in a dangerous neighborhood. Others wring what they can out of a labor market in which most of the jobs that pay a "family wage" continue to be reserved for men. Poverty is epidemic among single mothers and their children. But even those with cash income above the official poverty line are unlikely to be comfortably off.

A shortage of money is not the single mother's only problem, however. She also has an acute and painful shortage of time. A single parent must take on all of the time-consuming tasks that can be shared between parents in a two-parent family—shopping, errands, babysitting, handling finances, dealing with school affairs, and with illness. Single parenthood is also an acutely lonely state. Another adult is lacking to give company and to share the worries and the joys of parenthood.

Single parenthood presents a difficult problem for the mothers and children involved and for society at large. Because the traditional system of providing for children is eroding, leaving an increasing proportion of children out in the cold, new means of making adequate provision for the expenses of these children needs to be set up. If "fatherless children" and their mothers are to live above the poverty line, the present welfare system will have to be scrapped. It needs to be replaced by a radically reformed system of awarding and enforcing child-support payments and by improved access for single mothers to jobs that pay a "family wage."

THE GROWTH OF THE PROBLEM

In the United States in 1960, only 7 percent of families with children were maintained by women who did not have husbands living with them. By 1984, a total of 23 percent of families with children were in this situation. The progressive retreat of fathers from the homes of their children is going on in all population groups but is most advanced among blacks. Of all black families with children, 56 percent were maintained by women in 1984. Among whites, 17 percent of families with children were maintained by single mothers.[1]

The 12.6 million children living with husbandless mothers account for only a portion of the youngsters living apart from their biological father. About a quarter of the mothers of children with absent fathers are married to other men.[2] In all, about 30 percent of all children in the United States are currently living apart from their biological fathers.

The major events that create economically fatherless children—out-of-wedlock births, divorces, separations—are all increasing in frequency. Births to unmarried women were 20 percent of all births in 1983, up from 4 percent in 1970. For whites in 1983, a total of 13 percent of births were to unmarried women; for blacks 58 percent were out of wedlock in that year. Divorce rates also have grown. In 1960 there were 42 divorced (and unremarried) women for each 1,000 married women, but by 1984 there were 146.[3]

Both extramarital births and marital breakups are increasing, but the former are growing at a faster rate. In 1970, only 7 percent of single mothers had never been married. By 1984, more than one quarter of the children who were economically fatherless had been born out of wedlock, the rest being children of divorced, separated, or widowed mothers.[4] Death of a spouse has been dropping as a cause of single parenthood; it accounted for only 7 percent of single mothers in 1984.

THE DIFFICULTIES OF SINGLE PARENTHOOD

The economic difficulties of single mothers are reflected in the frequency of poverty among them. In 1983, a total of 48 percent of single mothers maintaining their own households were reported as having income below the government's official poverty line. Among white single mothers maintaining their own households, the poverty rate was 41 percent; among black single mothers, the rate was 63 percent.[5] By "single mothers" in this context we mean mothers who were currently living without husbands. This group of women includes the never-married as well as those reporting themselves married with husband absent, divorced, separated, or widowed.

One third of single mothers were not in the labor force in 1983, a high percentage of them living on low-level welfare grants. About 22 percent of single mothers who were in the labor force did not earn enough to keep them and their children above the official poverty line.[6]

United States government statistics on poverty among single mothers tend to underestimate the extent of the problem. The government officials who established the officially designated poverty line—the income the government says a family requires if it is to be considered nonpoor—took no account of the situation of the employed single mother. They made no allowance for out-of-pocket child-care expenses and assumed all meals could be prepared at home "from scratch." Many single mothers with earnings above the official poverty line should be counted as poor when the extra expenses they have due to their employment are taken into account.*

Even if the single mother earns a wage that puts her above the poverty level, she and her children are likely to live at a standard far below that enjoyed by households including an adult man. In the first quarter of 1986, the median weekly earnings of those women main-

* As single mothers and their children are an increasingly large share of the population at risk of poverty, the official definition of the amounts of income required to be nonpoor becomes more and more out of line with the real situation of the people in question. New methods of defining and counting the poor are clearly overdue. On the one hand, the borderline income should allow for decency in food, child care, housing, medical care, and so on. On the other, food stamps, medical insurance benefits, child-care benefits, and housing subsidies should be included in family income when a family's poverty status is determined.

taining families who were employed and who had no other earners in the family was $248. By contrast, married-couple families where only the husband had earnings enjoyed a median of $454 in the same period. But more than half of the married couples had both husband and wife at work, and for such couples the median weekly earnings were $706.[7] A considerable number of single mothers can achieve earnings that are above the poverty line. But most of them and their children will be firmly fixed at the low end of the income distribution and will lack the ability to buy goods and services most other families take for granted.

Single parents have demands on their time that are difficult to meet. If a single parent works full time, the time remaining apart from work is not really sufficient to accomplish the housekeeping and the personal-service chores parents have to do. Employed single parents have relatively little rest and leisure and have few opportunities of relief from the rigors of the job, housekeeping, and child care. Even where the single mother earns a wage that is at or above the average for male workers (something 22 percent of full-time women workers managed to do in 1983), she generally cannot use her income to buy services that would save her own time and allow her more rest or more attention to her job. There are certain tasks the parent cannot delegate, such as managing the household and taking a child to visit the doctor. For the employed single parent a child's periodic minor illnesses can turn an already difficult life into a nightmare; loss of pay and even loss of job may be threatened at each such occasion.[8]

It is no wonder that many single mothers, particularly the ones with poor job prospects, "cop out" from the rigors of a harried state of independence and go on welfare. When they do, they accept a sentence of extreme poverty and pariah status in return for an assured stipend, medical care, and the time to attend to their children's needs for nurturing and attention in a relatively leisurely way. An increasing share of the poor in the United States are single mothers who have accepted this pitiable fate as the best avenue open to them for survival.

So far we have been looking at the problems of single parenthood from the point of view of the parents themselves. However, the increase in the incidence of single parenthood is felt as a problem for society as a whole. These days, concern about the expense that must be borne by the taxpayers for the support of welfare clients has for the most part overwhelmed any humanitarian concern for their plight. The welfare population, including children, grew from 7.4 million in 1970 to 10.9 million in 1984. The cost to the taxpayers of supporting this population in 1984 ran about $73 billion per year for welfare benefits, food benefits, housing assistance, and medical insurance.[9] There is concern that widespread knowledge of the extent of dependency itself erodes the work ethic and encourages lax behavior. There is concern that the children brought up by single mothers will be prone to higher rates of delinquency and poor health, both of which impose costs on society at large. Researchers have not come up with conclusive evidence that children are harmed by living only with their mother. However, the poverty that frequently goes along with such a status can blight children's health, attitudes, and mental performance.[10]

MARRIAGE AND MALE PROVISION FOR CHILDREN

The traditional two-parent method of providing goods and services for the young calls on the child's biological mother to donate services to the child and for the child's presumed biological father to give money to buy sizable quantities of goods for the use of the child and its caregiver-mother. The mother is expected in turn to render personal services to the father, who is traditionally exempt from the direct donation of services to the mother or children. It is commonly taken for granted that this traditional method is the "natural" way of providing goods and services for human young. Yet the two-parent method of child support probably evolved millennia ago from the single-parent method of our primate ancestors. We seem to be in the process of change back to the single-parent method.

Both in the past and in the present, women have benefited from an alliance with a male who would make economic contributions to her and their children. Obviously, such arrangements provide advantages to males. When we look at the customs that grew up regulating these male-female alliances, the advantages on the male side of the ledger loom very large in most cultures. Men have not controlled free-born women in the way they controlled property or livestock or slaves. But they have been able to restrict them to subservience, confinement, and low status. Those who, in Engels' famous phrase, speak of a "world historic defeat for the female sex,"[11] do not think in terms of an alliance serving the needs of both sexes but in terms of a war of the sexes in which males subjugated females and reduced them to a status not far above that of slaves.

Whether we consider traditional marriage as an alliance for mutual advantage between a mother and a father, or as a system under which women are drafted into service for sexual and breeding purposes and as household drudges, marriage does accommodate at least some of the important interests of both mothers and fathers. Under the institution of marriage, each child would in normal circumstances be attached to an adult male who would make contributions over an extended period to his or her economic support.

Many of the institutions and restrictions of traditional society have the effect of reducing the number of children who are economically "fatherless"—that is, who are not receiving support from a man. The extended family, the institution of indissoluble marriage, a taboo on sex for unmarried women, and disgrace and deprivation for women bearing children out of wedlock and for the "illegitimate" children themselves all served the purpose of ensuring male contributions to most children and reducing the number of children lacking such contributions.

Marriage is the key institution in this system. Feminist criticism of marriage understandably has focused on the features most disadvantageous and demeaning to women in traditional marriage: on the traffic in women between fathers and bridegrooms, on the subordination and immurement of the wife within the home, and on the double standard with regard to sexual fidelity. However, granting these disadvantages, it is still possible to see women and children as historically, on balance, beneficiaries of stable marriage. Women have perforce had to tolerate those features of marriage that have been disadvantageous to them as the price they had to pay for those benefits. That price has in turn been affected by a woman's alternatives to staying with her present spouse: getting another husband, or getting a job.

A taboo on premarital sex for women was an important part of the social system minimizing the number of "fatherless" children. Obviously, the observance of the taboo keeps a woman from having children before obtaining the formalized pledge of a man's support. Its observance also restricted the supply of sex partners available to a man, thus encouraging him to contract a marriage that would supply economic support to a woman and her children. When a child was conceived outside of wedlock, vigorous and sometimes violent efforts were made to arrange the marriage of the mother and the father before the birth. Where a "shotgun wedding" could not be effected, the disgrace to the woman was shared by her parents and siblings as well as by the child.

The societal institutions built to keep down the number of children without the economic support of a male included structures to deal with children "left over" at the end of the marriage relationship. The extended family, which included adult male relatives of the couple, took up the economic burden of the widow and her children.*

Nothing can be more obvious than that the traditional institutions and mores that have kept the preponderance of children under the economic support of a male are declining. The factors responsible for that decline include better access to effective contraceptive devices and better opportunities for women in the labor market. A possible third factor in the decline of traditional institutions is the support for single mothers and their children available from the government.

BIRTH CONTROL AND THE DECLINE
OF TRADITIONAL INSTITUTIONS

One vital element in the decline of traditional institutions has been the development of more reliable and more easily used contraceptive devices. Access to contraceptives and to safe and legal abortion has also improved. Contraception and abortion surely must have been important in the genesis of the "sexual revolution," another name for the atrophy of the taboo against sex for women outside of marriage. The ready availability of contraception and abortion remove or at least reduce the chance that a woman will have to bear an extramarital child unwillingly as the result of any single act of sexual congress.

* If the extended family structure is strong, the system that minimizes "fatherless" children may be consistent with easy divorce. In Moslem countries, a husband may have a divorce for the asking; he may keep the children and send the woman back to her father or brothers. However, in the Christian West until recently, lifelong marriage has been the norm, with high barriers to divorce enforced by civil and religious authorities.

Women's participation in sex outside of marriage reduces the incentive for men to marry or to remain married. The reduction in the number of men who wish to marry has convinced some women that their only chance of achieving motherhood may be to have a child outside of wedlock.* Such a belief leads in some cases to a decision to carry an extramarital pregnancy (perhaps due to contraceptive failure) to term.

Black women have a lower chance than white women of being able to bring up a baby within a stable marriage to an economically successful man. In September 1985, only 79 percent of the black male population between twenty-five and fifty-four years old was employed. The comparable figure for white males was 91 percent, and the wage rates of white men were one third higher on average than the wage rates of black men.

The availability of measures to prevent the birth of unwanted children probably reduces somewhat the number of children born to those married people for whom divorce is foreshadowed by the unhappiness or dissatisfaction of one or both partners. Such children are at high risk of lacking economic support from their fathers. While prevention of these births lowers the number of children per divorced mother, the number of divorces is probably somewhat increased thereby.

The sexual revolution has brought greatly increased sexual activity to teenagers, but a high proportion of those sexually active are unprotected with contraceptive devices.[12] Moreover, the sexual partners of these teenage females usually are teenage males, who are not in a good position to give economic support to their children, even if they were inclined to do so.†

THE MOTHER'S RISING POTENTIAL EARNINGS

The progressive rise in wages for women has been an important cause of the move to a one-parent support system for children. A woman who supports herself and a child, independent of a man, has had access

---

* Other out-of-wedlock babies are born to gay women, and to women who become pregnant by men whom they do not consider suitable as husbands.

† A law passed in 1985 in Wisconsin makes a baby's maternal and paternal grandparents responsible for the baby's support while the baby's parents are unmarried teenagers.

to jobs that provide a standard of living far below average in most cases. But the rise in real wages has made it possible for a higher proportion of single parents to live above the poverty line. There is every reason to believe that real wages of both men and women will continue to rise. So as time passes it will become easier for single parents to live at any particular standard of comfort.

Before the trend toward single parenthood for women could gather momentum, the engagement of women in the marketplace for paid labor had to be well established. Wage rates for women had to rise to levels that made an appreciable number of single working mothers capable of supporting themselves and a child or two at a modest but decent standard. Very few single mothers are capable, given their present labor market opportunities, of achieving affluence or even solid comfort for themselves and their children. Nevertheless, a life at a standard above the poverty line is currently possible for a substantial fraction of single mothers if they work full time. That fraction will grow as real wages improve.

In 1983, about 84 percent of the women who worked full time earned enough to pay for day-care expenses for one child (about $1,650 annually) and to have enough money left over to maintain a standard above the government-designated poverty line for herself and one child. Half of the women working full time year round made $11,706, and at that wage or above, supporting one or two children at a modest standard becomes a reasonable possibility. Sixteen years previously, in 1967, when real earnings were lower, 67 percent of women full-time earners would have been able to live above the poverty line with one child and pay for day care.[13]

Each marriage or relationship has disadvantages for each party, and each party has alternatives to remaining in the relationship. The willingness of a woman to tolerate whatever disadvantages a marriage involves is conditioned by her economic alternatives, and the kind of life she and her children could have outside the marriage. The more a woman can hope for in the way of earnings, the more likely she is to leave a husband with whom she is unhappy.

The data on male violence toward their mates certainly suggest that a considerable number of women living with their husbands have ample cause for unhappiness.[14] As the possibilities of economic independence for women continue to increase and as the standard at which they can expect to live improves, we can expect that more of those women who suffer spousal violence as well as more of those with less dramatic grievances will elect to rupture their relationships.

Better economic prospects for mothers outside of marriage affect the behavior of husbands as well as wives. Knowing that their wives can support both themselves and the children reduces the guilt a husband feels when he leaves or takes the initiative to break up his marriage and fails to contribute to the subsequent support of his children. The probability that the ex-wife can eke out a living without his help also reduces the shame a man feels who acts in this way.

Conservative women such as Phyllis Schlafly have urged wives to spurn the opportunities to participate in the labor market and have deplored any governmental programs designed to improve the economic prospects of women outside of marriage. Such conservatives want to keep men's noses to the grindstone of family responsibilities and believe that this is furthered by the undivided devotion of the wife to her husband's comforts and orders and by the lack of any alternative for her. In this view, anything tending to reduce the fidelity of men to the task of support of wife and children is in the long run against the true interests of women. The conservatives viewed the Equal Rights Amendment as abolishing the legal obligation of the husband to support a housewife.[15]

There is a great deal of nostalgia for an era when the traditional family supposedly served as a dependable locus of loving comfort for both adults and children.[16] Those who feel this way regret the improvement in wives' economic alternatives to staying home and staying married. They ignore the plight of many a wife in a traditional marriage, passing her life under the orders of an irritable tyrant. They ignore the plight of the family whose single earner lost his job, sickened, died, or deserted. Some men who regret the passing of the traditional family are in truth mourning the passing of the historic privileges of the male sex.

The husband of a woman capable of financial independence at a fair standard of living must, if he wants to keep her, earn by his behavior her desire to continue in the relationship, just as she must earn his. It is entirely possible that there are more happy marriages today, rather than fewer, as men are less tempted to tyrannical behavior.

There are men and women who believe in equality but would like to find some way to reduce for women the attraction of opportunities outside the family. They believe a child needs a full-time mother. It is up to people who think this way to show us a new kind of partnership between mothers and fathers, with built-in guarantees of long-term sharing of financial burdens and long-term commitments to maintaining the relationship. Up to now, they have not done so.

THE WELFARE SYSTEM

The last line of defense for single mothers is the welfare system. Despite the low standard of living that mothers on welfare are allowed to have, it is frequently argued that the welfare system has played a part in promoting the increase in the number of children living with single mothers.[17] Poor and unemployed fathers may leave their families to make them eligible for welfare benefits. Fathers who have their own reasons for deserting may have less compunction about leaving, knowing that their children will not starve. Women can be active sexually outside of marriage and can carry any resulting pregnancies to term, knowing that the welfare system will provide benefits to set them up in independence. Married mothers can leave their husbands, knowing that welfare will provide. While such arguments seem plausible, careful statistical analysis suggests that the effect is in reality not large. David T. Elwood and Mary Jo Bane found little evidence that the availability of welfare benefits influenced the childbearing decisions of unmarried women. They may, however, increase the rate of divorce of very young women.[18]

The system of governmental help for single mothers and their children, popularly called "welfare," originated in the darkest years of the 1930s depression, when unemployment was epidemic and destitution common. Aid to Families with Dependent Children (AFDC) originally was intended to help widows and orphans until the more generous provision made for them under Social Security could be phased in.[19] As widows were enabled to leave AFDC, a new and, to most eyes, less respectable clientele came aboard. The widows, who were held personally blameless for their lack of male support, were replaced on the relief roles by unmarried mothers, who were commonly judged to have sinned, and by separated and divorced mothers, who had failed in their wifely duty of holding on to their husbands.

The AFDC rules originally denied benefits to a mother who had a husband or any other adult man living with her. Probably the unstated theory was that a man had to earn the right to get sexual and other services from a woman by supporting her and that a woman who was being supported at public expense should not be available to men. Under the "man-in-the-house rule," investigators conducted raids in the small hours of the night on the homes of welfare recipients, looking for men in their beds. An adult male's clothing in the closet was taken to be evidence of cohabitation with a man and could lead to a woman's removal from the benefit rolls.

The U.S. Supreme Court struck down the man-in-the-house rule in 1968. The state agencies that administer AFDC may not deny aid to children of a mother who cohabits with a man, if that man does not have legal responsibility for supporting the children. This gave eligibility for benefits to mothers living with a succession of "boy-friends" while allowing states to continue to deny benefits to mothers living with unemployed husbands. About half the states have adopted programs allowing welfare benefits to families whose "principal earner," usually the husband, is unemployed, but the family must be virtually destitute of assets to qualify. Only a tiny fraction of husband-wife families are on AFDC.[20]

The welfare system was set up in a period when married mothers were not expected to take paid jobs. Welfare was designed to allow the unmarried mother the right to choose to be a full-time home-maker—a pseudo-housewife supported by the government rather than by a husband. Women were to remain eligible for assistance as long as their youngest child was under eighteen. There was little encour-agement to take a job; any money that a welfare client earned was subtracted dollar for dollar from her welfare check. Yet in most states benefit levels never have been high enough to keep a mother and her children at the poverty line or even close to it.

Welfare beneficiaries get an AFDC cash grant and food stamps, which can be used instead of money in the supermarket to purchase most products. They and their children get health insurance under

Medicaid. About a quarter of them are in public or subsidized housing, and about a fifth have children who get free or subsidized school meals.[21] As of January 1985, in the fairly typical state of Pennsylvania, a mother and two children were entitled to a monthly AFDC grant of $364 plus food stamps worth $167. This allowed them a monthly spending rate of $531, only 77 percent of the poverty threshold.[22]

Only one state—Alaska—gives welfare recipients benefits sufficient to allow them to live at the poverty line. Another eight states give as much as 90 percent. Some states give notoriously low benefits. Texas's benefits are only 54 percent of the poverty-line income, and Mississippi and Alabama have benefits that are less than half the poverty-line income. In terms of purchasing power, the value of AFDC benefits has fallen sharply over the past fifteen years. In a typical state the benefits in 1985 bought 37 percent less than they bought in 1970.[23]

The choices facing the single mother who comes to depend on public assistance are bleak. For all practical purposes, she and her children can stay on welfare until her youngest child turns eighteen.* For as long as they stay, they are assured of food, a roof over their heads, and medical care. But they will live below the official poverty line, which means extreme deprivation. The mother may contemplate going off welfare by getting a job. If she does, the considerable effort she must devote to working may result in earnings that are not much larger than the AFDC and Medicaid benefits she will have to give up. Furthermore, taking a job requires additional expenses for child care, for carfare, and for suitable clothing. These expenses eat into her income and reduce the net benefits of leaving welfare. A mother of two children who went off welfare in 1985 would need to get a job paying $9,000 to have about the same cash disposable income she had on welfare. However, with the $9,000 job she would not be as well off as she was on welfare in two substantial respects: She would have lost her health benefits under Medicaid, and she would have lost the free time she had on welfare.[24] A mother who goes off welfare and then loses her job has the task of reestablishing herself on the welfare rolls. Until benefits can be started again, she might be completely destitute. That being on welfare discourages employment can be seen from the fact

---

* Mothers whose youngest child is six or over are now required to register for work, but if she chooses not to take a job, or not to keep one that has been assigned to her, the welfare authorities have been little inclined to throw her off the rolls.

that never-married mothers with young children are considerably less likely to have jobs than are mothers of young children who have husbands living with them. (See table 2–3, p. 25.)

As we have seen, about a third of the full-time jobs that women have open to them are not sufficient to support a family consisting of a mother and two children at a standard above the poverty line. A mother who left welfare for such a job would be making her situation worse because of the loss of benefits and the loss of her free time. The incentives to stay on welfare have made it into a "poverty trap" where the mother plays the part of a housewife but is supported by an ungenerous government agency rather than a middle-class husband. There is considerable circulation into and out of the welfare clientele, but some considerable fraction of women on the rolls stay there for long periods. A fraction of welfare mothers have daughters who become pregnant and set up as welfare mothers themselves.[25]

A disproportionate number of never-married mothers are black. Of black children in 1983, just over half were living with their not-currently-married mothers.[26] About a quarter of black children were living with mothers who had never been married. Here the problem of race in America interacts with sex-role problems. Past and present discrimination against blacks in schooling and employment makes their opportunities more constricted than those of white Americans. Black fathers are more likely to be unemployed than white fathers, and if employed are more likely to have an unstable job at low wages. Black women are more likely than white women to find the low standard of living that welfare provides to be the best choice among the set of undesirable prospects open to them. Some black women may view welfare as their only chance to become mothers and sustain the lives of their children. Hispanic women also suffer disproportionately from these problems.

In any relief program such as welfare, there is an inherent dilemma. Humanitarian considerations suggest a reasonably generous provision for the last-ditch relief of a mother and her children. The fact that children are involved makes generosity more compelling. Whatever the derelictions of their parents, the children are innocent victims who have not done anything to deserve severe deprivation. Nor will deprivation be likely to improve the children's character.

On the other hand, more generous benefits may mean that more mothers and children show up at the relief window. Probably few people actually plan to go on welfare; after all, welfare benefits have never been high enough to make anyone comfortable. Careful researchers have found no evidence that the higher benefits paid to welfare mothers in some states have caused a significant rise in dependency in those states.[27] Nevertheless, it is difficult to avoid the idea that the more meager the benefits, the harder people probably struggle to remain independent of welfare, and the harder those on welfare struggle to obtain some alternative means of support.

Most of those debating welfare policy see no alternative to keeping the present system, or something very like it. Thus, most of the arguments have been over the size of benefits and about who should be allowed to receive them. The standard liberal position favors larger benefits, the provision of benefits in the form of cash, and easier access to benefits. The liberal camp includes people who are still attached to the idea that women ought to be home with their children. They do not view welfare dependency as resulting from laziness and sin of the mothers. Rather they see its root cause to be the failure of our economic and social policies to reduce unemployment and low wages among men, particularly black men. Until these men can be enabled to bring home a "family wage" on a reliable basis, so as to be able to support wives and children themselves, generosity in welfare benefits seems to many liberals to be simple humanitarianism.

Those favoring a more generous version of the present welfare system ignore the change in the economic position of women since the Great Depression. Millions of single mothers currently support themselves and their children, something that would have been impossible in the 1930s. Millions of married mothers are employed as well. Prior to the 1970s it might have been persuasively argued that being home with her children was the normal place for a good and caring mother. Forcing a mother to abandon the full-time care of her children because she was poor and lacking a man's support would have been considered cruel. Now, however, the full-time mother is in the minority. The housewifelike position of the welfare mother no longer conforms to majority practice. The choice that so many mothers have made to take employment undermines the assumption that husbandless mothers can and should choose to devote themselves full time to motherhood and homemaking, at public expense.

Those who would expand benefits and eligibility under the current welfare system have failed to come to grips with the increasing proportion of children living with single parents. They have also failed to focus on the political impossibility, regardless of the party in power, of raising benefits to a level that would allow stay-at-home mothers and their children to live in the mainstream, above the poverty line.

Those favoring a more meager version of the present welfare system tend to see welfare mothers as a careless, lazy, sluttish, undeserving lot. Conservative policies under the Reagan Administration have moved to force mothers off welfare by limiting eligibility to those utterly destitute, by reducing the level of benefits, and by harassing those on the rolls. There have been scattered and largely unsuccessful attempts to force welfare clients to take nonpaying jobs to work off their benefits. Conservatives think that people presently poor would be better off if they were forced to sink or swim. The vast majority of people not eligible for welfare—women who are not mothers, and men—do manage to "swim," although the growing number of homeless people gives evidence that some do sink.

Conservatives have in the past had little interest in government programs designed to promote the employment of women in jobs that could get them off welfare and sustain them above the poverty line. On the other hand, neither have liberals—their idea of job training for women was limited for the most part to training for low-salaried, stereotypically female jobs such as data-entry clerks, maids, and typists.

In the late 1960s and early 1970s, under both Democratic and Republican presidents, attempts were made to recast the welfare system. Efforts were made to improve the lot of mothers on the rolls, yet to make it more attractive for them to leave the rolls, two somewhat contradictory goals.[28] Benefits were raised, some modest work incentives were incorporated, some training opportunities were added. However, the welfare population grew, and as it did, public distaste for supporting such large numbers of people became apparent. The pendulum swung away from generosity to welfare mothers.

Because of the difficulties in raising welfare benefits enough to allow welfare families a decent lifestyle, we never will be able to solve the problem of supporting single mothers and their children just by tinkering with the welfare system. Other forms of support for single mothers will have to be found that are less of a burden on the public purse, that encourage them to seek employment as other women do, and that create less spite toward single mothers. We need a policy package that has the potential of raising the standard of living of single parents and their children while at the same time reducing their dependence on public funds. The major elements of such a new policy package are 1) larger and more regular child support payments from fathers, 2) subsidized child care and medical care for employed single parents, and 3) better access to jobs with male-level wages for single parents. Such a package of policies would go far to cure the welfare problem.

CHILD SUPPORT PAYMENTS FROM ABSENT FATHERS

Currently, a majority of single mothers and their children do not receive from the fathers of those children regular, substantial payments to help with their support. A majority of such fathers make no child support payments whatever. The payments made are likely to be small and irregular. As Irwin Garfinkel, a leader in the movement to improve the size and reliability of child support payments, puts it, we need a system "designed to assure that all who parent children share their income with them."[29]

Most child support payments made currently have arisen out of a divorce. The divorcing parents may negotiate a written agreement that calls for a certain level of child support payments, or the judge in the divorce proceedings may set the level of the child support award. An award of child support also can be made for a child born out of wedlock. If a man's biological paternity is established in a judicial proceeding, then a judge may require him to make child support payments. The nature of the father's relationship with the mother of the child is not relevant. The law as currently interpreted does not distinguish between the support a man owes for the child resulting from a "one-night stand" and support he might owe as the result of a longer relationship.[30]

The Census Bureau surveyed women who had children whose father was living apart from them about child support payments re-

TABLE 10-1

Mothers Who Received Child Support Payments, 1983

	Number of Mothers (thousands)	Percent of Total
Women with children from an absent father	8,690	100.0
Received no child support	5,653	65.1
No award for 1983 payment	4,695	54.0
No payments made despite award	958	11.0
Received payments in 1983	3,037	34.9
Received full amount awarded	2,018	23.2
Received part of award	1,019	11.7

SOURCE: U.S. Bureau of the Census, Current Population Reports, *Child Support and Alimony: Current Population Report, 1983*, series P-23, no. 141 (Washington, D.C.: U.S. Government Printing Office, 1985) table A, p. 1.

ceived in 1983. These mothers were asked whether a court had issued an order awarding them child support payments, and if so, whether they were receiving the payments. (See table 10-1.)* Sixty-five percent of these mothers reported that they had received no child support payments whatever from the father in 1983. No court-ordered payments had been awarded for that year in 54 percent of the cases. In another 11 percent an award was in effect but the father had failed to make even a single payment. Another 12 percent reported that they received part of the payments they had been awarded. Only 23 percent of the mothers had an award that was fully obeyed by the father.

Of currently divorced mothers, 58 percent had awards entitling them to child support payments in 1983. Child support awards for children born out of wedlock are considerably more rare; only 12 percent of the never-married mothers had such awards. White mothers are far more likely to have awards than black mothers. Of black mothers, 23 percent had awards as compared to 55 percent of white mothers.

The failure to obtain child support from many absent fathers has been rationalized on two grounds. One argument commonly given is that the fathers who pay little or no child support are themselves poor

* Some of these women had remarried but still had children living with them fathered by someone other than their present husband.

and simply are unable to pay anything. Another is that the fathers of many children are unknown. It is, of course, true that some fathers are nonemployed teenagers, others are disabled, and still others have dropped out of sight. However, researchers have found that in a majority of cases, fathers could pay.

Absent fathers are not on average poorer than other men. Their average income is about equal to the average income of all male wage earners.[31] A study by Martha Hill of divorced couples showed that only in 10 percent of the cases where the mother was in poverty was the father also in poverty. Only 2.2 percent of ex-husbands would have become poor if they had been forced to share their incomes with their ex-wives and children so as to equalize living standards in the two households.[32] Fathers of children on AFDC in the years 1979–80 had an average annual income of about $11,000.[33]

The difficulty of identifying fathers also has been exaggerated. Thanks to advances in biochemistry and genetics in recent decades, the tests for paternity have been much improved. We have for some time been able to determine whether a particular man is or is not a child's father, with a low chance of error. The newest methods involve a direct examination of the child's genetic material, its DNA, and that of the suspected father. A decision can be made as to whether a particular man is or is not a child's father, with a probability of error smaller than one in a billion.[34]

Up to now, there have been grave deficiencies in the system responsible for making child support awards and enforcing them. Judges in divorce cases have had considerable discretion as to whether to make a child support award and as to the amount to be paid. Many awards have been far below any reasonable standard. Some judges have seen fit to make awards that were almost jokes—$7 per week per child is one example.*

In 1983, the average award was $2,521 per year, or about $1,430 per child. Awards for one child averaged about 10 percent of a white man's average full-time year-round earnings; for two children the award averaged about 14 percent.† Awards were on average about half of the amount an employed mother—with day care fees to pay—would have

---

* That is the size of the award given to Elaine Fromm, who went on to found the grassroots Organization for the Enforcement of Child Support.
† See tables 4–2 and 10–2.

TABLE 10–2

Child Support Due and Amounts Received by Mothers, 1983

	Number of Mothers* (thousands)	Average Child Support	
		Due	Received*
All mothers	3,995	$2,521	$1,779
One child	1,930	1,965	1,380
Two children	1,466	2,968	2,072
Three children	459	2,999	2,129
Four or more children	139	3,940	3,092

* Includes those due to receive payments but who received no payments.
SOURCE: U.S. Bureau of the Census, Current Population Reports, *Child Support and Alimony: 1983,* series P–23, no. 141 (Washington, D.C.: U.S. Government Printing Office, 1985), table 1, p. 7. The figures on support due by number of children are derived from unpublished Census tabulations.

to spend to keep a child fed, clothed, housed, and cared for at a poverty-level standard of living. After accounting for inflation, child support awards were smaller in 1983 than they had been in 1978.[35]

Low as awards were, actual collections were smaller still. Of the $10.1 billion due in child support payments for 1983, only $7.1 billion were received. This is hardly surprising in a culture where payment delinquency is a way of life. Many of us fail to make payments we owe for our cars, our department store bills, or on our credit-card purchases. The merchants to whom we owe money understand that collection is far from automatic. They program their computers to send us bills reminding us to pay. When we miss payments they add on interest penalties and send us letters containing threats that our credit ratings will suffer or our possessions will be seized. By contrast, parents owing child support have been expected to remind themselves faithfully to sit down and write a check each week or each month without the assistance of any of these reminders, penalties, or threats.

Where the father has been delinquent, the mother has had to hire an attorney to try to get the court system to make him pay. Being short of funds, she may not be able to do that. At best, she has to wait months for a court hearing of the case. Postponements, nonappearances, excuses, and promises to do better string the process out. A father brought in for a hearing before a judge after months or even years of delinquency may make partial restitution and promises of regular payment. However, it is not unusual for him to make a payment or two but thereafter cease paying anything, starting the whole cycle again. After one or two experiences with the expense, aggravation, and trouble of hauling a delinquent before a judge, and with the uselessness of doing so, many mothers simply give up on the process. When the mother and father live in different states, the problems are compounded.

Judges have the power to jail those who are delinquent in child support payments but seldom do so. They reason that a jailed father cannot earn anything, so that sending a father to jail cannot get support to a child. A study by David Chambers did show, however, that counties in which judges have a higher-than-average rate of jailing child support delinquents, the rates of delinquency are lower than average.[36] The jailed delinquents themselves never reform, he found, but their example does deter other delinquencies. However, even in counties with a high rate of jailing, delinquency was a common occurrence.

The reform of child support enforcement has been pushed by two groups: public officials who want to reduce AFDC expenditures for children whose fathers could contribute; and ex-wives, understandably furious at the deprivation they and their children are experiencing and their failure to secure what is by law theirs. Thus far, legislation has been passed on the national level to encourage the states, who remain in charge of marriage, divorce, and related issues, to improve their systems. Social Security and federal tax records now can be utilized to locate addresses for missing parents. The states are encouraged by federal grants to establish computerized billing and monitoring of payments, to secure awards for children on AFDC who do not have them, and to arrange for payments to be deducted from paychecks of delinquent parents by their employers. Legislation going into effect in 1985 encourages states to set up systems that start payroll deductions in the case of parents delinquent for a single month's payments.

In an increasing number of jurisdictions, employers are being required to deduct child support payments from their workers' pay from the onset of the child support award, without waiting for delinquency to occur. Where this is not done, there is a tendency for the newly separated or divorced father to consider his entire paycheck as his to spend. He then raises his standard of living, and it is hard for him to reduce his standard of living when the authorities catch up with him.

One result of stepped-up enforcement of child support is that mothers on welfare are being pressured to identify their children's fathers so they can be pursued for child support payments. If the child support payments are less than the welfare costs, then the money collected from the father simply goes to reimburse the government, with no net benefit to the children. This makes fathers of children on AFDC feel that their payments are "wasted." Some of the AFDC mothers maintain friendly relations with and get some informal support from the fathers of their children. This is said to be particularly true in the black community. Associations of this type, which may be of considerable value to the children, may end if the men are pressed by the authorities to make regular and formal child support payments. One can understand that such mothers may be reluctant to "finger" these men and see them pursued.[37] Such considerations are important, but the benefits to achieving a more regularized setup of child support enforcement probably outweigh the disadvantages.

More rigorous enforcement of child support obligations of fathers would make it more financially difficult for men to practice "serial polygamy"—engaging in a series of divorces and remarriages. It would also create greater interest by men in preventing births. Now a man can have the enjoyment of sex and whatever satisfaction might come from having offspring, leaving any financial responsibilities to the mother and to the community at large. If one night's contraceptive failure could bring in its wake eighteen years of heavy financial obligations, men's interest in contraceptive methods that they themselves use and control should increase.

If the extraction and delivery of child support payments are made more routine, the relations that separated fathers have with their children will undoubtedly be affected in many ways. As things are now, the financial problems are intertwined with the emotional problems in a way that complicates both. Many fathers probably experience guilt on account of their failure to keep up payments, and lose or evade contact with their children as a result. Children may become embittered because of their father's failure to send payments. On the other hand, many fathers accuse their ex-wives of denying them visitation with their children and claim to be withholding financial payments as punishment for this denial.

The poor state of child support enforcement has made the acceptance of custody of a child a financially punishing experience for women, and their lack of access to high-wage jobs has compounded the problem. Yet most women want custody. They have been the one in the family who has been responsible for almost all the child care, and in most cases that has served to attach them strongly to their children. It has been an article of faith that a good mother would never want to give up her children, while a good father would want to allow the children to stay with their mother. As a result, giving up custody of a child to the father has been repugnant and shameful to most women. That probably has changed little if at all in recent years.[38]

The rigorous enforcement of child support obligations on the noncustodial parent can be expected to increase fathers' disposition to request custody, but whether the effect will be major or minor is impossible to predict at this time. When fathers request custody, they are awarded it in a substantial number of cases.[39] The legal tradition that a child belongs with its mother unless her unfitness can be demonstrated is being eroded. The idea is spreading that neither parent should be presumed to be more fit for custody and that in each case custody should be determined "in the best interests of the children." Such a standard may in the future tip more child-custody decisions in favor of fathers. Judges may count the financially superior position of the contending father as an important point in his favor. In many cases the father will be remarrying, and the new wife may testify that she wants to stay home with the children. The children's mother will in many cases have no remarriage prospects and will have to take employment. If the judge counts all this in the father's favor, a low-wage mother will end up making child support payments to her high-wage ex-husband, while her ex-rival for his affections, now his wife, raises the children of the divorced mother.

So far reform efforts in the field of child support have been concentrated on enforcing the awards that have been made and getting awards for women who do not have them. Both of these lines of attack on the problem are indispensable if we are to progress toward a situation where "all who parent children share their income with them." However, research by the author and Mark Roberts indicates that such measures, desirable and necessary as they are, would by themselves not go very far toward the elimination of poverty among single mothers.[40] Many of the child support awards now being handed down by judges cover less than half of the cost of a child to the single parent. In addition to larger child support awards, single mothers need access to jobs with a male-level wage if they are to avoid a poverty stricken life on welfare. In the concluding section of this chapter I describe a package of measures that could take us a long way toward ending poverty among single mothers and their children.

ENDING THE POVERTY OF SINGLE PARENTS AND THEIR CHILDREN

The millions of single mothers became single mothers because of difficult events in their own lives—they went through out-of-wedlock births, or through separations and divorces. Some of them were unwise in their choice of a male companion; some were careless in using contraception; some were victims of other people's lack of wisdom, carelessness, or uncaring behavior. However we may deplore the lack of wisdom (or, if one wishes to define it that way, the immorality) of the behavior that made them single parents, we should not condone a life of poverty for them. Their children, who share their poverty, are certainly innocent of wrong doing or immorality. It is not likely that the trend toward single female parenthood could be reversed by harsh treatment of the single parents and their children. Preaching to women to be good wives and to men to be good husbands will not solve this problem, either.

Single motherhood is not a passing phenomenon in our community and in our economy. The children of single mothers are an increasing proportion of all our children. So we need to begin again to think about long-term solutions to their problems and about a set of policies that would allow single mothers to live in the mainstream of American life. First, they must be enabled to achieve incomes sufficient to keep them and their children from deprivation. Because of their unusually heavy burden of obligations, single mothers always will need special help. But they also need to be seen as honorable members of the community, earning their own way as the majority of other adults now are doing. We must begin soon to experiment with ways to wean welfare mothers from the pseudo-housewife status imposed by AFDC, to strengthen radically the inadequate system of child support payments, and to find ways to get these mothers access to jobs at a male-level wage scale.

The first step would be the adoption of a child support system that could replace welfare. Irwin Garfinkel has proposed a system in which each absent parent would pay to the state as a "child support tax" a share of his or her gross income: 17 percent for one child, 25 percent for two, 29 percent for three, 31 percent for four, 34 percent for five or more. The tax would automatically be withheld from pay. All children with an absent parent would be entitled to a payment from the state equal to what their absent parent had paid or to a guaranteed minimum, whichever was higher. This system is currently under trial in the state of Wisconsin.[41]

Unlike welfare payments, child support payments are not cut if the mother takes a job and earns a substantial income. So a child support system that reliably delivered substantial payments, such as the one proposed by Garfinkel, would not discourage single mothers from seeking employment, as welfare does. Indeed, single mothers would be expected to seek and take employment. This would be enforced by the abolition of welfare.

When the suggestion is made that single mothers now on welfare (about 3.7 million women in 1985)[42] would be better off in jobs, the objection is sometimes posed that jobs for them do not exist. Those who argue in this way seem to be implying that most of the welfare mothers would be unable to get jobs, or would be displacing others, and so ending the welfare system would simply increase the number of unemployed people by 3.7 million. This objection does not take account of the fact that, historically, the labor force has grown continuously, and that except in unusual times, new entrants have been absorbed. As new supplies of labor become available, the economy adapts, and the number of jobs grows. The growth of jobs is not perfectly synchronized with the growth of the labor force, and there are periods of economic ill health when the growth of jobs ceases. But over the longer term the labor force and employment grow at roughly the same rate. In the decade of the 1970s, the labor force grew by 23 million, of whom 13 million were women, and the number of jobs grew about proportionately. There is no reason to believe that the entry into the job market of single mothers coming off welfare would pose any problems of absorption not posed by the growth of the labor force from other sources.

Naturally, the absorption into the labor force of single mothers currently on welfare will be eased if economic policy can successfully keep unemployment rates low. Low unemployment rates and healthy economic growth are desirable for this reason, and for many other reasons as well. However, the idea that we cannot reform welfare until we have a special guarantee that jobs are available for welfare mothers is erroneous. One might as well say that no new young people should be allowed to come onto the labor force until new jobs have been earmarked for them.

There is a sense, however, in which the unemployment problem of single parents is more acute than that of other people. The consequences of a spell of unemployment are more severe for a single parent than for a spouse in a two-earner couple, or for a single person with no child to support. This suggests that the unemployment insurance system ought to be more generous to single parents in terms of size and duration of benefits.

A somewhat liberalized version of unemployment insurance ought to be made available to single parents. Like regular unemployment insurance, it would be limited in duration. But it would be available to single parents just entering the labor market. Adequate child support plus their earnings, supplemented by unemployment insurance, would keep a high percentage of single parents out of poverty.

In recognition of the special burdens of single parents, two additional programs should be instituted for them: a system of excellent, highly subsidized child care, and a system of free medical care for their children.

Finally and perhaps most importantly, single parents have a special need for good jobs—jobs in which it is possible to support a child or two above the poverty line. If most single parents were white men, good jobs would be open to them, and almost all of them would already be self-supporting and in comfortable circumstances. In actuality, of course, most of them are women, and many of them are black or Hispanic, so they suffer race and sex discrimination in employment. Effective programs including training, job creation, and affirmative action are needed to get single mothers into relatively well-paying jobs, which few of them now hold.

As the economy is now structured, men are able to take home

relatively large money rewards for their labor, as compared with women. High wages for men have traditionally been justified by the idea that they were earning a "family wage"—that is, a wage they were going to share with their nonearning wives and children. As the two-earner couple becomes common, a "family wage" for the husband loses whatever justification it once had. On the contrary, it is the growing corps of single female parents who need radically higher earnings to stay afloat.

But even were the wages of men and women to approach equality more rapidly than now appears to be in prospect, single female parents, who are currently among the economically weakest members of the community, still would carry a disproportionately large share of the burden for the reproduction of the human species. To the unshared physical burden of pregnancy and birth now have been added for an increasing number of women the unshared economic burden of rearing. Wise policy can help them with that burden in a way that will leave them independent and proud and that will not condemn their children to undeserved poverty.

CHAPTER 11

Keeping House:
The Economics and
Politics of Family Care

FAMILY WELL-BEING depends on the performance of the chores that create a safe, healthy, and comfortable life—putting meals on the table, caring for the children, keeping clothing and living quarters clean. The organization of family-care services is undergoing considerable change as the number of housewives dwindles. When the wife takes a paid job, the family has the problem of what to do about the services that the housewife has been providing. The wife may simply continue to do them, pretty much as before. Or the husband may increase the share of the housework he does. The couple can reduce the amount they have to do themselves by lowering their standard of housekeeping, or by purchasing a larger proportion of the family-care services they use. The choices the family makes in reorganizing family care are important ones. If the wife continues to do the same chores as before, plus her paid work, the overload may sour life for her and the whole family. Resort to the purchase of services on a large scale may change the whole tenor of family life.

Families are wrestling with these decisions as they try to find the lifestyle suitable to their taste and situation. As they do, they are forced to confront and reconcile the sometimes conflicting interests of husband and wife. How these problems are dealt with will establish the degree of fairness between the spouses, whether wives can live as full and free a life as husbands, the daily lives of children, the amount of friction between spouses, and the prevalence of divorce. Even the shape of the economy will be affected. If most family-produced services are replaced by purchased services, a large number of service jobs will be created, many of them in small enterprises.

As wives have increased their participation in paid employment they have reduced the time they spend in housework. Yet there seems to have been little increase in the contribution of services by husbands. To take up part of the slack, many families have increased their purchases of services. They are buying child care, and eat less home-cooked food. In many families, the daily life of a child is nothing like what it used to be, nor are meals.

The marketplace is responding to the changes in demand. New product lines—such as good-quality frozen dinners and the microwave ovens to defrost them—are being sold. New enterprises are springing up, offering to sell the services to families that the housewife used to perform. Fast-food restaurants selling hamburgers, chicken, and french fried potatoes; submarine sandwich shops; sushi bars; Chinese carryouts; and pizza palaces are taking Mother's place. So are child-care centers. The free market is filling the gap left by the departure of the full-time housewife and the unwillingness of men to take a greater share of the housework.

The question of which spouse was to do how much housework has only recently become a subject of discussion. In the past, it was clearly understood that females were marked out from birth to provide family-care services, while males were marked out as fully exempted from providing any. Indeed, males were considered to be disgraced if they did take part in family care. This system of providing for family care—the designation of females as a caste of home-service providers—appeared to be a simple matter of following biological dictates.

Up to now, and for some time into the future, biology ineluctably assigns to the wife the gestation and birthing of the family's infants. However, it is not pure and simple biology that assigned to her the responsibility for all subsequent care of the children within the home. Alternative arrangements certainly were and are viable in biological terms. However, if she was to do all of the child-minding, a great deal of that could be done simultaneously with cooking and cleaning. So the addition of the housework to the wife's child-care assignment served economic efficiency. Concentration of responsibility for housework in a single person also served the development of expertise and simplified the management of the home.

Until relatively recently a high proportion of urban husbands earned all or almost all of the family's money income, and a considerable proportion of them had a physically demanding job. So the assignment of all of the housework to the wife also served roughly to balance out the work assignments of the spouses. Even so, this traditional division of duties produced in many families a considerable disparity between the spouses in time and effort devoted to work and in time free for rest and leisure. The husband's work activities might be restricted to business hours or to a short agricultural season, while his wife, burdened perhaps with many children, with a disabled parent to attend to, and with primitive household equipment, might work long hours seven days a week. In a small minority of families, where domestic servants were employed, the wife might do little work of any kind.

In recent decades, housewives have on average had more leisure than their employed husbands. Housewives have spent less time in providing housework and other family services than the total time that employed husbands have spent at paid work, plus commuting, plus family chores. The situation is reversed when we look at wives with full-time jobs. They have had less rest and leisure than their husbands; most of them apparently have not been able to negotiate a significantly larger contribution to family service work from their husbands. Husbands have shared in the rise in the standard of living financed by the wife's earnings but have contributed little additional effort.

Wives have traded the disadvantages of the housewife status—monotony, overexposure to children, lack of direct access to money, little opportunity for expression and development of skills and talents—for a new set of disadvantages. The disadvantages of the employed wife—loss of leisure, increased management difficulties, a more harried and difficult schedule—must be preferable to the disadvantages of the housewife, or fewer women would have made the trade. Yet the disadvantages of the employed wife are substantial, and since her situation is now more directly comparable to that of her husband, inequities between the two are more obvious. The move to a greater dependence on purchases of services eases this problem but does not do away with it.

Most of us have not yet changed over to a lifestyle in which the burdens and benefits of paid employment and of family life are more evenly spread between husband and wife. The transition to a new style of providing family services provides ample occasion for conflict between the spouses. Selling the husband on doing more housework is not promoted by television advertising, the way store-bought fried chicken is.

ALTERNATIVE WAYS OF ORGANIZING FAMILY-CARE SERVICES

Family happiness is affected by the way in which the mundane necessities of eating, child care, and cleaning are taken care of. Human nature being what it is, no one mode of organizing family care guarantees happiness. Nor is adherence to any one mode necessary for happiness. We can certainly speculate, however, that some arrangements are more likely than others to produce unhappiness.

In some families a great deal of the family-care needs are met by unpaid work by family members; in other families relatively little is done internally, and needs are met by purchasing services for money from outsiders. The extent of housework-sharing between spouses also varies somewhat, although the wife does almost all of it in most families. Families change from one set of arrangements to another as children are born, as children grow up, as new job opportunities present themselves, and as new products appear and are advertised.

In the *housewife-maintaining family,* a large amount of unpaid housework is done, almost all of it by the wife, who does no productive work apart from housework. In such a family there will be few restaurant meals for the family, and the wife will cope with most of the labor of housecleaning and laundry herself. Such families use little paid child care apart from baby-sitters employed on occasional evenings to permit the wife to accompany the husband to an entertainment or social event. In the more affluent housewife-maintaining families there may be a part-time cleaning woman employed, but such a family tends to concentrate substantially all of the housework on the family-care specialist. She in turn may take on some highly labor-intensive tasks such as home baking, despite the relatively cheap substitutes available for convenient purchase. The husband's contribution of unpaid labor to the family is limited to occasional and highly intermittent tasks that are physically demanding, such as yardwork, and some that demand special expertise that by social convention is cultivated mostly by men, such as light carpentry. He may also play with the children on occasion, or occasionally do some shopping. The development of a parallel form of *househusband-maintaining family* still is in the early stages. In January 1986, 468,000 men were estimated to be out of the labor force because they were "keeping house," 22 percent more than in 1980.[1]

There are a few families in which the wife does no outside work but also does very little housework—defined here as meal preparation, meal cleanup, indoor and outdoor cleaning, laundry, and everyday shopping. Her family service consists mainly in the supervision of children, if any, and of paid servants. We can call this the *lady-of-leisure family*. Until thirty years ago, becoming a lady-of-leisure as the wife of a high-status man was the principal worldly ambition that parents had for their daughters.

Turning to two-earner families, we want to distinguish the case where the wife is employed part time (say, thirty hours per week or less, including commuting time) from the case where she has a full-time job. The family in which the wife works part time and the husband takes little hand in the housework I have dubbed the *semihousewife type*.

Where the wife is employed full time, there is likely to be considerable pressure to reduce unpaid housework and buy services. However, many families in which both spouses are employed full time continue to do a considerable amount of unpaid housework. Such families have the choice of having the wife do substantially all the housework, or having the husband take a nonnegligible share. (In theory, there is a third possibility—the husband might do almost all.) Families that rely mainly on unpaid services, where a wife employed full time does most of the housework, I have dubbed the *drudge-wife family.*

For the family in which both spouses work an approximately equal time for pay, an alternative to the drudge-wife style is to split the housework about half and half between the spouses. If the family buys relatively little in the way of housekeeping services, we might call this form the *two-housekeeper family.* This family prepares most of its own meals and may do a great deal of its own housecleaning and child care. Both spouses in this kind of family may work part time.

A variant of the two-housekeeper family is the *shiftwork family,* in which the husband and wife both work for pay, possibly full time, but have work hours that do not overlap, or that overlap minimally. The research of Harriet Presser and her associates has revealed that of families with children, with both spouses employed full time, 17 percent are in that situation.[2] Shiftwork families use little or no paid care. However, in such families the burden of the housework (which we have defined as exclusive of child care and baby-sitting) still may be on the wife. In a substantial proportion of such families the husband may do little more than baby-sit.

Couples may decide to meet a high proportion of their family-care needs by buying services for cash from outsiders. We can call this the *cash-paying style.* Some families with a cash-paying lifestyle live in apartment houses, which have no requirements for gardening or the management of appliance or structural repairs. They may have restaurants, child-care facilities, and laundries nearby.

Living in a single-family house in the suburbs is far less compatible with a cash-paying lifestyle. A few suburban two-earner families employ full-time domestic help, who provide a combination of cleaning, cooking, and within-the-home child-minding services. However, the data on the employment of household servants suggest that only a very small proportion of families manage to do this. Lacking a full-time servant, most suburban cash-paying families have a complicated and stressful time delivering their children to out-of-the-home care, have part-time cleaning help, and eat a considerable number of dinners bought at restaurants, fast-food outlets, or carry-out stores.

For completeness, mention must be made of the *kibbutz lifestyle,* which for our purposes can be defined as families banding together in cooperatives to provide family-care services jointly. The name comes, of course, from the kibbutzim established in Israel in the 1920s and still continuing. They provide joint child-care and feeding services for member families, with all of the labor performed by members. Members of an Israeli kibbutz cooperate in producing more than just family care. Each kibbutz has one or more "cash crops"—oranges, hotel services, jewelry—that kibbutzniks participate in producing.

The original idea of the kibbutz was that occupations would not be sex-stereotyped, that women and men would participate in producing the cash crop and in management, and that both sexes would participate in staffing for child care and in the cafeteria and cleanup work. In practice, the Israeli communes have resettled themselves into a traditional division of labor, with men working on "cash crops" and management, and women working on communal child-care and food services.[3]

In the United States, a kibbutz lifestyle adapted to the needs of married couples with children probably would not include the "cash crop" aspects of the Israeli version. There was the brief flourishing of a "commune" movement in the United States in the 1960s and early 1970s. However, in such communities, the difficulty of managing a business enterprise was added to the difficulty of joint housekeeping. Faced with this double burden of organization, the communes had short lives. Currently, the sharing of single-family dwellings by unrelated people appears to be on the rise in the United States, but apparently this is mostly confined to unmarried people without children. A share-the-chores lifestyle by couples with children or single parents might appeal to some people if an appropriate style of dwelling unit could be developed.

Table 11–1 summarizes the various family-care modes, classifying them by the amount of unpaid housework performed in the family and the extent of the sharing of that housework.

THE WAY FAMILIES OPERATE

In 1975 and 1976, the University of Michigan's Survey Research Center asked people in a sample of households to record in great detail the way they spent their time. The weekly time-use patterns for husbands

TABLE 11-1

Modes of Family-Care Organization (the number of spouses
working for cash is given in parentheses)

Equality of Housework Between Spouses	Amount of Unpaid Housework	
	Little	Much
Little	cash-paying nonegalitarian (2)	housewife-maintaining (1) semihousewife type (2) drudge-wife style (2) kibbutz with sex- segregated duties (1)
Much	cash-paying, egalitarian (2) lady-of-leisure (1)	two-housekeeper (2) shiftwork (2) egalitarian kibbutz (2)

and wives that were obtained have been used to tabulate the frequency
of the major modes of family care we have defined.

Of the couples sampled in the time-use survey, 44 percent were
housewife-maintaining. Only a very small group, about 6 percent, could
be classed as two-housekeeper families. The remaining families were
split into three modes: the semihousewife mode, the drudge-wife mode,
and the cash-paying mode.* (See table 11-2.) One salient feature of
table 11-2 is that housewives and semihousewives on average spend
less time doing work—either paid work or housework—than their
husbands. A second feature of the table is the low amount of housework
done by virtually all husbands.

* In making the tabulation, I included only those couples in which the husband averaged
over thirty hours per week of paid work and commuting. In dividing these couples into groups
by family-care mode, I first segregated those families in which the husband and wife together
did twelve or fewer hours per week of meal preparation and cleanup, indoor housecleaning, and
laundry, and assigned them to the "cash-paying" group. Of the families remaining after the cash-
paying families had been designated, those families in which the wives devoted five or fewer
hours a week to paid employment (defined as including commuting time and coffee breaks at
work) were classified as "housewife-maintaining." The "semihousewife" families were defined
as those among the remaining families in which the wife devoted more than five hours but no
more than thirty hours a week to paid employment. The families in which the wife devoted
more than thirty hours per week to paid employment and did more than 60 percent of the family-
service work—housework, child care, and other family chores—were designated as "drudge-
wife." The remaining families are classed as "two-housekeeper" families.

TABLE 11–2
Hours of Paid Employment and Housework by Husband and Wife in a Sample of American Married Couples, 1975–76

Family-Care Mode*	Number of Couples	Paid Employment† Husb.	Wife	Housework‡ Husb.	Wife	Other Family Work§ Husb.	Wife	All Work Husb.	Wife
Housewife-maintaining	128	51.0	0.1	4.0	31.6	8.2	17.6	63.2	49.3
Semihousewife	59	51.1	18.9	4.7	23.8	8.3	13.0	64.1	55.6
Drudge-wife	39	55.8	43.0	4.2	20.2	5.0	7.9	64.9	71.1
Cash-paying	48	48.3	31.9	4.0	11.7	8.9	9.8	61.2	53.5
Two-housekeeper	16	44.5	44.1	9.1	16.1	11.2	6.5	64.8	66.8
All couples	290	50.9	17.4	4.4	24.3	8.0	13.5	63.4	55.1

* For definition of family-care mode, see footnote, p. 262.
† Time devoted to paid employment includes commuting time and coffee breaks at work. Couples were included only if the husband averaged more than 30 hours per week at paid employment over the survey period.
‡ The definition of "housework" used in making the tabulation includes meal preparation and cleanup, indoor and outdoor cleaning, laundry, and every-day shopping.
§ The designation "other family work" includes other shopping, child care, baby-sitting, travel with children, medical care, gardening, pet care, household repair, other services, and associated travel.
Sources: Tabulated by the author from data derived from *Americans' Use of Time 1975–76* (Ann Arbor, Mich.: University of Michigan Survey Research Center). The inclusion of items in "housework" and "other family work" follows the usage of Joseph H. Pleck, *Working Wives, Working Husbands* (Beverly Hills, Calif.: Sage Publications, 1985), table 2.2, p. 36. What I call "housework," Pleck calls "basic housework."

Husbands of wives with full-time jobs averaged about two minutes more housework per day than did husbands in housewife-maintaining families, hardly enough additional time to prepare a soft-boiled egg. Only four of the 290 couples studied had arranged their affairs so that both husband and wife had full-time jobs and shared the housework fairly equally. One of the four was a cash-paying family with three children. The other three were classified as two-housekeeper families, and none of the latter had children requiring care at the time of the survey.*

Since only a tiny proportion of wives with paid employment in 1975–76 could count on a significant participation in housework by

* Among the 290 families with husbands employed more than thirty hours per week there are six lady-of-leisure families, which have been grouped in the tabulation with the cash-paying families.

the husband, the wife who wanted employment had essentially three choices, all of them with grave disadvantages. She could take on a full-time job, yet continue to do by herself a high proportion of the housework that a housewife would do. This would mean taking on the excessive hours of the drudge-wife, which average seventy-one hours a week. Alternatively, she could move the family in a cash-paying direction. This reduces the strain that derives from the husband's virtual nonparticipation in housework, but presumably at a high monetary cost, and at a possible cost in quality.

The third alternative of the wife whose husband was reluctant to increase his share of housework and other family chores was to take a part-time job. These jobs, especially the ones open to women, generally offer low pay, no fringe benefits, and little chance for promotion or interesting work. The situation of the semi-housewife may look equitable in table 11-2 because her total work time is lower than that of her husband. However, some of these women might have preferred and been able to manage more advantageous full-time jobs, had they been able to negotiate a bigger housework contribution from their husbands.*

The mode of family organization is influenced by the couple's age and whether they have children requiring time-consuming care (see table 11-3). Apparently almost half of young married people without children are in the cash-paying category. Of the older couples with no child-care responsibilities, far fewer are cash paying. Among younger couples, the arrival of children puts an end to the cash-paying lifestyle for most.

One way in which younger and older husbands are similar is in their avoidance of housework. Younger husbands appear to do even less housework than their older counterparts, although neither group of men averages as much as half an hour per day. Nor does the presence of small children appear to make much of a difference in the contribution of husbands to housework.

It is interesting to compare the results of the survey of 1975–76 with those reported for a survey done in 1967–68 (see table 11–4).[4] These comparisons have to be made with caution because of differences

* The same might be said of the women who chose to remain housewives. Some of them might have preferred sharing the family work and the paid work, and would have taken a job had husbands shown more willingness to do some housework.

TABLE 11–3

Family-Care Mode, by Husband's Age and Presence of Children, 1975–76

Family-Care Mode	Husband 35 or Under, Child-Care Time*		Husband Over 35, Child-Care Time*		All
	None	Some	None	Some	
Housewife-maintaining	10%	56%	34%	52%	44%
Semihousewife	24	20	21	19	20
Drudge-wife	17	12	17	12	13
Cash-paying	45	9	15	13	17
Two-housekeeper	5	3	13	5	6
All couples	100%	100%	100%	100%	100%
Number of couples	42	97	47	104	290

NOTES: For definitions and source, see table 11–1.
* Both spouses' time.

in survey methodologies. The results suggest, however, that husbands were raising their family work contributions over that time interval very slowly. But husbands of those women who devoted more than thirty hours per week to paid employment in 1975–76 still were doing little more family work than the husbands of housewives.

TABLE 11–4

Average Weekly Hours of "Family Work" by Spouses, 1967–68 and 1975–76

	Families with			
	Nonemployed Wives		Wives Employed Full Time	
	Husband	Wife	Husband	Wife
1967–68	11.2	56.7	11.2	33.6
1975–76	12.1	48.4	12.3	23.4

SOURCE: The 1967–68 figures are adapted from K. Walker and M. Woods, *Time Use: A Measure of Family Goods and Services* (Washington, D.C.: American Home Economics Association, 1976). The 1975–76 estimates were tabulated by the author. For the source of the 1975–76 estimates, see table 11–2.

Wives, whether employed or not, appear to have lowered their contributions to family work in the period between the two surveys. Furthermore, we know that in that interval many women switched their status; many housewives entered full-time employment. Housework went down by more than thirty hours per week on average for women who made such a transition. The move to replace unpaid services with purchased ones appears strong and broadly based.

Some of the couples who participated in the 1975–76 study were resurveyed in 1981–82.* It appears that these husbands increased their contributions by about an hour per week over the six-year interval.

WHY HUSBANDS' HOUSEWORK CONTINUES TO BE LOW

One way to achieve equity between the sexes—very possibly the only way—would be for women and men to take similar economic roles. By social custom husbands and wives would do the same amount of family-care work and devote the same time and energy to paid employment. The data we have on labor-force participation and time use shows that wives are moving in that direction; they are spending more time in employment and doing less housework. However, husbands are not meeting them halfway.

One explanation that has found favor with economists such as Gary Becker[5] is that a husband's time is so well paid for in the marketplace (largely because of discrimination against women workers, I have argued) that his time is too valuable to be devoted to housework. In the jargon of economists, husbands have a comparative advantage at paid work, and wives have a comparative advantage at housework. Looking back at table 11–2, one can see that the husbands on average do not sacrifice any of their paid labor time when the family moves

* The 1981–82 sample is smaller and represents a relatively low response rate. The tabulation of housework hours is on a somewhat different basis than that reported in tables 11–3 and 11–4. See F. Thomas Juster, "A Note on Recent Changes in Time Use," in F. Thomas Juster and Frank P. Stafford, eds., *Time, Goods and Well-Being* (Ann Arbor, Mich.: Institute for Social Research, University of Michigan, 1985), pp. 313–32.

from the housewife-maintaining mode to the semi-housewife mode. Husbands in drudge-wife families actually devote more time to employment than do those in housewife-maintaining families. On the other hand, in cash-paying and two-housekeeper families, the husbands devote somewhat less time to employment.

The comparative advantage argument says that there would be a financial loss if the family moved in an egalitarian direction—if the husband substituted housework time for on-the-job time. However, it does not explain husbands' low contributions to family-care services in the numerous cases where the wife's total work time is greater than the husband's. In such cases, he might even things up timewise by contributing more services without lowering his time in employment. Nor does the comparative-advantage theory explain why husbands give so small a proportion of the time they devote to family-care chores to housecleaning, cooking, dishwashing, and laundry—the central and despised "housework" chores—and confine their contributions to child care, shopping, yardwork, and household repair.

A more adequate explanation of men's failure to increase housework time has to include an account of the dynamics of family decision-making. The unequal distribution of the housework burden may start at the time of the marriage. Whether it does or not, things certainly go in that direction if the wife quits her job when she has a baby, or reduces her hours in paid employment. The problem is that if the wife resumes full-time employment, it is almost impossible for her to shift part of the burden to the husband's shoulders.

One important and obvious reason that the renegotiation of the housework burden has been difficult is that people do not find housework enjoyable.[6] Both men and women rate cleaning the house as an activity that they like less than most other uses of their time. Shopping also gets a low rating from both sexes. Cooking gets a higher rating from women, and doing repairs gets a higher rating from men. Apparently activities that take some expertise rate high with the sex customarily having the skill to work at them efficiently and produce a good product, and low with the opposite sex. (Cooking for a family is, of course, far more time-consuming than doing repairs—by a factor of about three.[7]) Both sexes claim that caring for children and socializing with them are among their favorite activities, and the time-use surveys show that those husbands who do make contributions to family-care services share child care with far greater frequency than they share cleaning, cooking, or doing the laundry.

It is very difficult for a wife to get a husband to increase the time he spends doing something he dislikes. He may refuse her request outright, or he may simply ignore her suggestion. Or he may say he will do it but fail to do it, or do it grudgingly or sloppily or tardily. He may do it for a while and then stop. Then the wife has the choice of asking him again (he will define that as nagging) or of giving up and continuing to do the tasks she had wanted to get off her own shoulders.[8]

In the marketplace, people change their ways and their activities when sufficient financial incentives are offered. Within the family, the essence of the wife's problem is that the only incentive she has to offer for the husband's compliance is the cessation of her requests for more help. However, these requests have a negative side for her, too, because they fuel hostility and add to the burden of keeping the marriage going. To a woman who recently has had a baby, the idea that the marriage is headed for the rocks will understandably be painful. Thus all the husband has to do is resist the requests for help for a while; eventually they will cease.

It is easier for the wife to take the initiative in getting some of the household tasks replaced by purchases than it is for her to get the husband to provide more services. The wife who wants to cook less and wash fewer dishes might unilaterally start to make it a practice to buy a pizza or some other kind of take-out food instead of making a dinner dish from scratch. If she has full control of the family's cash, then she does the rebudgeting. If she has a food allowance, then her husband may only grudgingly increase it. However, it is he who must in this case make requests for changed behavior. If he persists in such requests, it is he who is defined as causing trouble for the marriage.

Almost half of the wives classified as drudge-wives express a desire for more help from their husbands,[9] and such wives may be in the process of bringing pressure on their husbands for change. A husband who hates housework might think himself happiest if his wife continues to do it all without complaint. However, most husbands, faced with the choice of continuing to receive pressure to do more, pitching in and performing more services himself, or acceding to greater purchases of services, may lean toward the latter.

When a couple changes the mode of providing family-care services, the final arrangement of tasks and budgets may be quite different from what was anticipated by the person who initiated the change. The husband who thought that the sole result of his suggestion that the wife consider an outside job was that he was going to take better vacations may end up eating more fast food and under pressure to do more housework. The wife who thought she was going to exchange housework time for market-work time may find that she has merely added to her work burden, while the family budget for durable goods has enlarged itself irreversibly. She may end up as a drudge-wife, with very little she can do about it short of marital breakup.

ECONOMIC POWER AND THE DIVISION OF HOUSEWORK

Husbands are in a good material position to resist employed wives' demands for a more equal division of hours of housework because of the difference in their salaries. It is a rare wife who makes enough at a job to support herself and her children in any degree of comfort. If she carries the fights about housework too far and the couple separates or divorces, her standard of living is going to be severely cut.[10] Her social status also will be reduced without a husband. By contrast, the income the husband has to devote to himself will increase, and he will be wooed by the many single women eager for husbands.

Power in any relationship, including marriage, tends to flow to the partner who can most easily replace the other. It is much easier for the husband to replace the family-care services of the wife than for the wife to replace the financial contributions of the husband. Divorced women looking for husbands find a shortage of suitable partners, with the odds worsening as they age. Men die on average at a younger age than women do, and men generally look for and succeed in attracting women who are younger than they are.

The way the disparity in economic power works to keep the housework fastened on the woman is that repeated requests for a change in the sharing of housework may bring in return a threat on the part of the husband to leave. The disparity in raw economic power between men and women is one basis for the adoption by about a quarter of working couples in the United States of the drudge-wife family style. But the disparities in economic power between men and women are being reduced faster than the housework burden is shifting.

SEX-ROLE IDEOLOGIES

The influence of sex-role ideologies on the nonsharing of housework has been perceptively described by Myra Marx Ferree, a sociologist who has done extensive interviewing on this subject:

> One constraint employed women have to struggle against in negotiating a more favorable division of labor is their husbands' perceptions of housework as demeaning and unmasculine. The individual man who does not share that perception is nonetheless likely to believe that his buddies do, and all-male social gatherings may reflect and reinforce this rejection of housework as unfit for "real men." . . . For a wife to let other people know what chores her husband does around the house "would make the man seem like he was henpecked."[11]

Ferree emphasizes that when husbands take up housework in individual families, the news of it is suppressed, and the help such news might give to other wives in the process of their negotiations never gets delivered. Each wife fights in isolation. This observation suggests that if the housework issue became a subject of public discussion—perhaps through TV comedies, letters to advice columns in newspapers, articles in women's magazines—members of a drudge-wife family might lose face.

Husbands with an egalitarian attitude toward sex roles do little or no more housework on average than husbands who adhere to a traditional ideology.[12] Either ideology is unimportant, which is difficult to believe, or as Ferree suggests, individuals base their actions on what they perceive to be the dominant ideology rather than on their own ideology.

Ferree also comments tellingly on the situation of the middle-class woman who, because of her husband's high salary, cannot cite a pressing financial need to do paid work. In effect, her work is defined as unnecessary and as interfering with homemaking activities the family wants continued.

> [Her] employment is then defined not as a *contribution* to the family but a *cost* the family bears, more or less willingly, as a consequence of the woman's desire for a job. In essence, under these conditions, the job itself becomes a privilege, and if a woman desires it for "personal" reasons, she will have to pay for it. She may pay by becoming the supermother and superwife who can demonstrate that her job "doesn't hurt anything," does not interfere with her meeting family demands. She may promise . . . that "dinner will still be on the table."[13]

THE ETHICS OF INTRAFAMILY ECONOMIC RELATIONS

Husbands sometimes respond to the requests of their employed wives for more housework contributions with the assertion that they are bringing in more than half of the family's money income, and so the wife should do more than half of the housework. This rejoinder may be simply a reminder of the power that better access to economic resources bestows on the husband. Or it may just be a rationalization cynically designed to shut down the argument. On its face, however, such an argument is an expression of an ethical point of view: It is the importation of a market idea of fairness into family life.

The market ethic is that things ought to trade at their market-determined price, that a trade at any other price is both inefficient and exploitative, and that anything is up for sale. The market ethic imported into civics says that a person should be able to hire someone at market rates to replace himself in the Army. The market ethic imported into the family says that a family member should be able to buy himself out of spending certain hours doing housework. At what price should the purchase of freedom occur, according to the market ethic? At the market price for those services, of course.

Because of the husband's high salary, he brings to the family enough money to match the wife's cash contribution, plus a good deal more. With this excess cash contribution, he claims the right to purchase his freedom from doing half of the housework. By the ethics of the marketplace, even the husband who is allowed to buy his freedom is exploited, because he is paying a very high price for the hours of labor at which he is "hiring" the wife to replace him. The husband who is not allowed to buy his freedom—who contributes lots of money and half the housework, too—is exploited even worse, under market ethics.

Under market ethics, contributions to the family are valued in money terms. The wife's big contribution of time is valued at her low market-set wage rate. By this method of valuation, the husband in the drudge-wife family who does no housework whatever is considered to have contributed much more than the wife, who bears a greater work burden in terms of hours.

An alternative to the market ethic is what we might call the sharing ethic. Each spouse's contribution might be valued as proportional to the total time the person devoted to the family's economic well-being— time devoted to a paid job (including commuting) and time devoted to housework. Each hour would be valued inversely to the pleasure the activity gave. By this method of valuation, a husband working at an interesting and lucrative job would be contributing less to the family than his wife working at a painfully boring job, if that were the best she could get. The sharing ethic would have him do more of the housework than she in that case. The sharing ethic's measurements are for internal use only. In the market, including today's marriage market, he is worth a great deal more.

Which standard reflects justice? To try to answer that question, we have to appeal to what most people consider the essence of family life—love, caring, companionship, consideration, continuity, familiarity. In the predominant culture of the United States, sharing equally in purchased consumer goods is commonplace for spouses. The sharing ethic calls for carrying that idea farther and moving toward equality for the spouses in the pleasurability of their time.

In some other cultures, where the spouses do not look to each other for sociality and support and where the wife is maidservant-*cum*-breeder of the husband's children, even equality of material living standards has not been achieved. In Japan, for example, the husband has large areas of consumption that the wife does not share but that are done in company with male friends or colleagues. Wives seldom are seen in restaurants with their husbands, and husbands take pleasure trips, including trips abroad, in company with other males. What in the West is an occasional "night out with the boys" for the husband has in Japan remained at the center of males' sociability.[14]

Surely, the sharing ethic is closer to the American ideal of family than the market ethic. Under the former, the husband is sharing with the wife his good fortune in the market's evaluation of his services. Under the latter, the husband is importing into the family the disparate valuations of their labor and extracting advantage from his own market superiority. Market ethics make family life look like market life—no friendship, just get what you can out of the person you are dealing with.

THE FUTURE OF HOUSEWORK

The housewife-maintaining family is giving way, but which form will replace it as the dominant mode of organization of family care is not clear. Neither the drudge-wife family nor the semihousewife type offer an egalitarian alternative. As yet only a tiny fraction of married couples lead lives where both spouses have parity in market work and family work. Even those couples I have classified as cash-paying load most of the least pleasant activities on the back of the wife. At least for such couples, the amount of housework is low, so perhaps the uneven allocation matters less.

It is possible that we are in a transition phase and that we are in the process of passing on to a different and more egalitarian arrangement. However, no one could predict with any certainty whether and how rapidly American families will begin to move toward having each adult take part in neatening up the mess we and our children inevitably make as we lead our daily lives. In the Soviet Union, which has the dubious distinction of pioneering in the "double day" for the wife, the failure of husbands to participate on an equal basis in housework has persisted for more than half a century, despite the fact that over that period most Soviet wives have held full-time jobs. While something that persists half a century may in retrospect prove to be a transitional phase, it is a distressingly slow transition.

In the United States and the capitalist West, a free, competitive economy makes possible the movement of resources into producing housework substitutes in step with families' increasing willingness to buy housework substitutes. It is possible that much of the housework problem will dissolve by a process of "industrialization." The prospects for that—the conditions under which it might take place, the effects on the economy, and the special problems of the industries involved— are the subjects of the next chapter.

CHAPTER 12

"Industrializing"
Housework and Child Care

T HE REPLACEMENT of unpaid housework by family-care services that have been purchased has recently speeded up due to the entry of more and more married women into paid work. The "industrialization" of child care and food services, and perhaps of housecleaning services as well, can be thought of as the ultimate episode—and the logical conclusion—of a process that began millennia ago. Before economies based on regularized exchange were well established, the only way to consume some product or service was to have a family member (or perhaps a tribe member) produce it. As economies have developed over the centuries, more and more products for family consumption have come to be supplied by purchase and fewer by within-the-family production. Housework and child care are the major do-it-yourself products that remain; if they are absorbed into the exchange economy, only self-chauffeuring, some amateur house-painting, backyard vegetable gardening, and a few other minor hobbies will be left.

The coming of the industrial revolution in the late eighteenth century and the urbanization it engendered speeded up the decline of production in the home for direct family use, particularly for city people. Most sewing left the home, and purchased clothing became the rule. The raising of water from a well by the bucket was replaced by the marvelously cheap services of water authorities. Centrally provided energy services changed the nature of the home activities producing heat, lighting, and cooking and reduced the time such activities took. While country people might continue to do much of their own butchering, food preserving, and baking, city dwellers could not. Schools have partially replaced home care for children. Institutions such as hospitals and old-age homes have replaced some in-home care of the sick and the disabled. Most recently, entertainment activities with a significant do-it-yourself component—conversation, reading, games— have given way to commercially produced electronic entertainment.*

Every transfer of the production of services from the home to an industrialized or commercial setting changes the size and shape of the economy. Establishments that produce and sell prepared food and out-of-home child care are growing rapidly. The sale for money of house-cleaning services also may be growing, after a century or so of shrinkage. The growth of these industries creates paid jobs, some of which are taken by women coming onto the labor market. The industrialized production process generally is different from the at-home process: for one thing, efficiency is gained by producing in large batches. And as Clair Brown has noted, home production requires that each home have its own equipment, which is idle much of the time.[1] An industrialized process is more mechanized than a home-based process yet may require less total societal investment in mechanical equipment. Each piece of equipment a business buys is more intensively used.

When we replace some self-produced services with purchased services, family life changes. The services we buy tend to be quite different than the home-produced services they are replacing. Fast food differs from home-cooked food; a child's experience in a day-care center is nothing like the experience of a housewife's child. The purchased services may be judged to be better or worse than the homemade ones

---

* There has been some reverse flow, where production for sale has been replaced by unpaid production by family members. One is the decrease in the use of servants—the decline in the number of servants per household. Another is the replacement of the bus and the train by the private car driven by a family member. The latter is connected to suburbanization, and the former may also be to some extent.

they are replacing, but different they certainly are, and less individualized. There is a loss of the "mother's touch." As a cook, Mother may produce meals lacking taste and variety; as a child-minder she may be petulant or negligent or anxiety-producing. Nevertheless, she is one's own mother, and commercial substitutes for her services, even of excellent quality, do not have the same psychological significance. Aside from the actual differences in the services themselves, the purchase of services has tended to reduce the contacts that family members have with each other. Day care is the most obvious example of that. The purchase of prepared food seems to reduce the number of meals that are shared by family members. When the only source of dinner was the main dish Mother had prepared, everybody gathered around the table for it. Now individual family members can pick up their own take-out food and eat it by themselves or with friends. Of course, the quality of the time family members spend with each other may have improved as its quantity has diminished.

The first prediction of the complete industrialization of housework was heard from Russian revolutionaries. The idea undoubtedly came from the women in their ranks. Lenin is quoted in 1920 as saying:

> We are establishing communal kitchens and public eating-houses, laundries and repair shops, infant asylums, kindergartens, children's homes, educational institutes of all kinds. In short, we are seriously carrying out the demand in our program for the transference of the economic and educational functions of the separate household to society. That will mean freedom for the women from the old household drudgery and dependence on man. . . .[2]

The Soviet leaders' proclaimed intentions to replace private housework with socially provided services was not achieved. Their commitment to the relief of women from drudgery was apparently not a very deep one. Rather, their commitment was to the growth of heavy industry. The Soviet state did provide child-care facilities sufficient to permit the full-time employment of most urban adult women. This the Soviet planners felt was necessary to relieve a chronic labor shortage. However, complaints about the inadequacy of places and the consequent scrambling for informally provided substitutes are common. Replacements for other kinds of housework in the Soviet Union have not materialized.[3]

Housekeeping in a socialist state continues to be more difficult than in market economies because of long lines at retail stores, and lower income levels. Soviet husbands remain notorious for their low contribution to family-care chores.

In the 1920s the Soviet Union was not the only place where the idea of doing away with private housework was being promoted. Kibbutzim were being organized in Israel by people devoted to a socialist, collectivist way of life. The kibbutzim were set up to minimize private housework and to replace it by collectively organized food preparation and child-care services.* Most people in Israel have never joined a kibbutz, however, and apparently the newer immigrants are not drawn to the existing kibbutzim or to the formation of new ones. Nor has the kibbutz style of life spread beyond Israel. The Israeli kibbutz offers people an all-or-nothing collectivism that appeals to a small minority.

With the exceptions of Sweden and France, most of the Western capitalist countries remain behind the Eastern European socialist economies in the extent to which child-care centers are provided and used. But the capitalist West is catching up with the socialist East in the use of out-of-the-home child care. At the same time the commercial availability of other housework-replacing services is increasing in the West, as the demand for them swells. In a centrally planned economy like that of the Soviet Union, no line of production can expand without a politically negotiated provision for it in the state economic plan. Thus, while the Soviet Union was the first to promise the abolition of private unpaid housework, the capitalist countries, with their highly flexible response to demand, are moving toward it faster.

Of the family-care services being switched to an industrialized basis, the least problematical is food service. The transfer of house-cleaning services from a do-it-yourself basis to a commercial basis is retarded by organizational and ideological problems. Free enterprise is vigorously enlarging the part of the child-care industry that sells its services for money. Here, in addition to quality problems, there are long-standing, highly controversial demands that this industry should be organized on a subsidized basis and run by the government. Finally, we can envisage the rise of a new type of integrated service establish-

---

* The kibbutz is not, however, just an organization for getting housework done collectively. People participating in the kibbutz are required to take a share in the work of the kibbutz's own enterprises and to rely for their cash income on an egalitarian share of the income of those enterprises. They cannot participate in the regular labor market and cannot reap any benefits from special training or talents or work effort.

ment that could replace the management functions of the housewife as well as her cleaning, cooking, and child-care functions: the service-mall apartment complex.

THE PURVEYING OF PREPARED FOOD

The industry that sells prepared food is an ancient one; visitors to Pompei, the Roman city buried and preserved by volcanic ashes in A.D. 79, can see the remains of numerous commercial bakeries. A billboard advertising a commercial brand of the Roman condiment *liquamen* also was found there. Canning was invented in the beginning of the nineteenth century. Many canned foods, such as soups and stews and sauces, go through extensive processing and cooking in the cannery. Canning allowed consumers to replace some home-cooking activities by the purchase of cooking services performed in a factory. The sale of prepared frozen "dinners" dates from the 1950s; the recent invention and spread of microwave ovens, which speed the heating of frozen dinners for serving, has increased their popularity. Recently, mass-produced frozen dinners of high quality have become available.

Restaurants probably go back to the inns set up to accommodate travelers. Ordinaries, meant to serve local people, were common in large English towns by the sixteenth century; most of their customers probably were men who lacked a woman "to look after them." In France, after the Revolution, many of the chefs who had cooked for aristocrats opened restaurants. The self-service cafeteria is an American invention. By the 1930s, a New York chain of cafeterias called Automats—which incorporated in their design a wall full of coin-in-the-slot vending machines—had as their advertising slogan "Less work for Mother." Fast-food restaurants—which feature cheapness, uniform limited menus, no wait, and no plates or cutlery that require washing—are phenomena of the 1960s. The sale of restaurant food for off-premises consumption is growing rapidly, with outlets springing up in suburbs.

Sales of food by restaurants have been one of the fastest-growing segments of the post-World War II economy. Between 1952 and 1982, restaurant sales, corrected for inflation, grew by 220 percent, as compared with a growth of 160 percent over the same period in total consumer spending.[4]

HOUSECLEANING FOR PAY

The number and proportion of people telling the census-taker they were employed as domestics in private households have been going down since the turn of the century. In 1900, there were 1.6 million people who worked as servants, or one for every ten households. By 1950 there was one servant for every twenty-eight households, and by 1983 the Census Bureau reported one for every eighty-six households.[5] Most of the two million people (mostly women) who were doing domestic work in private households for pay in January 1986 did not work full time for one employer, but split up their services among as many as ten households.

One of the problems in replacing housework by the wife with purchased housework is ideological. It is not unusual to hear, especially from women of a left-of-center political orientation, expressions of disdain toward the wife who has a well-paid job with high time demands who hires a woman to do housework for pay. Such a wife is condemned for passing along *"her* shitwork" to another woman, and stands accused of joining men in oppressing women. Few of the people who express themselves in this way emphasize a greater effort to engage husbands in doing part of "the shitwork." The only alternative to that is for every woman to do "her" own.

The negative attitude toward hiring people to do housecleaning services may spring from the low status of such work. In the past, when class differences were more keenly felt, hiring oneself out as a servant sealed one's permanent assignment to a place close to the bottom of the social order. In addition, race and sex discrimination relegated most black women to domestic jobs, lowering the social status of such jobs even farther. The low status of paid domestics has persisted, whatever the decline in class consciousness or feelings of race superiority. People may feel embarrassed to be procuring someone to do what they perceive to be demeaning work. Hiring a servant has some of the unpleasant aspects of becoming a slum landlord. In both cases, one has to make transactions that are conditioned by the poverty of the people one is dealing with. Just as the slum landlord offers a substandard apartment to a poor person with no alternative, so the person hiring a servant offers a low wage, based on the worker's poor alternatives.

However, a change in the status of housework may be in the offing. It is not uncommon now for college students to do housecleaning part time. The high status that college students expect to occupy in society may reduce any anxieties that they will lose face by performing housework. For them, it is more lucrative than working in fast-food establishments at the minimum wage, in part because the housecleaners who work for individual families find it easy to evade income and Social Security taxes on their earnings. Whatever the reason that students have taken these jobs, the result may be that the stigmatization attached to performing it will diminish.

Some of the millions of illegal immigrants now in the United States also do housework. Neither the native tax evaders nor the illegal immigrants (some of whom may be evading taxation as well as detection by the immigration authorities) are probably well counted by the Census Bureau. So although the official statistics on employment do not show it, it is possible that the amount of housework being done for pay is currently rising.

One of the factors keeping the amount of paid housework low is that the homes of many potential customers are in affluent suburbs, far from the residential locations of the potential workers. The poor state of public transportation makes transportation to the job for the houseworkers difficult, time-consuming, and expensive. Transportation problems also reduce the reliability of the service, a crucial issue for working parents. However, as real wage levels rise, more domestic workers have their own cars and are able to transport themselves to their jobs in the suburbs. Nevertheless, a move of middle-class families back to central cities probably would increase considerably the purchase of housecleaning services.

Another one of the factors that damps down the sale of housework is the individualized nature of the market for such services. Large numbers of people shrink from advertising for strangers from the less-favored groups in the population to come to their house, from conducting interviews, checking references, setting pay, supervising and criticizing the work, firing those who are unsatisfactory, and then starting all over again. The personal nature of the relationship of the employer to the household servant also is daunting to both.

These problems might be alleviated if people bought their household services from business firms that took on all the chores of personnel procurement and management. There does appear to be a modest-sized growth of small local business firms that offer housecleaning services.* For some reason that merits psychological research, frequently they adopt whimsical names such as Maid to Order, Maid in the U.S.A., or Maiday. Their charges are high relative to the cost of hiring an individual, in part because the firms and their employees must pay taxes. However, they do take care of recruitment and supervision, work quickly using teams, and offer reliability and high standards.

The provision of cleaning services for office buildings, restaurants, hotels, stores, and schools, which include kitchen areas and toilet facilities, are apparently dealt with in a satisfactory way. These establishments have employees specialized to that purpose, or make contracts with firms that specialize in providing such services. We are already paying for cleaning services for our daytime environments. The prices we pay for the products sold from offices and stores, and the bill for the food we eat in restaurants, include an allowance for cleaning charges. Eventually many of us will want to pay for the cleaning of our nighttime and weekend environments as well. However, a significant expansion in paid-for housecleaning will require a recongregation of affluent people in a central-city environment. The service-mall apartment complex we discuss in this chapter would provide an environment that would make the hiring of housecleaning services easier and cheaper.

---

* This industry is as yet too small to be distinguished with a line of its own in the Census of Business.

USE OF OUT-OF-HOME CHILD CARE

The trends in child care since the 1950s are shown in table 12–1. Child-care centers have shown the most rapid growth compared to other forms of care. They served 4.5 percent of children of mothers employed full time in 1954; by 1982 they were serving 19.9 percent. The number of children cared for in group centers has been growing since 1970 at about 9 percent per year. Two reasons can be given: The number of mothers employed full time is increasing, and the proportion of such mothers choosing that mode of care is increasing.

Despite the rapid growth of child-care centers, they continue to serve a distinct minority of children of employed mothers. A higher proportion of employed mothers send their children to "family day care," provided by a woman who takes a few small children into her own home to be cared for, perhaps along with her own children. Of mothers employed full time, almost a quarter use family day care. (In table 12–1, family day care is represented by "care in another home by nonrelative.")

A considerable majority of families with employed mothers now make some cash expenditures for child care, although some manage to avoid this by using care by the husband, a grandmother, or another relative. Of mothers employed full time, 79 percent pay some cash. Even where grandparents or other relatives are relied on, cash payments sometimes are made.[6]

ATTITUDES TOWARD OUT-OF-HOME CHILD CARE

Attitudes toward out-of-home child care are determined in part by what people think is good for children. They are also influenced by the importance people give to women's autonomy—whether they think women have the same right as men to be a parent without leaving paid work and thus the right to avoid, if they wish, a stint in the

TABLE 12–1

Child-Care Arrangements Used by Families with
Employed Mothers, 1958–82*

Type of Child-Care Arrangement	(percent)			
	1982	1977	1965	1958
Mother Employed Full Time				
Total	100.0	100.0	100.0	100.0
Care in child's home	27.2	28.6	47.2	56.6
By father	10.9	10.6	10.3	14.7
By other relative	10.9	11.4	18.4	27.7
By nonrelative	5.4	6.6	18.5	14.2
Care in another home	46.3	47.4	37.3	27.1
By relative	20.8	20.8	17.6	14.5
By nonrelative	25.5	26.6	19.6	12.7
Child-care center	19.9	14.6	8.2	4.5
Child cares for self	†	0.3	0.3	0.6
Mother cares for child while working	6.6	8.2	6.7	†
All other arrangements	0.3	0.8	0.4	11.2
Mother Employed Part Time				
Total	100.0	100.0	100.0	100.0
Care in child's home	41.2	42.7	47.0	N.A.
By father	21.3	23.1	22.9	N.A.
By other relative	13.3	11.2	15.6	N.A.
By nonrelative	6.6	8.4	8.6	N.A.
Care in another home	35.7	28.8	17.0	N.A.
By relative	16.4	13.2	9.1	N.A.
By nonrelative	19.3	15.6	7.9	N.A.
Child-care center	7.9	9.1	2.7	N.A.
Child cares for self	†	0.5	0.9	N.A.
Mother cares for child while working	15.1	18.5	32.3	N.A.
All other arrangements	0.1	0.4	—	N.A.

* Data prior to 1982 are restricted to children of ever-married mothers. Data for 1965
and 1958 are for children under six; for 1977 and 1982 data are for children under five.
† Included with all other arrangements.
SOURCE: U.S. Bureau of the Census, *Current Population Reports, Trends in Child Care
Arrangements of Working Mothers,* P–23, no. 117 (Washington, D.C.: U.S. Government
Printing Office, 1982), p. 6, and Current Population Report, *Child Care Arrangements of
Working Mothers: June 1982,* series P–23, no. 129 (Washington, D.C.: U.S. Government
Printing Office, 1983), p. 4.

housewife status when they have children. It would be a mistake to
imagine that attitudes on such issues are unaffected by economic incentives. To some degree, attitudes follow majority practice, which is
apt to change when the economic environment changes.

Only a few decades ago, a mother was considered neglectful unless she waited until her youngest child had graduated from high school before taking a full-time job. A mother was told that it was crucial to her child's development that she be in the house at the moment the child came home from school so that the child might tell her about the events of the school day. Later it became respectable for a mother to go to work when her last child entered elementary school. We appear to be entering a period where mothers have society's permission to avoid any and all full-time housewifery. This last development depends on an acceptance of day care as a satisfactory way of caring for preschool children.

One striking change in the climate of opinion is the turnabout in the thinking of "experts" on the harmful effects of the mother's employment on the child. Prior to 1976, the most widely used baby-care manual, that of Dr. Benjamin Spock, had this to say:

> If a mother realizes clearly how vital [good mother care] is to a small child, it may make it easier for her to decide that the extra money she might earn, or the satisfaction she might receive from an outside job, is not so important after all.[7]

The 1976 edition and subsequent editions of Spock's *Baby and Child Care* abandoned this attitude completely. The book now advises,

> Parents who know they need a career or a certain kind of work for fulfillment should not simply give it up for their children . . . [but should] work out some kind of compromise between their two jobs and the needs of their children, usually with the help of other caregivers.[8]

One amusing turnaround is in the lessons taught by "monkey research." In the 1960s much publicity was given to the report of a researcher who had deprived a monkey infant of its mother. The monkey mother was replaced in the cage by a heated post swathed in terrycloth, on which was mounted a bottle of milk. The unfortunate infant was wont to cling to the post in moments of stress. To no one's surprise, the monkey brought up by the terrycloth post developed severe psychological problems. From our current perspective, it is hard to see how the results of that experiment could be considered relevant to the effects on children of maternal employment. However, at the time it was considered highly relevant, and the publicity it got strengthened the presumption that the full-time presence of the mother was indispensable if the child were to develop normally. By 1974, however, monkey studies were being quoted to show that even a male monkey might make a splendid "surrogate mother" for a monkey infant.[9]

There continues to be, of course, some rearguard agitation against purchased child care. Selma Fraiberg's 1977 book *Every Child's Birthright* argues that every child is entitled to full-time mothering. A recent book on day care by Marian Blum, a Wellesley College psychologist, is a compendium of untoward practices and incidents observed in day-care centers: the children who cry when brought to the center, the use of harnesses for taking children on walks, the mass-production feeding, the long hours that children must spend without privacy or quiet, the occasional delinquencies of center staff who may fall asleep or walk off the job. Somewhat facetiously, she invites a comparison of the children at a day-care center to Soviet prisoners in a slave-labor camp. Some of the things that Blum faults seem trivial, such as the color-coded bottles to keep formulas apart. Others seem serious and point to the need for reforms. Such problems include children's unmet needs for quiet and individualized attention, and the difficulties created when parents bring sick children to a day-care center.[10]

GOVERNMENT INVOLVEMENT WITH OUT-OF-HOME CHILD CARE

Federal and local governments are involved with out-of-home child care on three counts: maintaining quality standards, improving availability, and reducing the price to the parents. In some cities the local authorities themselves run child-care centers. In the past there has been considerable agitation for a more active governmental role in providing or subsidizing preschool child care, and it may well revive once the current wave of conservatism passes.

Governmental regulations on quality are enforced by city and county authorities in the United States. For the most part, they pertain to issues of health and safety: appropriate space, bathroom facilities, the avoidance of overcrowding, and cleanliness of food service. Recent widespread publicity on the sexual abuse of children in a few day-care centers has provoked demands that there be official regulation of personnel selection.

In the United States, governmental payments for preschool child care, either through subsidy or through outright provision of free service, is a highly controversial subject. What little has been provided came from programs arising out of the "war on poverty" that began in the mid-1960s. Some child-care programs were aimed at improving the cognitive development and health of low-income preschool children. Others have been designed to encourage low-income single mothers to take jobs, to reduce welfare costs to the public. However, in 1971, a broader program almost became law. The Congress passed a bill setting up a federal child-care program, with universal access and with a sliding-fee schedule based on parents' income. Perhaps to camouflage the benefits such a bill would confer on mothers, the bill was entitled the Comprehensive Child Development Act. President Nixon vetoed it, declining, as he said in his veto message, to "commit the vast moral authority of the National Government to the side of communal approaches to child rearing over against the family-centered approach."[11]

Despite President Nixon's veto of the 1971 child-care bill, public spending for child care continued to increase. By 1977, the federal government was spending $1.7 billion a year for child-care programs that served about 2 million children. The Reagan Administration, starting in 1981, has cut back on these programs to a considerable degree.

Other countries have been far more active in providing governmental funds to finance the care of preschool children.[12] As we have noted, the Eastern European socialist countries, believing that their economies need the full-time labor of women, have been particularly active; among capitalist countries, Sweden and France have done the most. France has a large system of public child-care centers. The youngest are cared for in *crèches,* which are highly subsidized. Older preschool children are cared for, free of charge, in *écoles maternelles,* which are provided with accredited teachers who lead the children in activities designed to enhance their enjoyment of the senses—sight, hearing, taste, and smell. A large proportion of French preschool children attend the *écoles maternelles;* even children whose mothers are not employed attend them in considerable numbers. Apparently their educational programs are considered by parents to be beneficial to the children.

JUSTIFICATIONS FOR GOVERNMENTAL PROVISION OF CHILD CARE

Many feminists favor governmental financial support for high-quality child care; They think it would help both mothers and children. The children would be helped by saving them from the inadequate care to which some of them are consigned in the absence of government aid. Government-sponsored child care would help mothers by redressing the traditional difference between the sexes in child-care responsibilities.

Current economic arrangements and social assumptions allow men to fulfill the duties and have the pleasures of parenthood without sacrificing their right or ability to pursue economic and vocational interests. Men customarily go to their jobs unencumbered by the worry that their children will not be well cared for. Those fathers who are single parents usually have salaries high enough to enable them to buy child care.

High-quality child care provided at no charge by government would confer on female parents the right and ability to pursue their economic betterment (and their children's) less encumbered by child-care worries. Single mothers, whose rate of pay is on average too low to stretch to high-quality child care and who lack a husband's financial help, are particularly torn between the needs of their children for care and the need of the family for the mother's earnings. However, the suggestion that mothers need freedom from the encumbrance of child care touches a sensitive nerve. Many people cannot bring themselves to believe that mothers could ever under any circumstances find their children an encumbrance.* So most emphasis tends to be put on the benefits to children.

In the United States, the demand for government-run and government-paid-for child care runs up against two sources of opposition. One obvious source is the people devoted to the perpetuation of the system of sex roles that prescribes that women be homemakers, a system that accords the husband primacy in the family on the basis of his role as sole earner. The second source of opposition in the United States is from those who think that as a rule people ought to obtain what they need or want from profit-making private enterprises out of their own incomes rather than from government organizations at public expense. Free or subsidized provision of any product by the government has the effect of forcing those citizens who have no call or need to use the product to subsidize those who do. Advocates for publicly provided and publicly paid-for child care for preschool children have the burden of demonstrating that it is a proper exception to that rule.

Of course, free public schools for children are provided by governments everywhere, including the business-oriented United States. Can the rationale that justifies them also be used to justify free child care? After all, the addition of a public child-care system would simply tack on additional years of attendance at public institutions for children. The common explanation given for public provision of free schools is that it helps the whole country economically and politically to have a literate citizenry. The primary benefit of education does go to the student. But there is an external or spillover effect that benefits everyone taking part in the advanced economy that universal education makes possible. A second, less frequently cited, yet certainly valid argument for free public schools is that they save the children of poor parents from being fatally disadvantaged throughout their adult lives by the lack of an education. The free schools mitigate the rigors of an economic and social system that condemns children of poverty-stricken parents to live in poverty.

* Some people believe that women should return to the enthusiastic embrace of full-time motherhood, at least for a child's first few years. Others think that fathers and mothers should arrange their lives to share jointly in the care of their children at home. Perhaps more male and female parents should be encouraged to give up time from their outside-the-home endeavors. (See the discussion of long paid child-rearing leaves in chapter 9 and shift work families in chapter 10.) However, neither a revivification of the housewife role nor a two-housekeeper lifestyle could be brought about by act of Congress, as universally available subsidized child care could be. The suggestion that a parent be paid a professional-level salary by the government to take care of a child at home is probably outside the bounds of political possibility for the near future.

The concern for poor children does lend some support to subsidized child care. Research suggests that children from poor home environments benefit from spending time in a high-quality child-care center.[13] There is a chance to catch and attend to health and emotional problems that might plague the child for its whole life and that might lead later to behavior costly to society as a whole. Helping the children provided part of the rationale for some early-childhood programs, such as Head Start.

However, it would be hard to base an argument favoring the extension of government-sponsored care from poorer children to all children just on the analogy to public schools. Rather, the argument has to depend on the gains to mothers available in no other way and on the structure of the child-care industry. The absence of a high-quality "brand-name product" in child care that operates at a price that parents in moderate circumstances are willing to pay produces situations for mothers exemplified in the following account:

> Last year was a nightmare for Carol Berning. Each day after dropping off her two pre-school children at the baby sitter's, the 34-year-old consumer research manager for Procter & Gamble went to work with a knot in her stomach. Instead of analyzing data for such products as Tide, Cascade and Ivory Liquid, she found herself staring at her youngsters' pictures and worrying. Their sitter had been letting them play in the street, and worse, she was taking them on unscheduled trips across the Ohio River to Kentucky. Then, unexpectedly, the sitter resigned and the chore of finding a replacement was soon absorbing much of Mrs. Berning's workday. . . .[14]

Berning's "nightmare" is without doubt authentic, and experiences like hers must at one time or another be the lot of parents who depend on family day care. But she appears from the context to have a well-paying job. Why doesn't she buy the kind of care that would present fewer or no nightmarish experiences? Is it up to the taxpayers to arrange some better alternative for her children, and for the taxpayers to pay for it?

The argument for government provision of child care open to all children is based in the last analysis on its assured quality. Government-run centers would allow parents to bypass family day care of the type used by Berning. Family day care provided by individuals in their homes is rather like the little girl in the nursery rhyme: When it is good it is very, very good, and when it is bad, it is horrid. The problem is that parents cannot with assurance distinguish ahead of time the good from the bad. They hope to be lucky—to take advantage of the low cost, yet to find a provider who will give their child a good environment. More parents choose family day care than choose a child-care center. Most of the providers of family day care probably do a good job. Children can be treated more individually in very small groups, and for very young children the likelihood of catching an illness is lower. Managerial expenses are minor, and the facilities are the living quarters of the provider and therefore are essentially free to the day-care business. (Tax evasion by family day-care operators probably also reduces costs to parents; it is really a stolen government subsidy.)

Family day care may be both best and cheapest as long as things are going normally. However, independent family day care is more risky and less dependable than institutional child care. Unassisted private individuals cannot be as dependable as organizations, which can routinely arrange for backups in case of illness or other problems. The lack of oversight of the independent family day care operator and the defenselessness of the children open them to abuses. Moreover, when a parent has to change providers, finding new providers, evaluating them, and deciding which to use is a nerve-racking and time-consuming task.

A government program might provide institutional child care, on a free basis, or with fees geared to family income. It is likely that unsupervised and unaffiliated family day-care providers would be run out of business, and there would be both gains and some losses from that. Some excellent child-care establishments might be eliminated. On the other hand, there probably would be a reduction in the number of children receiving inadequate care in downright dangerous situations. Such a program would simplify the lives of employed mothers, doing away with difficult and costly searches and allowing them the luxury of carrying out their jobs in relative peace. Whether public opinion would support a substantial child-care program on such a rationale remains to be seen. But putting a floor under quality for the sake of both parents and children certainly is a worthy objective of public policy.

Public child care would help women just entering the labor market and those women who become unemployed. It would greatly facilitate their job search. Freely available child care also would permit women with a low potential wage to avoid welfare. Free public child care never could be justified solely or mainly on the ground that it reduces welfare costs. But there would be a gain in independence and respectability for low-earning single mothers. They would have at least a chance to advance to a better job.

In the 1960s and early 1970s, governmental provision of child care tended to be justified on the grounds that child-care facilities simply were not available and that government had to make them available to enable many women who wanted jobs to take them. In the 1980s these rationales sound rather anachronistic—both the number of mothers of young children in jobs and the capacity of the child-care industry have grown rapidly, with only limited governmental help. Obviously, the cheaper and more easily available child care is, the faster will the remaining at-home mothers come into the market for paid jobs. However, the ideas that lack of governmental provision of child care, and an inability of private child care to expand, would keep a large percentage of women off the job market have proven to be false.[15]

Free or subsidized child care, which reduces the cost to the parents of having children, may increase people's willingness to have and rear children. Government subsidy of reproduction is something that may become an open issue as the birth rate drops farther. In France, worries about population size have been a government preoccupation for generations, and this probably explains at least in part the generosity of government provision for child care. Even if there is no desire by the public to increase the birth rate, it is possible to argue plausibly that parents are performing a public service by doing the work of bringing up the next generation. However, once subsidies for children becomes the avowed intent, then the form of the aid becomes an issue, and there are many possible forms. Cash allowances, free medical care, and paid time off for parents will strike some as more worthy means of support than subsidized child care in away-from-home centers.

A revival of political activity for a more extensive governmental program of providing child care to middle-class parents must await the return of an administration espousing an egalitarian sex-role ideology and a willingness to undertake more extensive domestic spending programs. It is unlikely that such a program could be advocated and sold to the nation as enabling mothers of preschool children to work, since

over half of them already do, and the private sector h
ability to expand the number of child-care centers. Free
care for the children of the entire population would have
by a concern to put a floor under the quality of child care,
parents from having to depend on trouble-prone private child care,
and as a way to assist parents with the trouble and expenses of bringing
up children.

OTHER WAYS OF SUBSIDIZING CHILD CARE

As a substitute for direct subsidies to providers of child care, some
governmental assistance with child care has been given through
concessions on the income tax. Single parents and two-earner couples
have been allowed a credit on their federal income taxes for a portion
of their child-care expenses. Reimbursement through rebates on taxes
is not the same thing as having a well-trusted center in which children
can be placed while the mother looks for a job, before she knows what
job she will get. In any case, current moves to simplify the tax code
by removing credits and deductions make help with child-care through
the tax system less likely.

Some employers have provided subsidized child care to their employees. Procter & Gamble, the employer of Carol Berning, whose
day-care troubles we referred to earlier, is one of the employers who
recently started to do so.[16] The employer may simply help the employee
to pay for day care in a facility unconnected to the employer's enterprise,
or may actually set up and run a child-care center, perhaps on the
employer's premises.

From the employer's point of view, setting up a high-quality day-
care center for employees' children is a good way to lower labor turnover, to allow employees to work without distractions occasioned by
child-care problems, and to reduce absenteeism. However, employers
also can gain simply by including financial help with child care purchased on the open market as a fringe benefit. Under current tax law,
employees are exempt from taxation on employer-provided child-care

benefits, as is the case with health insurance and numerous other in-kind benefits. Such fringe benefits are worth more to the employee than the equivalent amount of cash wages would be and so are a cheap way for the employer to provide the employee with a given amount of after-tax income.

Government subsidies for employer-run day care do not help the unemployed, who need a place for their children while they conduct a job search. Nor do they help those parents who work for an employer too small or too marginal to establish a child-care center for employees. If government subsidies were available to all parents on the same basis, there could be no objection to having some of the child-care centers on the premises of large employers. However, a child-care subsidy restricted to those who worked for an employer providing child care is unfair to a large number of parents.

IMPROVING THE QUALITY OF CHILD CARE

Critics of institutional child-care centers have described the problems of caring for young children in large groups. Among the most difficult issues are the long hours some children have to spend in a noisy environment, and the problem of dealing with sickness. Marian Blum explains why so many ill children show up at day-care centers:

> [Y]oung parents . . . are faced with dilemmas when their children are ill. Their jobs are important and their employers are annoyed if they stay home to care for a sick child. Because there are no emergency services or grandmothers around, some parents tend to minimize illnesses and send sick children to day care. In the early morning household rush, it is easy for parents—consciously or unconsciously—to ignore the beginnings of an illness.[17]

The result is that the day-care centers designed for well children find themselves dealing with children who have coughs and running noses, diarrhea, or nausea. The other children are put at risk, and infections spread.

Some thought has been given to child-care setups that deal better with the need of children for quiet in the course of a long day, and the problem of illness. Myra Strober has proposed what she calls an "integrated system" of child care that combines several modes of care into one operating system. It would have at its core a child-care center with accommodation for up to seventy-five children. A network of supervised, closely regulated (and taxpaying) family day-care homes would be attached to the center. The latter would keep the youngest children all day and some of the others part of the day. The family day-care homes could be used for meals and naps. Certain family day-care centers associated with the system could be designated as infirmaries that, under the supervision of local pediatricians, could deal with ill children.[18] In the next section, I shall discuss a form of housing—high-service housing—that would be a particularly good setting for integrated child care of the type envisaged by Strober.

Another way to solve the illness problem would be for child-care centers to send out workers to care for ill children in their homes, or to maintain sick bays.

HIGH-SERVICE HOUSING—THE FAMILY CARE MALL

As time goes on, American families are buying more and more of their family-care services, thus trading some of their money income for greater freedom from housework chores. This trade is easiest for those who live in urban multifamily dwellings. In some apartment houses the services of housecleaners who go from one unit to another can be contracted for. Apartment houses are likely to have restaurants as well as establishments that clean clothes nearby, and possibly child-care facilities, too.

At the present time, the convenience of having a large number of services available under one roof and one management is available for older people. A considerable number of apartment houses now are being built in metropolitan areas for affluent and still physically independent elderly people. Generally they have community dining facilities and offer housecleaning and laundry services. These facilities are not available to younger people; in fact, they and their children are expressly barred by the rules of most of these establishments.

One possibility for helping young parents with children to get their family care done efficiently would be to build residential centers set up to provide many of the services being provided to the affluent elderly, plus child care. The Swedes have set up some housing complexes that offer such service; one name for them in Sweden is "family hotel." The name is suggestive—an enumeration of the services that hotels provide shows that even families who purchase a high quantity of services might be enabled to go a lot farther in that direction if residential buildings with hotel-like services were to become available.

In a hotel, the living quarters are neatened up and cleaned by people paid to do that work, and the hiring, scheduling, quality control, and supervision of the cleaners are done by the hotel's management employees. The hotel supplies interior decoration, and it buys and renews the furnishings and linens. It manages the maintenance of the building and of the appliances. Laundry service is available. The hotel maintains one or more restaurants on the premises, whose services replace food shopping, cooking, and dishwashing. Sometimes contracts can be signed for a certain number of fixed-menu meals at reduced prices. A hotel will cater parties for the entertainment of guests of the hotel residents. The hotel staff will take messages and are there to accept deliveries when the residents are out. Finally, many hotels will arrange for baby-sitters. Obviously, affluent two-earner families already purchase many of the services that a hotel offers, but only a tiny minority of families actually live permanently in a building designed for family residence whose management coordinates the provision of all of them.

The first Swedish family hotel, also called a "collective house" or *servicehus,* was built in the 1930s for 120 families at the instigation of Alva and Gunnar Myrdal. It had a restaurant, a laundry, and a child-care center. In a sense, its success killed it: People whose children grew up refused to move out. As a result, patronage of its service facilities fell off, and they were forced to close. The building still exists as a conventional apartment house.

Projects built subsequently along this line continue to function in Sweden. A typical project might have apartments for more than one thousand families. It would offer from a central kitchen meals that could be eaten in a dining room or in one's apartment; day care for children from six months to seven years; activities and day rooms for older people; laundries, clinics, and a "front desk" staffed by people who arrange for baby-sitting, housecleaning, and errand-running. It is notable that the Swedes have seen provision of these projects as a way they can integrate a high-service environment for elderly people with services to employed parents.[19]

These establishments reportedly have their drawbacks. One problem is noise. A large complex might house over a thousand children under fifteen. The management of restaurants for such complexes has been a problem, apparently both for the restaurant and for the residents. The residents understandably would rather not commit themselves to pay for and eat large numbers of meals from the restaurant, but the existence of the restaurant is predicated on the assumption that they will. For all of these problems, however, the Swedish service houses have long lists of people waiting to get into them.

American versions of the service house might consist of a large apartment house built over a "service mall." The integrated child-care system described by Strober might function quite efficiently in such a setting. The child-care center would be part of the service mall, while people who contracted to provide family day care might be especially recruited as tenants. Sick children might be accommodated in their own apartment under the care of specially trained practical nurses. The service mall might contain a pediatrician's office, a fast-food establishment, an Oriental-food take-out, a high-style cafeteria, a dry cleaner, the child-care center, and the service desk, which would help residents with arrangements for housecleaning. If the service mall were open to the general public, the problem of forcing the residents to use the services would be reduced.

The management of a service mall apartment complex would be rather tricky—one would have to balance giving the residents some freedom of choice in whether to patronize the establishments of the service mall with the necessity of making those establishments viable. The price of the apartments would have to be structured to discourage the residence of those who did not intend to use the provided services. The location would have to be chosen carefully.

In the United States, the central city has largely been stripped of middle-class families with children, who after World War II went to the suburbs in search of space and greenery and the financial benefits of home-owning. They also wanted to get away from crime and from the problems they perceived with schools that had a high proportion of disadvantaged black youngsters. However, for the two-earner family, and especially for the family with two parents with demanding careers, carrying on life in a single-family house in the suburbs has been extremely difficult. We do not know what proportion of such couples might opt for an urban high-service environment—would choose to give up the greenery and the space and the privacy to be able to stop commuting and avoid the endless juggling to provide family-care services. But at least some might opt for service-mall housing, were it to come into existence.

The extent to which service-rich housing develops depends to some extent on the entrepreneurship of American developers. It also depends on the amount of progress we make in solving the problems that currently render the city unattractive and dangerous. A better integration of blacks into the American economy, better methods of fighting crime, rehabilitation of public transportation, and improvements in urban school systems would facilitate a move toward an end to housework—initially for a few pioneers, later for everyone.

CHAPTER 13

A Policy Agenda for
the Sex-Role Revolution

$\mathbf{A}$S THE REVOLUTION in sex roles proceeds, it becomes more and more obvious that many of the policies, institutions, attitudes, and habits that belong to the old system are out of place in the new. Whatever purpose they formerly served, under current conditions they create difficulties and injustices. Reserving the best jobs for men is an example of a habit that does not accord with today's notions of fairness, nor with unmarried women's need for a decent standard of living. Today we should not be saddled with a welfare system that sets up single mothers to play the part of housewives—lacking only husbands and decent incomes. The age-old custom that men are waited on by women within the family and take little or no part in providing household services has to be changed if women are to have lives as comfortable and enjoyable as those of men.

Some customs get changed when large numbers of individuals or families, acting without much or any public discussion, respond to changes in the economic incentives. Reducing the need for housework by purchasing prepared food has gone on gradually and quietly, spurred on by the advertising of those selling the food. This change, which has helped many women, did not require an ideologically charged campaign. In fact, such a campaign might well have hurt more than it helped.

Some of the work of changing long-standing habits and practices in the workplace, the school, and the home does have to be speeded by agitation—consciousness-raising, as it is called in feminist circles. There should be active and ongoing discussions on a broad range of sex-role issues, with both women and men taking part. We need public discussion on what kinds of behavior should be classifed as sexual harassment and what is to be done about it, on what level of child support payments would be fair, on how the employed wife's double burden is to be alleviated. These issues are being aired now, for the most part under the guise of fiction—in television comedies, in movies, in novels. That is better than nothing, but it is not enough.

For some of the needed changes, consciousness-raising can be only the prelude to the government action that is required. Only the government can threaten penalties that will motivate more employers to allow women to compete fairly for the most interesting and best-paid work. Government practices themselves need reforming. We should not go on with a governmental welfare system that chains millions of women and children to poverty. Nor should child support enforcement be left to a judicial system that is not adapted to ensure the monthly delivery of relatively small sums to millions of people. Government should set the standards for the child-care industry and set up centers of its own. A new government insurance program is needed to help families who give birth to a disabled child—a risk of disaster that all prospective parents face.

It is not easy to devise social policy changes that do more good than harm. Examples of failed or flawed policy initiatives litter the stage. No-fault divorce looked like a civilized way for equal adults to deal with marital incompatibility. Its implementation has cut adrift millions of middle-aged and elderly housewives who had every right to believe they had been guaranteed a comfortable home for life. Well-meaning efforts to reform welfare failed miserably to lead single-mother families out of poverty. Instead they provoked a reaction that has left poor single mothers and their children radically worse off. Government encouragement of home ownership drained off the vitality of the central cities, which at their best provide the most comfortable environment for the two-earner family and the single-parent family.

Given the difficulties of finding and implementing policies that will help more than hurt, we need a spirit of experimentation. New ideas are best tried out on a small scale, with the results carefully observed. Resources have to be found and devoted to research. Demonstration projects have to be mounted. Unsuccessful projects have to be analyzed, and campaigns run to get successful projects reproduced. Interest in particular policies that promise improved conditions must be kept up over a time-span of decades.

The women and men who see the need for policy changes have lacked a forum for discussion. Partly as a result, we have done little to establish sensible priorities and then to concentrate our efforts on the most important issues. In the past decade, a great deal of the energy of feminists went into efforts at reforms that, while positive, could have only minor effect or could help only small numbers of people.

The issues I have highlighted—fairness in the workplace, a better system for helping single parents, a better sharing of household and child-care tasks—are central, if women's situations are to be significantly improved. Feminists have up to now devoted remarkably little energy to exposing abuses in these areas, formulating remedies, fighting to strengthen the laws, and then fighting to get the laws energetically and intelligently applied.

At this writing, a conservative national administration is in office in the United States and will hold power until January 1989. It is attempting to dismantle even the present inadequate system of anti-discrimination enforcement. There is no likelihood that it would want to move positively on most of the other items on the feminist agenda, with the possible exception of those that promise to reduce government expenditures. This does not mean that assembling such an agenda is a fruitless task. On the contrary, unless a sensible agenda is established, the next opportunity for realizing gains may be wasted, as past opportunities have largely been wasted.

A TWELVE-POINT POLICY AGENDA

The following policy agenda draws together the most important of the suggestions made in earlier chapters, plus some additional ones. It starts with a group of five measures that would promote equality in the workplace for women and men. Of all policy initiatives, these surely have the highest priority. For women to have equal access to the work that is most interesting and best paid is obviously worthwhile for its own sake. Moreover, the other problems that women have will become more tractable once women have better jobs. Good jobs are especially needed for women who become single parents, a steadily increasing fraction of all mothers. Good jobs for women will finance the purchase of services to replace self-performed housework. When women earn more, they will have more power in the family, so equality between husband and wife in doing household chores should be easier to achieve.

1. IMPROVE ENFORCEMENT OF FAIRNESS IN PLACEMENT AND PROMOTION

Most employees still separate the sexes by function in the workplace, and certain jobs continue to be virtually off-limits to women. The Equal Employment Opportunity Commission (EEOC), charged with enforcing the Civil Rights Act, has not been fully effective in inspiring employers to change this kind of behavior. If the tax laws of the United States were enforced as slackly as the antidiscrimination laws currently are, very few people would pay any taxes.

The Internal Revenue Service (IRS) gets business firms and individuals to obey the tax laws by requiring annual reports, by scrutinizing the reports closely, and by investigating those whose reports do not conform to the law or look suspicious. It assesses fines and initiates prosecutions when it establishes violations. People are worried about how the IRS is going to react to their tax return. By contrast, the EEOC gets reports on employment by race and sex from employers but makes little or no use of them for enforcement purposes. The operations of the EEOC have had little effect on the behavior of employers, because employers who disobey the law have little cause to fear that the EEOC will come after them.

There continue to be firms that hire very few women college graduates and that place the ones they do hire in clerical jobs. There are firms that deny women workers on-the-job training given to men. Many firms are reluctant to have women supervising both men and women. The EEOC must develop audit devices that reveal such practices, and it must go after firms that practice them.

The bulk of resources for antidiscrimination enforcement should be focused on large-scale employers. Each branch of each large firm should have an EEOC audit officer attached to its case, just as it has an IRS agent looking at its tax compliance. If we can make wholesale progress against sex and race discrimination in large establishments, which tend to dominate the labor market, then time-consuming enforcement actions against small employers will become less necessary.

Among the employers who need to be pushed harder to abolish sex and race discrimination are the federal, state, and local government agencies. They are large employers, and although they probably discriminate less than private industry does, their record is far from good. The antidiscrimination-enforcement agencies and organizations interested in civil rights should monitor their progress.

The program of monitoring the employment practices of establishments that sell to the federal government or that get grants or contracts should also be strengthened. Withdrawing eligibility for federal funds from a higher proportion of noncooperating employers would be bound to increase the rate of compliance.

Business firms need better guidance in developing their personnel policies to conform to laws against discrimination. A new breed of business consultants is needed. They would specialize in helping firms to get rid of current practices, whether formal or informal, that disadvantage women and blacks. They would be equipped to teach an employer how to locate individuals within the organization who discriminate and to reeducate them or neutralize their influence. Such consultant firms might employ psychologists, social workers, and education specialists as well as personnel experts and lawyers. Winning plaintiffs in large class-action discrimination cases could ask the judge in the case to assign such a consultant group to monitor the offending employer for a few years and to help in a transition to a nondiscriminatory system.

2. REALIGN WAGE RATES BASED ON COMPARABLE DUTIES

A considerable number of state and local government agencies are realigning the wages they pay to their own employees, raising the wages in the occupations in which women predominate. This is occurring through political pressure and shows what skillful agitation that hits a responsive chord can accomplish, even in a relatively hostile political climate. The next target is the federal government.

Wage realignment in the public sector will affect occupational wage levels in the private sector. However, if wage realignment is to be applied directly to the private sector, a strategy of attack must be formulated. A wholesale approach rather than individual lawsuits or firm-by-firm negotiations would make for faster progress. The U.S. Department of Labor or the National Academy of Sciences should issue guidelines concerning relative wages for important occupations. The agency would rate a small number of widely used occupations, some predominantly female and some predominantly male. The occupations would be rated with respect to intelligence required, extent of knowledge required, responsibility, and working conditions. Guidelines in the form of wage ratios would be based on the agency's own study.

Government contractors should be required to realign their wages according to the guidelines to remain eligible for contracts. Even if enforcement powers were lacking, the existence of the guidelines, and knowledge by women employees of what they say, might cause enough ferment in the workplace to make employers interested in applying them. The U.S. Supreme Court may in the future decide that the realignment of wages in conformance with job evaluations is positively required under the Civil Rights Act in certain cases. However, the Supreme Court's permission is not needed for the legislature-backed realignment of wages in public-sector jobs nor the issuance of wage guidelines by a federal agency.

3. END SEX SEGREGATION IN VOCATIONAL AND ENGINEERING EDUCATION

Many blue-collar and technical occupations continue to be virtually closed to women. The schools or courses where the skills needed in these occupations are taught remain all-male. Public high-school courses that teach people construction trades or how to be machinists or repair engines or electronic equipment have very few if any female students. While the boys are learning high-paying trades, the girls are learning cosmetology, haircutting, typing, or data entry. They are headed for a lifetime of low-wage, dead-end jobs.[1]

Sexual harassment by male students of girls who do try to make it through the technical courses probably is not uncommon. Vocational education teachers of "male" courses probably do not want trouble among their students, and in any case consider the present situation natural and normal and nothing to worry about.

Girls of high-school age are extremely vulnerable to peer pressure to behave in ways that appear to validate their identity as women. They now perceive the technical occupations as outside their permissible repertoire. Campaigns must be mounted to convince high-school girls that technical and crafts occupations are open to them and that these occupations have important advantages that the typically female occupations do not. Most of all, they must be convinced that they will not be desexed if they participate in them. Where the schools themselves are inhospitable to training girls in crafts and technical subjects, local feminist groups must organize to force them to change. Compulsory courses in construction skills, mechanical subjects, cooking, and baby care for students of both sexes should be instituted in high schools.

Union-run apprenticeship programs that continue to welcome only white males should be targets for desegregation. The high-school vocational education teachers who refer only males for apprenticeship slots need reeducation.

Engineering continues to be a large and lucrative profession that is largely male. While women students are flooding into law, medicine, business, and the sciences, the increase of women among engineering students has been small. While engineering is something one studies in college rather than high school, what goes on in high schools is crucial to the recruitment of engineering students under the present system. One does not come to an engineering major as one might come to a history or economics major, or even a mathematics or physics major. Most people enter those majors as college sophomores or juniors, after a period of trying out courses to see where their talents and tastes lie. By contrast, one must apply to be an engineering major from high school. It probably never occurs to the vast majority of high-school girls that they might have an enjoyable career as an engineer. Once they get to college, there is no way they can explore a course or two to find out if they have the talent and taste for engineering. The engineering department usually is not interested in having them transfer into the program. So eighteen-year-old girls are shut out of the program because they did not know enough at seventeen to apply. The result is that engineering is the one field not having a sizable influx of women.

The solution to the exclusion of women from engineering must be outreach to the high-school students plus a restructuring of engineering curricula to allow for transfer after the freshman year. These reforms would help many male students as well.

4. END DISCRIMINATION AGAINST PART-TIME WORKERS

Employers customarily treat part-time workers differently than full-time workers—the former get less hourly pay for the same work. Most often, part-time workers are deprived of the fringe benefits their employers pay other workers—credits toward pensions, health insurance, vacations, pay for holidays, and paid sick leave. They are not considered in line for promotion.

The poor treatment of part-time workers affects women most of all. Of all employed women over twenty years old in the first half of 1985, a total of 19 percent were reported to be employed part time; for employed men the corresponding figure was 5 percent.[2] In some cases, that poor treatment of part-time workers may be motivated by the fact that the workers involved are women, who, because of discrimination, have a weak position in the labor market.

Some, perhaps most, women workers with part-time jobs prefer part-time work. However, there are some circumstances where women have part-time jobs because of employer discrimination. Employers may offer women applicants part-time jobs but offer similarly qualified male applicants far more advantageous full-time jobs. While this occurs in retail sales, it also is not uncommon on university campuses. There male professionals may be hired into regular full-time faculty slots that carry the possibility of promotion and permanence, while women find themselves being offered and being forced to take lower-status part-time appointments that are "nontenure track" and that pay less for more teaching.

The poor pay and benefits that part-time jobs carry penalize those workers—male or female—who would like to devote less than the standard number of hours to paid work in order to have more time for themselves or their families. It makes difficulties for couples who want to share family and child care and who would be willing to make a modest sacrifice of money income in return for ample time for their home duties. It makes the cost of such a trade-off prohibitive.*

Legislation ending discrimination against part-time workers would require that they receive prorated fringe benefits and that their hourly pay be equal to that of full-time workers performing similar duties. It would not allow workers to set their hours unilaterally but would guarantee those assigned part-time work by their employer the same treatment full-time workers receive. Such legislation would raise costs to employers and raise some prices. It would add to the burden of governmental interference with business, something that should not be done lightly. However, if discrimination against part-timers is not outlawed, the problem, which is already an important source of disadvantage to women workers, will grow worse.

5. CAMPAIGN AGAINST SEXUAL HARASSMENT

Sexual harassment on the job is designed to keep women in what sexists believe to be their place. It is practiced against women who hold traditionally female occupations and against those who try to hold jobs and perform well in jobs that are traditionally men's.

Women in jobs that are traditional for them, such as secretaries, are nagged, cajoled, and threatened for sexual favors. While the harasser may rationalize that he is just having fun, at least part of the aim is to demonstrate his power in the very act of enjoying its perquisites. This kind of harassment may make it distasteful for a women to stay in a particular job that might otherwise be advantageous. Thus she is presented with the unpleasant alternative of putting up with the harass-

---

* It is presumably to evade the penalties against part-timeness that the idea of full-time job between two people has evolved. However, this is merely an awkward : a problem that has been artificially created by the discriminatory treatment of part-tin

ment, possibly giving in to it, or quitting and having to look for another job, where the situation may repeat itself.

With women in jobs atypical for them, harassment takes the form of derisive insult masked as an invitation to sexual activity. Its purpose is to show contempt for the woman and to disabuse her of the notion that she is being received as just another human being on the job. Those who do it take pleasure in torturing the woman psychologically while she remains, but their real aim is to get rid of her.

Sexual harassment has important negative economic consequences for women in both kinds of jobs. Employers who tolerate sexual harassment of their female employees can be sued under the Civil Rights Act, and this has happened in some cases. However, surveys indicate that sexual harassment is quite common, and progress against it through lawsuits is very slow.[3] Feminist organizations need to organize campaigns against employers who permit sexual harassment. Employers must be induced to establish and enforce a rule making sexual harassment an offense that can get the harasser fired.

The next three agenda items are a package of reforms to help single parents, many of whom are currently in poverty and who at best lead difficult lives. They present a set of reforms designed to replace the present welfare system that would shift most of the cost of supporting single parents to their own earnings and to the earnings of the absent parent. For the majority, welfare payments from the government would be replaced by child-support payments from the biological parent not living with the child. The single parent would be expected to get most of her (or his) income from earnings. However, a specially designed form of unemployment insurance would deal with the income needs of the single parent just entering the labor force, and in case of job loss. A welfarelike program would be a final bulwark against destitution, but if the system worked well, it would be used by very few. If this package of programs worked as anticipated, it would allow single parents to escape the poverty trap that now catches so many of them. At the same time, it might save public funds and so might appeal to conservatives.

Black men and white men would pay a higher share of the support for their biological offspring than they do now. Almost all white men can afford it, and so can a high proportion of black men. However, the race discrimination that detracts from the earnings of black men needs to be fought with increasing vigor and better-designed procedures.

6. NATIONAL ADOPTION OF A DEDUCTION-BASED UNIFORM CHILD-SUPPORT PLAN

There are four major problems with our current system of child-support payments for single parents. Child-support awards do not exist for many children living with one parent. Many of the awards are very small. The system, which is supposed to make sure that those who owe child-support payments make the actual payments faithfully, is lax and inefficient. Cases that cross state boundaries are virtually impossible to resolve in a timely and satisfactory way.

We need a system that will get rid of all four of those problems. A system that, if applied nationally, promises to do that is going into operation in the state of Wisconsin. The Wisconsin plan allows for uniform awards based on the absent parent's income and the number of children. Awards are the same for children born out of wedlock as for children of divorced or separated parents. For each child born out of wedlock, a judicial determination of parenthood is to be made based on biochemical tests. Enforcement will be on the basis of automatic deductions from pay, which will go into a state fund. Each single custodial parent will draw from the fund what has been contributed by the absent parent. Parents whose absent counterpart pays little or nothing get a minimum payment.

In 1983, child-support awards averaged about 14 percent of the income of the average adult man; about 71 percent was paid. Under the Wisconsin schedule, awards would be 50 percent higher. All single parents would receive payments; total child support dollars received would about quadruple.[4] Payments under the Wisconsin system would be about equal to the U.S. average of welfare benefits. However, child-support payments would not diminish if the single parent worked, so they would not deter work, as welfare payments currently do. A salary, plus child-support payments on the level mandated by the Wisconsin system, plus some help with child-care expenses would suffice to keep almost all single parents and their children out of poverty.

7. SET UP SPECIAL UNEMPLOYMENT INSURANCE
   FOR SINGLE PARENTS

Single parents need a more generous system of unemployment insurance than that currently available to the general run of workers.[5] Under the present program, a spotty work record reduces benefits. An unemployed person who never has had a job or who has not had one within the past year gets no unemployment insurance benefits.

However, single parents need to be supported while they are looking for their first job. Single parents are more likely to have spotty work records because they are juggling a lot of responsibilities. The difficulties they may have with child care, their children's health problems, and transportation problems make them particularly vulnerable to unemployment. Single parents may lose jobs, have to quit jobs, or have to refuse to take jobs because the duties or hours or locations are incompatible with their parental responsibilities. Thus their spells of unemployment may be more frequent and last longer than those of other workers.

Special unemployment insurance for single parents would pay a benefit to single parents looking for their first job. It would have more lenient rules for paying benefits to people with intermittent work records. Perhaps benefits might be more generous and the maximum period lengthened as compared with the regular program.

It may be objected that a special unemployment insurance of this sort for single parents would be a welfare program masquerading under a more respectable name. However, this is not really the case. The major difference between welfare and unemployment insurance is that welfare has no time limit, while unemployment insurance ordinarily is limited to twenty-six weeks. Welfare recipients currently are urged to seek work or training, but usually it is understood that if they do not do so, they can receive benefits as long as they have children under eighteen. By contrast, the special version of unemployment insurance for single parents would have a time limit, just as the regular version does.

A backup system would have to come into existence for single parents who ran out of unemployment insurance coverage. Benefits probably should not be sums of money but should consist of help with the rent plus meals for parent and child.

8. ESTABLISH A PUBLICLY FUNDED, HIGH-QUALITY CHILD-CARE SYSTEM

The third part of the package to replace welfare for single parents would be a publicly funded, high-quality child-care system that would be available without cost to single parents. Children of two-parent families should be made welcome at subsidized rates.

Single parents in particular need access to free child care when they are looking for jobs—when they are just coming on to the labor market, or when they have lost a job and are looking for another. In such a situation they could not pay for child care yet need it to devote themselves to the job search.

It would be desirable to have the child care set up for single parents' children accessible to other children. That would promote racial integration and high standards of care. The standards set for public child care might serve as mandatory standards for privately run child care as well.

The final four agenda items would improve family life. They would promote a reduction in housework chores, and a sharing between men and women of those that remain. They include provision of more family time for workers, and greater access to facilities for purchasing the services they need.

9. LOWER STANDARD HOURS OF DAILY WORK

There has not been a drop in the standard hours of work per day since the 1930s, when the law was passed requiring employers to pay premium wages for hours over eight hours per day or over forty hours per week. A major benefit of a reduction in standard hours is that parents would have more time to spend with their children. It would also give both women and men more time to participate in housework. Flextime programs—giving workers the right within limits to define their own hours—would also contribute to the easier and more equitable organization of family life. So would a ban on revolving shifts.

Economically, lower hours would mean a trade-off of money wages for free time. The lower hours could be phased in, taking the place of a rise in money wages that would otherwise take place.

Lower hours would make long commutes less advantageous, because the ratio of paid work time to unpaid commuting time would fall. While this would be a serious disadvantage to those committed to living far from their work, it would encourage central-city living, which is more advantageous to single parents and two-earner parent couples.

10. ESTABLISH SUBSIDIES FOR APARTMENT COMPLEXES WITH RESIDENT CHILD-CARE FACILITIES

Builders should be encouraged to plan new apartment housing designed for parents that would include child-care facilities and other family-care services on the premises. As I have suggested, they might be called service-mall apartments. In the existing Swedish version of this type of housing, the child-care center and the restaurant are under the apartment-house management. In the United States, such facilities might be rented out to entrepreneurs, and people who live in other housing might be allowed to patronize them. A "front desk" would take messages and packages and arrange for housecleaning.

In the United States, the traditional way of encouraging innovative and risky projects is by giving them special tax treatment.

11. ESTABLISH A NEW ETHIC OF SHARING FAMILY-CARE WORK BETWEEN MEN AND WOMEN

The relief of employed wives from a disproportionate share of housework is of very great importance to the well-being of women, yet it does not appear explicitly on the agenda of feminist organizations. Popular magazines angled toward working married women generally shun it. As a topic of conversation, it is avoided because it brings into the open the unresolved grievances that lurk in family life. Talking it over with friends washes the family's dirty linen in public. However, as more and more married women emerge into full-time jobs, questions concerning the distribution of housework among family members must come to the foreground. Sharing of housework between spouses should become a publicly-acknowledged norm.

In Sweden the national government under Olaf Palme officially encouraged the increase in participation of husbands and fathers in the

work of the home. Men along with women are given opportuniti.
to take paid child-care leave when they become new parents. In the
United States, discussion of the problem on television and in newspapers
and magazines would contribute to changes in attitudes. Fictional
treatments of the problem probably are helpful as well.

12. HELP FAMILIES WITH AN IMPAIRED CHILD BY
    AN INSURANCE FUND

Giving birth to an impaired child is a hazard that every potential
parent faces. To the ordinary difficulties and expense of parenthood
are added additional ones, often of overwhelming magnitude. The
burden almost always falls on the mother. She may be forced to give
up any hope of leading an ordinary life with ordinary pleasures—
travel, study, work she would like to do—in order to take care of an
impaired child. Since we all share the danger of giving birth to such
a child, we should band together to share the cost so it is not concentrated on the unlucky.

Public facilities for impaired children exist, but their poor quality
makes it difficult for a conscientious parent to use them. Private facilities
are beyond the reach of most families. We need vastly improved and
expanded publicly funded residential facilities to take care of children
who are impaired, for those parents who would like to use them.

AN INTELLIGENT FOCUS FOR OUR EFFORTS

Some women and men argue that reformist efforts on behalf of justice
for women such as the ones I am advocating here are a delusive waste
of time. They characterize affirmative action, child support, and housework-sharing as trivial, or perhaps only of interest to white, middle-
class women. True feminism, they say, requires us to spend a high
proportion of our energy on really important issues such as peace,
racism, and capitalism.

Nothing, it is urged, could exceed peace in importance, and besides,

killed in a nuclear war will be women. Others suggest
give priority to ending political and racial oppression
ound—again reminding us that half the people being
men. These issues certainly are worthy of the energy
 ....son or goodwill. However, none of these campaigns would do
anything toward ending the institutions and customs that oppress
women. If the cause of women in this world is to advance, then the
energies of at least some people must be devoted primarily to advancing
it. And anything that advances American women—even American
middle-class women—contributes by example to the advancement of
women of all classes all over the world.

Marxist radicals contend that unless our whole economic and social
system is rebuilt along better lines, nothing real or worthwhile can be
accomplished. Capitalism—private property and private enterprise—
is, they contend, at the root of most of the evil in the world. The
problems of women, as well as racism, poverty, imperialism, and mil-
itarism all derive, they claim, from capitalist exploitation. Since this is
the case, they argue, nothing short of the elimination of the capitalists
and of their power for doing evil will solve our problems definitively.
So we must put our efforts toward the complete overthrow of capitalism
rather than wasting them on peripheral issues such as fair employment
practices.

Those devoted to such a complete restructuring of society go on
to say that any reform on behalf of women that did not address the
fundamental problem of capitalism, if it did anything at all, would
help only white, middle-class women. It would not relieve the miseries
of black women, working-class women, women in Third World
countries.

The reforms I have advocated here would not get rid of all injustices
in the world. But a revolution that destroyed capitalism would be
unlikely to do that either. The example given us by the socialist countries is hardly an inspiring one. These reforms I have cited would help
a lot of women toward independence, out of poverty, toward greater
respect, and out from under the dual burden of wage work and housework. These reforms, while difficult to achieve, would be more
achievable than a revolution that ended capitalism. A success in favor
of women, even if its beneficiaries were for a time largely limited to
white, middle-class women in the United States, would eventually

help women of other races, other classes, other countries by example.

Other women argue that many of the reforms I advocate, particularly those in the labor market, contemplate that women would compete in men's worlds on men's terms. But, they say, men's terms should be unacceptable to truly civilized people. The womanly virtues of nurturing, tenderness, cooperation, and consideration should become the standards by which both women and men should operate and be judged. Women should not accept, they say, the harsh, competitive, dog-eat-dog environment men have created. Instead of asking that women be accorded a fair chance to compete and succeed in that environment, we should be working to change it. Women, they say, should never adopt the brutal characteristics men have cultivated, even if it means women can never successfully compete with men.

The answer to that objection is that those women who do want to compete with men under the current rules and customs deserve the chance to compete fairly. The world might well be a better place if women and men adopted a less severely competitive style of behavior. However, it is hard to change the rules of a club from outside the clubhouse. For now, competitive behavior is necessary to get into the clubhouse.

Those of us who are beneficiaries of the sex-role revolution have time on our side. The changes we are seeing in the economic sex roles are the inevitable results of a progressive economy and advancing technological change. Sooner or later the policies and institutions appropriate to the new arrangements in the family, in child-rearing, and in the workplace will be realized and built. It is our job to see that they are built with justice, common sense, and humanity, and sooner rather than later.

Appendices

Appendix A

TABLE A–1
Ranking of 335 Occupations by the Percentage of their Workers who are Women, 1984*

Rank	Occupation	Employ-ment (thousands)		Percent Women	Percent of All Workers in this and Higher-Ranked Occupations	
		Men	Women	Women	Women	Men
1.	Dental hygienists	†	25	100.00	.08	.00
2.	Child-care workers	1	133	99.25	.53	.00
3.	Prekindergarten and kindergarten teachers	2	203	99.02	1.21	.01
4.	Secretaries	59	3,070	98.11	11.47	.14
5.	Receptionists	11	432	97.52	12.91	.17
6.	Dental assistants	3	82	96.47	13.19	.17
7.	Typists	26	637	96.08	15.32	.23
8.	Licensed practical nurses	13	283	95.61	16.26	.26
9.	Private household cleaners and servants	8	163	95.32	16.81	.28
10.	Registered nurses	52	923	94.67	19.89	.40
11.	Health record technologists and technicians	2	34	94.44	20.01	.41
12.	Teacher aides	9	150	94.34	20.51	.43

* Based on employment of full-time workers in detailed occupations of more than 25,000 workers.

TABLE A–1 (Continued)

		Employ- ment (thousands)		Percent	Percent of All Workers in this and Higher- Ranked Occupations	
Rank	Occupation	Men	Women	Women	Women	Men
13.	Dieticians	3	49	94.23	20.67	.43
14.	Welfare service aides	2	26	92.86	20.76	.44
15.	Textile sewing machine operators	54	687	92.71	23.05	.56
16.	Telephone operators	14	164	92.13	23.60	.60
17.	Personnel clerks, except payroll and timekeeping	5	57	91.94	23.79	.61
18.	Data-entry keyers	26	280	91.50	24.73	.67
19.	Bank tellers	36	349	90.65	25.89	.75
20.	Stenographers	4	36	90.00	26.02	.76
21.	Bookkeepers, accounting, and auditing clerks	131	1,167	89.91	29.92	1.06
22.	Dressmakers	4	34	89.47	30.03	1.07
23.	Nursing aides, orderlies, and attendants	100	760	88.37	32.57	1.30
24.	Speech therapists	5	37	88.10	32.69	1.31
25.	Material recording, scheduling, dist. clerks, N.E.C.	3	22	88.00	32.77	1.32
26.	Eligibility clerks, social welfare	8	51	86.44	32.94	1.34
27.	Special-education teachers	21	132	86.27	33.38	1.38
28.	Billing clerks	18	110	85.94	33.75	1.43
29.	Hairdressers and cosmetologists	32	194	85.84	34.40	1.50
30.	Librarians	22	133	85.81	34.84	1.55
31.	Library clerks	7	41	85.42	34.98	1.57
32.	Child-care workers	23	129	84.87	35.41	1.62
32.	Interviewers	20	110	84.62	35.78	1.67
34.	Billing, posting, and calculating machine operators	4	22	84.62	35.85	1.67
35.	Elementary-school teachers	186	981	84.06	39.13	2.10
36.	Health aides, except nursing	42	209	83.27	39.83	2.20
37.	Physical therapists	8	39	82.98	39.96	2.22
38.	Information clerks, N.E.C.	19	91	82.73	40.26	2.26
39.	Payroll and timekeeping clerks	27	129	82.69	40.69	2.32
40.	Folding machine operators	5	23	82.14	40.77	2.33
41.	Cashiers	160	715	81.71	43.16	2.70
42.	Waiters and waitresses	96	429	81.71	44.59	2.92
43.	File clerks	41	178	81.28	45.19	3.02
44.	Public-transportation attendants	6	25	80.65	45.27	3.03
45.	Health specialties teachers	7	27	79.41	45.36	3.05
46.	General office clerks	101	374	78.74	46.61	3.28
47.	Records clerks	25	92	78.63	46.92	3.34

TABLE A–1 (Continued)

Rank	Occupation	Employ-ment (thousands)		Percent Women	Percent of All Workers in this and Higher-Ranked Occupations	
		Men	Women		Women	Men
48.	Shoe machine operators	12	42	77.78	47.06	3.36
49.	Administrative support occupations, N.E.C.	107	363	77.23	48.27	3.61
50.	Sales workers, apparel	37	125	77.16	48.69	3.70
51.	Statistical clerks	19	64	77.11	48.91	3.74
52.	Cost and rate clerks	15	50	76.92	49.07	3.77
53.	Clinical laboratory technologists and technicians	53	173	76.55	49.65	3.90
54.	Winding and twisting machine operators	21	67	76.14	49.87	3.94
55.	Maids and housemen	88	279	76.02	50.81	4.15
56.	Office machine operators, N.E.C.	8	25	75.76	50.89	4.16
57.	Order clerks	40	121	75.16	51.30	4.26
58.	Legal assistants	29	80	73.39	51.56	4.32
59.	Investigators and adjusters, except insurance	75	206	73.31	52.25	4.50
60.	Electrical and electronic equipment assemblers	93	247	72.65	53.08	4.71
61.	Kitchen workers, food preparation	20	52	72.22	53.25	4.76
62.	Solderers and braziers	11	28	71.79	53.34	4.78
63.	Hotel clerks	17	42	71.19	53.48	4.82
64.	Food counter, fountain, and related occupations	23	56	70.89	53.67	4.87
65.	Management-related occupations, N.E.C.	58	136	70.10	54.13	5.01
66.	Recreation workers	14	32	69.57	54.23	5.04
67.	Sales workers, other commodities	176	388	68.79	55.53	5.44
68.	Bill and account collectors	24	52	68.42	55.70	5.50
69.	Hand packers and packagers	70	151	68.33	56.21	5.66
70.	Sales counter clerks	22	46	67.65	56.36	5.71
71.	Health technologists and technicians, N.E.C.	53	108	67.08	56.72	5.83
72.	Insurance adjusters, examiners, and investigators	67	130	65.99	57.16	5.99
73.	Laundering and dry-cleaning machine operators	39	74	65.49	57.41	6.08
74.	Supervisors, general office	125	232	64.99	58.18	6.36
75.	Computer operators	231	419	64.46	59.58	6.89
76.	Knitting, looping, taping, weaving machine ops.	14	25	64.10	59.67	6.93

TABLE A-1 (Continued)

Rank	Occupation	Employ-ment (thousands)		Percent Women	Percent of All Workers in this and Higher-Ranked Occupations	
		Men	Women	Women	Women	Men
77.	Supervisors, financial records processing	27	48	64.00	59.83	6.99
78.	Radiologic technicians	33	58	63.74	60.02	7.06
79.	Inhalation therapists	18	31	63.27	60.12	7.11
80.	Managers, medicine and health	33	55	62.50	60.31	7.18
81.	Graders and sorters, except agricultural	33	53	61.63	60.48	7.26
82.	Social workers	144	230	61.50	61.25	7.59
83.	Supervisors, food preparation and service occ.	63	99	61.11	61.58	7.73
84.	Religious workers, N.E.C.	16	25	60.98	61.67	7.77
85.	Typesetters and compositors	20	31	60.78	61.77	7.82
86.	Pressing machine operators	40	62	60.78	61.98	7.91
87.	Therapists, N.E.C.	13	20	60.61	62.04	7.94
88.	Transportation ticket and reservation agents	32	49	60.49	62.21	8.01
89.	Supervisors, personal service	10	15	60.00	62.26	8.04
90.	Cementing and gluing machine operators	16	22	57.89	62.33	8.07
91.	Personal service occupations, N.E.C.	22	30	57.69	62.43	8.12
92.	Personnel, training, and labor-relations specialists	132	164	55.41	62.98	8.43
93.	Packaging and filling machine operators	166	203	55.01	63.66	8.81
94.	Optical goods workers	22	25	53.19	63.74	8.86
95.	Expediters	48	53	52.48	63.92	8.97
96.	Counselors, educational and vocational	77	83	51.87	64.20	9.15
97.	Photographic process machine operators	36	38	51.35	64.32	9.23
98.	Production inspectors, checkers, and examiners	332	345	50.96	65.48	9.99
99.	Mail clerks, except postal service	67	68	50.37	65.71	10.15
100.	Cooks, except short-order	395	397	50.13	67.03	11.06
101.	Sales workers, shoes	22	22	50.00	67.11	11.11
102.	Food batchmakers	13	13	50.00	67.15	11.14
103.	Animal caretakers, except farm	20	20	50.00	67.22	11.18
104.	Production coordinators	90	89	49.72	67.51	11.39
105.	Teachers, N.E.C.	80	79	49.69	67.78	11.57
106.	Miscellaneous textile machine operators	35	34	49.28	67.89	11.65

TABLE A–1 (Continued)

Rank	Occupation	Employ-ment (thousands)		Percent Women	Percent of All Workers in this and Higher-Ranked Occupations	
		Men	Women		Women	Men
107.	Street and door-to-door vendors	33	32	49.23	68.00	11.73
108.	Real-estate sales	135	130	49.06	68.43	12.04
109.	Secondary-school teachers	544	523	49.02	70.18	13.29
110.	Bookbinders	17	16	48.48	70.23	13.33
111.	Miscellaneous printing machine operators	16	15	48.39	70.28	13.37
112.	Psychologists	43	40	48.19	70.42	13.47
113.	Underwriters and other financial officers	279	258	48.04	71.28	14.11
114.	Bartenders	97	89	47.85	71.58	14.33
115.	Public-relations specialists	66	58	46.77	71.77	14.48
116.	Personnel and labor-relations managers	56	49	46.67	71.94	14.61
117.	Misc. food-preparation occupations	135	118	46.64	72.33	14.92
118.	Weighers, measurers, and checkers	30	26	46.43	72.42	14.99
119.	Biological technicians	25	21	45.65	72.49	15.05
120.	Managers, properties and real estate	102	85	45.45	72.77	15.28
121.	Editors and reporters	96	80	45.45	73.04	15.50
122.	Sales workers, furniture and home furnishings	53	44	45.36	73.19	15.62
123.	Dispatchers	86	69	44.52	73.42	15.82
124.	Short-order cooks	20	16	44.44	73.47	15.87
125.	Economists	58	46	44.23	73.62	16.00
126.	Sales occupations, other business services	187	146	43.84	74.11	16.43
127.	Attendants, amusement, and recreation facilities	35	27	43.55	74.20	16.51
128.	Assemblers	555	422	43.19	75.61	17.79
129.	Medical scientists	16	12	42.86	75.65	17.83
130.	Advertising and related sales	59	44	42.72	75.80	17.96
131.	Postmasters and mail superintendents	15	11	42.31	75.84	18.00
132.	Buyers, wholesale and retail trade, ex. farm prod.	89	65	42.21	76.05	18.20
133.	Miscellaneous hand working occupations	18	13	41.94	76.10	18.24
134.	Accountants and auditors	620	443	41.67	77.58	19.67
135.	Molding and casting machine operators	53	36	40.45	77.70	19.79

TABLE A–1 (Continued)

Rank	Occupation	Employment (thousands)		Percent Women	Percent of All Workers in this and Higher-Ranked Occupations	
		Men	Women		Women	Men
136.	Technical writers	27	18	40.00	77.76	19.85
137.	Dental laboratory and medical appliance technicians	21	14	40.00	77.81	19.90
138.	Painters, sculptors, craft artists, art printmakers	51	33	39.29	77.92	20.02
139.	Designers	160	102	38.93	78.26	20.39
140.	Officials and administrators, public administration	248	158	38.92	78.78	20.96
141.	Statisticians	16	10	38.46	78.82	20.99
142.	Administrators, education and related fields	237	147	38.28	79.31	21.54
143.	Supervisors, cleaning and building service workers	70	42	37.50	79.45	21.70
144.	Purchasing agents and buyers, N.E.C.	137	80	36.87	79.72	22.01
145.	Stock and inventory clerks	291	165	36.18	80.27	22.68
146.	Financial managers	218	123	36.07	80.68	23.18
147.	English teachers	16	9	36.00	80.71	23.22
148.	Waiters/waitresses assistants	68	38	35.85	80.84	23.38
149.	Tailors	18	10	35.71	80.87	23.42
150.	Art, drama, and music teachers	19	10	34.48	80.90	23.46
151.	Computer programmers	306	161	34.48	81.44	24.17
152.	Physicians assistants	28	14	33.33	81.49	24.23
153.	Science technicians, N.E.C.	35	17	32.69	81.55	24.31
154.	Postal clerks, except mail carriers	164	79	32.51	81.81	24.69
155.	Technicians, N.E.C.	125	60	32.43	82.01	24.98
156.	Barbers	21	10	32.26	82.04	25.02
157.	Business and promotion agents	26	12	31.58	82.08	25.08
158.	Production testers	39	18	31.58	82.14	25.17
159.	Bakers	44	20	31.25	82.21	25.27
160.	Engineering technicians, N.E.C.	124	56	31.11	82.40	25.56
161.	Hand printing, coating, and decorating occupations	20	9	31.03	82.43	25.61
162.	Insurance sales	251	110	30.47	82.80	26.18
163.	Miscellaneous machine operators, N.E.C.	630	274	30.31	83.71	27.63
164.	Management analysts	37	16	30.19	83.77	27.72
165.	Supervisors and proprietors	1,341	570	29.83	85.67	30.80
166.	Computer systems analysts and scientists	201	85	29.72	85.95	31.26
167.	Actors and directors	36	15	29.41	86.00	31.35

TABLE A–1 (Continued)

Rank	Occupation	Employment (thousands)		Percent Women	Percent of All Workers in this and Higher-Ranked Occupations	
		Men	Women		Women	Men
168.	Machine operators, not specified	212	88	29.33	86.30	31.83
169.	Biological and life scientists	41	17	29.31	86.36	31.93
170.	Managers and administrators, N.E.C.	2,865	1,180	29.17	90.30	38.52
171.	Operations and systems researchers and analysts	99	39	28.26	90.43	38.74
172.	Machine feeders and offbearers	56	22	28.21	90.50	38.87
173.	Slicing and cutting machine operators	118	46	28.05	90.66	39.14
174.	Securities and financial services sales	126	49	28.00	90.82	39.43
175.	Punching and stamping press machine operators	87	33	27.50	90.93	39.63
176.	Bus drivers	149	56	27.32	91.12	39.98
177.	College and university teachers, subject not spec.	72	26	26.53	91.21	40.14
178.	Chemical technicians	51	18	26.09	91.27	40.26
179.	Crushing and grinding machine operators	40	14	25.93	91.31	40.35
180.	Pharmacists	79	27	25.47	91.40	40.53
181.	Purchasing managers	63	21	25.00	91.47	40.68
182.	Supervisors, computer equipment operators	27	9	25.00	91.50	40.74
183.	Printing machine operators	299	96	24.30	91.82	41.43
184.	Traffic, shipping, and receiving clerks	304	92	23.23	92.13	42.13
185.	Lawyers	237	71	23.05	92.37	42.67
186.	Managers, marketing, advertising, and pub. relations	259	77	22.92	92.63	43.27
187.	Chemists, except biochemists	73	21	22.34	92.70	43.44
188.	Supervisors, distribution, sched., adjusting clerks	115	32	21.77	92.80	43.70
189.	Inspectors, testers, and graders	87	24	21.62	92.88	43.90
190.	Stock handlers and baggers	273	74	21.33	93.13	44.53
191.	Messengers	58	15	20.55	93.18	44.66
192.	Janitors and cleaners	1,002	258	20.48	94.04	46.97
193.	Sales workers, hardware and building supplies	109	28	20.44	94.14	47.22
194.	Photographers	51	13	20.31	94.18	47.33
195.	Announcers	20	5	20.00	94.20	47.38
196.	Sales workers, radio, television, hi-fi, appliances	85	21	19.81	94.27	47.58

TABLE A–1 (Continued)

Rank	Occupation	Employment (thousands)		Percent Women	Percent of All Workers in this and Higher-Ranked Occupations	
		Men	Women		Women	Men
197.	Inspectors and compliance officers ex. construction	124	30	19.48	94.37	47.86
198.	Misc. metal-, plastic-, stone-, glassworking mach. ops.	25	6	19.35	94.39	47.92
199.	Physicians	178	42	19.09	94.53	48.33
200.	Correctional institution officers	132	31	19.02	94.63	48.63
201.	Administrators, protective services	35	8	18.60	94.66	48.71
202.	Drilling and boring machine operators	23	5	17.86	94.68	48.76
203.	Musicians and composers	28	6	17.65	94.70	48.83
204.	Laborers, except construction	766	163	17.55	95.24	50.59
205.	Upholsterers	33	7	17.50	95.26	50.67
206.	Vehicle washers and equipment cleaners	121	25	17.12	95.35	50.95
207.	Misc. material moving equipment operators	127	26	16.99	95.43	51.24
208.	Butchers and meat cutters	179	36	16.74	95.55	51.65
209.	Mathematical science teachers	26	5	16.13	95.57	51.71
210.	Judges	21	4	16.00	95.58	51.76
211.	Painting and paint spraying machine operators	142	27	15.98	95.67	52.08
212.	Architects	48	9	15.79	95.70	52.19
213.	Sales reps, commodities, ex. retail (inc. sales engs.)	1,020	191	15.77	96.34	54.54
214.	Metal plating machine operators	27	5	15.63	96.36	54.60
215.	Grinding, abrading, buffing, polishing machine ops.	114	21	15.56	96.43	54.86
216.	Supervisors, motor vehicle operators	22	4	15.38	96.44	54.91
217.	Mail carriers, postal service	194	35	15.28	96.56	55.36
218.	Drafting occupations	245	41	14.34	96.70	55.92
219.	Athletes	30	5	14.29	96.71	55.99
220.	Lathe and turning machine operators	72	12	14.29	96.75	56.16
221.	Supervisors, production occupations	1,108	182	14.11	97.36	58.71
222.	Meter readers	39	6	13.33	97.38	58.80
223.	Guards and police, except public service	403	61	13.15	97.59	59.72
224.	Electrical and electronic technicians	219	33	13.10	97.70	60.23

TABLE A–1 (Continued)

Rank	Occupation	Employment (thousands)		Percent Women	Percent of All Workers in this and Higher-Ranked Occupations	
		Men	Women	Women	Women	Men
225.	Surveying and mapping technicians	49	7	12.50	97.72	60.34
226.	Production helpers	57	8	12.31	97.75	60.47
227.	Air traffic controllers	23	3	11.54	97.76	60.52
228.	Chemical engineers	49	6	10.91	97.78	60.64
229.	Sheriffs, bailiffs, and other law-enforcement officers	70	8	10.26	97.80	60.80
230.	Photoengravers and lithographers	35	4	10.26	97.82	60.88
231.	Data processing equipment repairers	90	10	10.00	97.85	61.09
232.	Miscellaneous plant and system operators	27	3	10.00	97.86	61.15
233.	Geologists and geodesists	37	4	9.76	97.87	61.23
234.	Farm workers	610	65	9.63	98.09	62.64
235.	Sales workers, parts	122	12	8.96	98.13	62.92
236.	Supervisors, guards	31	3	8.82	98.14	62.99
237.	Supervisors, mechanics, and repairers	223	21	8.61	98.21	63.50
238.	Garage and service-station-related occupations	152	14	8.43	98.26	63.85
239.	Mining machine operators	33	3	8.33	98.27	63.93
240.	Farm managers	44	4	8.33	98.28	64.03
241.	Telephone installers and repairers	218	19	8.02	98.35	64.53
242.	Mechanical controls and valve repairers	24	2	7.69	98.35	64.58
243.	Industrial engineers	181	15	7.65	98.40	65.00
244.	Sales workers, motor vehicles and boats	195	16	7.58	98.46	65.45
245.	Police and detectives, public service	382	31	7.51	98.56	66.33
246.	Civil engineers	192	15	7.25	98.61	66.77
247.	Engineering teachers	26	2	7.14	98.62	66.83
248.	Electrical and electronic engineers	436	33	7.04	98.73	67.83
249.	Taxicab drivers and chauffeurs	82	6	6.82	98.75	68.02
250.	Physicists and astronomers	28	2	6.67	98.75	68.08
251.	Supervisors, farm workers	42	3	6.67	98.76	68.18
252.	Truck drivers, light	342	24	6.56	98.84	68.97
253.	Sawing machine operators	72	5	6.49	98.86	69.13
254.	Freight, stock, material movers, hand, N.E.C.	389	26	6.27	98.95	70.03

TABLE A–1 (Continued)

Rank	Occupation	Employ-ment (thousands)		Percent Women	Percent of All Workers in this and Higher-Ranked Occupations	
		Men	Women		Women	Men
255.	Industrial truck and tractor equipment operators	376	22	5.53	99.02	70.89
256.	Mixing and blending machine operators	89	5	5.32	99.04	71.10
257.	Groundskeepers and gardeners, except farm	326	18	5.23	99.10	71.85
258.	Telephone line installers and repairers	55	3	5.17	99.11	71.97
259.	Welders and cutters	510	27	5.03	99.20	73.15
260.	Drivers—sales workers	193	10	4.93	99.23	73.59
261.	Misc. electrical and electronic equip. repairers	60	3	4.76	99.24	73.73
262.	Separating, filtering, clarifying machine ops.	61	3	4.69	99.25	73.87
263.	Mechanical engineers	237	11	4.44	99.29	74.41
264.	Supervisors, police and detectives	65	3	4.41	99.30	74.56
265.	Machinists	478	22	4.40	99.37	75.66
266.	Engineers, N.E.C.	180	8	4.26	99.40	76.08
267.	Clergy	227	10	4.22	99.43	76.60
268.	Sheet metal workers	117	5	4.10	99.45	76.87
269.	Elect. repairers, communications, industrial equip.	121	5	3.97	99.47	77.14
270.	Painters, construction and maintenance	226	9	3.83	99.50	77.66
271.	Specified mechanics and repairers, N.E.C.	336	13	3.72	99.54	78.44
272.	Machinery maintenance occupations	26	1	3.70	99.54	78.50
273.	Construction inspectors	54	2	3.57	99.55	78.62
274.	Airplane pilots and navigators	54	2	3.57	99.56	78.75
275.	Glaziers	27	1	3.57	99.56	78.81
276.	Lathe and turning machine setup operators	27	1	3.57	99.56	78.87
277.	Pest control	28	1	3.45	99.57	78.93
278.	Cabinetmakers and bench carpenters	28	1	3.45	99.57	79.00
279.	Forestry and conservation scientists	29	1	3.33	99.57	79.06
280.	Not specified mechanics and repairers	121	4	3.20	99.59	79.34
281.	Petroleum engineers	31	1	3.13	99.59	79.41

TABLE A–1 (Continued)

Rank	Occupation	Employ-ment (thousands)		Percent Women	Percent of All Workers in this and Higher-Ranked Occupations	
		Men	Women	Women	Women	Men
282.	Extruding and forming machine operators	31	1	3.13	99.59	79.49
283.	Crane and tower operators	94	3	3.09	99.60	79.70
284.	Supervisors, firefighting and fire prevention	33	1	2.94	99.61	79.78
285.	Supervisors, related agricultural occupations	66	2	2.94	99.61	79.93
286.	Industrial machinery repairers	506	15	2.88	99.66	81.09
287.	Household appliance and power tool repairers	35	1	2.78	99.67	81.17
288.	Furnace, kiln, and oven operators, except food	106	3	2.75	99.68	81.42
289.	Millwrights	86	2	2.27	99.68	81.62
290.	Small-engine repairers	44	1	2.22	99.69	81.72
291.	Construction laborers	565	12	2.08	99.73	83.02
292.	Stationary engineers	97	2	2.02	99.73	83.24
293.	Carpet installers	49	1	2.00	99.74	83.35
294.	Grader, dozer, and scraper operators	99	2	1.98	99.74	83.58
295.	Truck drivers, heavy	1,536	31	1.98	99.85	87.11
296.	Supervisors, extractive occupations	50	1	1.96	99.85	87.23
297.	Timber cutting and logging occupations	50	1	1.96	99.85	87.34
298.	Office machine repairers	55	1	1.79	99.86	87.47
299.	Construction trades, N.E.C.	112	2	1.75	99.86	87.73
300.	Automobile body and related repairers	128	2	1.54	99.87	88.02
301.	Locomotive operating occupations	64	1	1.54	99.87	88.17
302.	Tool- and diemakers	130	2	1.52	99.88	88.47
303.	Drywall installers	74	1	1.33	99.88	88.64
304.	Carpenters	826	11	1.31	99.92	90.54
305.	Aircraft engine mechanics	84	1	1.18	99.92	90.73
306.	Plumbers, pipefitters, and steamfitters	363	4	1.09	99.94	91.56
307.	Electricians	559	6	1.06	99.96	92.85
308.	Automobile mechanics	636	6	.93	99.98	94.31
309.	Operating engineers	127	1	.78	99.98	94.60
310.	Helpers, construction trades	141	1	.70	99.98	94.93
311.	Supervisors, N.E.C.	318	2	.62	99.99	95.66
312.	Bus, truck, and stationary engine mechanics	320	2	.62	100.00	96.40

TABLE A–1 (Continued)

Rank	Occupation	Employ-ment (thousands) Men	Women	Percent Women	Percent of All Workers in this and Higher-Ranked Occupations Women	Men
313.	Heating, air conditioning, and refrigeration mechanics	181	1	.55	100.00	96.81
314.	Aerospace engineers	74	†	‡	100.00	96.98
315.	Firefighting occupations	160	†	‡	100.00	97.35
316.	Heavy-equipment mechanics	152	†	‡	100.00	97.70
317.	Farm-equipment mechanics	37	†	‡	100.00	97.79
318.	Supvsrs., electricians, and power trans. installers	36	†	‡	100.00	97.87
319.	Brickmasons and stonemasons	98	†	‡	100.00	98.09
320.	Electrical power installers and repairers	103	†	‡	100.00	98.33
321.	Plasterers	26	†	‡	100.00	98.39
322.	Concrete and terrazzo finishers	68	†	‡	100.00	98.55
323.	Insulation workers	49	†	‡	100.00	98.66
324.	Roofers	106	†	‡	100.00	98.90
325.	Sheet-metal duct installers	29	†	‡	100.00	98.97
326.	Structural metal workers	50	†	‡	100.00	99.08
327.	Drillers, oil wells	53	†	‡	100.00	99.21
328.	Mining occupations, N.E.C.	37	†	‡	100.00	99.29
329.	Boilermakers	33	†	‡	100.00	99.37
330.	Water and sewage treatment plant operators	38	†	‡	100.00	99.45
331.	Power plant operators	51	†	‡	100.00	99.57
332.	Railroad conductors and yardmasters	36	†	‡	100.00	99.65
333.	Railroad brake, signal, and switch operators	48	†	‡	100.00	99.77
334.	Excavating and loading machine operators	63	†	‡	100.00	99.91
335.	Garbage collectors	39	†	‡	100.00	100.00

† Fewer than 500.
‡ Less than .005.
SOURCE: U.S. Bureau of Labor Statistics, unpublished tabulations from the Current Population Survey.

Appendix B

SUPPLY AND DEMAND FOR LABOR IN A SEX-SEGREGATED LABOR
MARKET: A SIMPLIFIED NUMERICAL EXAMPLE

To understand how the exclusion of women from the "men's
turf" can lower the wages set for the jobs women hold, we will construct and analyze an example—an economy so simple that it has just
two occupations. The supply and demand for labor in the two occupations will determine the wages in each. First we will look at the
wage levels to be expected if employers do not make any distinction
among workers by sex. Then we can see what difference occupational
segregation by sex would make to wages in each occupation and to
the wages of men and women.

Instead of calling our two occupations Blues and Pinks, we shall
call them "machine operators" and "service workers." We are going
to assume that at any time there is a prevailing wage in each occupation,
and employers find out what that is by looking at the want ads in the
newspapers.

In the real economy, as well as in our example, there is no fixed
number of jobs in each occupation. The amount of each kind of labor
employers will want to hire will depend on the wage they have to pay
for workers in that occupation. The higher the prevailing wage in an
occupation, the fewer workers employers will want to hire to do that
kind of work. Expensive labor means expensive products, which in
turn means fewer sales for that type of product, less production, and
less labor hired to produce it. If labor in an occupation is relatively
cheap, its use can be expanded to relatively lower-priority tasks. If it
is expensive, employers will want to restrict its use to the higher-
priority tasks and so will hire fewer people in that line.

For illustrative purposes, we have made up as examples "demand
schedules" for our two occupations, which are shown in table B–1.
For the machine operators, a prevailing wage of $300 per week is
assumed to cause employers to want to hire eight thousand of them.
If the wage were $200 per week for machine operators, employers

would want to hire an additional six thousand of them, or fourteen thousand in all.*

For service workers, the demand schedule we are assuming calls for a lower level of hiring at each wage than the demand schedule we have invented for carpenters. For example, at a wage of $200 for service workers, employers are assumed to want to hire four thousand of them, while, as we have said, at a wage of $200 for machine operators, employers would want to hire fourteen thousand machine operators. In reality, as in our example, the demand schedules for any two occupations will differ. The demand for their labor depends on the nature of the products the two occupations contribute to producing, the desires of the public to spread its income among those products, and the efficiency with which the two kinds of labor can be used in making the various products to which they contribute. The more kinds of products a certain type of labor can contribute to, the more workers of that type will be demanded by employers at a given wage.

For our example, we need to make some assumptions about the supply of labor. We need to specify how many people will want to work at each wage and also what they will be competent to do. As to competence, we will start out with the seemingly unrealistic assumption that all of the workers can do either job equally well. After seeing the implications of that assumption, we can throw it overboard and see what difference that makes.

With respect to numbers willing to work, table B–1 gives hypothetical supply schedules for male and for female labor. At a wage of $300 a week, twelve thousand men and ten thousand women are assumed to be available to take jobs, or twenty-two thousand persons in all. At a wage of $200 a week, eighteen thousand persons, consisting of ten thousand men and eight thousand women, would be available. The supply of labor to an occupation depends on the skills and education required by employers and whether employers demand any particular sex identity for workers in that occupation.

We are going to make the usual assumptions that economists make

* In reality, demand schedules for particular occupations vary from economy to economy and from time to time. Moreover, in a real situation, it is very difficult for economists to determine what a demand schedule looks like at any particular time, and very subtle methods are used to make very imperfect estimates of them. None of this has prevented economists from using the concept as the basis of much reasoning about economic processes, and I am following this tradition here.

TABLE B–1
Illustrative Supply and Demand Schedules for a Two-Occupation Economy

Illustrative Demand Schedules

Machine Operators		Service Workers		Total Demand (under assumption of equal wages)	
Weekly Wage	Number of Workers Demanded (thousands)	Weekly Wage	Number of Workers Demanded (thousands)	Weekly Wage in Both Occupations	Number of Workers Demanded (thousands)
$300	8	$300	0	$300	8
250	11	250	1	250	12
200	14	200	4	200	18
150	17	150	7	150	24
100	20	100	10	100	30

Illustrative Supply Schedules

Males		Females		Total Supply	
Weekly Wage	Number of Workers Supplied (thousands)	Weekly Wage	Number of Workers Supplied (thousands)	Weekly Wage in Both Occupations	Number of Workers Supplied to Both Occupations (thousands)
$300	12	$300	10	$300	22
250	11	250	9	250	20
200	10	200	8	200	18
150	9	150	7	150	16
100	8	100	6	100	14

about occupational wages—that they will go down if the supply of labor to the occupation exceeds the demand, and up in the opposite case. Thus wages are assumed to move until the supply of labor equals the demand in each occupation.*

We are now ready to look at occupational differences in wages in the very simple situation we have posited. We will consider two simple

* We are obviously abstracting from the unemployment problem. We are also abstracting from the reality that, for morale purposes, it is difficult for employers to adjust wages downward. However, in times of inflation, real wages can fall without money wages falling.

cases. In each case we will assume different conditions, and therefore each will yield different results in terms of wage rates and in terms of how workers are distributed between the two occupations.

THE CASE OF NO SEX DISCRIMINATION

Let us assume that employers act on a sex-neutral basis and welcome men and women into both occupations. Under this assumption, market forces would be expected to eliminate any difference in wages between machine operators and service workers. If any difference in wages did show up, workers in the lower-paid occupation would try to shift to the higher-paid occupation. We are assuming there would be no bar to such movement, due to lack of training or skill, or because of any distaste for the occupation or due to custom. Nor are employers assumed at this point to throw up any bars to the flow of workers by excluding anyone for reason of sex. The attempt of workers to enter the higher-paying occupation would increase the supply of workers to it and decrease the supply of workers to the lower-paying occupation. This would go on until the wages in the two occupations were once again equal.

Since wages in the two occupations can, under our assumptions, be assumed to be the same except for temporary lapses, it makes sense to compile a "Total Demand" schedule, which is the total amount of labor employers would be willing to hire at various wage levels with identical wages in the two occupations. We can also compile a "Total Supply" schedule of *people* available to employers at each wage. These schedules are shown in the last two columns of table B–1.

In this case, the considerations of supply and demand would suggest that the wage in both occupations and for both sexes would be $200 a week. This is the wage at which the number of workers sought by employers would be equal to the number of workers who wanted jobs in the labor market as a whole. This solution is shown diagrammatically in the left-hand panel of figure B–1. There would be fourteen thousand people in machine operator jobs and four thousand in service worker jobs, and the wage would be the same in both jobs. Both men's and women's wages would be $200. In such a labor market, we would expect to see men and women in both occupations.

Figure B-1
Supply and Demand in Unsegregated and Segregated Labor Markets

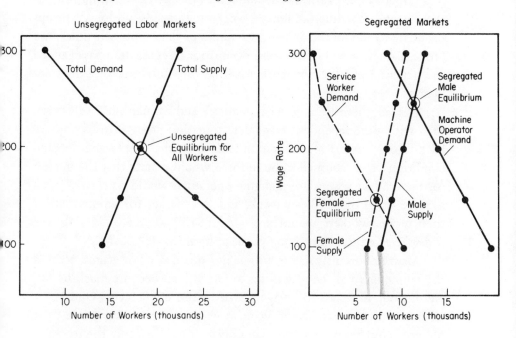

THE CASE OF SEX SEGREGATION OF OCCUPATIONS

Let us now change the assumptions about how employers operate, and assume that employers maintain the practice of restricting women to service worker jobs. We will continue to assume that men and women do not differ in skills, or in preferences for one job over another. Employers might pursue such a policy, which would have to be labeled "discriminatory" by any reasonable definition of that term, for reasons given in chapter 5. Competitive pressures could allow employers to persist in such behavior, for reasons given in chapter 6.

Whatever the psychological or sociological or economic reasons for employers to insist on the sex segregation of occupations, the supply-and-demand situation that resulted from this employer behavior would be very different from that in the labor market where occupational segregation was absent and employers paid no attention to sex, as under our previous assumptions. The demand schedule for machine operators would become pure and simple the demand schedule for male workers, and similarly the demand schedule for service workers would become the demand schedule for female workers. It would no longer be appropriate to add up the demand schedules or the supply schedules into "total market" schedules, because occupational segregation has changed the structure of the labor market so that the "total market" does not operate.

Instead, there are now separate men's and women's labor markets, each with an independent wage determination process. In fact, going back to our numerical example in table B–1, the supply-and-demand conditions now assumed to be in force would dictate that the market for men, all of whom are machine operators, would be cleared at an average wage of $250 per week, and the market for women, all of them service workers, would be cleared at $150 per week. This outcome is displayed in the right-hand panel of figure B–1.

Most importantly, there will be no equalization of wages, because the employers will be unwilling to let women become machine operators and compete the wage down to the $200 level. Under our assumptions, no man would want to be a service worker (even if he did not mind being in a "woman's occupation") because the pay is so bad.

The service occupation under segregation is relatively crowded. see p. 12? Instead of having four thousand workers, it has to accommodate seven thousand, at a much lower wage.

DIFFERENT TALENTS, DIFFERENT TASTES

Suppose we now drop the assumptions that all workers are indifferent to which occupation they pursue and that all are equally competent in both. In fact, let us assume that the men are more inclined to being machine operators and the women to service work. If no women could be or would want to be a machine operator, then the segregation could not be attributed to discrimination. However, if some of the women would be willing and able to switch fields, then the gap in pay between the two occupations would narrow. In the numerical example presented here, the wage gap between the two occupations would completely disappear if half of the women left service work and got jobs as machine operators.*

* In the real labor market the proportion of women who would have to switch to previously male-type jobs for wage equality to occur between men and women with equal human capital might be closer to Estelle James's estimate of one third. Where the men's segment of the labor market consists of several occupations, women would not have to colonize all of them to the same degree. See Estelle James, "The Income and Employment Effects of Women's Liberation," in Cynthia Lloyd, ed., *Sex, Discrimination, and the Division of Labor* (New York: Columbia University Press, 1975), pp. 379–400.

Notes

Chapter 1

1. Heidi I. Hartmann, "The Unhappy Marriage of Marxism and Feminism: Towards a More Progressive Union" in *Women and Revolution,* Lydia Sargent, ed. (Boston, Mass.: South End Press, 1979), pp. 1–41.

2. Alice-Kessler-Harris, *Out to Work: A History of Wage-Earning Women* (New York: Oxford University Press, 1982).

3. On relations between husbands and wives, see Carl N. Degler, *At Odds: Women and the Family in America from the Revolution to the Present* (New York: Oxford University Press, 1980).

4. The originator of this argument, cited by many economists, is Gary S. Becker. However, Becker himself appears to be undecided as to the importance of sex discrimination. See *The Economics of Discrimination* (Chicago, Ill.: University of Chicago Press, 1957).

5. See Solomon W. Polachek, "Occupational Self-Selection: A Human Capital Approach to Sex Differences in Occupational Structure," *Review of Economics and Statistics,* vol. 58, no. 1 (February 1981):60–69. For a refutation, see Paula England, "The Failure of Human Capital Theory to Explain Occupational Sex Segregation," *Journal of Human Resources,* vol. 17, no. 3 (Summer 1982):358–70.

6. Dorothy Atkinson, Alexander Dallin, and Gail Warshofsky Lapidus, eds., *Women in Russia* (Stanford, Calif.: Stanford University Press, 1977).

7. See chapter on Japan by Tadashi Hanami in Alice H. Cook, Val R. Lorwin, and Arlene Kaplan Daniels, *Women and Trade Unions in Eleven Industrialized Countries* (Philadelphia, Penn.: Temple University Press, 1984), pp. 215–38.

Chapter 2

1. Thorstein Veblen, *The Theory of the Leisure Class* (New York: Macmillan, 1912).

2. Alice Kessler-Harris, *Out to Work: A History of Wage-Earning Women in the United States* (New York: Oxford University Press, 1982).

3. Linda J. Waite, David E. Kanouse, and Thomas J. Balschke, *Changes in the Lifestyles of New Parents* (Santa Monica, Calif.: Rand, 1984).

4. Kessler-Harris, *Out to Work: A History of Wage-Earning Women in the United States,* p. viii.

5. Deborah Fallows, who believes that mothers should stay home with their children, understands this dodge, and attempts to debunk the "need" rationale for mothers to take employment. *A Mother's Work* (Boston, Mass.: Houghton Mifflin Company, 1985).

6. See Myra Marx Ferree, "Sacrifice, Satisfaction and Social Change: Employment in the Family" in Karen Brodkin Sacks and Dorothy Remy, eds., *My Troubles Are Going to Have Trouble with Me* (New Brunswick, N.J.: Rutgers University Press, 1974), pp. 61–79.

7. Maxine L. Margolis, *Mothers and Such: Views of American Women and Why They Changed* (Berkeley, Calif.: University of California Press, 1984), chap. 4.

8. John P. Robinson, "Changes in the Time Use: An Historical Overview," in F. Thomas Juster and Frank P. Stafford, eds., *Time, Goods, and Well-Being* (Ann Arbor, Mich.: Institute for Social Research, University of Michigan, 1985), pp. 289–312. Joann Vanek, piecing together earlier time use studies, concluded that in 1965 housewives were spending the same time in housework as their predecessors over the previous fifty years. See Joann Vanek, "Time Spent in Housework," *Scientific American,* vol. 231 (May 1974):116–20.

9. Clair (Vickery) Brown, "Home Production for Use in a Market Economy" in Barrie Thorne and Marilyn Yalom, eds., *Rethinking the Family: Some Feminist Questions* (New York: Longman, 1982), pp. 151–67.

10. U.S. Bureau of Labor Statistics, *Consumer Expenditure Survey: Interview Survey, 1980–81* (Washington, D.C.: Department of Labor, April 1985), bulletin 2225.

11. Valerie K. Oppenheimer, *The Female Labor Force in the United States: Demographic and Economic Factors Governing its Growth and Changing Composition,* (Westport, Conn.: Greenwood Press, 1979).

12. Margery Davies, *Women's Place Is at the Typewriter* (Philadelphia, Penn.: Temple University Press, 1982).

13. See Myra Strober and Carolyn Arnold, "The Dynamics of Occupational Segregation by Gender: Bank Tellers (1950–80)" in Clair Brown and Joseph A. Pechman, eds., *Gender in the Workplace* (Washington, D.C.: Brookings Institution, 1987).

14. Jean Lipman-Blumen, "Role De-Differentiation as a System Response to Crisis: Occupational and Political Roles of Women," *Sociological Inquiry,* vol. 43, no. 2 (1973): 105–29.

Chapter 3

1. *Historical Statistics of the United States: Colonial Times to 1957* (Washington, D.C.: U.S. Government Printing Office, 1960), p. 24; *Statistical Abstract of the United States, 1981* (Washington, D.C.: U.S. Government Printing Office, 1980), p. 62.

2. National Center for Health Statistics, *Advance Report of Final Natality Statistics, 1983,* vol. 34, no. 6, supplement (September 20, 1985), p. 13.

3. The discussion here and in the next two sections is based in part on Jeanne Clare Ridley, "Family Planning and the Status of Women in the United States" (undated, mimeographed), which was brought to my attention by Harriet Presser.

4. Nancy Folbre, "Of Patriarchy Born: The Political Economy of Fertility Decisions," *Feminist Studies*, vol. 9, no. 2 (Summer 1983):261–80.

5. Warren C. Sanderson, "Qualitative Aspects of Marriage, Fertility and Family Limitation in Nineteenth Century America: Another Application of the Coale Specifications," *Demography*, vol. 16, no. 3 (August 1979):339–58.

6. Pascal K. Whelpton and Clyde V. Kiser, *Social and Psychological Factors Affecting Fertility* (New York: Milbank Memorial Fund, 1950).

7. Margaret Sanger, *An Autobiography* (New York: Dover, 1971).

8. Robin Maranz Henig, "The Sterilization Option," *The Washington Post*, March 19, 1986 (health section), p. 10.

9. The cases are *Griswold* v. *Connecticut*, 381 U.S. 113 (1965) and *Eisenstadt* v. *Baird*, 405 U.S. 438 (1972).

10. The landmark case on abortion was *Roe* v. *Wade*, 410 U.S. 113 (1973). Data on abortions from *Statistical Abstract of the United States, 1985* (Washington, D.C.: U.S. Government Printing Office, 1984), p. 67.

11. *Statistical Abstract of the United States, 1985*, p. 66.

12. Carol Cassell, *Swept Away: Why Women Fear Their Own Sexuality* (New York: Simon & Schuster, 1984).

13. Paul T. Schultz, *The Economics of Population* (Reading, Mass.: Addison-Wesley, 1981).

14. Alice Nakamura and Masao Nakamura, *The Second Paycheck: An Analysis of the Employment and Earnings of Married Women* (New York: Academic Press, 1985).

15. Ridley, "Family Planning and the Status of Women in the United States."

16. Kingsley Davis, "The Future of Marriage," *Bulletin of the American Academy of Arts and Sciences*, vol. 36, no. 8 (May 1983):33.

17. *Statistical Abstract of the United States, 1985*, p. 36.

18. Barbara Ehrenreich, *The Hearts of Men: American Dreams and the Flight from Commitment* (Garden City, N.Y.: Doubleday & Company, 1983).

19. Marcia Guttentag and Paul F. Secord, *Too Many Women: The Sex Ratio Question* (Beverly Hills, Calif.: Sage Publications, 1983).

20. U.S. Bureau of the Census, Current Population Reports, *Marital Status and Living Arrangements: March 1984*, series P–20, no. 399 (Washington, D.C.: U.S. Government Printing Office, 1984), p. 7 and p. 9.

21. Ernest A. T. Barth and W. B. Watson, "Social Stratification and the Family in Mass Society," *Social Forces*, vol. 45 (1967):392–402.

22. Simone de Beauvoir, *The Second Sex* (New York: Alfred A. Knopf, 1953).

23. Betty Friedan, *The Feminine Mystique* (New York: W. W. Norton, 1963).

Chapter 4

1. U.S. Department of Labor, U.S. Bureau of Labor Statistics, "Weekly Earnings of Wage and Salary Workers: Fourth Quarter 1985," USDL *86–46*.

2. For an example of exposition of the argument that discrimination is a relatively minor contributor to the gap between men's and women's wages, see a widely used labor economics textbook by Belton M. Fleisher and Thomas J. Knieser, *Labor Economics: Theory, Evidence, and Policy*, third ed. (Englewood Cliffs, N.J.: Prentice-Hall, Inc., 1985), pp. 405–13.

3. *Bullock* v. *Pizza Hut, Inc.,* 429 F. Supp. 424 (1977).

4. Francine Blau, *Equal Pay in the Office* (Lexington, Mass.: D.C. Heath & Co., 1977). See also the discussion of the research of Bielby and Barron reviewed in chapter 5.

5. Andrea H. Beller, "Trends in Occupational Segregation by Sex and Race, 1960–1981" in Barbara F. Reskin, ed., *Sex Segregation in the Workplace* (Washington, D.C.: National Academy Press, 1984), pp. 11–26.

6. Jacob Mincer and Solomon W. Polachek, "Family Investments in Human Capital: Earnings of Women," *Journal of Political Economy,* vol. 82, no. 2, part 2 (March/April 1974):S76–S108.

7. For a comprehensive review of statistical studies on the earnings gap see Janice F. Madden, "The Persistence of Pay Differentials: The Economics of Sex Discrimination" in *Women and Work, An Annual Review,* vol. 1 (Beverly Hills, Calif.: Sage Publishing, 1985), chap. 3.

8. Jacob Mincer and Solomon W. Polachek, "Family Investments in Human Capital: Earnings of Women," *Journal of Political Economy,* vol. 82, no. 2, part 2 (March/April 1974):S76–S108.

9. Gary S. Becker, "Human Capital, Effort, and the Sexual Division of Labor," *Journal of Labor Economics,* vol. 3, no. 1, part 2 (January 1985):S33–S58. The quotation is from p. S35.

10. Equal Employment Opportunity Commission, *A Unique Competence: A Study of Equal Employment Opportunity in the Bell System* reprinted in the *Congressional Record* (February 17, 1972), pp. E1234–E1272. A useful summary of this document is presented in Barbara Allen Babock, Ann E. Freedman, Eleanor Holmes Norton, and Susan C. Ross, *Sex Discrimination and the Law* (Boston, Mass.: Little, Brown & Co., 1975). See also Phyllis Wallace, ed., *Equal Employment Opportunity and the AT&T Case* (Cambridge, Mass.: MIT Press, 1976).

11. Quoted in Babock et al., p. 289.

12. See Barbara R. Bergmann, "The Common Sense of Affirmative Action," in *Selected Affirmative Action Topics in Employment and Business Set-Asides,* vol. 1 (U.S. Commission on Civil Rights, March 6–7, 1985), pp. 29–32.

13. P. A. Goldberg, "Are Women Prejudiced Against Women?" *Trans-Action* (April 1968):28–30. The literature on these studies is reviewed in Sharon Toffey Shepela and Ann T. Viviano, "Some Psychological Factors Affecting Job Segregation and Wages" in Helen Remick, ed., *Comparable Worth and Wage Discrimination* (Philadelphia, Penn.: Temple University Press, 1984), pp. 47–58.

Chapter 5

1. The experiences of Shaun Meredith are in *Generations* (Winter 1985). The Southeast Women's Employment Coalition, P.O. Box 1357, Lexington, Ky. 40590.

2. Herbert Hill, "Race and Ethnicity in Organized Labor: The Historical Sources of Resistance to Affirmative Action," *The Journal of Intergroup Relations,* vol. 12, no. 4 (Winter 1984):5–49.

3. William T. Bielby and James N. Barron, "A Woman's Place Is With Other Women: Sex Segregation Within Organizations" in Barbara F. Reskin, ed., *Sex*

Segregation in the Workplace (Washington, D.C.: National Academy Press, 1984), pp. 27–55.

4. Bielby and Barron, p. 43.

5. Bielby and Barron, p. 48.

6. To anyone seeking an understanding of sex roles, Susan Brownmiller's book *Femininity* (New York: Simon & Schuster, 1984) is indispensable.

7. For an account of women coal miners see Calvin Trillin, *Killings* (New York: Viking Penguin, Inc., 1985), pp. 149–59.

8. Sandra L. Bem and Daryl J. Bem, "Does Sex-Biased Job Advertising 'Aid and Abet' Sex Discrimination?" *Journal of Applied Social Psychology*, vol. 3, no. 1 (1973):6–18.

9. Rosabeth Kanter, *Men and Women of the Corporation* (New York: Basic Books, 1977).

10. Lester C. Thurow, "Why Women Are Paid Less than Men," *The New York Times*, March 8, 1981, sect. II, p. 2.

11. William Foot Whyte, "The Social Structure of the Restaurant," *American Journal of Sociology*, vol. LIV (January 1949):302–10.

12. Some of the discussion in this section is based on the review of the literature in Patricia A. Roos and Barbara F. Reskin, "Institutional Factors Contributing to Sex Segregation in the Workplace" in Barbara F. Reskin, ed., *Sex Segregation in the Workplace: Trends, Explanations, Remedies* (Washington, D.C.: National Academy Press, 1984), pp. 235–60. The reader is referred there to an excellent bibliography of original studies.

13. This experience was related by one of my students.

14. *Parker v. Siemens-Allis, Inc.*, 601 F. Supp. 1377 (1985).

15. *King v. New Hampshire Department of Resources and Economic Development*, 562 F. 2d 80 (1977).

16. Quoted in Suzanne C. Carothers and Peggy Crull, "Contrasting Sexual Harassment in Female- and Male-Dominated Occupations" in *My Troubles Are Going to Have Trouble with Me* (New Brunswick, N.J.: Rutgers University Press, 1984), pp. 219–20.

17. U.S. Merit Systems Protection Board, *Sexual Harassment in the Federal Workplace: Is It a Problem?* (Washington, D.C.: Government Printing Office, March 1981), p. 47.

18. Catherine MacKinnen, *Sexual Harassment of Working Women: A Case of Sex Discrimination* (New Haven, Conn.: Yale University Press, 1979).

19. *Morgan v. Hertz Corp.*, 542 F. Supp. 123 (1981), p. 127.

20. See Carothers and Crull, "Contrasting Sexual Harassment in Female- and Male-Dominated Occupations."

21. U.S. Merit Systems Protection Board, *Sexual Harassment in the Federal Workplace: Is It a Problem?*

22. Peter Doeringer and Michael J. Piore, *Internal Labor Markets and Manpower Analysis* (Lexington, Mass.: D.C. Heath and Co., 1971). See also James E. Rosenbaum, *Career Mobility in a Corporate Hierarchy* (Orlando, Fla.: Academic Press, 1984).

23. Sandra Peterson-Hardt and Nancy D. Perlman, "Sex-Segregated Career Ladders in New York State Government; A Structural Analysis of Inequality in Employment" (State University of New York at Albany, N.Y.: Center for Women in Government, working paper 1, October 1979, mimeographed).

24. *Kyriazi v. Western Electric Co.*, 461 F. Supp. 894 (1978), p. 910.

25. *Morgan v. Hertz Corp.*

26. Solomon W. Polachek, "Occupational Self-Selection: A Human Capital Approach to Sex Differences in Occupational Structure," *Review of Economics and Statistics*, vol. 58, no. 1 (February 1981):60–69.

27. Paula England, "The Failure of Human Capital Theory to Explain Occupational Sex Segregation," *Journal of Human Resources* (Spring 1982):358–70.

28. Valerie K. Oppenheimer, *The Female Labor Force in the United States: Demographic and Economic Factors Governing Its Growth and Changing Composition* (Westport, Conn.: Greenwood Press, 1979).

29. Myra Strober and Carolyn Arnold, "The Dynamics of Occupational Segregation by Gender: Bank Tellers (1950–80)" in Clair Brown and Joseph A. Pechman, eds., *Gender in the Workplace* (Washington, D.C.: Brookings Institution, 1987).

30. Women employees surveyed in the data used in the Corcoran-Duncan study mentioned in chapter 4 had spent 12 percent of their time with their present employer in training, while men had spent 20 percent. See table 4–5.

31. A review of studies on turnover rates by sex is given in Paula England, "Socio-Economic Explanations of Job Segregation" in Helen Remick, ed., *Comparable Worth and Wage Discrimination* (Philadelphia, Penn.: Temple University Press, 1984), pp. 37–38.

32. The discussion in this section parallels that in Barbara R. Bergmann and William Darity, Jr., "Social Relations in the Workplace and Employer Discrimination," *IRRA 33rd Annual Proceedings, 1980*. There the same analysis is applied to segregation by race, which we believe has a similar etiology.

33. For a review of the literature on apprenticeship, see Barbara F. Reskin and Heidi I. Hartmann, eds., *Women's Work, Men's Work: Sex Segregation on the Job* (Washington, D.C.: National Academy Press, 1986), pp. 100–103.

Chapter 6

1. See discussion of study by Corcoran and Duncan in chapter 4, table 4–5, p. 78. Mary Corcoran and Gregory J. Duncan, "Work History, Labor-Force Attachment, and Earnings Differences Between the Races and Sexes," *Journal of Human Resources*, vol. XIV (Winter 1979):3–20.

2. See discussion of study by Corcoran and Duncan in chapter 4, table 4–5. In a number of sex discrimination cases, blacks have argued that one way they were discriminated against was by being denied overtime work that was given to similarly situated white workers.

3. Solomon W. Polachek, "Occupational Self-Selection: A Human Capital Approach to Sex Differences in Occupational Structure," *Review of Economics and Statistics*, vol. 58, no. 1 (February 1981):60–69.

4. Gary S. Becker, "Human Capital, Effort, and the Sexual Division of Labor," *Journal of Labor Economics*, vol. 3, no. 1, part 2 (January 1985):S33–S58.

5. William T. Bielby and James N. Barron, "A Woman's Place is with Other Women: Sex Segregation Within Organizations" in Barbara F. Reskin, ed., *Sex Segregation in the Workplace* (Washington, D.C.: National Academy Press, 1984), pp. 27–

55. For earlier research with a similar result, see Francine D. Blau, *Equal Pay in the Office* (Lexington, Mass.: D.C. Heath & Co., 1977).

6. Sometimes economists speak of a single labor market divided into segments based on sex, and also on class and race differences. Workers cannot move from one segment to another. The idea of a "dual market" is similar. Peter Doeringer and Michael J. Piore, *Internal Labor Markets and Manpower Analysis* (Lexington, Mass.: D.C. Heath & Co., 1971).

7. Estelle James, "The Income and Employment Effects of Women's Liberation" in Cynthia Lloyd, ed., *Sex, Discrimination, and the Division of Labor* (New York: Columbia University Press, 1975), pp. 379–400.

8. For a more technical discussion of these issues, see Barbara R. Bergmann, "Occupational Segregation, Wages and Profits when Employers Discriminate by Race or Sex," *Eastern Economic Journal*, vol. 1 (April/July 1974):561–73.

9. Francine D. Blau, *Equal Pay in the Office* (Lexington, Mass.: D.C. Heath & Co., 1977).

10. This has been documented for British establishments in Rosemary Crompton and Gareth Jones, *White-Collar Proletariat: Deskilling and Gender in Clerical Work* (Philadelphia, Penn.: Temple University Press, 1984).

11. In conversation, Heidi Hartmann noted that this was the case with male clerical workers at the National Academy of Sciences in Washington.

12. Barbara R. Bergmann and Myles Maxfield, Jr., "How to Analyze the Fairness of Faculty Women's Salaries on Your Own Campus," *AAUP Bulletin* (Autumn 1975): 262–65.

13. Testimony given in *Lemons* v. *City and County of Denver*, 17 FEP Cases 906 D. Col. (1978).

14. *County of Washington* v. *Gunther*, 452 U.S. 967 (1981).

15. *Scott* v. *Océ Industries, Inc.*, 536 F. Supp. 141 (1982).

16. See Rosabeth Kanter, *Men and Women of the Corporation* (New York: Basic Books, 1977), chaps. 1, 4, 6, and 10.

17. Claudia Goldin, "The Gender Gap in Historical Perspective" in *Comparable Worth: Issue for the 80s* (Washington, D.C.: U.S. Commission on Civil Rights, 1984), pp. 3–19.

18. Paula England and George Farkas, *Households, Employment, and Gender: A Social, Economics, and Demographic View* (New York: Aldine, 1985), chap. 7.

19. Gary S. Becker, in *The Economics of Discrimination* (Chicago, Ill.: University of Chicago Press, 1957), first made the argument that discriminators would be competed to death. As previously noted, he currently appears agnostic concerning the existence of discrimination against women.

20. *Morgan* v. *Hertz Corporation*, 542 F. Supp. 123 (1981).

21. For example, Theodore Caplow, *The Sociology of Work* (Minneapolis, Minn.: University of Minnesota Press, 1954).

22. Becker, *The Economics of Discrimination*.

23. Becker, *The Economics of Discrimination*.

24. *Bourque* v. *Powell Electrical Manufacturing Company*, 617 F. 2d. 61 (1980).

25. *Strecker* v. *Grand Forks County Social Service Board*, 640 F. 2d 96 (1980).

26. Perhaps this is a better interpretation of Gary S. Becker's discrimination coefficient. See Becker, *The Economics of Discrimination*.

27. Employment figures by occupation from *Historical Statistics of the United States: Colonial Times to 1957* (Washington, D.C.: Government Printing Office, 1960),

p. 74, and the *Statistical Abstract, 1982–83* (Washington, D.C.: Government Printing Office, 1982), p. 388.

28. Compare Valerie K. Oppenheimer, *The Female Labor Force in the United States: Demographic and Economic Factors Governing the Growth and Changing Composition* (Westport, Conn.: Greenwood Press, 1979).

29. Estelle James, "The Income and Employment Effects of Women's Liberation."

Chapter 7

1. Researchers have found the result of enforcement activities to be positive but not large. See, for example, Randall W. Eberts and Joe A. Stone, "Male-Female Differences in Promotions: EEO in Public Education," *Journal of Human Resources* (Fall 1985): 504–21. Also see Charles Brown, "The Federal Attack on Labor Market Discrimination: The Mouse That Roared" in *Research in Labor Economics,* Ronald G. Ehrenberg, ed., vol. 5 (Greenwich, Conn.: JAI Press, 1982), pp. 33–68.

2. U.S. Code 206 (d) (1) (1970).

3. Michael Evans Gold, "A Tale of Two Amendments: The Reasons Congress Added Sex to Title VII and Their Implication for the Issue of Comparable Worth," *Duquesne Law Review,* vol. 19 (Spring 1981):453–477.

4. Barbara Allen Babock, Ann E. Freedman, Elinor Holmes Norton, and Susan C. Ross, *Sex Discrimination and the Law* (Boston, Mass.: Little, Brown & Co., 1975), chap. 2.

5. Quoted in Babock et al., p. 231.

6. 303 F. Supp. 54 M.D. Ala. (1969).

7. Edmund S. Phelps, "The Statistical Theory of Racism and Sexism," *American Economic Review,* vol. 62 (September 1972):659–61.

8. *Manhart* v. *City of Los Angeles,* 435 U.S. 702, 98 S. Ct. 1370, 55 L. Ed. 2d 657 (1978).

9. Affidavit of the author in *Spirt* v. *TIAA-CREF.* This case resulted in the equalization by sex of pension benefits for retired faculty members.

10. *Evans* v. *Sheraton Park Hotel,* 5 FEP Cases 393 (D.D.C., 1972).

11. *Sibley Memorial Hospital* v. *Wilson,* 6 FEP Cases 1029 (D.C. Cir., 1973).

12. *Diaz* v. *Pan American World Airways, Inc.,* 442 F. 2d. 385 (5th Cir., 1971), as cited in Babock et al.

13. Alice Kessler Harris, *Out to Work: A History of Wage-Earning Women* (New York: Oxford University Press, 1982), p. 164.

14. *Rosenfeld* v. *Southern Pacific Company,* 444 F. 2d 1219 (9th Cir., 1971).

15. *Griggs* v. *Duke Power Co.,* 401 U.S. 424, 91 S. Ct. 849, 28 L. Ed. 2d 158 (1971).

16. *Stotts* v. *Memphis Fire Department,* 104 S. Ct. 2578 (1985).

17. *Laffey* v. *Northeast Airlines, Inc.,* 6 FEP Cases 902 (D.D.C., 1973).

18. For a discussion of sexual harassment as a form of sex discrimination, and the legal issues involved, see Catherine MacKinnen, *Sexual Harassment of Working Women* (New Haven, Conn.: Yale University Press, 1979).

19. *Fleur* v. *Cleveland Board of Education,* 326 F. Supp. 1208 (N.D., Ohio, 1972), 414 U.S. 632, 94 S. Ct. 791. For a discussion see Babock, et al., pp. 308–329.

20. The Pregnancy Disability Act of 1978.

21. Herbert Hill, "The Equal Employment Opportunity Commission: Twenty Years Later," *Journal of Intergroup Relations,* vol. XI, no. 4 (Winter 1983):45–72. U.S. General Accounting Office, *The Equal Employment Opportunity Commission Has Made Limited Progress in Eliminating Employment Discrimination* (Washington, D.C.: U.S. Government Printing Office, 1976), pp. 38–39.

22. "EEOC Reports Accomplishments for Fiscal 1985," *The Washington Post,* December 4, 1985, p. A25.

23. The text of these regulations is in 43 FR 49240, *Federal Register,* July 1, 1984.

24. A modestly optimistic assessment is given by Jonathan S. Leonard, "What Promises Are Worth: The Impact of Affirmative Action Goals," *The Journal of Human Resources,* vol. 20, no. 1 (Winter 1985):3–20. But see also U.S. General Accounting Office, *The Equal Employment Opportunity Program for Federal Nonconstruction Contractors Can Be Improved* (Washington, D.C.: General Accounting Office, 1975). Also see James J. Heckman and Kenneth I. Wolpin, "Does the Contract Compliance Program Work? An Analysis of Chicago Data," *Industrial and Labor Relations Review,* vol. 29, no. 4 (July 1976):544–64.

25. *Steelworkers* v. *Weber,* 443 U.S. 193 (1979).

26. Thomas Sowell, *The Economics and Politics of Race* (New York: William Morrow, 1983).

27. Peter C. Robertson, "Why the Bosses Like to be Told to Hire Minorities," *The Washington Post,* November 10, 1985, p. D1.

28. Patrick Fenton, "The Way Police Exams Used to Be," *The New York Times,* July 27, 1985, p. 23.

29. Cynthia Fuchs Epstein, *Women in Law* (New York: Basic Books, 1981). See also Rosabeth Kanter, *Men and Women of the Corporation* (New York: Basic Books, 1977).

30. See documentation for Great Britain in Rosemary Crompton and Gareth Jones, *White Collar Proletariat* (Philadelphia, Penn.: Temple University Press, 1984).

31. *Statistical Abstract of the United States, 1985* (Washington, D.C.: U.S. Government Printing Office, 1984), p. 324.

Chapter 8

1. ". . . loonier than *Loony Tunes*" was the comment of Clarence Pendleton, chair of the U.S. Commission on Civil Rights. For an able and measured presentation of opposing views with rebuttals, see Michael Gold, *A Debate on Comparable Worth* (Ithaca, N.Y.: Industrial and Labor Relations Press, 1983).

2. *Borque* v. *Powell Electrical Manufacturing Co.,* 617 F 2d 61 (1980). In this case, the manager was refusing to pay a woman the salary a man received in an identical position.

3. Helen Remick, "Comparable Worth and Wages" (Manoa, Hawaii, Industrial Research Center, University of Hawaii, 1984).

4. A review of job evaluation schemes and of problems inherent in using them is presented in Donald J. Treiman, "Job Evaluation: An Analytic Review" (Washington, D.C.: National Academy of Sciences, 1979). Now that job evaluation is being recommended as the methodology of choice by those favoring pay equity, a more critical eye is being cast on its characteristics by experts in wage administration and industrial relations.

5. William J. Fox, "Purpose and Validity in Job Evaluation," *Personnel Journal,* vol. 41 (October 1962):432–37.

6. Mark Killingsworth makes this suggestion in "Statement on Comparable Worth," testimony before the Joint Economic Committee, U.S. Congress (April 10, 1984).

7. *Lemons* v. *City and County of Denver,* 17 FEP Cases 906 (D. Col, 1978), 620 F 2d (10th Cir.), *cert. denied,* 449 U.S. 888 (1980).

8. Alice Cook, Arlene Kaplan Daniels, and Val R. Lorwin, *Women and Trade Unions in Eleven Industrialized Countries* (Philadelphia, Penn.: Temple University Press, 1984).

9. Robert S. Gregory and Ronald C. Duncan, "The Relevance of Segmented Labor Market Theories: The Australian Experience of the Achievement of Equal Pay for Women," *Journal of Post Keynesian Economics,* vol. 3 (Spring 1981):404–28.

10. R. G. Gregory and Vivian Ho, "Equal Pay and Comparable Worth: What Can the U.S. Learn from the Australian Experience?" (unpublished draft, 1984).

11. Gregory and Duncan, "The Relevance of Segmented Labor Markets Theories." Their findings, as summarized in Gregory and Ho, are:

> . . . aggregate female employment relative to that of male employment in Australia has not been *significantly* affected by a 30 percent increase in female pay. Since the introduction of equal pay and comparable worth female employment has continued to grow at a faster rate than male employment although for both groups the employment rate has slowed considerably. . . . The unemployment of women in Australia has continued to fall relative to that of men and also appears not to have been affected to a great degree. In both countries [the United States and Australia], female unemployment is marginally above that of male unemployment . . . there has been some difference in the relationship between the growth of full time and part time jobs in each country. In Australia a large amount of the job growth for females has been in part time jobs. This has not been true in the U.S. . . . It is also important to note that the Australian experience is not unique. The equal pay experiments in the U.K. have generated similar results: Large increases in female pay with little relative employment loss.

12. Gregory and Ho, "Equal Pay and Comparable Worth."

13. U.S. Bureau of Labor Statistics, "Over 121 Million Persons Worked in 1984," *USDL 85–328* (August 16, 1985).

14. June C. O'Neill, "The Comparable Worth Trap," *Wall Street Journal,* January 20, 1984, p. 28.

15. *Economic Report of the President, February 1984,* table B–21, pp. 244–45. These figures represent magnitudes before taxes on incomes and profits.

16. The split in wage income between men and women is based on earnings data by sex published by the U.S. Bureau of the Census in Current Population Reports, *Money Income of Households, Families, and Persons in the United States, 1982,* series P–60, no. 142 (Washington, D.C.: U.S. Government Printing Office, 1984), table 54, pp. 194–95. I have not attempted to correct for the fact that the Census data covered only money earnings, which may be distributed between males and females somewhat differently than noncash benefits.

17. For year-round, full-time workers in 1982, the Current Population Survey shows men with mean annual earnings of $23,637, and women with earnings of $14,327. I

have taken these figures to be representative of wage rates. Closing one third of the gap in these earnings wc uld have required that women's mean annual wage should raise by $3,103, or 21.7 percent. This percentage was applied to the estimated female wage bill of $541 billion to produce the estimate that the rise required would have been $117 billion.

18. *Economic Report of the President, February 1985,* table B–41, p. 279.

Chapter 9

1. These figures are derived from tables A–4 and A–22, U.S. Bureau of Labor Statistics, *Employment and Earnings* (February 1986).

2. John Kenneth Galbraith, *Economics and the Public Purpose* (Boston, Mass.: Houghton Mifflin, 1973), chap. 4.

3. Unpublished tabulation from the Census' Current Population Surveys.

4. *Statistical Abstract of the United States, 1985* (Washington, D.C.: U.S. Government Printing Office, 1984), table 179, p. 113. The figure is for 1981.

5. U.S. Department of Justice, *A Survey of Spousal Violence Against Women in Kentucky* (Washington, D.C.: Law Enforcement Assistance Administration, 1979).

6. C. Lopate, "Pay for Housework," *Journal of Social Policy,* vol. 5 (January 1974): 27–31.

7. The Swedish Institute, "Child Care Programs in Sweden," *Fact Sheets on Sweden* (Stockholm: September 1984).

8. Andrew Cherlin, *Marriage, Divorce, Remarriage: Social Trends in the United States* (Cambridge, Mass.: Harvard University Press, 1981).

9. U.S. Bureau of the Census, Current Population Reports, *Marital Status and Living Arrangements: March 1983,* series P–20, no. 389 (Washington, D.C.: U.S. Government Printing Office, 1984).

10. These numbers are derived from unpublished data based on a survey taken in 1980 by the U.S. Bureau of the Census.

11. U.S. Bureau of the Census, Current Population Report, *Divorce, Child Custody, and Child Support,* series P–23, no. 84 (Washington, D.C.: U.S. Government Printing Office, June 1979).

12. Lenore J. Weitzman, *The Divorce Revolution* (New York: The Free Press, 1985).

13. U.S. Bureau of the Census, Current Population Reports, *Child Support and Alimony, 1983,* series P–23, no. 141 (Washington, D.C.: U.S. Government Printing Office, 1985), table E.

14. The discussion here and in the next paragraph follows the ideas of Isabel V. Sawhill, "Developing Normative Standards for Child-Support Payments" in Judith Cassetty, ed., *The Parental Child Support Obligation* (Lexington, Mass.: Lexington Books, 1983), pp. 79–114.

15. Sawhill, "Developing Normative Standards for Child Support Payments," pp. 91–92.

16. This idea also has been developed by Judith Cassetty in *Child Support and Public Policy* (Lexington, Mass.: D. C. Heath and Co., 1978).

17. The Swedish Institute, "Taxes in Sweden," *Fact Sheets on Sweden* (Stockholm: March 1985).

18. Rolande Cuvillier, "The Housewife—An Unjustified Financial Burden on the Community," *Journal of Social Policy,* vol. 8 (January 1979):1–26.

19. For detailed discussions of all of the major alternatives to the present system of computing Social Security benefits, see Richard V. Burkhauser and Karen C. Holden, eds., *A Challenge to Social Security: The Changing Roles of Women and Men in American Society* (New York: Academic Press, 1982).

Chapter 10

1. *Statistical Abstract of the United States, 1982–83* (Washington, D.C.: U.S. Government Printing Office, 1983), table 73, p. 52; U.S. Bureau of the Census, Current Population Reports, *Household and Family Characteristics: March 1984* (Washington, D.C.: U.S. Government Printing Office, 1984), series P–20, no. 398, p. 4.

2. Number of children from U.S. Bureau of the Census, Current Population Reports, *Marital Status and Living Arrangements: March 1984,* series P–20, no. 399 (Washington, D.C.: U.S. Government Printing Office, 1985), p. 4. Percentage remarried from U.S. Bureau of the Census, Current Population Reports, *Child Support and Alimony: 1983,* series P–23, no. 141 (Washington, D.C.: U.S. Government Printing Office, 1985), p. 7.

3. National Center for Health Statistics, *Advance Report of Final Natality Statistics, 1983,* Monthly Vital Statistics Report, vol. 34, no. 6 (Hyattsville, Md.: Public Health Service, 1985), p. 3; U.S. Bureau of the Census, Current Population Reports, *Marital Status and Living Arrangements: March 1984,* series P–20, no. 399 (Washington, D.C.: U.S. Government Printing Office, 1985), p. 3.

4. U.S. Bureau of the Census, Current Population Reports, *Marital Status and Living Arrangements: March 1984,* p. 4. The proportion of children living with never-married female single parents was 24 percent in 1984, but the proportion who were born out of wedlock is probably somewhat higher. Some of the mothers reported as divorced or separated had out-of-wedlock children before or after the marriage they reported as terminating. Some never-married mothers may have misreported themselves.

5. U.S. Bureau of the Census, Current Population Reports, *Characteristics of the Population Below the Poverty Level: 1983,* series P–60, no. 147 (Washington, D.C.: U.S. Government Printing Office, 1985), p. 117.

6. U.S. Bureau of Labor Statistics, *Number of Working Mothers Now at Record Levels,* USDL 84–321 (June 26, 1984).

7. U.S. Bureau of Labor Statistics, *Employment and Earnings Characteristics of Families: First Quarter 1986* USDL 86–152 (April 21, 1986).

8. See Clair (Vickery) Brown, "The Time-Poor: A New Look at Poverty," *The Journal of Human Resources,* vol. XII, no. 1 (Winter 1977):27–48.

9. This includes expenditures at all levels of government—federal, state, and local. *Statistical Abstract of the United States, 1985* (Washington, D.C.: U.S. Government Printing Office, 1984), table 593, p. 357.

10. See Heather L. Ross and Isabel V. Sawhill, *Time of Transition: The Growth of Families Headed by Women* (Washington, D.C.: The Urban Institute, 1975). Chapter 6 has an extensive review of the research literature on the effects on children of living

with single mothers. They refer to "a paucity of evidence that marital mobility and single-parent headship harm children . . ." (p. 153).

11. Frederich Engels, *Origin of the Family,* quoted in *The Woman Question: Selections from the Writings of Karl Marx, Frederich Engels, V. I. Lenin, Joseph Stalin* (New York: International Publishers, 1970), p. 16.

12. Carol Cassell, *Swept Away: Why Women Fear Their Own Sexuality* (New York: Simon & Schuster, 1984), see chapter 8, "Good Girls and Bad Contraception."

13. Estimated by the author from data on distribution of money earnings in U.S. Bureau of the Census, Current Population Reports, *Money Income and Poverty Status of Families and Persons in the United States: 1983,* series P–60, no. 145 (Washington, D.C.: U.S. Government Printing Office, 1984), table 11, p. 16, and U.S. Bureau of the Census, Current Population Report, *Income in 1967 of Persons in the United States,* series P–60, no. 60 (Washington, D.C.: U.S. Government Printing Office, 1968), p. 50. Child-care costs were roughly put at $1,000 per child in 1978 by the Congressional Budget Office ("Childcare and Preschool: Options for Federal Support" [September 1978], p. 64), and these have been carried forward and back by using the consumer price index for services other than medical.

14. U.S. Department of Justice, "A Survey of Spousal Violence Against Women in Kentucky," Law Enforcement Assistance Administration, July 1979.

15. Phyllis Schlafly, *The Power of the Positive Woman* (New York: Harcourt, Brace, Jovanovich, 1977).

16. Christopher Lasch, *Haven in a Heartless World* (New York: Basic Books, 1977).

17. Charles Murray, *Losing Ground* (New York: Basic Books, 1984).

18. Elwood and Bane found that the major effect of welfare benefits was to set up single mothers in their own household. So welfare benefits that have little effect on the number of single mothers can have a major effect on the number of single mothers on welfare. David T. Elwood and Mary Jo Bane, "The Impact of AFDC on Family Structure and Living Arrangements" (Cambridge, Mass.: Harvard University, February 1985).

19. This account of the history of welfare relies on Ross and Sawhill, *Time of Transition,* chap. 5, and on Irwin Garfinckel and Sara McLanahan, *A New American Dilemma: The Plight of Single Mothers and Their Children* (Washington, D.C.: Urban Institute Press, 1986). The original name of the program was Aid to Dependent Children. It was set up under the Social Security Act of 1935, which also set up Unemployment Insurance and Old Age and Survivor's Insurance (OASI, later OASDI, popularly known as "Social Security"). Widows of men who had Social Security coverage, the vast majority, now receive benefits under the latter program.

20. Ross and Sawhill, *Time of Transition,* p. 97.

21. U.S. Bureau of the Census, Current Population Reports, *Economic Characteristics of Households in the United States: Third Quarter 1983,* series P–70, no 1 (Washington, D.C.: U.S. Government Printing Office, 1984), table 8, p. 23.

22. Committee on Ways and Means, U.S. House of Representatives, "Background Material and Data on Programs Within the Jurisdiction of the Committee on Ways and Means" (February 22, 1985), p. 348.

23. Committee on Ways and Means, "Background Material and Data," pp. 347 and 353.

24. Committee on Ways and Means, "Background Material and Data," p. 343. This calculation includes food stamps in with cash income.

25. For extended comments on the welfare system see Nancy Folbre, "The Pauperization of Motherhood: Patriarchy and Public Policy in the United States," *Review of Radical Political Economics,* vol. 16 (Winter 1984):72–88. On the circulation of women in and out of the welfare population, see Mary Jo Bane and David Elwood, "The Dynamics of Dependence: The Routes to Self-Sufficiency" (Cambridge, Mass.: Urban Systems Research and Engineering, June 1983). Nancy Barrett's "The Welfare Trap" (unpublished) presents ideas on welfare similar to those I express here.

26. U.S. Bureau of the Census, Current Population Report, *Marital Status and Living Arrangements: March 1984,* series P–20, no. 399 (Washington, D.C.: U.S. Government Printing Office, 1985), p. 4.

27. Bane and Elwood, "The Dynamics of Dependence."

28. Henry Aaron, *Why Is Welfare So Hard to Reform?* (Washington, D.C.: The Brookings Institution, 1973).

29. Statement made orally. For an elaboration, see Irwin Garfinkel and Sara McLanahan, *A New American Dilemma: The Plight of Single Mothers and Their Children.*

30. Whether children born out of wedlock have a legal right to receive support from their fathers has now been definitively answered in the affirmative. See Harry D. Krause, *Child Support in America: The Legal Perspective* (Charlottesville, Va.: The Mickie Company, 1981).

31. Ron Haskins, Andrew W. Dobelstein, John S. Akin, and J. Brad Schwartz, "Estimates of National Child Support Collections Potential and the Income Security of Female-Headed Families." Report to the Office of Child Support Enforcement (University of North Carolina at Chapel Hill, Bush Institute for Child and Family Policy, January 1, 1985), pp. 11–12.

32. Martha S. Hill, "What Absent Fathers Do and Could Provide" (Ann Arbor, Mich.: University of Michigan, 1985), pp. 10 and 20.

33. Haskins, Dobelstein, Akin, and Schwartz, "Estimates of National Child Support Collections Potential," p. 11.

34. Barbara E. Dodd, "DNA Fingerprinting in Matters of Family and Crime," *Nature,* vol. 318 (December 12, 1985):506–7.

35. The size of awards is reported in U.S. Bureau of the Census, Current Population Report, *Child Support and Alimony: 1983,* series P–23, no. 141 (Washington, D.C.: U.S. Government Printing Office, 1985), p. 3. For poverty thresholds see U.S. Bureau of the Census, Current Population Reports, *Money Income and Poverty Status of Families and Persons in the United States: 1983,* series P–60, no. 145 (Washington, D.C.: U.S. Government Printing Office, 1984). For child-care costs, we again rely on Congressional Budget Office, "Child Care and Preschool: Options for Federal Support."

36. David Chambers, *Making Fathers Pay* (Chicago, Ill.: University of Chicago Press, 1979).

37. Carol Stack and Herbert Semmel, "The Concept of Family in the Black Community," Subcommittee on Fiscal Policy, Joint Economic Committee of the Congress (November 4, 1973).

38. Lenore J. Weitzman, *The Divorce Revolution* (New York: The Free Press, 1985), see chap. 8.

39. Lenore J. Weitzman, *The Divorce Revolution.*

40. Barbara R. Bergmann and Mark Roberts, "Income for the Single Parent: Work, Child Support, and Welfare" in Clair Brown and Joseph Pechman, eds., *Gender in the Workplace* (Washington, D.C.: The Brookings Institution, 1987).

41. Tim Corbett, "Child Support Assurance: Wisconsin Demonstration," *Focus,* vol. 9, no. 1 (Spring 1986):1–5. Madison, Wisc.: University of Wisconsin, Institute for Research on Poverty.

42. Congressional Budget Office, unpublished estimate.

Chapter 11

1. U.S. Bureau of Labor Statistics, *Employment and Earnings* (February 1986), p. 15.

2. Harriet B. Presser and Virginia S. Cain, "Shift Work Among Dual-Earner Couples with Children," *Science,* vol. 219 (February 18, 1983):876–79.

3. Some Israeli kibbutzim appear to be on the road to abandoning the communal provision of eating and child care. See Stephanie Cleverdon, "On the Brink: Three Attempts to Liberate Women," *Working Papers for a New Society* (Spring 1975), for a feminist view of the way kibbutzim have evolved in dividing labor by sex. For a more detailed account from authors who believe that the biological differences between the sexes dictate work assignments, see Lionel Tiger and Joseph Shepher, *Women in the Kibbutz* (New York: Harcourt, Brace, Jovanovich, 1975).

4. A good review of past surveys of time use and of sociologists' interpretations of them is to be found in Shelley Coverman, "Explaining Husbands' Participation in Domestic Labor," *Sociological Quarterly,* vol. 26 (Spring 1985):81–97.

5. Gary S. Becker, *A Treatise on the Family* (Cambridge, Mass.: Harvard University Press, 1981).

6. John Robinson, *How Americans Use Time: A Social-Psychological Analysis of Everyday Behavior* (New York: Praeger, 1977). See also Andrew Harvey and David Elliot, *Time and Time Again* (Ottowa, Canada: Employment and Immigration, 1983).

7. Tabulation by the author from the 1975–76 study *Americans' Use of Time.*

8. See the classic article on this subject by Pat Mainardi, "The Politics of Housework" in Robin Morgan, ed., *Sisterhood Is Powerful* (New York: Random House, 1970), pp. 447–54.

9. Of all such women, 46.7 percent said they would like their husbands to do more housework (tabulation by the author from the 1975–76 study *Americans' Use of Time*).

10. Lenore J. Weitzman, *The Divorce Revolution* (New York: The Free Press, 1985).

11. Myra Marx Ferree, "Sacrifice, Satisfaction and Social Change: Employment and the Family" in Karen Brodkin Sacks and Dorothy Remy, eds., *My Troubles Are Going to Have Trouble with Me* (New Brunswick, N.J.: Rutgers University Press, 1984), p. 73.

12. See Coverman, "Explaining Husbands' Participation in Domestic Labor," for a review of findings. Most researchers have found little or no positive effect for egalitarian attitudes. Coverman herself finds that men with more egalitarian attitudes appear to do amounts that are below average when other influences on their housework contribution are accounted for. See also Joseph H. Pleck, "Husbands' Paid Work and Family Roles: Current Research Issues," *Research in the Interweave of Social Roles: Jobs and Families,* vol. 3 (Greenwich, Conn.: JAI press, 1983), pp. 251–333.

13. Ferree, "Sacrifice, Satisfaction and Social Change," p. 73.

14. John David Morley, *Pictures from the Water Trade: Adventures of a Westerner in Japan* (Boston, Mass.: Atlantic Monthly Press, 1985).

Chapter 12

1. Clair Brown, "Home Production for Use in a Market Economy" in Barrie Thorne with Marilyn Yalom, eds., *Rethinking the Family: Some Feminist Questions* (New York: Longman, 1982), pp. 151–67.

2. The quotation is from an interview with Lenin by the German Socialist leader Klara Zetkin as given in K. Marx, F. Engels, V. I. Lenin, and J. Stalin, *The Woman Question: Selections from the Writings of Karl Marx, Frederick Engels, V. I. Lenin, Joseph Stalin* (New York: International Publishers, 1970), p. 94.

3. Norton T. Dodge, *Women in the Soviet Economy* (Baltimore, Md.: The Johns Hopkins Press, 1966), chap. 5. See also the chapters by Gail Warshorfsky Lapidus, Janet C. Chapman, and Bernice Madison in Dorothy Atkinson, Alexander Dallin, and Gail Warshorfsky Lapidus, eds., *Women in Russia* (Stanford, Calif.: Stanford University Press, 1977). For a comparison of women in the Soviet Union with those in Sweden and Israel, see Stephanie Cleverdon, "On the Brink: Three Attempts to Liberate Women," *Working Papers for a New Society* (Spring 1975):28–36.

4. *Survey of Current Business* (July 1983).

5. Data for 1900 and 1950 from *Historical Statistics of the United States, Colonial Times to 1957* (Washington, D.C.: U.S. Government Printing Office, 1960), and for 1983 from *Statistical Abstract of the United States, 1985* (Washington, D.C.: U.S. Government Printing Office, 1984). It is likely that these figures underestimate the number of private-household workers, since there has been sizable illegal immigration since 1950. A considerable number of female illegal immigrants serve in this capacity, and are likely to miss being counted by the statistical agencies. In 1986, estimates of illegal immigrants ranged from two million to fifteen million persons, according to the *Economic Report of the President, February 1986*, p. 219.

6. U.S. Bureau of the Census, Current Population Reports, *Child Care Arrangements of Working Mothers: June 1982*, series P–23, no. 129 (Washington, D.C.: U.S. Government Printing Office, 1983), table 5, p. 30.

7. I have relied here on the survey of expert opinion compiled in Maxine L. Margolis, *Mothers and Such: Views of American Women and Why They Changed* (Berkeley, Calif.: University of California Press, 1984). This quote is from p. 71.

8. Quoted in Margolis, *Mothers and Such*, p. 89.

9. Margolis, *Mothers and Such*, pp. 91–92.

10. The full title of Fraiberg's book is *Every Child's Birthright: In Defense of Mothering* (New York: Basic Books, 1977), and Blum's is *The Day-Care Dilemma: Women and Children First* (Cambridge, Mass.: Lexington Books, 1983). Curiously, both subtitles seem designed to imply a prowoman attitude; in fact, subtitles that conveyed the author's attitudes more accurately would be, respectively, *In Castigation of Part-Time Mothering* and *Children First, Mothers Last*. One of Blum's chapters is titled "A Day in the Life of Ivy Denison," a takeoff on the Alexander Solzhenitsyn book on life in a Siberian prison camp titled, *A Day in the Life of Ivan Denisovich*.

11. Carolyn Teich Adams and Kathryn Teich Winston, *Mothers at Work: Public Policies in the United States, Sweden and China* (New York: Longman, 1980), p. 67.

12. Sheila B. Kamerman and Alfred J. Kahn, eds., *Child Care, Family Benefits and Working Parents: A Study in Comparative Policy* (New York: Columbia University Press, 1981).

13. Edward F. Zigler and Edmund W. Gordon, eds., *Day Care: Scientific and Social Policy Issues* (Boston, Mass.: Auburn House Publishing Co., 1982).

14. William Meyers, "Child Care Finds a Champion in the Corporation," *The New York Times,* August 4, 1985, section 3, p. 1.

15. The evidence on the extent to which difficulties in finding and paying for child care actually prevent the entry of mothers into the labor force is mixed and difficult to interpret. In a survey conducted in 1982, nonemployed mothers with children under five were asked if they would "look for work if child care were available at a reasonable cost," 26 percent said they would do so. On the other hand, in a survey conducted a number of years earlier, of mothers who were asked why they did not hold a job, only 1.5 percent of wives, and 11.8 percent of single mothers said the reason was that they couldn't arrange for child care. The 1982 survey is reported in U.S. Bureau of the Census, Current Population Reports, *Child Care Arrangements of Working Mothers: June 1982,* table H, p. 18. The earlier survey, which refers to the year 1975, is reported in *Child Care and Preschool: Options for Federal Support* (Washington, D.C.: Congressional Budget Office, 1978), table 14. See also, Harriet B. Presser and Wendy Baldwin, "Child Care as a Constraint on Employment: Prevalence, Correlates, and Bearing on the Work and Fertility Nexus," *American Journal of Sociology,* vol. 85, no. 5 (March 1980):1202–13.

16. Meyers, "Child Care Finds a Champion in the Corporation."

17. Blum, *The Day-Care Dilemma,* p. 67.

18. Myra H. Strober, "Formal Extrafamily Child Care: Some Economic Observations" in Cynthia Lloyd, ed., *Sex, Discrimination and the Division of Labor* (New York: Columbia University Press, 1954), pp. 346–78.

19. For brief discussions of housing projects in Sweden and England that had a variety of family care services on the premises, see Delores Hayden, *Redesigning the American Dream* (New York: W. W. Norton & Company, 1984). See also Ellen Perry Berkeley, "The Swedish Servicehus," *Architecture Plus* (May 1973):56–59, which served as the source of the discussion in the text.

Chapter 13

1. Barbara F. Reskin and Heidi I. Hartmann, eds., *Women's Work, Men's Work* (Washington, D.C.: National Academy Press, 1986), chap. 4.

2. U.S. Bureau of Labor Statistics, *Employment and Earnings* (Washington, D.C.: U.S. Department of Labor, July 1985), table A–45, p. 49. In the figure in the text, workers employed part time for "economic reasons"—that is, whose employers have lowered their hours because of slack demand—are included with full-time workers.

3. U.S. Merit Systems Protection Board, *Sexual Harassment in the Federal Workplace: Is It a Problem?* (Washington, D.C.: March 1981).

4. U.S. Bureau of the Census, Current Population Report, *Child Support and Alimony: 1983,* series P–23, no. 141 (Washington, D.C.: U.S. Government Printing Office, 1985), pp. 2–3; welfare average from January 1984 report of the Ways and Means Committee of the U.S. Congress, p. 345.

5. For a description of the unemployment insurance program, see U.S. Department of Labor, *Comparison of State Unemployment Insurance Laws* (January 6, 1985).

Bibliography

Aaron, Henry. *Why Is Welfare So Hard to Reform?* Washington, D.C.: The Brookings Institution, 1973.

Adams, Carolyn Teich and Kathryn Teich Winston. *Mothers at Work: Public Policies in the United States, Sweden and China*. New York: Longman, 1980.

Americans' Use of Time (1975–1976). Ann Arbor, Michigan: University of Michigan, Survey Research Center.

Atkinson, Dorothy, Alexander Dallin, and Gail Warshorfsky Lapidus, eds. *Women in Russia*. Stanford, California: Stanford University Press, 1977.

Babcock, Barbara Allen, Ann E. Freedman, Elinor Holmes Norton, and Susan C. Ross. *Sex Discrimination and the Law*. Boston, Massachusetts: Little, Brown & Company, 1975.

Bane, Mary Jo and David Elwood. *The Dynamics of Dependence: The Routes to Self-Sufficiency*. Cambridge, Massachusetts: Urban Systems Research and Engineering, June 1983.

Barrett, Nancy. "The Welfare System as State Paternalism," Washington, D.C.: American University, 1984.

Barth, Ernest A. T. and W. B. Watson, "Social Stratification and the Family in Mass Society," *Social Forces*, vol. 45 (1967):392–402.

Becker, Gary S. *The Economics of Discrimination*. Chicago, Illinois: University of Chicago Press, 1957.

———. "Human Capital, Effort, and the Sexual Division of Labor," *Journal of Labor Economics*, vol. 3, no. 1, part 2 (January 1985):S33–S58.

———. *A Treatise on the Family*. Cambridge, Massachusetts: Harvard University Press, 1981.

Beller, Andrea H., "Trends in Occupational Segregation by Sex and Race, 1960–1981" in Barbara R. Reskin, ed., *Sex Segregation in the Workplace*, pp. 11–26. Washington, D.C.: National Academy Press, 1984.

Bem, Sandra L. and Daryl J. Bem, "Does Sex-Biased Job Advertising 'Aid and Abet' Sex Discrimination?," *Journal of Applied Social Psychology*, vol. 3, no. 1 (1973):6–18.

Bergmann, Barbara R., "The Common Sense of Affirmative Action," in *Selected Affirmative Action Topics in Employment and Business Set-Asides*, vol. 1 (Washington, D.C.: U.S. Commission on Civil Rights, March 6–7, 1985).

———. "Occupational Segregation, Wages and Profits When Employers Discriminate by Race or Sex," *Eastern Economic Journal*, vol. 1 (April/July, 1974):561–73.

Bergmann, Barbara R. and William Darity, Jr., "Social Relations in the Workplace and Employer Discrimination," IRRA 33rd Annual Proceedings, 1980.

Bergmann, Barbara R. and Myles Maxfield, Jr., "How to Analyze the Fairness of Faculty Women's Salaries on Your Own Campus," *AAUP Bulletin* (Autumn 1975):262–65.

Bergmann, Barbara R. and Mark Roberts, "Income for the Single Parent: Work, Child Support, and Welfare" in Clair Brown and Joseph Pechman, eds., *Gender in the Workplace*. Washington, D.C.: The Brookings Institution (1987).

Berkeley, Ellen Perry, "The Swedish Servicehaus," *Architecture Plus* (May 1973):56–59.

Bielby, William T. and James N. Barron, "A Woman's Place Is With Other Women: Sex

Segregation Within Organizations" in Barbara F. Reskin, ed., *Sex Segregation in the Workplace,* pp. 27–55. Washington, D.C.: National Academy Press, 1984.

Blau, Francine. *Equal Pay in the Office.* Lexington, Massachusetts: D. C. Heath & Company, 1977.

Blum, Marian. *The Day-Care Dilemma: Women and Children First.* Lexington, Massachusetts: Lexington Books, 1983.

Brown, Charles E., "Equalizing Differences in the Labor Market," *Quarterly Journal of Economics* (February 1980):113–34.

———. "The Federal Attack on Labor Market Discrimination: The Mouse That Roared" in Ronald G. Ehrenberg, ed., *Research in Labor Economics,* vol. 5., pp. 33–68. Greenwich, Connecticut: JAI Press, 1982.

Brown, Clair (Vickery), "Home Production for Use in a Market Economy" in Barrie Thorne and Marilyn Yalom, eds., *Rethinking the Family: Some Feminist Questions,* pp. 151–67. New York: Longman, 1982.

———. "The Time-Poor: A New Look at Poverty," *The Journal of Human Resources,* vol. 12, no. 1 (Winter 1977):27–48.

Brownmiller, Susan. *Femininity.* New York: Simon & Schuster, 1984.

Burkhauser, Richard V. and Karen C. Holden. *A Challenge to Social Security.* New York: Academic Press, 1982.

Caplow, Theodore. *The Sociology of Work.* Minneapolis, Minnesota: University of Minnesota Press, 1954.

Carothers, Suzanne C. and Peggy Crull, "Contrasting Sexual Harassment in Female- and Male-Dominated Occupations," in *My Troubles Are Going to Have Trouble With Me,* pp. 219–20. New Brunswick, New Jersey: Rutgers University Press, 1984.

Cassell, Carol. *Swept Away: Why Women Fear Their Own Sexuality.* New York: Simon & Schuster, 1984.

Cassetty, Judith, *Child Support and Public Policy.* Lexington, Massachusetts: D. C. Heath & Co., 1978.

Chambers, David. *Making Fathers Pay.* Chicago, Illinois: University of Chicago Press, 1979.

Cherlin, Andrew. *Marriage, Divorce, Remarriage: Social Trends in the United States.* Cambridge, Massachusetts: Harvard University Press, 1981.

Cleverdon, Stephanie, "On the Brink: Three Attempts to Liberate Women," *Working Papers for a New Society* (Spring 1975):28–36.

Committee on Ways and Means, U.S. House of Representatives, "Background Material and Data on Programs Within the Jurisdiction of the Committee on Ways and Means." Washington, D.C., February 22, 1985.

Congressional Budget Office. *Child Care and Preschool: Options for Federal Support.* Washington, D.C.: Congress of the United States, 1978.

Cook, Alice, Arlene Kaplan Daniels, and Val R. Lorwin. *Women and Trade Unions in Eleven Industrialized Countries.* Philadelphia, Pennsylvania: Temple University Press, 1984.

Corbett, Tim, "Child Support Assurance: Wisconsin Demonstration," *Focus,* vol. 9, no. 1 (Spring 1986):1–5. Madison, Wisconsin: University of Wisconsin, Institute for Research on Poverty.

Corcoran, Mary and Gregory J. Duncan, "Work History, Labor-Force Attachment, and Earnings Differences Between the Races and Sexes," *Journal of Human Resources,* vol. XIV (Winter 1979):3–20.

Coverman, Shelley, "Explaining Husbands' Participation in Domestic Labor," *Sociological Quarterly,* vol. 26 (Spring 1985):81–97.

Crompton, Rosemary and Gareth Jones. *White-Collar Proletariat: Deskilling and Gender in Clerical Work.* Philadelphia, Pennsylvania: Temple University Press, 1984.

Cuvillier, Rolande, "The Housewife—An Unjustified Financial Burden on the Community," *Journal of Social Policy,* vol. 8 (January 1979):1–26.

Davies, Margery. *Women's Place Is at the Typewriter.* Philadelphia, Pennsylvania: Temple University Press, 1982.

Davis, Kingsley, "The Future of Marriage," *Bulletin of the American Academy of Arts and Sciences,* vol. 36, no. 8 (May 1983):33.

Degler, Carl N. *At Odds: Women and the Family in America from the Revolution to the Present.* New York: Oxford University Press, 1980.

de Beauvoir, Simone. *The Second Sex.* New York: Alfred A. Knopf, 1953.

Dodd, Barbara E., "DNA Fingerprinting in Matters of Family and Crime," *Nature,* vol. 318 (December 12, 1985):506–07.

Dodge, Norton T. *Women in the Soviet Economy.* Baltimore, Maryland: The Johns Hopkins Press, 1966.

Doeringer, Peter and Michael J. Piore. *Internal Labor Markets and Manpower Analysis.* Lexington, Massachusetts: D. C. Heath & Company, 1971.

Eberts, Randall W. and Joe A. Stone, "Male-Female Differences in Promotions: EEO in Public Education," *Journal of Human Resources* (Fall 1985):504–21.

The Economic Report of the President, February 1986. Washington, D.C.: U.S. Government Printing Office, 1986.

Ehrenreich, Barbara. *The Hearts of Men: American Dreams and the Flight from Commitment.* Garden City, New York: Doubleday & Company, 1983.

Elwood, David T. and Mary Jo Bane. *The Impact of AFDC on Family Structure and Living Arrangements.* Cambridge, Massachusetts: Harvard University, February 1985.

England, Paula. "The Failure of Human Capital Theory to Explain Occupational Sex Segregation," *Journal of Human Resources,* vol. 17 (Spring 1982):358–70.

———. "Socioeconomic Explanations of Job Discrimination" in Helen Remick, ed., *Comparable Worth and Wage Discrimination.* Philadelphia, Pennsylvania: Temple University Press, 1984.

England, Paula and George Farkas. *Households, Employment, and Gender: A Social, Economic, and Demographic View.* New York: Aldine, 1985.

Epstein, Cynthia Fuchs. *Women in Law.* New York: Basic Books, 1981.

Equal Employment Opportunity Commission. *A Unique Competence: A Study of Equal Employment Opportunity in the Bell System.* Reprinted in the *Congressional Record* (February 17, 1972):E1234–E1272.

Fallows, Deborah. *A Mother's Work.* Boston: Houghton Mifflin Company, 1985.

Fenton, Patrick. "The Way Police Exams Used to Be," *The New York Times,* July 27, 1985, p. 23.

Feree, Myra Marx, "Sacrifice, Satisfaction and Social Change: Employment and the Family" in Karen Brodkin Sacks and Dorothy Remy, eds., *My Troubles Are Going to Have Trouble With Me,* pp. 61–79. New Brunswick, New Jersey: Rutgers University Press, 1974.

Fleisher, Belton M. and Thomas J. Kneiser. *Labor Economics: Theory, Evidence, and Policy.* Third ed. Englewood Cliffs, New Jersey: Prentice-Hall, Inc. 1985.

Folbre, Nancy, "Of Patriarchy Born: The Political Economy of Fertility Decisions," *Feminist Studies,* vol. 9, no. 2 (Summer 1983):261–80.

———. "The Pauperization of Motherhood: Patriarchy and Public Policy in the United States," *Review of Radical Political Economics* vol. 16 (Winter 1984):72–88.

Fox, William M., "Purpose and Validity in Job Evaluation," *Personnel Journal,* vol. 41 (October 1962):432–37.

Fraiberg, Selma. *Every Child's Birthright: In Defense of Mothering.* New York: Basic Books, 1977.

Friedan, Betty. *The Feminine Mystique.* New York: W. W. Norton, 1963.

Galbraith, John Kenneth. *Economics and the Public Purpose.* Boston: Houghton Mifflin, 1973.

Garfinkel, Irwin and Sara McLanahan. *A New American Dilemma: The Plight of Single Mothers and Their Children.* Washington, D.C.: Urban Institute Press, 1987.

Gold, Michael Evans. *A Debate on Comparable Worth.* Ithaca, NY: Industrial and Labor Relations Press, 1983.

———. "A Tale of Two Amendments: The Reasons Congress Added Sex to Title VII and Their Implication for the Issue of Comparable Worth," *Duquesne Law Review,* vol. 19 (Spring 1981): 453–77.

Goldberg, P. A., "Are Women Prejudiced Against Women?," *Trans-Action* (April 1968):29–30.

Goldin, Claudia, "The Gender Gap in Historical Perspective" in *Comparable Worth: Issue for the 80s,* pp. 3–19. Washington, D.C.: U.S. Commission on Civil Rights, 1984.

Gregory, Robert G. and Ronald C. Duncan, "The Relevance of Segmented Labor Market Theories: The Australian Experience of the Achievement of Equal Pay for Women," *Journal of Post Keynesian Economics,* vol. 3 (Spring 1981):404–28.

Gregory, Robert G. and Vivien Ho, "Equal Pay and Comparable Worth: What Can the U.S. Learn from the Australian Experience?" (unpublished, 1984)

Guttentag, Marcia and Paul I. Secord. *Too Many Women: The Sex Ratio Question.* Beverly Hills, California: Sage Publications, 1983.

Hartmann, Heidi I., "The Unhappy Marriage of Marxism and Feminism: Towards a More Progressive Union" in *Women and Revolution,* pp. 1–41, ed., Lydia Sargent. Boston, Massachusetts, South End Press, 1979.

Harvey, Andrew and David Elliot. *Time and Time Again.* Ottawa, Canada: Employment and Immigration, 1983.

Haskins, Ron, Andrew W. Dobelstein, John S. Akin, and J. Brad Schwartz, "Estimates of National Child Support Collections Potential and the Income Security of Female-Headed Families," *Report to the Office of Child Support Enforcement.* Chapel Hill, North Carolina: University of North Carolina, Bush Institute for Child and Family Policy, January 1, 1985.

Hayden, Delores. *Redesigning the American Dream.* New York: W. W. Norton & Company, 1984.

Hayghe, Howard, "Rise in Mothers' Labor Force Activity Includes Those with Infants," *Monthly Labor Review,* vol. 109, no. 2 (February 1986):43–45.

Heckman, James J. and Kenneth I. Wolpin, "Does the Contract Compliance Program Work? An Analysis of Chicago Data," *Industrial and Labor Relations Review,* vol. 29, no. 4 (July 1976): 544–64.

Henig, Robin Maranz, "The Sterilization Option," *The Washington Post,* March 19, 1986, health section, p. 10.

Hill, Herbert, "The Equal Employment Opportunity Commission: Twenty Years Later," *Journal of Intergroup Relations,* vol. XI, no. 4 (Winter 1983):5–49.

———. "Race and Ethnicity in Organized Labor: The Historical Sources of Resistance to Affirmative Action," *The Journal of Intergroup Relations,* vol. 12, no. 4 (Winter 1984):5–40.

Hill, Martha S. "What Absent Fathers Do and Could Provide." Ann Arbor, Michigan: University of Michigan, 1985.

Historical Statistics of the United States: Colonial Times to 1957. Washington, D.C.: U.S. Government Printing Office, 1960.

Holden, Karen C., ed. *A Challenge to Social Security: The Changing Roles of Women and Men in American Society.* New York: Academic Press, 1982.

James, Estelle, "The Income and Employment Effects of Women's Liberation" in Cynthia Lloyd, ed., *Sex, Discrimination, and the Division of Labor,* pp. 379–400. New York: Columbia University Press, 1975.

Juster, F. Thomas, "A Note on Recent Changes in Time Use," in F. Juster and Frank P. Stafford, eds., *Time, Goods, and Well-Being,* pp. 313–322. Ann Arbor, Michigan: Institute for Social Research, University of Michigan, 1985.

Kamerman, Sheila B. and Alfred J. Kahn, eds. *Child Care, Family Benefits and Working Parents: A Study in Comparative Policy.* New York: Columbia University Press, 1981.

Kanter, Rosabeth. *Men and Women of the Corporation.* New York: Basic Books, 1977.

Kessler-Harris, Alice. *Out to Work: A History of Wage-Earning Women in the United States.* New York: Oxford University Press, 1982.

Killingsworth, Mark, "Statement on Comparable Worth," Joint Economic Committee, U.S. Congress, April 10, 1984.

Krause, Harry D. *Child Support in America: The Legal Perspective.* Charlottesville, Virginia: The Michie Company, 1981.

Lasch, Christopher. *Haven in a Heartless World.* New York: Basic Books, 1977.

Leonard, Jonathan S., "What Promises Are Worth: The Impact of Affirmative Action Goals," *The Journal of Human Resources,* vol. XX, no. 1 (Winter 1985):3–20.

Lipman-Blumen, Jean, "Role De-Differentiation as a System Response to Crisis: Occupational and Political Roles of Women," *Sociological Inquiry,* vol. 43, no. 2 (1973):105–29.

Lopate, C., "Pay for Housework," *Journal of Social Policy,* vol. 5 (January 1974):27–31.

MacKinnon, Catherine. *Sexual Harassment of Working Women: A Case of Sex Discrimination.* New Haven, Connecticut: Yale University Press, 1979.

Madden, Janice I., "The Persistence of Pay Differentials: The Economics of Sex Discrimination" in *Women and Work, An Annual Review,* vol. 1. Beverly Hills, California: Sage Publishing, 1985.

Mainardi, Pat, "The Politics of Housework" in Robin Morgan, ed., *Sisterhood Is Powerful,* pp. 447–54. New York: Random House, 1970.

Margolis, Maxine L. *Mothers and Such: Views of American Women and Why They Changed.* Berkeley, California: University of California Press, 1984.

Meyers, William, "Child Care Finds a Champion in the Corporation," *New York Times,* section 3, August 4, 1985.

Mincer, Jacob and Solomon W. Polachek, "Family Investments in Human Capital: Earnings of Women," *Journal of Political Economy,* vol. 82, no. 2 (March/April 1974):S79–S108.

Morley, John David. *Pictures from the Water Trade: Adventures of a Westerner in Japan.* Boston, Massachusetts: Atlantic Monthly Press, 1985.

Murray, Charles. *Losing Ground: American Social Policy, 1950–1980.* New York: Basic Books, 1984.

Nakamura, Alice and Masao Nakamura. *The Second Paycheck: An Analysis of the Employment and Earnings of Married Women.* New York: Academic Press, 1985.

National Center for Health Statistics. *Advance Report of Final Natality Statistics, 1983.* Washington, D.C.: National Center for Health Statistics. *Monthly Vital Statistics Report* vol. 34, no. 6. Hyattsville, Maryland: Public Health Service, 1985.

O'Neill, June, "The Comparable Worth Trap," *The Wall Street Journal,* January 20, 1984, p. 28.

Oppenheimer, Valerie K., *The Female Labor Force in the United States: Demographic and Economic Factors Governing Its Growth and Changing Composition.* Westport, Connecticut: Greenwood Press, 1979.

Peterson-Hardt, Sandra and Nancy D. Perlman, "Sex-Segregated Career Ladders in New York State Government: A Structural Analysis of Inequality in Employment." Albany, New York: State University of New York, Center for Women in Government, working paper I, October 1979, mimeographed.

Phelps, Edmund S., "The Statistical Theory of Racism and Sexism," *American Economic Review,* vol. 62 (September 1972):659–61.

Pleck, Joseph H., "Husbands' Paid Work and Family Roles: Current Research Issue," *Research in the Interweave of Social Roles: Jobs and Families,* vol. 3. Greenwich, Connecticut: JAI Press, 1983.

———. *Working Wives, Working Husbands.* (Beverly Hills, Calif.: Sage Publications, 1985.

Polachek, Solomon W., "Occupational Self-Selection: A Human Capital Approach to Sex Differences in Occupational Structure," *Review of Economics and Statistics,* vol. 58, no. 1 (February 1981):60–69.

Presser, Harriet B. and Wendy Baldwin, "Child Care as a Constraint on Employment: Prevalence, Correlates, and Bearing on the Work and Fertility Nexus," *American Journal of Sociology,* vol. 85, no. 5 (March 1980):1202–13.

Presser, Harriet B. and Virginia S. Cain, "Shift Work Among Dual-Earner Couples With Children," *Science,* vol. 219 (February 18, 1983):876–79.

Helen Remick, ed., *Comparable Worth and Wage Discrimination.* Philadelphia, Pennsylvania: Temple University Press, 1984.

Remick, Helen, "Comparable Worth and Wages." Manoa, Hawaii: Industrial Research Center, 1984.

Reskin, Barbara F. and Heidi J. Hartmann, eds., *Women's Work, Men's Work: Sex Segregation on the Job.* Washington, D.C.: National Academy Press, 1986.

Ridley, Jeanne Clare, "Family Planning and the Status of Women in the United States" (undated manuscript).

Robertson, Peter C., "Why the Bosses Like to Be Told to Hire Minorities." *The Washington Post,* November 10, 1985, p. D1.

Robinson, John P., "Changes in the Time Use: An Historical Overview" in F. Thomas Juster and Frank P. Stafford, eds., *Time, Goods, and Well-Being,* pp. 289–312. Ann Arbor, Michigan: Institute for Social Research, University of Michigan, 1985.

———. *How Americans Use Time: A Social-Psychological Analysis of Everyday Behavior.* New York: Praeger, 1977.

Roos, Patricia A. and Barbara F. Reskin, "Institutional Factors Contributing to Sex Segregation in the Workplace" in Barbara F. Reskin, ed., *Sex Segregation in the Workplace: Trends, Explanations, Remedies,* pp. 235–60. Washington, D.C.: National Academy Press, 1984.

Rosenbaum, James E. *Career Mobility in a Corporate Hierarchy.* Orlando, Florida: Academic Press, 1984.

Ross, Heather L. and Isabel V. Sawhill. *Time of Transition: The Growth of Families Headed by Women.* Washington, D.C.: The Urban Institute, 1975.

Sanderson, Warren C., "Qualitative Aspects of Marriage, Fertility and Family Limitation in Nineteenth Century America: Another Application of the Coale Specifications," *Demography,* vol. 16, no. 3 (August 1979):339–58.

Sanger, Margaret. *An Autobiography.* New York: Dover, 1971.

Sawhill, Isabel V., "Developing Normative Standards for Child-Support Payments" in Judith Cassetty, ed., *The Parental Child Support Obligation,* pp. 79–114. Lexington, Massachusetts: Lexington Books, 1983.

Schlafly, Phyllis. *The Power of the Positive Woman.* New York: Harcourt, Brace, Jovanovich, 1977.

Schultz, Paul T. *The Economics of Population*. Reading, Massachusetts: Addison-Wesley, 1981.
Scott, A. C., "The Value of Housework for Love or Money?," *Ms. Magazine* (June 1972):56–58.
Shepela, Sharon Toffey and Ann T. Viviano, "Some Psychological Factors Affecting Job Segregation and Wages" in Helen Remick, ed., *Comparable Worth and Wage Discrimination*, pp. 47–58. Philadelphia, Pennsylvania: Temple University Press, 1984.
Sowell, Thomas. *The Economics and Politics of Race*. New York: William Morrow, 1983.
Stack, Carol and Herbert Semmel, "The Concept of Family in the Black Community," Subcommittee on Fiscal Policy. Washington, D.C.: Joint Economic Committee of Congress, November 4, 1973.
Strober, Myra H., "Formal Extrafamily Child Care—Some Economic Observations" in Cynthia Lloyd, ed., *Sex, Discrimination and the Division of Labor*, pp. 346–78. New York: Columbia University Press, 1954.
Strober, Myra H. and Carolyn Arnold, "The Dynamics of Occupational Segregation by Gender: Bank Tellers (1950–1980)" in Clair Brown and Joseph A. Pechman, eds., *Gender in the Workplace*. Washington, D.C.: Brookings Institution, 1987.
The Swedish Institute. "Child Care Programs in Sweden," *Fact Sheets on Sweden*. Stockholm, September 1984.
———. "Taxes in Sweden," *Fact Sheets on Sweden*. Stockholm, March 1985.
Thornton, Arland and Deborah Freedman. "The Changing American Family," *Population Bulletin*, vol. 38, no. 4 (October 1983):17.
Thurow, Lester C., "Why Women are Paid Less Than Men," *The New York Times*, section 2, March 8, 1981, p. 2.
Tiger, Lionel and Joseph Shepher. *Women in the Kibbutz*. New York: Harcourt, Brace, Jovanovich, 1975.
Tilly, Louise A. and Joan W. Scott. *Women, Work and Family*. New York: Holt, Rinehart and Winston, 1978.
Treiman, Donald J., "Job Evaluation: An Analytic Review." Washington, D.C.: National Academy of Sciences, 1979.
Treiman, Donald J. and Kermit Terrell, "Sex and the Process of Status Attainment: A Comparison of Working Women and Men," *American Sociological Review*, vol. 40 (April 1975):174–200.
Trilling, Calvin. *Killings*. New York: Viking/Penguin, Inc., 1985.
U.S. Bureau of the Census. Current Population Reports. *Characteristics of the Population Below the Poverty Level: 1983*, series P–60, no. 147. Washington, D.C.: U.S. Government Printing Office, 1985.
———. *Child Care Arrangements of Working Mothers: June 1982*, series P–23, no. 129 (1982).
———. *Child Support and Alimony, 1983*, series P–23, no. 141 (1985).
———. *Divorce, Child Custody, and Child Support*, series P–23, no. 84 (1979).
———. *Economic Characteristics of Households in the United States: Third Quarter 1983*, series P–70, no. 1 (1983).
———. *Household and Family Characteristics: March 1984*, series P–20, no. 398 (1984).
———. *Income in 1967 of Persons in the United States*, series P–60, no. 60 (1969).
———. *Marital Status and Living Arrangements, March 1983*, series P–20, no. 389 (1984).
———. *Marital Status and Living Arrangements, March 1984*, series P–20, no. 399 (1985).
———. *Money Income of Households, Families, and Persons in the United States, 1984*, series P–60, no. 151 (1986).
———. *Money Income and Poverty Status of Families and Persons in the United States: 1983*, series P–60, no. 145 (1984).
———. *Money Income of Households, Families, and Persons in the United States, 1982*, series P–60, no. 142 (1984).
———. *Trends in Child Care Arrangements by Working Mothers*, series P–23, no. 117 (1982).
U.S. Bureau of Labor Statistics. *Consumer Expenditure Survey: Interview Survey, 1980–1981*. Bulletin 2225. Washington, D.C.: U.S. Department of Labor, April 1985.
———. *Employment and Earnings Characteristics of Families: First Quarter, 1986*, USDL 86–152, April 1986.
———. *Employment and Earnings*. (Monthly.)
———. *Labor Force Statistics Derived from the Current Population Survey*, vol. I, bulletin 2086 Washington, D.C.: U.S. Department of Labor, 1982.

———. *Number of Working Mothers Now at Record Levels,* 84-321 USDL.

U.S. Department of Health and Human Services. *Social Security Handbook,* 8th edition. Washington, D.C.: U.S. Government Printing Office, 1984.

U.S. Department of Justice. *A Survey of Spousal Violence Against Women in Kentucky.* Washington, D.C.: Law Enforcement Assistance Administration, 1979.

U.S. Department of Labor. *Comparison of State Unemployment Insurance Laws.* Washington, D.C.: January 6, 1985.

U.S. General Accounting Office. *The Equal Employment Opportunity Commission Has Made Limited Progress in Eliminating Employment Discrimination.* Washington, D.C., 1979.

———. *The Equal Employment Opportunity Program for Federal Nonconstruction Contractors Can Be Improved.* Washington, D.C., 1975.

U.S. Merit Systems Protection Board. *Sexual Harassment in the Federal Workplace: Is It a Problem?* Washington, D.C.: U.S. Government Printing Office, March 1981.

Vanek, Joann, "Time Spent in Housework," *Scientific American,* vol. 231 (May 1974):116–20.

Veblen, Thorstein. *The Theory of the Leisure Class.* New York: Macmillan, 1912.

Waite, Linda J., "U.S. Women at Work," *Population Bulletin,* vol. 36, no. 2. Washington, D.C.: Population Reference Bureau, Inc., May 1981.

Waite, Linda J., David E. Kanouse, and Thomas J. Blaschke. *Changes in the Lifestyles of New Parents.* Santa Monica, California: Rand, 1984.

Walker, K. and M. Woods. *Time Use: A Measure of Family Goods and Services.* Washington, D.C.: American Home Economics Association, 1976.

Wallace, Phyllis, ed. *Equal Employment Opportunity and the AT&T Case.* Cambridge, Massachusetts: MIT Press, 1976.

Ways and Means Committee of the U.S. Congress. "Background Material and Data on Programs Within the Jurisdiction of the Committee on Ways and Means." Washington, D.C., U.S. Government Printing Office, February 22, 1986.

Weitzman, Lenore J. *The Divorce Revolution.* New York: The Free Press, 1985.

Whelpton, Pascal K. and Clyde V. Kiser. *Social and Psychological Factors Affecting Fertility.* New York: Milbank Memorial Fund, 1950.

Whyte, William Foot, "The Social Structure of the Restaurant," *American Journal of Sociology,* vol. LIV (January 1949):302–10.

Willis, Norman D. with Ann O. Worcester, "State of Washington, Comparable Worth Study, September 1974," Norman D. Willis & Associates, 1974.

The Woman Question: Selections from the Writings of Karl Marx, Frederick Engels, V. I. Lenin, Joseph Stalin. New York: International Publishers, 1970.

Zigler, Edward F. and Edmund W. Gordon, eds. *Day Care: Scientific and Social Policy Issues.* Boston, Massachusetts: Auburn House Publishing Company, 1982.

INDEX